Nonprofit Institutions in America

Recent Studies and Dissertations

STUART BRUCHEY
University of Maine
General Editor

A Garland Series

"Shifting Sands Beneath the State"

Unemployment, the Labor Market, and the Local Community 1893–1922

PETER C. SEIXAS

Garland Publishing, Inc.
New York & London
1993

Library of Congress Cataloging-in-Publication Data

Seixas, Peter C., 1947–
"Shifting sands beneath the state": unemployment, the labor market, and the local community, 1893–1922 / Peter C. Seixas.
p. cm. — (Nonprofit institutions in America)
Originally presented as the author's thesis (Ph. D.).
Includes bibliographical references and index.
ISBN 0-8153-0943-0 (alk. paper)
1. Unemployment—New York (State)—Yonkers—History. 2. Labor market—New York (State)—Yonkers—History. 3. Labor policy—New York (State)—Yonkers—History. 4. Poor—New York (State)—Yonkers—History.
I. Title. II. Series.
HD5726.Y65S45 1993
331.1'09747277—dc20 92-38642
CIP

Printed on acid-free, 250-year-life paper
Manufactured in the United States of America

Contents

Preface

Since completing my work on unemployment as a problem in social history in 1988, my research interests have shifted to the problems of teaching and learning history. The opportunity to circulate this previously unpublished dissertation in a Garland Press series is therefore most welcome. If some of the secondary sources I cite have been superseded by more recent work, the central questions which I address in this history are still most current.

I am indebted to Jim Feldman and the staff at the Yonkers Family Service Society for providing access to the Yonkers Charity Organization Society papers; to Rick Beard and the staff at the Hudson River Museum for access to the Alexander Smith papers and the Museum collections; to Karolyn Wrightson of the Westchester County Historical Society; to Mary Pisano of the Yonkers Woman's Institute; to Dean Grandin and Michael Rebic of the Yonkers Community Development Agency; and to Dianne Courtney and the staff at the Yonkers Public Library.

Among many archivists who aided in this project, Eleanor Lewis of the Sophia Smith Collection, Dale Mayer of the Hoover Presidential Library, Anne Millbrooke of the United Technologies Archives, and Richard Strassberg of the Labor Management Documentation Center at Cornell University were particularly helpful. U.C.L.A. and the Herbert Hoover Presidential Library Association provided grants which helped in the initial and final stages, respectively. Permission to use quotations from the Yonkers *Herald* and *Statesman* has been granted by the Westchester Rockland Newspapers. Most of Chapter 3 appeared in *Social Research* Vol. 54, No. 2, and is reprinted here with permission.

Joy and George Dryfoos provided warm hospitality and a bed on one of my Yonkers trips. Camaraderie and criticism came from members of the Vancouver Labour History Works-in-Progress Seminar. I benefitted from several discussions with Alex Keyssar. Katherine Kish Sklar and Sanford Jacoby gave encouragement and support as well as criticism. Eric Monkkonen guided me in the project from its inception: his interest and excitement have been crucial. Steve Fraser, Ellis Hawley, and Michael Katz gave thoughtful comments on the completed dissertation. Robin Van Heck did a most thorough job of formatting for the Garland edition.

My parents, Judith S. Seixas and the late Frank A. Seixas, provided such a succession of gifts and loans of things both tangible and intangible that it is impossible to list them or to thank them adequately.

Susan Inman has provided loving encouragement and support. Without her encouragement, I would not have started this project; and without her support, I could not have finished it.

Introduction:
The Geographic Scale of Unemployment as a Historiographic Problem

"The unemployed have aptly been called 'the shifting sands beneath the State.' Surely there is no condition which more immediately demands the attention of Congress than that of unemployment, which is . . . sapping the very basis of our national efficiency and germinating the seeds of revolution."

—U.S. Commission on Industrial Relations[1]

At the turn of the twentieth century economists and reformers attempted to isolate the specific problem of unemployment from the more general problem of poverty.[2] The idea that people needed relief, protection, or correction was not new. But the idea that some people were out of work as victims of the process of capitalist development, faulty distribution of labor, or of economic cycles was. In their efforts to define unemployment, Progressives attempted to separate two policy areas: one affecting "dependent" unemployables needing relief or rehabilitation; and another affecting erstwhile wage-earners whose poverty could be attributed to problems with the nation's industrial system.[3] The effort consumed much of reformers' energies at the turn of the century, despite mounting evidence from their own investigations that the two were inextricably linked, that "dependence" was an almost normal aspect of working-class life.[4]

Traditionally responsibility for the poor had been local. Though there was a strong ideological current which dictated individuals' responsibility for their own welfare, destitute individuals and families did not generally starve: they were provided for in the local community.[5] In the nineteenth century United States, this welfare arrangement bore a significant relationship to the political economy, which likewise rested on the local community. Local factory owners, bankers and merchants often played prominent roles in the town's charities. The family-owned entrepreneurial firm rarely had manufacturing plants located in more than one city: elites' charitable impulses—whether motivated by social control, religious, or other concerns—were generally focused in their own towns and cities.

In nineteenth century America high levels of working class mobility complemented the local rootedness of the dominant classes. But this movement was of so little concern to the articulate, that its exposure by historians in the 1970s constituted a major "discovery."[6] Towards the end of the century, however, there were numerous signs of strain in the old order, including new concern about tramps and the mobile unemployed, increasing interest in state-wide mechanisms to control local welfare efforts, growth in the state institutions to deal with some forms of dependency, and the development of voluntary associations for interchange of ideas about charity and corrections.[7]

The locally-based social stabilization mechanisms of the nineteenth century began to appear inadequate at roughly the same time as the organization of capital underwent a major transformation. Between 1898 and 1902 there were 3,653 corporate mergers directly involving between one quarter and one third of the entire U.S. manufacturing capital stock. The largest firms increased immensely in size, and in some cases controlled unprecedented shares of the national market in their own products.[8] The larger factories which produced for the new corporations helped to accelerate the growth of densely populated industrial cities, and to attract increasing numbers of immigrants. The family-owned entrepreneurial firm gave way to control through corporate stock and finance capital and ownership was thus frequently removed from the local community.

While the new nationally based corporations potentially undermined the local social stabilization projects of the nineteenth century, they made possible the consideration of stabilization on a scale which transcended the local community. First, some corporate managers took an interest in promoting labor loyalty and productivity beyond the local paternalism of the nineteenth century.[9] Secondly, some of the fortunes of the new corporations began to be steered towards philanthropic social reform projects operating on a vastly enlarged scale.[10] Finally, the drive towards expertise and efficiency in the corporation became an explicit model for nascent professionalism in the social reform spheres.[11] In this setting unemployment and underemployment emerged as the prime cause of poverty, partially remediable not through character reform but through reform of industrial policies.[12]

The central question of this study is: how did the change in scale (from local to national) on which the dominant individual firms operated in the United States affect understandings of the labor market and responsibility for employment and unemployment? The key actors were employers, social reformers, state officials and workers, none of which, of course, was a monolithic group with a unified perspective.

The tension between local solutions to social problems and reform efforts on a broader scale is a major consideration in answering the question. While eighteenth and nineteenth century labor and welfare history can appropriately focus within a local arena—the success of recent local studies in nineteenth century working-class history is in part dependant upon this historical reality—Progressive era studies are more difficult to contain within the local setting.[13] The geographic scale of employment reform was, in fact, a major point of contention: those who saw unemployment as a "problem of industry" approached it as a national problem. Those who saw it as a problem of dependency, character, relief or charity were generally content to leave it in local hands.[14] Debates about the problem of unemployment invariably confronted the local/national issue, and activities undertaken—or not undertaken—reflected the outcomes of those debates.

A second major theme of this study is the tension between "private" and "public" approaches to the solution of perceived social and economic problems. The definition of "private" and "public" realms are themselves contingent and historically constructed.[15] Those policy areas which are acknowledged as "public" come under the direct purview and control of legitimately constituted public authority, the state; "private" concerns do not.[16] While unemployment had consequences seen as affecting public concerns, reform might mean restrictions on employment policies which were close to the center of "private" capitalist prerogatives. State involvement with unemployment was thus a particularly contentious issue, and most employers fought bitterly any initiative which they thought might extend state authority in dealing with unemployment. Reformers generally accommodated these fears by urging businessmen to reform their own management practices rather than expanding state capacities and jurisdiction to deal with the problem.[17] Information gathering and dissemination were high on the list of reformers' agendae throughout the period precisely because they entailed minimal expansion of state offices. The information which the state gathered—for employment bureaus in the beginning of the period and on business cycle data towards the end—could be given to businessmen and workers for them to make their own decisions.

An important connection existed between the public/private debate and the local/national debate. Those who sought to restrict the impact of publicly constituted authority might support public activities at the local level only: local commissioners of charity for giving relief to dependents, local employment bureaus for the unemployed, local health officers to inspect factories, and local vocational counselling programs for young people. These measures posed no threat to the large national corporations. Since the latter operated beyond the level of the individual community, they could and did hold communities hostage to their own economic interests: local elected officials who acted against those interests were seen as endangering the economic well-being of the community.[18]

American labor historians and social welfare historians have generally approached these themes in relation to unemployment before the 1930s only tangentially.

Unemployment in Labor History

John R. Commons was acutely aware of the transformation in the scale of industry at the turn of the century, and of its impact on local owners and workers. "Industry has markedly changed, during these last forty years," he wrote in 1935, "from neighborhood relations of employers and laborers to absentee relations of millions of investors and millions of laborers, with the banker as their middleman."[19] In this setting, Commons' associates saw the channeling of labor opposition into a narrowly defined "pure-and-simple" business unionism as a positive development, as an opportunity to incorporate workers into the values of middle-class American acquisitive individualism. "Americanism," wrote Commons, "has a new meaning of opportunities for promotion and investment within a capitalist system that seems to create wealth faster than it can be consumed." And, he added, "Upon the unions falls the first burden of 'Americanizing' the immigrants."[20]

Commons acknowledged the extensive impact of the problem of unemployment on workers. As early as 1901, he testified that unemployment was "the most serious of all industrial problems."[21] When his *History of Labor* volumes covering 1896 to 1932 were published in 1935, they not surprisingly gave particular attention to the issue. Don Lescohier and Florence Peterson wrote extensive sections covering the depression of the 1890s, Coxey's army, and the AFL advocacy of shorter hours as a solution to unemployment, in addition to presenting the available statistics on historical unemployment rates. They reviewed the American Association for Labor Legislation's Program for the Prevention of Unemployment, William Leiserson's research and recommendations in New York State, Wesley Mitchell's report on business cycles, and Herbert Hoover's 1921 unemployment conference as laying the theoretical groundwork for action during the 1930s.[22] The authors' location in the midst of the avalanche of federal programs to deal with unemployment exacerbated the Commons school's tendency to view positively the achievements of American labor in the late nineteenth and early twentieth century—achievements made possible in large part by reformers' support of conservative trade unions and progressive managers, and through their united ability to expand state institutions to cope with and contain industrial problems and conflicts. "Never in American history," wrote Lescohier, "did industry, relief organizations, and local, state, and federal government rise and grapple with an unemployment emergency as they did in the 1930s."[23]

It was exactly this coalition, celebrated by the Commons school, which the proponents of the "corporate liberalism" thesis attacked head-on in the 1960s. James Weinstein and Gabriel Kolko claimed that worker opposition had been channeled into conservative trade unionism as a consequence of self-interested manipulation by sophisticated corporate members of the National Civic Federation, with the cooperation of collaborators like Samuel Gompers in the context of a liberal state. As R. Jeffrey Lustig puts it: "Influenced by the carrot (of NCF sponsorship) and the stick (of heavy reprisals), the AFL finally submitted to a view of labor not as an autonomous force but as a subordinate factor in the existing arrangements of production."[24]

Since proponents of the corporate liberalism thesis assume that management initiatives and those of the state were motivated by congruent interests, they make insufficient distinction between the two. Any apparent advances made by labor in better wages, bonuses, pensions, benefits, union recognition, health and safety regulations, education, job security and profit-sharing, are interpreted as more "carrots" delivered by an undifferentiated state-management coalition in order to increase productivity and reduce opposition.

The assumption of the almost automatic responsiveness of the state to corporate needs makes scrutiny of public/private relationships difficult. Steve Fraser complicates the corporate liberals' oversimplified relationship "between organized labor, industry and the state," articulating the differences between the ideas of "corporatists," dominant in the 1920s, who saw the need for expanded coordination but who wanted to accomplish it without an expansion of the state, and those of "Keynesians" who saw the same need and looked to the state to accomplish it.[25] Attention to the autonomous role of the state in the social reform process should add further to our understanding of these relationships.[26]

Like the Commons school, Weinstein understands Progressive activity as a precursor to the New Deal, but unemployment reform occupies only a minor chapter in the corporate liberal thesis. William Leiserson's suggestions in testimony to the U.S. Commission on Industrial Relations in 1914, Weinstein notes, were small contributions to "the transformation of the federal government into an agency of rationalization and stabilization of the existing industrial system."[27] Corporate liberalism thesis proponents in fact deal only marginally with workers themselves: like the Commons associates—perhaps even moreso—they are primarily concerned with the political activity of the leaders of organized labor.

Harry Braverman's *Labor and Monopoly Capital* shares with the proponents of the corporate liberalism thesis a dismal assessment of the fate of workers' control in the early twentieth century. Braverman concludes that Frederick Winslow Taylor's principles of scientific management provided the guidelines for the reorganization of production in such a way that control of the work-process was intentionally removed from the worker. Workers lost control not only of the tools but of the manner of their performance of labor. Braverman sees workers as victims whose "critical, intelligent, conceptual faculties" were being stripped from them by capital.[28] Engineers designed the work-process down to the minute detail. Industrial psychologists, sociologists and personnel managers designed supplementary programs to deal with residual human resistance which might be offered by workers. But more important in the habituation of the worker to the new conditions, in Braverman's words, are

> the destruction of all other ways of living, the striking of wage bargains that permit a certain enlargement of the customary bounds of subsistence for the working class, the weaving of the net of modern capitalist life that finally makes all other modes of living impossible.[29]

Braverman's workers are "first of all raw material for exploitation."[30]

Braverman's treatment of unemployment comprises an essential element in this analysis. The working class "is seized, released, flung into various parts of the social machinery and expelled by others, not in accord with its own will or self-activity, but in accord with the movement of capital."[31] The accumulation process itself produces the reserve armies. Quoting Marx, Braverman asserts, "The greater the social wealth, the functioning capital, the extent and energy of its growth, and therefore, also the absolute mass of the proletariat and the productiveness of its labor, the greater is the industrial reserve army."[32] Braverman grounds these theoretical assertions, however, in a brief empirical investigation of the historical record only since the end of World War II.

American working class history of the past decade and a half—heir to the radical impulse of the corporate liberal and Braverman interpretations—has nevertheless been fueled largely by the rejection of the passive picture of workers painted by those schools. Built on foundations laid by British historian E.P. Thompson, it emphasizes the ability of the working class to respond actively to the imposition of capitalist relations of production.[33] In the process, in this literature, the working class "made itself," by standing on the firm ground of its own pre-capitalist cultural legacy. As an argument about working class formation, Thompson's work itself and that of his American followers has dealt primarily with the late eighteenth and nineteenth centuries.

Extending the Thompsonian paradigm into the twentieth century has been problematic. Craig Calhoun argues that the "working class culture" Thompson discovered rested on the strengths of a pre-capitalist artisanal culture, and that once capitalist relations of production were fully established, the remnants of this culture disintegrated into a mass culture dominated by capitalist controlled institutions.[34] In the counter-Thompsonian view of the twentieth century, the working class became increasingly integrated into the capitalist social order: bureaucratic unions, rather than generating a culture of resistance, helped to adjust workers to living under the conditions of corporate capitalism.[35]

David Montgomery is at the forefront in combatting the "incorporation" thesis as it applies to the late nineteenth and early twentieth centuries. He emphasizes "the initiatives of the workers themselves rather than the ways in which they were manipulated by those in authority over them."[36] He documents workers' resistance to the employer strategies of welfare capitalism, scientific management and personnel management. Montgomery has identified both individual resistance and more widespread organized and articulate opposition which workers mounted in order to maintain shop-floor control over their own jobs.[37] Braverman's total working class defeat becomes in Montgomery, a hard-fought "battle for the control of the workplace."[38]

Montgomery and Ronald Schatz' "Facing Lay-offs" brings the notion of an active working class to the problem of unemployment.[39] They argue that a major change in the shape of unemployment occurred in the 1930s as a result of the successful demands of the industrial unions that lay-offs be governed by seniority as a first principle. In the late 1930s, the new unions maintained "unprecedented involvement" in the struggles of the unemployed. But prior to that time, workers struggled to keep control over lay-offs in their own hands, often sharing the burden collectively through slowdowns. The seniority principle was first and foremost a defense against arbitrary layoff and recall. Montgomery and Schatz' interpretation offers an ideologically comforting and understandably welcome counterpoint to its immediate predecessors, in which workers were either duped, defeated, or non-existent.[40]

Despite Montgomery's studies, it still remains to be seen how successfully the Thompsonian project will be extended into a twentieth century American context. As we turn from labor history to social welfare history, the beginning of the twentieth century poses a corresponding historical divide.

Unemployment in Social Welfare History

How has the historiography of poverty and social welfare dealt with the transformation in the scale of industry and the organization of the economy which took place around the turn of the century? For a number of reasons, very little of it has directly confronted this issue.[41]

Much of the important recent work simply does not deal with the time period. For solid historical reasons, most studies deal either with the eighteenth and nineteenth centuries *or* with the twentieth. Local studies characterize the former.[42] Michael Katz referred to the local studies as an "emerging" field in 1983, but did not note the overwhelming predominance of pre-twentieth century subjects among them.[43] Social historians of poverty and welfare make their subject manageable by limiting their investigations to single cities.

There are some important exceptions. Gary B. Nash's *The Urban Crucible: Social Change, Political Consciousness, and the Origins of the American Revolution* deals with pre-revolutionary poverty and its impact on the Revolution in Boston, New York and Philadelphia. Nash uses an interweaving of three local histories to make a grand argument about the role of the urban poor in political change.[44] Michael Katz' *Poverty and Policy in American History* is a collection of studies based largely on records generated at the state level. He demonstrates repeatedly the refusal of nineteenth century commentators to recognize the structural roots of dependency in American society.[45] Ending his examination in the late nineteenth century, Katz does not have to explain the Progressive publicists' "discovery" of the structural roots of dependency and their centrality in the welfare campaigns of the early twentieth century.[46]

A methodological divide separates the local studies from the histories of twentieth century welfare and poverty. None of the major contributions to welfare history in the twentieth century is a local study. Instead, there are histories of the development of the profession, the transformation of institutions, and campaigns for reform legislation.[47] James T. Patterson's traditional approach provides a typical combination of intellectual developments and public policy.[48] His survey of welfare reform before 1930 consists of two short chapters. The first uses Robert Hunter's *Poverty* as a starting point to survey the definition and extent of poverty in the first three decades of the century; the second surveys reform thought from the settlements, the charity organization movement, the A.A.L.L. and the obstacles posed by persisting localism and voluntarism. While he commends Hunter for a "structural" view of poverty, he does not himself give any account of the early twentieth century economic changes which gave poverty—and philanthropy—its new forms.

Other monographs on the dynamics of the reform process in the twentieth century treat the nation as a unit: they focus on reform movements in New York City—as does John McClymer's *War and Welfare: Social Engineering in America, 1890–1925*—or administrative developments in Washington, D.C.—as does Guy Alchon's *The Invisible Hand of Planning: Capitalism, Social Science, and the State in the 1920s*—because these were centers of national power, not because they provide illustrative case studies.[49]

A number of surveys span the nineteenth-twentieth century transition: how they manage to cross that divide merits close examination. Older studies, with a purely institutional and policy focus were not confronted with a major problem. David M. Schneider and Albert Deutsch, for instance, deal with policy change in New York State from 1609 to 1940, simply noting multiple transformations in the roles of the state over the course of time.[50] James Leiby's *History of Social Welfare and Social Work in the United States* has the avowed purpose of showing "how policies and agencies came into being and changed over the years and how they gave form to general notions about personal and social problems."[51] By looking backwards for the "origins of modern welfare practices," Leiby sets his problem in a presentist context: what were the past's influences "on the main features of contemporary policies and programs."[52] He deals with philanthropy, state boards of charity, large institutions, and the nascent social science organizations between 1850 and 1900. He summarizes the transition from the nineteenth to the twentieth century:

> . . . by 1912 the nineteenth century concern about paupers, criminals, and institutions for their relief or correction was somewhat eclipsed by a bold new notion of "social welfare" that addressed itself to impersonal causes of poverty and injustice and looked toward a more just and equal society. So philanthropy and social policy were brought closer together.[53]

Though it was published in 1978, Leiby's work ignores the literature suggesting anti-democratic implications of the development of social work and reform activities. As in many surveys, urbanization, industrialization, and immigration serve, in a vague and unexamined way, as the social background against which developments in the field of social welfare took place. Leiby's approach is sufficiently institutional to avoid major methodological problems—or breakthroughs—in the transition from the nineteenth to the twentieth century.

The transition is difficult to locate at all in the thematic chapters of Walter Trattner's *From Poor Law to Welfare State*. That on "Scientific Charity" is a survey of developments from 1865 to 1900, though the reasons for the choice of dates are not clear. Trattner includes two pages of cursory summary of the "economic revolution" of these years, including an extended quotation from Charles and Mary Beard on the growth of manufacturing.[54] In one on child welfare, we learn simply that, "of all those who required help . . . children seemed the most deserving. Moreover, the social upheaval resulting from large-scale immigration and rapid industrial and urban growth was especially hard on children."[55] There is no inquiry into the changing nature of the labor market having an impact upon poverty nor on reformers' goals in shaping welfare policy.[56]

Udo Sautter's article on public works as a remedy for unemployment before the New Deal offers a brief and simple explanation for the twentieth century trend away from local responsibility:

> Experience over the subsequent years showed . . . that the old poor-law tradition of exclusive local-welfare responsibility was no longer adequate. Private and civic actions alone proved insufficient for the alleviation of distress caused by joblessness, and the intervention of state and federal governments became unavoidable in the view of many close to the charity scene.[57]

Paul Boyer's *Urban Masses and Moral Order* covers one hundred years of voluntary philanthropic and reform efforts between 1820 and 1920 by middle and upper classes to establish and maintain social moral control of the new urban "masses."[58] Boyer's interest in "voluntarist and extra-legal" campaigns by organized groups precludes an account of the expansion of state mechanisms to deal with the problems of industrial capitalism. Boyer focuses on well-known reform thinkers in major American cities. While his cities grow larger during the century of his account, their role within the American political economy does not change, nor do the shape and function of labor markets undergo any transformation. Rather, a broadly described process of "industrialization, urbanization, and immigration," inspire a succession of programs, through which middle class reformers cope with their fears of disorder and immorality. By 1920 urbanism is sufficiently accepted that reformers no longer rely on a recreation of small-town social relations as a solution to urban problems. Middle-class urbanism, not the transformation of the political economy, is the most significant change in Boyer's early twentieth century.

The intellectual content of Boyer's Progressive reformers differed importantly from their nineteenth century predecessors, in that they sought "broad programs utilizing a full panoply of governmental power and aimed at a fundamental restructuring of the urban environment."[59]

Progressive environmentalism was split between a negative, coercive branch which sought elimination of saloons and brothels, and a positive branch which sought better housing, parks and playgrounds. But Boyer provides a meager explanation, as Michael Katz has pointed out, for why environmentalism supplanted campaigns aimed at the reform of individuals around the turn of the century.[60] Boyer's interest lies in the contours of reform thought, and his contribution lies in demonstrating the continuity of its themes. He, too, bypasses the issue of the reasons for change in the Progressive era. The sources of ideological continuity and change in Boyer lie more in the realm of other ideas (e.g. religion and the memory of small-town life) than in social change, economic reorganization, or political struggle.

John Garraty's *Unemployment in History* is a survey of "economic thought and public policy" with an international scale covering ideas on unemployment from Greece (briefly) to the present in Europe and North America.[61] This important exposition is not, however, a social history. It is an investigation of "how the condition of being without work has been perceived and dealt with": Garraty does not investigate how changing social and economic conditions—sometimes in the small, local context—might have contributed to the intellectual and policy changes he does explore. For example, Garraty shows how the theories of Charles Booth and William Beveridge contributed to an understanding of poverty linked to the problem of unemployment and underemployment.[62] But he does not ask how changes in the scale of the political economy might have helped to create a receptive audience for their theories.

Katz and Keyssar

Two recent works do address many of the shortcomings of these earlier monographs. Michael Katz's *In the Shadow of the Poorhouse* is divided into three chronological sections, "The Poorhouse Era" on the nineteenth century, "Building the Semiwelfare State" through the 1920s with a final chapter on the thirties, and "From the War on Poverty to the War on Welfare," on the postwar era.[63] The first of these benefits most from the wealth of Katz's original research, while the second two thirds rely more heavily on secondary sources.

Katz is sensitive to the nineteenth century localism of welfare efforts. In his account, "the shock of 1893 reshaped political alignments, escalated the war between capital and labor, and changed the direction of social reform."[64] The obvious inadequacy of nineteenth century principles of relief led to "the discovery of unemployment."[65] At the same time, the escalating war between capital and labor and increasing competition and economic uncertainty among the largest firms led to a search for new managerial strategies and new efficiencies. This search produced not only the modern corporation, but also an increase in state regulation of the economy, scientific management, and the spread of welfare capitalism.[66]

Katz comes very close to explaining the timing of the new understanding of reform, and specifically unemployment reform. Relying on the work of Harry Braverman, which provides the basis for some of his observations on the growth of institutions in the nineteenth century, Katz posits that management wanted to clear "the labor market of workers newly made unproductive by technological development."[67]

> Anxious to rid their factories and offices of workers insufficiently speedy and productive, yet afraid of the impact on the work ethic of a large, demoralized class of casual labor, management looked for ways to eliminate unwanted workers not only from their workplaces but, as well, from the workforce.[68]

Among the tactics to achieve these goals were, according to Katz, abolition of child labor, immigration restriction, forced retirement, and eugenics.

This proposition has the capacity to link industrial developments in the 1890s to the reorganization of the labor market and thence to various reform movements. Katz' support for this grand explanation is rather thin, probably unconvincing for those who see the child-saving movement as motivated by a concern for children rather than corporate profitability. Katz himself seems ambivalent about whether workers were driven out of the labor market altogether, or merely into "ghettos of unskilled dead-end employment at its margins."[69] Such jobs, as child-savers themselves emphasized, had *always* been children's place in the labor market, and were not a new development.

But there is more support for his thesis than Katz presents. While managers were not at the forefront, reformers and economists concerned with the problem of unemployment called attention to the demoralization and the erosion of workers' discipline which unemployment and underemployment produced.[70] Following Charles Booth and William Beveridge in England, one of the key planks in the prewar unemployment reform campaign was the "decasualization" of labor. The strategy called for reorganization of work into well-paid, stable, full-time jobs. "Where a system of employment is such as to keep two men perpetually half-employed though one regular man would serve, that system must in the public interests be changed. . . ."[71] Beveridge advocated that workers who remained surplus after such reorganization be institutionalized or forced to emigrate.[72] Beveridge's influence was fundamental in the United States: American labor economist Don D. Lescohier wrote that Beveridge's work was "the foundation upon which all subsequent writers have builded."[73] Largely because of Beveridge's influence in the first decades of the twentieth century, employment exchanges—and not unemployment insurance or business cycle reform—were at the center of the reform program.

Over the first two decades of the twentieth century, American reformers and economists rewrote their prescriptions so as to appeal to those who held power in American industry and finance. Katz is aware of both efforts to centralize responsibility for public welfare, and of the political and administrative barriers to effective centralization. Mistrust of the "public" sphere, despite a long history of involvement in relief; mistrust of the poor; and the perceived need to use welfare policy to regulate the labor market, all continue to shape the political struggles over welfare policy.[74]

Alexander Keyssar's *Out of Work: The First Century of Unemployment in Massachusetts* is the second major ground-breaking survey which covers both nineteenth and twentieth century developments in policies related to unemployment. Keyssar chooses the state of Massachusetts as the geographic limits of his study for "practical" reasons. On the one hand a "national study was simply not feasible." On the other, Keyssar found that the single community was inappropriate both because of the wide variations in levels of unemployment from town to town, and because he did not want to miss the political debates about unemployment which took place in the state legislature.[75] While Keyssar's study does not itself change geographic scale as it moves from the nineteenth to the twentieth centuries, it leaves open the possibility of an examination of that crucial moment in the transformation of scale of labor markets and reform efforts.

Most of *Out of Work* concerns the extent and impact of unemployment on the working class and working-class responses to unemployment. Between 1830 and 1870 the proletarianization of labor created the condition we now understand as unemployment. After 1930 another major change took place as labor became segmented, and the burden of unemployment was shifted disproportionately onto certain sectors of the labor market. Between those two periods, from 1870 to 1930, with very little change in the experience and impact of unemployment, Keyssar finds an almost random "democratic sharing of misfortune" throughout the working class.[76]

On the other hand, he notes "a sea change" in middle class thinking about unemployment between 1908 and the early 1920s.[77] That unemployment was chronic and that cyclical depressions were a regular feature of the economy became widely acknowledged. He attributes the new middle-class awareness of the problem to the increased numbers of unemployed (even if percentages did not increase) and to the gradually increasing seriousness of the problem as urbanization, immigration and industrialization cut off more of the unemployed from sources of support other than wage labor. Unemployment, Keyssar explains, "seems to have attained a critical mass that made it impossible to ignore," while the theoretical contributions of William Beveridge and Wesley Mitchell gave shape to the reform impulse.[78]

Katz and Keyssar both cross the methodological boundary between the nineteenth and twentieth centuries in important ways. Katz' survey uses the local studies done by himself and others, but begins to put them into the context of changes in the labor market of the corporate era and the politics of the twentieth century. Keyssar's reconstruction of unemployment statistics provides the background for a multi-faceted picture of working-class response to chronic and pervasive underemployment. While transcending the historical division between the centuries, these two works also transcend the disciplinary divide between social welfare history and labor history. Katz persistently argues that workers and dependents must be seen as part of the same story. And Keyssar actually brings the methodology of the new working-class history to the study of the problem of unemployment.

Yonkers, New York and the Study of Unemployment

This study probes the impact of the transformation from the largely locally based economy of the nineteenth century to the nationally based economy of the twentieth, with respect to the problem of unemployment. The methodology aims particularly to examine the interaction between local developments and extra-local forces. Among the latter I include the multi-branch corporations with markets nation- or world-wide; metropolitan reform organizations and university social science departments, which belonged to a nation-wide network; and state and federal politicians and officials whose purview extended beyond the local community.

My approach bridges those most commonly used for nineteenth and twentieth century histories in order to analyze the turn-of-the-century transition. I concentrate on a local case study, but move back and forth between that case and developments among metropolitan reform theorists, and political, economic, and ideological change beyond the local level. Social change in the manufacturing city at the turn of the century was a product of both local and extra-local forces, and I have attempted to draw a picture of their interaction.

The small manufacturing city of Yonkers, New York is the locus of the study. Relatively few people have ever studied Yonkers. Ernest Ludlow Bogart, whose examination of working-class housing in Yonkers was published in 1898, noted that "in the desire for large results the smaller towns may be altogether overlooked," and expressed concern that "no presentation of the facts as they exist in our small manufacturing towns has been made."[79] Ten years later, when the Russell Sage Foundation sponsored a garden school in Yonkers, it noted the location as "an exceptional opportunity to test the possibilities . . . in a town typical in size of many American cities, while near enough to New York City to be easily accessible to those who might desire to study what was accomplished there."[80]

Located immediately north of New York City on the Hudson River, Yonkers was the only city of its size to share a border with New York City. Growing from a population of 32,033 in 1890 to 100,176 in 1920, Yonkers was both interesting and accessible to metropolitan reformers based in New York City in the early twentieth century. Five major manufacturing industries dominated the city: Otis Elevator, Alexander Smith Carpets, Waring Hats, and two sugar refineries. Otis had a largely skilled male workforce; Smith's and Waring's were predominantly female; while the refineries employed exclusively male and largely unskilled immigrants. (See chapters 1 and 2.)

Management of all of the industries with the exception of Waring (which went bankrupt in 1924) was affected by the corporate reorganization of the 1890s, but the presence of the elevator shops is particularly important for the design of this study. Otis became integrated into a national "elevator trust" and provides the clearest example of corporate organization in its twentieth century form.[81] Otis Chairman William Delavan Baldwin thereafter became directly involved in explorations of broad labor market management campaigns, serving as representative on the advisory board to the State Employment Bureau and Chairman of the New York City Mayor's Committee on Unemployment.[82]

There is a problem with any local case, in that no city is "typical." I am less concerned here with the fact, documented by Keyssar, that local unemployment rates varied from city to city, than the suggestion by Katz that the relative power of various constituents of local elites—factory owners, merchants, and wealthy professionals—may have led to differing responses to the problem of unemployment.[83] With this caveat in mind, I maintain hope that the dynamics I have discovered in Yonkers' relationship to the metropolis, the state, and the nation, will suggest fruitful lines of further inquiry. Here, in summary, is what I have found:

In the late nineteenth century local male elites frequently took responsibility for local social stability and expressed their concern through major contributions of time and money to local charitable and philanthropic organizations. In so doing they hoped to sustain the idea of a community in which they were the "natural" leaders in towns and cities where class divisions threatened that image.[84] In Yonkers, they supported the Yonkers Woman's Institute which became a focal point for a new group of female social reformers during the depression of the 1890s. By 1900 these reformers had created a new infrastructure for social stabilization and largely supplanted factory owners in local projects (chapter 1).

The composition and concerns of the local manufacturing elites were directly affected by the economic reorganization of the turn of the century. Their increasing integration into a national economy made them less dependent upon the local community and less involved in community organizations. Nevertheless, an ideology of "localism" persisted (and was actively promoted) in the small city through the first decade of the twentieth century. This ideology held that unemployment (and other social problems) could and should be dealt with by the local community and that workers should remain cooperative and quiescent in the interest of boosting local industries. Localism before World War I was one aspect of the "incorporation" discussed above. One expression of this localism was the heightened concern with workers' mobility and the attempt to bind previously mobile workers to the local community. To the new furor over "tramps" in the 1890s was added a rash of studies of labor turnover—never previously perceived as a problem—in the following decades[85] (chapter 2).

In metropolitan centers, however, university-based economists and social reformers influenced by European developments began to formulate theories of poverty and unemployment which rejected "localism" and looked toward a broadly organized administrative distribution of labor. Since the depression of the 1890s local public works had been an accepted way of dealing with high unemployment levels. But involving state and federal governments with such projects continued to meet strong resistance. Reformers accordingly shaped their analyses to appeal to the new nationally-based corporate and financial elites (chapter 3).

Metropolitan social reformers based in New York City had an important opportunity during the depression of 1913–1915 under the reform administration of John Purroy Mitchel. Their theories, oriented towards "unemployment in normal times," did not meet the test of a cyclical depression. But their failure led to a reformulation which began to deal with cyclical depression. The vaguely suggested economic coordination by industrial associations and high finance suggested by Mitchel's Committee on Unemployment in 1917 foreshadowed Herbert Hoover's post-war solutions (chapter 4).

The depression, followed quickly by wartime industrial mobilization disrupted labor markets, with major consequences for the reform program on two levels. First, at the state and federal levels, the reformers' proposals for labor market organization became politically attractive. Second, the labor market disruptions in an ideological context of militant nationalism spelled the end of "localism" (chapter 5).

During the war, employers supported nationalistic campaigns in part as a way to combat radicalism and union militance. But the breakdown of localism seemingly opened the door to permanently increased state activity at the state and national levels. While national industry had little to fear from strictly local public involvement in regulating the economy, employers vigorously and successfully opposed extension of labor market management mechanisms into the post-war era (chapters 6 and 7).

When the first major postwar economic downturn hit in 1920, the new twentieth century social, economic, and ideological arrangements were expressed in Herbert Hoover's Unemployment Conference of the following year. Hoover understood the importance of national planning for efficiency and productivity in the economy, but remained opposed to state involvement. He called on business to play the leading role in planning efforts at the national level. As a counterbalance, in order to maintain faith in individual economic initiative and community self-reliance apparently threatened by national planning, he resurrected and actively promoted a new variation of the localist ideology (chapter 8).

Between the 1890s and 1920s, business depressions were times of exacerbated fears and threats of class conflict. The presence of large numbers of men and women unable to find work undermined the assumptions upon which capitalism operated. These periods were thus the occasion for new thinking about charity, philanthropy and social welfare as attempts to mediate class relations. By the 1920s, philanthropic, corporate and state officials attempted such mediations far beyond the local level. Yet in their rhetoric they returned to the importance of the "community." To understand both the transformation of the *reality* of the "community" and the curious resilience of the *idea* of "community" as a crucial element in dealing with the problem of unemployment, we turn first to an examination of the small city during the crisis of the 1890s.

Notes

1. *Final Report and Testimony* (Washington: G.P.O., 1916), 38.

2. Alexander Keyssar, *Out of Work: The First Century of Unemployment in Massachusetts* (Cambridge: Cambridge University Press, 1986), 2–5. Sanford Jacoby identifies the seminal American definition in Davis R. Dewey, "Irregularity of Employment," American Economic Association Publication No.9, October and December 1894. Sanford Jacoby, *Employing Bureaucracy: Managers, Unions, and the Transformation of Work in American Industry, 1900–1945* (New York: Columbia University Press, 1985), 105. See also Jose Harris, *Unemployment and Politics: A Study in English Social Policy, 1886–1914* (Oxford: Clarendon Press, 1972), 4; Raymond Williams, *Keywords: A Vocabulary of Culture and Society* (New York: Oxford University Press, 1976), 273–275; Amos Warner, *American Charities: A Study in Philanthropy and Economics* (N.Y: Thomas Crowell, 1894), 180–181; Carlos Closson, "Notes on the History of 'Unemployment' and Relief Measures in the United States," *Journal of Political Economy* 3 (Sept., 1895), 461–469.

3. See e.g., Frances A. Kellor, "Organizing to Fight Unemployment Effectively," *Survey*, 31, 20 (Feb.14, 1914), 611.

4. The "normality of dependence" is a paraphrase from Michael B. Katz, *Poverty and Policy in American History* (New York: Academic Press, 1983, 183); Alexander Keyssar, *Out of Work*, passim. See also, e.g., Orlando F. Lewis, "Vagrancy in the United States," National Conference of Charities and Correction *Proceedings*, 1907, 64ff.; Annie Marion MacLean, *Wage Earning Women* (New York: Macmillan, 1910); Alice Willard Solenberger, *One Thousand Homeless Men: A Study of Original Records* (New York: Russell Sage, 1911); William M. Leiserson, "Unemployment in the State of New York," PhD. Diss., Columbia University, 1911.

5. In 1900, according to Katz, seven eighths of relief in New York State was *public* and *local*, Michael B. Katz, *In the Shadow of the Poorhouse: A Social History of Welfare in America* (New York: Basic Books, 1986), 45, also see 3–57.

6. Stephen Thernstrom, *The Other Bostonians: Poverty and Progress in the American Metropolis, 1880–1970* (Cambridge: Harvard University Press, 1973). For reviews, see Howard P. Chudacoff, "Success and Security: the Meaning of Social Mobility in America," *Reviews in American History* 10, 4 (Dec., 1982), 101–112; Eric Monkkonen, "The Dangers of Synthesis," *American Historical Review* 91, 5 (Dec., 1986), 1146–1157, esp. 1149.

7. Eric Monkkonen, *Walking to Work: Tramps in America, 1790–1935* (Lincoln: University of Nebraska Press, 1984); Katz, *In the Shadow*, 148–149, David Rothman, *Conscience and Convenience: the Asylum and Its Alternatives in Progressive America* (New York: Little, Brown, 1980); James Leiby, *A History of Social Welfare and Social Work in the United States* (New York: Columbia, 1978), 90–135.

8. David Gordon, Richard Edwards, and Michael Reich, *Segmented Work, Divided Workers: The Historical Transformation of Labor in the United States* (Cambridge: Cambridge University Press, 1982), 107–108; Alfred Chandler, *The Visible Hand: The Managerial Revolution in American Business* (Cambridge: Harvard University Press, 1977), 332–376.

9. Daniel Lustig, *Corporate Liberalism: The Origins of Modern American Political Theory* (Berkeley: University of California Press, 1982), 113–115; Stuart D. Brandes, *American Welfare Capitalism, 1880–1940* (Chicago: University of Chicago Press, 1970); James Weinstein, *The Corporate Ideal in the Liberal State, 1900–1918* (Boston: Beacon, 1968).

10. Guy Alchon notes that the founders of the Russell Sage Foundation argued that it "could act for the nation just as the charity organization societies acted for the larger cities." *The Invisible Hand of Planning: Capitalism, Social Science, and the State in the 1920s* (Princeton: Princeton University Press, 1985), 12.

11. This reverses the formulation in Robert Wiebe, *The Search for Order, 1877–1920* (New York: Hill and Wang, 1967). See Daniel T. Rodgers, "In Search of Progressivism," *Reviews in American History*, 10,4 (Dec., 1982), 113–132; John F. McClymer, *War and Welfare: Social Engineering in America, 1890–1925* (Westport, CT: Greenwood Press, 1980), 32.

12. After 1905 "problems of industry" generated increasing interest at meetings of the National Conference of Charities and Correction. Watson, 384.

13. E.g., Daniel J. Walkowitz, *Worker City, Company Town: Iron and Cotton-Worker Protest in Troy and Cohoes, New York, 1855–1884* (Urbana: University of Illinois Press, 1981), 13; Leon Fink, *Workingmen's Democracy: the Knights of Labor and American Politics* (Urbana: University of Illinois Press, 1983), 14

14. On a related question of the geographic scale of reform, see William Graebner, "Federalism in the Progressive Era: A Structural Interpretation of Reform," *Journal of American History* 64 (1977), 331–357.

15. Morton Horwitz, "*The Transformation of American Law, 1780–1860* (Cambridge: Harvard University Press, 1977); W. Norton Grubb and Marvin Lazerson, *Broken Promises: How Americans Fail Their Children* (New York: Basic Books, 1982); Katz, *Poverty and Policy*, 188; Robert B. Reich, *The Next American Frontier* (New York: Times Books, 1983), 3–21; Louis Hartz, *Economic Policy and Democratic Thought: Pennsylvania 1776–1860* (Chicago: Quadrangle, 1968); Oscar Handlin, *Commonwealth: A Study of the Role of Government in the American Economy, Massachusetts 1774–1861* (New York: New York University Press, 1947).

16. Definitions of "public" and "private" policy areas are not related to the scope of the impact: the "private" investment decisions of a national corporation may have more far-reaching impact than the "public" decision of a local school board.

17. Roy Lubove, *The Struggle for Social Security, 1900–1935* (Cambridge: Harvard University Press), 144–174 and passim; Daniel Nelson, *Unemployment Insurance: The American Experience, 1915–1935* (Madison: University of Wisconsin Press, 1969), 3–46.

18. For theoretical contributions on this phenomenon from two vastly different perspectives see Charles Lindblom, *Politics and Markets: The World's Political-Economic Systems* (New York: Basic Books, 1977); and Adam Przeworski, "Material Bases of Consent: Economics and Politics in a Hegemonic System," in Maurice Zeitlin, ed., *Political Power and Social Theory*, 1 (1980), 21–66.

19. John R. Commons, "Introduction," in Commons and Associates, *History of Labor in the United States*, vol. III (New York: Macmillan, 1935), xxvii.

20. John R. Commons, "Introduction," xii, xvii.

21. Commons and Associates, *History of Labor in the United States*, vol. III (New York: Macmillan, 1935), 126.

22. Commons and Associates, *History of Labor in the United States*, vol. III, 114–269.

23. Commons and Associates, *History of Labor in the United States*, vol. III, 156.

24. James Weinstein, *The Corporate Ideal in the Liberal State: 1900–1918* (Boston: Beacon Press, 1968), 172 and passim; Weinstein and David W. Eakins, *For a New America: Essays in History and Politics from Studies on the Left, 1959–1967* (New York: Vintage, 1970); Ronald Radosh, "Labor and the American Economy: the 1922 Railroad Shop Crafts Strike and the 'B&O Plan'" in Jerry Israel, ed., *Building the Organizational Society: Essays on Associational Activities in Modern America* (New York: Free Press, 1972), 73–87; R. Jeffrey Lustig, *Corporate Liberalism: The Origins of Modern American Political Theory, 1890–1920* (Berkeley: University of California Press, 1982), 144; Ellis W. Hawley, "The Discovery and Study of a 'Corporate Liberalism,' *Business History Review* 52, 3 (Autumn, 1978), 309–320.

25. Steve Fraser, "From the 'New Unionism' to the New Deal," *Labor History*, 25, 3 (Summer, 1984), 405–430.

26. Theda Skocpol, "Bringing the State Back In: Strategies of Analysis in Current Research," in Peter B. Evans, Dietrich Rueschemeyer, and Theda Skocpol, eds., *Bringing the State Back In* (Cambridge: Cambridge University Press, 1985), 3–37; Stephen D. Krasner, "Approaches to the State: Alternative Conceptions and Historical Dynamics," *Comparative Politics* 16, 2 (Jan., 1984), 223–246.

27. Weinstein, 212.

28. Harry Braverman, *Labor and Monopoly Capital: The Degradation of Work in the Twentieth Century* (New York: Monthly Review Press, 1974), 139.

29. Braverman, 151.

30. Braverman, 377.

31. Braverman, 378.

32. Braverman, 388.

33. E.P. Thompson, *The Making of the English Working Class* (New York: Vintage, 1963); Herbert Gutman, *Work, Culture, and Society in Industrializing America: Essays in American Working-Class History* (New York: Vintage, 1977). For reviews of the literature see David Montgomery, "Trends in Working-Class History," *Labour/Le Travail* 19 (Spring, 1987), 13–22; Sean Wilentz, "Artisan Origins of the American Working Class," *International Labor and Working Class History* 19 (Spring, 1981), 1–22.

34. Craig Calhoun, *The Question of Class Struggle* (Chicago: University of Chicago Press, 1982). See also Lawrence Goodwyn, *Democratic Promise: The Populist Moment in America* (Oxford: Oxford University Press, 1976).

35. James Cronin's introduction to a jointly edited volume articulates the objective of extending the concerns of the Thompsonian "new labor history" into the twentieth century. James E. Cronin, "Rethinking the Legacy of Labor, 1890–1925" in James Cronin and Carmen Sirianni, eds., *Work, Community and Power: The Experience of Labor in Europe and America, 1900–1925* (Philadelphia: Temple University Press, 1983), 3–19. Bryan Palmer, whose work has followed Thompson's, has noted the difficulty in extending the Thompsonian approach into the twentieth century.

36. David Montgomery, *Workers Control in America: Studies in the History of Work, Technology, and Labor Struggles* (New York: Cambridge University Press, 1979), 4. Despite his rejection of Braverman's passive picture of labor, Montgomery acknowledges that "the discussion of work relations [in the twentieth century] has pivoted on the meaning of Taylorism, with Harry Braverman's *Labor and Monopoly Capital* providing the definitive text." Montgomery, "Trends in Working-Class History," *Labour/le Travail* 19 (Spring, 1987), 17.

37. Montgomery, *Workers' Control*, passim; Montgomery, "New Tendencies in Union Struggles and Strategies in Europe and the United States, 1916–1922," in Cronin and Sirianni, eds., *Work, Community and Power*. On the impact of these management initiatives, see also Sanford Jacoby, *Employing Bureaucracy: Managers, Unions, and the Transformation of Work in American Industry,1900–1945* (New York: Columbia University Press, 1985); Daniel Nelson, *Managers and Workers: Origins of the New Factory System in the United States, 1880–1920* (Madison: University of Wisconsin Press, 1975); Stuart Brandes, *American Welfare Capitalism, 1880–1940* (Chicago: University of Chicago Press, 1979); Gerald Zahavi, "Negotiated Loyalty: Welfare Capitalism and the Shoeworkers of Endicott-Johnson, 1920–1940," *Journal of American History* 70, 3 (Dec., 1983), 602–620.

38. Montgomery, *Workers' Control*, 4.

39. David Montgomery and Ronald Schatz, "Facing Layoffs" in Montgomery, *Workers' Control*, 139–152.

40. See also Keyssar, *Out of Work*, 293–298.

41. Clarke A. Chambers, "Toward a Redefinition of Welfare History," *JAH* 73, 2 (September, 1986), 407–433.

42. Raymond A. Mohl, *Poverty in New York, 1783–1825* (New York: , 1971); John K. Alexander, *Render Them Submissive: Responses to Poverty in Philadelphia, 1760–1800* (Amherst: University of Massachusetts Press, 1980); Priscilla Ferguson Clement, *Welfare and the Poor in the Nineteenth-Century City: Philadelphia, 1800–1854* (Rutherford, N.J.: Fairleigh Dickinson University Press, 1985); Eric Monkkonen, *The Dangerous Class: Crime and Poverty in Columbus, Ohio, 1860–1885* (Cambridge: Harvard University Press, 1975).

43. Micahel B. Katz, *Poverty and Policy in American History* (New York: Academic Press, 1983), 184.

44. Gary B. Nash, *The Urban Crucible: Social Change, Political Consciousness, and the Origins of the American Revolution* (Cambridge: Harvard University Press, 1979).

45. Katz, *Poverty and Policy,* 183.

46. David J. Rothman, *The Discovery of the Asylum: Social Order and Disorder in the New Republic* (Boston: Little, Brown and Company, 1971) is part of another subfield, explaining the growth of institutions in the Jacksonian era. The penitentiaries, mental hospitals and almshouses in the Jacksonian era. These institutions, initially expressions of optimism about the possibility of creating order amidst the disordering forces of nascent commercial and industrial capitalism, quickly degenerated. Because he deals with institutions and their intellectual roots, Rothman can tell the story on a national scale.

47. Roy Lubove, *The Professional Altruist: The Emergence of Social Work as a Career, 1880–1930* (Cambridge: Harvard University Press, 1965); Roy Lubove, *The Struggle for Social Security, 1900–1935* (Cambridge: Harvard University Press, 1965); Daniel Nelson, *Unemployment Insurance: The American Experience, 1915–1935* (Madison: University of Wisconsin Press, 1969); Irving Bernstein, *A Caring Society: The New Deal, the Worker, and the Great Depression* (New York: Houghton, Mifflin Co., 1985).

48. James T. Patterson, *America's Struggle Against Poverty, 1900–1980* (Cambridge: Harvard University Press, 1981).

49. Guy Alchon, *The Invisible Hand of Planning: Capitalism, Social Science and the State in the 1920s* (Princeton: Princeton University Press, 1982); John F. McClymer, *War and Welfare: Social Engineering in America, 1890–1925* (Westport, CT: Greenwood Press, 1980). Also see Edward Berkowitz and Kim McQuaid, *Creating the Welfare State: The Political Economy of Twentieth Century Reform* (New York: Praeger, 1980).

50. David M. Schneider and Albert Deutsch, *The History of Public Welfare in New York State, 1867–1940* (Chicago: University of Chicago Press, 1941). A prior volume by Schneider, published in 1938, covered the period from 1609 to 1866.

51. James Leiby, *A History of Social Welfare and Social Work in the United States* (New York: Columbia University Press, 1978), 1.

52. Leiby, 5.

53. Leiby, 144.

54. Walter Trattner, *From Poor Law to Welfare State: A History of Social Welfare in America* (New York: Free Press, 1974), 75–77.

55. Trattner, 97.

56. Similarly unanalytical, but far more helpful for my study is Paul Ringenbach, *Tramps and Reformers, 1873–1916: The Discovery of Unemployment in New York* (Westport, CT: Greenwood Press, 1973).

57. Udo Sautter, "Government and Unemployment: The Use of Public Works Before the New Deal," *Journal of American History* 73, 1 (June, 1986), 62.

58. Paul Boyer, *Urban Masses and Moral Order in America 1820–1920* (Cambridge: Harvard University Press, 1978).

59. Boyer, 190.

60. Katz, *Poverty and Policy*, 200.

61. John A. Garraty, *Unemployment in History: Economic Thought and Public Policy* (New York: Harper and Row, 1978).

62. Garraty, *Unemployment in History*, 110–113; 134–139.

63. Michael Katz, *In the Shadow of the Poorhouse: A Social History of Welfare in America* (New York: Basic Books, 1986).

64. Katz, *In the Shadow,* 147.

65. Katz, *In the Shadow,* 149.

66. Katz, *In the Shadow,* 179–181.

67. Katz, *In the Shadow,* 181.

68. Katz, *In the Shadow,* 181.

69. Katz, *In the Shadow,* 181.

70. See Chapter 3, below.

71. William Beveridge, *Unemployment: A Problem of Industry* (London: Longman's, Green and Company, 1908), 204.

72. William Beveridge, *Unemployment: A Problem of Industry*, 204–208; Michael Freeden, *The New Liberalism: An Ideology of Social Reform* (Oxford: Clarendon Press, 1978), 184–185. Also see Jose Harris, *Unemployment and Politics: A Study in English Social Policy, 1886–1914* (Oxford: Clarendon Press, 1972); Harris, *William Beveridge: A Biography* (Oxford: Clarendon Press, 1977).

73. Lescohier, *The Labor Market* (New York: Macmillan, 1923), vii.

74. Katz, *In the Shadow,* 290–291 and passim.

75. Keyssar, *Out of Work,* xv.

76. Keyssar, *Out of Work,* 109.

77. Keyssar, *Out of Work,* 262.

78. Keyssar, *Out of Work,* 263, 264.

79. Ernest Ludlow Bogart, "The Housing of the Working People in Yonkers," *Economic Studies*, 3, 5 (Oct., 1898), 273–274. Bogart's Yonkers roots may have influenced his choice of the particular city. *Who Was Who in America* Vol. 3, 1951–1960 (Chicago: Marquis, 1960), 86. Like Bogart, my childhood in the Yonkers region admittedly played a part in my own interest.

80. "The Fairview Garden School of Yonkers: Report for the Period Ending Sept. 30, 1910," Folder 170, Box 11, RSF Papers.

81. Chandler calls machinery-making "the largest and, in many ways, the most representative big business in early twentieth century America." *The Visible Hand,* 357.

82. See Chapters 4 and 5.

83. Katz, *In the Shadow,* 43; Keyssar, 121–122.

84. In that I understand that the "community" of Yonkers was an ideological construct of the local elites from the time of the beginning of this study, I am not writing another account of the "breakdown of community" of the kind attacked by Thomas Bender in *Community and Social Change in America* (Baltimore: Johns Hopkins University Press, 1978), 45–120. Bender shows how recent historical writing has located "the" breakdown of community in almost every decade of American history from the 1600s to the 1930s.

85. Stephen Thernstrom, *The Other Bostonians* (Cambridge: Harvard University Press, 1973). Katz notes the "hardened wall between residents and strangers" as a result of the new concern over worker mobility; Michael Katz, *In the Shadow*, 148; Jacoby, *Employing Bureaucracy*, 115–126.

1

The Depression of the 1890s and the Transformation of Yonkers Charity

In the 1890s, the owners of the factories of Yonkers exercised a preeminent role in local philanthropy. Remembering the wrath of a community united against them in the 1880s, they assumed leadership in the unemployment crisis of 1893–1894 and mounted a massive program of paternalism which would convincingly affirm for two decades their commitment to the community.[1] Ironically, however, they constructed the most significant monuments to their community commitment on the eve of the demise of their active involvement in local affairs. As their firms became integrated into the new world of corporate capitalism, owners and managers left Yonkers for New York City and largely abandoned direct interest in charity for local workers and their families.[2] Those managers who maintained an active role in promoting social stability through industrial reform and social welfare did so on a much broader scale, without the local focus on Yonkers.

As the male factory-owning elite scaled down its local leadership role, however, a new group of reforming women took on many of its functions and extended them in new directions. They coalesced around a nucleus in the decade-old Yonkers Woman's Institute, which quickly became the center of reform and social welfare activity in Yonkers. The women, some of them wives and daughters of the old male elite, gathered local support as their husbands and fathers turned to other concerns. They led movements in school, housing, health, recreation and, in a minor way, employment reform. Their success in extending the scope of local philanthropy drew in part from their proximity to the centers of local power. But it was also enhanced by the ideology of feminine domesticity, which provided a special role for middle-class women in maintaining home, child, and family, and by extra-local contact with other reform organizations.[3]

Two processes thus took place simultaneously in Yonkers in the 1890s. First, the factory-owners reached the pinnacle of their community-oriented philanthropic efforts, solidifying an image of their own benevolence, responsibility and leadership which endured until the First World War. Secondly, a new group, largely composed of women, developed a new set of institutions to mediate class relations outside of the factories.

Information-gathering, which was central in nineteenth century Charity Organization activity, became even more so in their social reform movements of the early twentieth. As Yonkers reformers extended and transformed local philanthropic organizations, they, like their counterparts elsewhere, increasingly saw solutions to the problem of poverty in the gathering of information on the poor. By the turn of the century knowledge of the poor became, to a remarkable degree, an end in itself. How much information the poor could or would give about their past became a measure of their worthiness; how much information a charitable agency had on its clients became the measure of its efficiency; and how much information a government had on its citizens became a measure of its domestic security.[4]

The depression of the 1890s, the catalyst for both of these processes, caused both real hardship and fears of potential social disorder. With forty percent of the manufacturing establishments of the country shut down, unemployment was unprecedented. "The question," said Frank D. Watson, an early student of the charity organization movement, "of how work could be furnished for the unemployed was raised on all sides."[5] The problem was not only how to provide work and relief for local residents, but how to protect the local communities from the "armies of the unemployed" descending from elsewhere. The recent waves of Eastern and Southern European immigration, labor and political unrest, and Coxey's "armies" only increased the fears.

Across the country, local emergency measures took a variety of forms. Many communities based relief efforts on previously existing Charity Organization societies.[6] The societies had been founded because of "discontent with the prodigality and inefficiency of public relief, and the chaotic state of private charity."[7] The "fundamental law" of charity organization, according to the founder of the first American C.O.S., "is expressed in one word. INVESTIGATE."[8] Investigation, registration and cooperation" [i.e. sharing information with other agencies] were the "main features" of charity organization, according to Watson.[9]

The first C.O.S.s in the United States were founded in Buffalo and Boston in 1877. By 1892, the latter had 767 friendly visitors at its disposal to enter the homes of the poor. New York's had opened its doors in 1882. Ten years later, it had a yearly income of $41,000 and 170,000 families on record, acting as a major clearing house for information on the poor.[10] Of the fifty-five local societies which reported to the Charity Organization committee of the National Conference of Charities in 1893, Boston's and New York's were merely among the largest. Most operations were much smaller. In 1891 the Yonkers C.O.S. reported an income of $829, no paid staff, and no friendly visitors.[11]

Even where large and relatively wealthy societies did exist, the magnitude of the crisis in 1893–94 strained their resources. During that winter many communities set up local emergency relief committees, which existing C.O.S.s joined. The emergency committees coordinated relief agencies, raised and distributed funds, and supervised work relief.[12] Whenever possible, C.O.S. participants used these committees to promote their principles—emphasizing the necessity of investigating the backgrounds of all applicants for any form of relief.

C.O.S. workers found themselves at odds with many of the groups trying to provide relief, labelling such groups "indiscriminate." The C.O.S. supporters argued that newspaper campaigns for relief funds, bread and soup lines, hand-outs of fuel, and free lodging without proper investigation of the lodgers only attracted the mobile unemployed—and thus created for the community more of the problems which they were intended to solve. Newspaper publicity about the problems of unemployment and the collection of funds or goods for distribution to the poor were singled out for vehement attack by the Charity Organization movement. According to Leah Hannah Feder, writing approvingly of the C.O.S. positions, "Chicago became the Mecca for tramps and vagrants when it advertised free food and lodging."[13] In the disapproving words of Josephine Shaw Lowell, founder of the New York C.O.S., "the larger the funds given in relief in any community, the more pressing is the demand for them."[14] The C.O.S. campaign for information collection and investigation was, however, basically a success. Feder treats the mid-1890s as the period when "study and measurement begin."[15] Investigation seemed to promise a relatively inexpensive path to social stability. Thus, in the fall of 1893 a Yonkers newspaper expressed hope that an investigation by the Association for the Improvement of the Condition of the Poor would help put the

Society "in condition to take care of New York's poor, wherever and whenever the need arises," and thus put an end to "ugly mutterings" and "anxiety about the future."[16]

When the worst of the depression was over, the charity organization societies thus found their position strengthened. Though they stirred opposition from those who saw them as the agents of wealthy philanthropists retarding more substantial social reform, even those critics subscribed to the central C.O.S. objects of gathering, organizing, and systemizing information about the poor. While the decade saw the development of new charity organization societies and the growth of old ones, the impact of the movement was greater than this growth and development would indicate.[17] At the same time, the C.O.S. of the mid-1890s was only an historical way-station in the development of new information-gathering techniques and institutions. The extension of the movement itself created a demand for more standardization and coordination of records and information, as well as yet more advanced techniques and institutions for amassing them.

Yonkers, New York, situated just north of New York City, had a population of 32,000 in 1890.[18] Its wealthiest residents, who built spectacular houses on terraces overlooking the Hudson River, comprised both local industrialists and representatives of New York City's industrial, financial, and professional elites. But most of the city's population was dependent upon the large local factories for work. Ernest Bogart, a young economist who took an early interest in Yonkers remarked that "perhaps the most striking fact . . . is the large percentage of those engaged in manufactures."[19] The largest firm was the huge Alexander Smith Carpet Company. Established by Smith in 1865, the carpet works now employed 4,000 workers, putting it among the country's twenty-five largest factories, and supplied 90 percent of the world's Moquette carpet demand.[20] The Waring Hat Company, the largest of several Yonkers hat factories, employed 1,700 workers making nearly 15,000 fur and wool hats daily.[21] Rapid urban expansion propelled the successful Otis Brothers Elevator Company, a local concern since the 1850s, into spectacular growth and reorganization as it absorbed eight other elevator companies to become a nation-wide elevator "trust."[22]

Many of the workers were foreign born, largely Irish but increasingly from Eastern and Southern Europe. Immigrants and children of immigrants lived in close proximity to the factories, making up with their families seven tenths of Yonkers' population.[23] While

Bogart claimed that there were "no real slums, as in New York," the density of workers' housing ranked with the largest cities in the U.S. at the time.[24] He observed that the majority of workers' houses were "of a severe, square box-like type, without the slightest pretension to beauty or individuality," and he found streets in which they were situated "depressing in the extreme."[25] Over half of the families in Bogart's sample of the working-class population had lived in Yonkers more than ten years, and fully three quarters had lived there at least five. Of the small (8%) percent who had been there less than two years, most lived on two streets, Clinton and Washington, identified as having a concentration of recently immigrated "Slavonic population." Bogart assumed that this concentration represented a recent influx and not necessarily ongoing geographic mobility among immigrants.[26] He found that almost nine percent of the population sample were boarders or lodgers—mostly single men—living with unrelated families. On troubled Clinton Street about one fourth of the population were boarders, a proportion more than three times higher than that for Bogart's sample as a whole.[27]

Thus, while boosters promoted Yonkers as a "community," the city was in fact home to a number of very distinct groups. Among the wealthiest, there was, and continued to be, a split between those whose income was based largely on sources in Yonkers—its factories, real estate, utilities, and banks, and—those who had homes in Yonkers but had professional and managerial positions in New York City. In the 1890s, the former dominated local politics, clubs, and philanthropy. Because of their material dependence upon the Yonkers working class, they had much more interest in shaping solutions to the social problems like those exposed by Bogart's study. Alexander Smith's descendants and their spouses were at the center of this group. Smith had died in 1878, (on the night he was elected to the U.S. House of Representatives) leaving a son, Warren, who became president of the company, and a daughter, Eva, married to William F. Cochran, treasurer, part-owner, heir to half of the Smith fortune and director of the First National Bank of Yonkers. Ownership continued in the Cochran family, through William and Eva's three sons, Alexander Smith (president 1902– 1909), William Francis, and Gifford Alexander (president 1909– 1914), and three daughters, Anna, Elinor, and Elizabeth. In this generation, only Anna and her husband Thomas Ewing, Jr. remained active in mill management and in Yonkers affairs.[28]

The Otises and Warings occupied similar positions in Yonkers society in the 1890s. Elisha Graves Otis had died in 1861, leaving his nine-year old elevator company to his two sons, Charles and Norton, who ran the company until its reorganization under William Delavan Baldwin in the 1890s. Norton was elected Yonkers mayor and New York State assemblyman and died in 1905 as a member of the U.S. Congress. Among several local philanthropic positions, Otis was President of the St. John's Riverside Hospital.[29] John T. Waring established his hat-making factories during the mid-century decades and prospered, building the opulent "Greystone," one of the largest residences in the City, on thirty three acres on North Broadway. In the 1870s, reversals swept away his fortune, but within a few years, he was back in Yonkers in the hat business while serving as a director of the First National Bank of Yonkers, and donating heavily to various Yonkers philanthropies.[30]

Joining these factory-owning families on the boards of local banks, clubs, and philanthropies were people like William Allen Butler, a prominent Yonkers judge, John Oliver, publisher of the Republican Yonkers *Statesman*, William W. Scrugham, president of the Yonkers Gas Light Company and director (later president and Chairman of the Board) of the First National Bank of Yonkers, and Walter W. Law, partner in W. and J. Sloane Company, exclusive wholesale agents for Alexander Smith carpets.[31] There was also a group of wealthy residents with no direct business ties to Yonkers, which nevertheless took a major interest in the Yonkers workers, largely from a religious motivation. Thus, John C. Havemeyer, son of New York City's Mayor William Havemeyer, a major owner of sugar refineries, railroads and real estate around the country was the founding president of the Yonkers Y.M.C.A.[32]

Those whose wealth segregated them from the Yonkers working class, whose work was in New York City, and whose religion did not otherwise spur them towards an interest in the "less fortunate," had minimal involvement in the "community" which the Yonkers-based industrialists and their friends promulgated during the 1890s.

In the 1880s, local industrialists had established a skeletal institutional framework for dealing with the poor and working class. A local branch of the Y.M.C.A. was founded in 1881, with John C. Havemeyer as its first president. In May 1883, a year after the New York City Charity Organization Society was founded, the new Yonkers

C.O.S. installed Norton P. Otis as the first president. William F. Cochran, son-in-law of Alexander Smith and treasurer of the company, joined Otis on the Executive Committee. The aims of the C.O.S. were "to prevent street begging, to curtail indiscriminate giving, and generally to improve the condition of the poor." Using the pioneering Buffalo C.O.S. as a model, the organizers assured all those concerned that goals would be met through a thorough "system of registration and inspection."[33]

The 1880s saw the last organizing effort in the Alexander Smith works until the 1930s. A successful campaign by the Knights of Labor in 1884–1885 ended in a strike which closed the mills for five months and united much of the city against the Smith management. Thereafter, the Smith family undertook a broad program of paternalistic measures. The first of these were directed specifically toward the carpet workers, further contributing to the faltering Knights of Labor local. In summer 1886, the Company granted Saturdays as half-holidays and began construction of four rows of workers' housing on the hillside west of the Moquette weaving mills.[34]

Other Smith family activity was directed more broadly toward the "community." In 1894, in the depths of the depression, Reverend James Freeman helped to establish a "club for workingmen," the Hollywood Inn. The club operated on a small scale in two different locations over the next two years. In April, 1896, William F. Cochran offered to build a large new building for the club at Hudson Street and South Broadway. "It is seldom," observed Freeman, "that you hear of a capitalist taking such interest in the toiling masses of everyday workingmen."[35]

Plans, drawings and excavation complete, the cornerstone was ready for laying on Labor Day, 1896. The ceremony provided a golden opportunity for Yonkers' factory-owners to celebrate their interdependence with their workers: "Capital and labor are mutually indispensible," blared the *Statesman.* "In the long run, whatever raises one class in the world raises all. . . ."[36]

The newspaper called the laying of the cornerstone "the most important event in the City of Yonkers today—the workingmen's holiday." Four hundred and fifty people shared the platform, including Cochran, John T. Waring, Norton P. Otis, the mayor, aldermen, ministers and "delegations from almost every organization in the city." Streets in the neighborhood were thronged with an estimated three to four thousand people, including the Iron Molders' and Brick Layers'

Unions. For the workingman, Cochran offered the building as a "rest, retreat, and home;" for working youth, as a place "such as will draw him away from places of vice, and give him sentiments which will help to make him grow to be an honest man and a useful member of society."[37]

General Horace Porter followed Cochran, with praise for the owner of the palatial North Broadway residence, "Duncraggan," for his "contact with workingmen." Porter continued with a warning:

> Now this is a land in which we expect everyone to work. . . . We want no drones in our national hive. . . . A man who does not work we place somewhere between an imbecile and a tramp.[38]

The reaction of the unemployed in the crowd, if any, was not recorded—only laughter and applause. Yet the celebration came only a week after Alexander Smith's worsted spinning mills shut down, throwing 700 out of work on top of retrenchments in other departments, at a time when business of all kinds was described as "dull throughout the country."[39]

Cochran's Hollywood Inn was the greatest in the series of the late nineteenth century philanthropic projects. They were expressions of the factory owners' determination to avoid another situation such as that which confronted Smith in the strike of 1885. Such paternalism promoted an image of the factory owners and their close associates as the "natural" benevolent leaders of a "community" which was in fact increasingly divided along class and ethnic lines.

The Yonkers Free Library For Self-Supporting Women, founded in 1880 by Mary Marshall Butler, her sister Harriet, and eight other "earnest young women representing families prominent in the settlement and development of Yonkers," seemed at first to be a related if somewhat more modest project.[40] Butler's father, Judge William Allen Butler, provided much of the financial support. Mary Marshall Butler regarded religion as her inspiration and continued to frame her goals in the language of religion as she oversaw the growth of the Library. But despite early appearances, this embryonic organization became, as the Yonkers Woman's Institute, a home to the key groups which emerged to mediate class relationships once the factory owners themselves withdrew from their central role in local philanthropy.

The Library's form and function remained essentially unchanged for a decade. In 1882, Butler organized a club for the working women who used the Library. The Library Association sponsored social evenings, musical entertainment, Saturday afternoon outings, and classes in dressmaking, cooking and current events. At the end of the decade, a small red brick house donated in 1883 was still adequate, housing a library and parlor on the first floor and classrooms on the second.[41] Just as the local C.O.S. sought interchange with parallel local efforts elsewhere, the Library Association became a charter member of the Association of Working Women's Societies.[42]

Plans for expansion began as early as 1887 with the initiation of a building fund campaign. The success of the campaign depended to a large degree on the contributions of the wealthiest members of Yonkers society, including the local factory owners. Of the $38,015 raised by 1894, $30,000 came in subscriptions of $1,000 or more. Warren B. Smith, president of the Alexander Smith Carpet Company, gave $10,000; William Allen Butler gave another $6,500; Walter W. Law contributed $5,000; while the Alexander Smith agents, William and John Sloane, donated $2,500. The Waring family, supporting the 1894 revitalization of the Yonkers Y.M.C.A. with $15,000, gave only $500.[43]

The new building opened in April 1893 on the eve of the depression. It was a substantial three-story brick structure with room for much more than classrooms and library. In addition to the library, office, and social parlor, the main floor had two store-fronts which were rented out for revenue. The second floor contained a large lecture hall with a seating capacity of 300. And the third floor housed the classrooms, a kindergarten room and school kitchen.[44] When the depression hit Yonkers, this building was headquarters for local efforts to deal with it.

Yonkers was effected by the depression of 1893–94 in ways not unlike communities across the nation. By this time, large industries dominated the city's economic life and other work opportunities within the city were limited when these shops closed or laid off workers.[45] One of the major supplements to household income—the renting of rooms to boarders—was equally vulnerable to shop closures, since most of the boarders themselves worked in the local factories.[46] Furthermore, since these closures effected such a large proportion of the Yonkers population, they had crippling effects on Yonkers' stores and retailers.

Late in July 1893 the Smith Carpet works went on half-time. "At present all is veiled in uncertainty," the Yonkers *Statesman* reported. "The proprietors may find it necessary to shut down entirely."[47] The paper counselled Yonkers workingmen "to carefully husband their resources. Keep out of saloons. Hold every dollar for rational use."[48] On August 1, Smith Carpets shut down for the first time in its history. At the same time, Waring Hat laid off 1,000 of its workers; Waring made further cuts in the next weeks. Otis cut its work week to four days. Depression hit Yonkers like a whirlwind.[49]

Men and women whose livelihoods depended entirely upon the large factories met on street corners and discussed the situation. According to the *Statesman* they felt that they literally faced starvation, as shopkeepers would not or could not extend credit to the unemployed.[50] The *Herald* noted:

> A very large proportion of the employes are single men and women with no family ties to keep them in Yonkers during a spell of protracted idleness. . . . A complete suspension of work for a long and indefinite period would undoubtedly result in many of these hands leaving the city.[51]

The paper expressed confidence that the firm, in seeking to avoid such an exodus, would run on half-time rather than have a protracted and complete closing. Fear and concern, however, were not confined to workers: the lay-offs created the conditions for social unrest which seemed to threaten the America on which Yonkers wealth was built, and the wealthy of Yonkers mobilized accordingly.

It took about a month before reports of severe hardship became a part of the public record. On September 1, the *Statesman* carried a lead editorial, "Feed the Hungry."

> Yesterday, one of our leading physicians visited the *Statesman* office, and asked us to announce that, owing to want of employment, whole families in this city are now suffering the pangs of hunger. . . . In the evening, a well-known citizen called upon us, and related facts which also went to prove that there is widespread anxiety and suffering among those who depended upon our suspended industries for daily bread.
>
> The sooner there is some recognized organization to extend relief to the needy, the better. . . . From this time forward, until the wheels of industry are again put in motion, the needy army of unemployed people will continue to grow. An organization of our more favored citizens should be put in charge of extending judicious relief. . . .

> The object of this article is to bring the facts before our people, in the hope of inspiring practical results.[52]

The response was immediate. William F. Cochran (treasurer of Alexander Smith and President of the new Yonkers Board of Trade) called a special meeting of the Board to organize relief efforts. Simultaneously, William Allen Butler called for a Relief Committee, "in which all the religious, charitable and public-spirited organizations of the city shall be represented."[53] Butler's suggestion was taken up by Yonkers' Mayor Weller, who issued a proclamation and invitation to a public meeting. From that meeting came the committee which coordinated emergency relief efforts for the Yonkers unemployed over the next six months.

The twenty-four Yonkers groups who sent representatives to the meeting give us a sense of the organizational structure of the city at the time. About half of the people at the meeting (including W.D. Baldwin, future president of Otis Elevator) represented churches. Butler's daughter, Mary Marshall Butler, represented the Yonkers Woman's Institute. *Statesman* publisher John Oliver and future Republican mayor John E. Andrus attended. Other organizations included Cochran's Board of Trade, the Salvation Army, the Society for the Prevention of Cruelty to Children, the Y.M.C.A., the Charity Organization Society, a couple of fraternal orders, and one union, the Bricklayer's and Plasterer's Union.[54]

Though Mayor Weller called the meeting, he did so as the city's first citizen, not because there was any official mandate for municipal action in such affairs. He rejected outrightly the idea of the city's hiring the unemployed on public works as both undesirable and impossible. (In fact, though there was pressure from organized labor for state authorization of municipal public works for unemployment relief, no enabling legislation had been passed.)[55]

The meeting set up a smaller committee, with just one representative from each of the constituent organizations; in turn it delegated responsibilities to a working committee, which met regularly at the Yonkers Woman's Institute to supervise collection and disbursing of funds. The committee coordinated its efforts with those of the Charity Organization Society and the Yonkers Commissioner of Charities, in part by having the C.O.S. secretary and the Commissioner serve actively on the committee. Contrary to the strategies advocated by the C.O.S.s in larger cities, appeals for money appeared regularly in the local papers over the following months, along with names of contributors and numbers of people helped.

One month after it was established, the Committee had identified one thousand unemployed working people in Yonkers whom it deemed worthy and in need of assistance. The Committee was spending about $200 per week, largely for food distributions. Though it urged Yonkers' "working people who are so fortunate as to be employed [to] contribute regularly a small share of their earnings," most contributions came in larger amounts from wealthier residents. At the same time, the C.O.S. was giving food relief to 300, and the Commissioner of Charities to 750. With the Smith mills among others still closed in December, the *Statesman* referred to one third of the industrial population of Yonkers being out of work,[56]

The committee's relief efforts took a variety of forms. At first it purchased food to be prepared and distributed by Women's Christian Temperance Union volunteers at Temperance Hall. Soup and bread was thus distributed in September. Soon, however, it added a system of food vouchers to be spent on a list of approved groceries at local stores. Clothing was collected and distributed, and some authorizations were made for the purchase of coal.[57]

In January, the Smith mills began slowly and sporadically to go back to work. The announcement that the Moquette mills would re-open sent one thousand people to the mills before seven o'clock on the morning of January 3. (A large part of the throng, the *Statesman* noted, were Hungarians). Some of the old hands were re-hired, but no new workers were taken on. "Probably 700" went back to work on the first day, at a reduction of about twenty percent in the piece rate.[58] A week later, the tapestry, worsted, and print mills reopened, drawing from the crowd of "two or three hundred girls" gathered about the doors, but hiring old hands first.[59] By the end of the month a labor force of two thousand was working. The *Statesman* reported, "Work at the Smith Carpet Works is very irregular. Sometimes a girl will work two or three days, and then be laid off. Expert hands get the preference, and those not expert are not working."[60] Nevertheless, the relief committee began to see a tapering off of applications, and by the end of March, applications for relief had fallen off 75 percent.

A final meeting of the committee was held on March 28 at the Woman's Institute. It reported having received $5,969 and having disbursed $5,484 to 462 families, with an estimated 2,210 individuals.

Remaining money was turned over to the Yonkers C.O.S., and the committee's work was deemed to have been completed.[61]

Though the acute peak of shutdowns had subsided by the Spring of 1894, unemployment continued to be a large-scale problem for the next several years. While the entire carpet works did not shut down again, major portions of it did, and there were continued reports of hardship in the area and in neighboring New York City.[62] The Depression profoundly affected the thinking of those with the resources to shape institutions for dealing with the poor. From the account so far, the Mayor's Relief Committee appears to have represented simply the exercise of a consensus of opinion among the wealthy of Yonkers to help those who were thrown out of work by the Depression. Yet there was a deep ambivalence toward the working class underlying this cooperative philanthropic effort. While the Yonkers *Statesman* ran daily appeals for contributions to the Mayor's Relief Committee through the fall and winter of 1893–94, it also printed a steady stream of editorials against encouraging tramps and pauperism with indiscriminate charity. The basic character of the American worker was portrayed as being both worthy and unworthy, both hard-working and lazy, both loyal and potentially traitorous. No wonder there was such attention paid to the separation of the deserving and the undeserving poor.

On the one hand, in the eyes of *Statesman* publisher John Oliver, while a number of the unemployed were thrown out of work because of poor business conditions (created, he charged, by Democratic tariff reform), many more were not working simply out of their own laziness. Early in January 1894 he reprinted an article from the *North American Review* entitled "Begging as a Fine Art," which claimed that begging was a healthful, lucrative, and anxiety-free occupation for those too lazy for honest work.[63] Citing J.J. McCook's study of tramps, he concluded, "it is easy to see that the real reason why a large majority of tramps choose this mode of life is laziness or lack of mental force."[64] The problem with indiscriminate charity was that many workers would prefer to collect alms than to work. In February, basing his calculations roughly on a New York City Police survey, Oliver estimated that one quarter to one third of New York City's unemployed quit work voluntarily in order to collect relief. He warned, "relief, indiscriminately given, swells this class of the unemployed amazingly."[65] Invoking an American version of the principle of less eligibility, Yonkers C.O.S.' Thomas Cornell explained that his organization discouraged pauperism by keeping relief food "more simple than the recipients could themselves have provided with previous self-denial and economy."[66] Cornell went further: among those genuinely thrown out of work by the poor business conditions, only the improvident became destitute and hungry:

> Only a small proportion of the families of workingmen for years past have been unable, with reasonable prudence, self-denial and economy, to lay of their earnings some small savings from month to month and year to year, towards a competence in old age, and to lift them over temporary lack of work, as at present. . . .[67]

These writers portrayed poverty as moral failure, and a moral failure to which most working people were particularly susceptible. On the other hand, the paper portrayed American workers as people who would not respond to anarchist agitation. "Those persons who go about seeking to persuade workingmen—manual laborers—that their wages are insufficient and their condition deplorable, will succeed in securing some listeners. But among industrious, thrifty, sensible Americans, they will not win many followers." America, after all, was a land of opportunity where industrious workers could buy their own small homes in the suburbs.[68] This ambivalence about American workers was evident in the Yonkers reporting of the migration of one thousand unemployed miners to Chicago in the summer of 1893. The depression had struck hard and early in the silver mining areas of Colorado. When between ten and twenty thousand unemployed drifted into Denver, the railroads offered free transportation from the region.[69] The *Statesman*'s first article quoted one of the men sympathetically:

> We came from Colorado . . . every workingman who can get out of the state is going. The men in this crowd are not tramps. They are mechanics and workers. We have beaten our way on freight trains to Chicago. We separate here and expect to get work somewhere.[70]

The City of the Chicago opened a public works project, digging a canal to drain the Chicago River into the Mississippi and, more importantly, to drain the army of unemployed from the streets of Chicago where preparations were under way for the World's Columbian Exposition. A month and a half after the article on their arrival, the *Statesman* reported that the men were too lazy to dig ditches and had quit the work after a few hours of shovelling: "Listening to anarchistic harangues on the Lake

Front was more to their liking than earning a living by the sweat of their respective brows."[71] Here, the moral failure of poverty was linked to the dangers of radicalism: workers who were radicals were so because they were too lazy to work.

Even more frequently, radicalism was associated with immigration. Unrestricted immigration from southern and eastern Europe, the *Statesman* editorialized, brought "ignorant masses with resentment against owners of capital . . . who support Socialism and anarchism," unlike the "worthy and thrifty immigrants from Great Britain, Germany, the Netherlands and Scandinavia."[72] Interestingly, immigrants' radicalism was sometimes associated not with laziness and profligacy but with "economical habits and slavish industry:" Russian and Polish workmen, having driven from the New York City needle trades the "native born and persons born in the Great Nations of Europe," were listening to anarchists at "riotous assemblies." They refused to accept, the paper explained, that their unemployment was due to the insoluble problem of business depression: "how to provide employment for everyone to his satisfaction is a problem which no nation has ever successfully solved, because it is incapable of solution. . . ."[73] In a similar vein, the *Statesman* carried an editorial on strikes and disorders in the West, blaming radicalism on unassimilable immigrants:

> These western miners . . . are really not Americans at all; like their brethren in Pennsylvania, they are mostly Poles, Hungarians, or other foreigners who have little or no conception of the duties of American citizenship. Nor does it appear that they are ever likely to learn. . . .[74]

Eastern and Southern European immigrants were thus frequently assailed in the pages of the *Statesman* for radicalism in the West, anarchism in Chicago, "Coxeyism" in Washington, and riot and disorder as close as New York City, the gateway to the country. Noticeably rare in the pages of the *Statesman*, were similar attacks on the local immigrant population.

The Yonkers picture of the American worker is made considerably more complex when we examine the city's second newspaper, the Democratic Yonkers *Herald*. Its front page news stories were frequently more overtly partisan than those of the *Statesman* in these years. The *Herald* supported organized labor, and gave a prominent place to union news, but was nevertheless fiercely anti-radical, anti-black, and anti-immigrant.[75] As the panic gathered steam around the country in late summer 1893, the *Herald*, like its counterpart, headlined the dangers of radicalism. It warned that Denver was "overrun with tramps," that Newark's unemployed were parading "with a black flag," that "the anarchistic element" was in control of the labor organizations in New Haven, and that the unemployed threatened riot in Chicago.[76]

On the other hand, the local mill shut-downs produced a different response in the *Herald* than in the *Statesman*. The former countered the *Statesman* charges that the closings would mean hardship for the workers.

> Many of the factory hands employed by the Smith Carpet Company are indignant at the statements which have appeared in the *Statesman* regarding the privations which they are likely to suffer from being out of work. Most of them are prudent and thrifty and they consider the insinuation that they are improvident a direct insult.[77]

The paper assumed, like Thomas Cornell, that thrifty workers could ride out a period of unemployment, but used this to defend the character of the Carpet mill employees.[78] When there were reports of destitution and hardship in Yonkers, the *Herald* pointed the finger at Eastern European immigrants. It quoted Committee member Michael Walsh, who laid "the blame for the outrageous stories . . . about want in the city at the doors of the Hungarians and Slavs."

> "They are a people," said he, "who will always make a rush when they think they can get something for nothing. Ninety per cent of the applications for relief come from this class. The very day after the formation of the relief committee these people came in droves to the office of the Commissioner of Charities."[79]

Contradictions in descriptions of the workers and in the basic facts (one day Smith had 5,000 operatives, the next 3,600) cast doubt on the *Herald*'s veracity, and reinforce the notion that its news articles were constructed most fundamentally as *ad hoc* defences of the Democratic administration under which the nation-wide depression took place.[80]

While the *Herald* pressed for immigration restrictions, the *Statesman*'s antidotes to the threats posed by immigrants and radicals in the larger cities of the United States rested upon enhancing the ability of the government to maintain information on the migrating and immigrating poor.[81] In New York City, there was the "inevitable" presence of vast numbers of "detached individuals from the interior and from beyond the seas." The *Statesman* considered these to be "people who need looking after" and suggested, "it is important that something should be known of the character and circumstances of every person either permanently residing or temporarily staying within the city." The massive surveillance required for this project in New York City would necessitate, suggested the *Statesman*, district supervisors under police authority. Not only would it provide knowledge of the city's residents, temporary and permanent; it would also discourage the potential migrant who would know that he would be "'spotted', immediately upon his arrival in the city, and made to give an account of himself."[82]

The use of the police for social investigation was not a new idea: New York City's Mayor Gilroy had turned to his police to conduct a house-to-house survey of the unemployed and their needs for assistance in January 1894. Both their authority and their familiarity with the neighborhoods recommended the police for this task. Yet this survey, and those like it in other cities, were criticized because of the potential for political influence and the lack of experience and training of policemen in gathering social data.[83] In fact, the police surveys of the 1890s marked not the beginnings of a new function for the police but the end of a more typically nineteenth century police function.[84] What Oliver, the *Statesman*, and the concerned elites of New York and Yonkers were seeking was a troop of investigators, armed—like the police—with official authority but also possessed of special training in gathering information on the poor.

Yonkers presented a somewhat different set of problems from those of New York and other larger cities. The difference did not stem from a paucity of local immigrants, with roughly one third of the population foreign-born and another third children of foreign-born parents. Nor, if assimilability was based on country of origin, did Yonkers immigrants pose less of an assimilation problem: the 1890s saw particularly heavy immigration from Southern and Eastern Europe. The Polish-born population of Yonkers jumped 330 percent (from 115 to 500), while the Hungarian-born population jumped from 440 to 1387 over the decade. Italian-born population soared from 132 in 1890 to 898 in 1900.[85] The difference lay rather in the elite's ability to know the poor, the unemployed, the immigrants in a smaller community. In a city the size of Yonkers, with the resources available to and through its local elites, the task was eminently possible. For that reason, the local poor, though receiving indirect admonishment in the form of frequent editorials about their co-nationals in other cities, were not generally perceived as a collective threat.

As the local immigrant population swelled, those who actively sought to maintain social stability did so in large part by maintaining a high level of information on the poor. Their ability to accomplish this end depended both restrictions on the influx of the mobile unemployed, and on surveillance of the more residentially stable poor population.

The first of these tasks was similar to though simpler than the problem for larger cities. The *Statesman* editorialized:

> Especially at the present time is it necessary to refrain [from giving indiscriminate alms] so as to empty the city of these wandering tramps. Unless men and women who ought to know better stop this casual giving, we shall have the city crowded with tramps and full of beggars all summer.[86]

In the winter, authorities could keep track many of the homeless unemployed wandering through Yonkers as they sought lodging in the police station. In the summer, however, the numbers dwindled as the young men in their twenties who made up the bulk of the winter numbers went elsewhere (perhaps employed, perhaps sleeping outdoors), leaving only the older men. Through the 1890s, police recorded the names, ages and birthplaces of an annual average of over 2,600 men (and a scattering of women) reaching a peak in 1894–95, with 3,377.[87] Theodore Silkman, President of the Board of Police, expressed concern about the conditions in that year:

> In front [of the basement], under the sidewalk there is a place where tramps are accomodated; there is a large platform on which they lie, and if they desire to turn over, they must give a signal and turn altogether. The basement is perhaps 22X50 and 50 persons are often down there at a time . . . the atmosphere is calculated to destroy the appetite of any normal person.[88]

When New York City was quicker than Yonkers to close their police lodging houses, Yonkersites feared that "5,000 parasites" would descend upon the suburbs and there were calls for Yonkers authorities to redouble efforts to arrest "professional tramps."[89] The *Herald* concurred on the "tramp problem": "One thing is certain . . . [the tramp] is growing more numerous, more bold, more lawless, and more menacing to life and property."[90]

If the centerpiece of the local efforts to deal with the homeless unemployed was to keep them out of Yonkers, the focus of efforts to deal with immigrant boarders and working-class families was to gather information. The Yonkers Woman's Institute, uniquely poised to coordinate efforts to deal with the problems of the depression itself, was transformed during the 1890s to spearhead this operation. Efforts directed initially toward coordinating relief and coping with the problem of unemployment among working women led the Institute women to expand into a broadly-based social service organization which could maintain and coordinate information on a variety of aspects of the lives of the poor. Further, the Woman's Institute became an operating base for reform campaigns which sought to have the local and state governments assume increasing responsibility for these functions. In this process, the Yonkers factory owners largely removed themselves from the front lines of local charitable activities, and turned over these functions to a full-time corps of volunteer and professional women.

At the time of the opening of the new Woman's Institute building in 1893, these new directions were still unclear. More people turned out for the entertainments and social evenings, but in spite of the hiring of more teachers for classes, there was no marked increase in the number of class participants, nor was there significant growth in the Institute Club, the successor to Butler's Library Association for Working Girls.[91]

The participants in the Woman's Institute Club were similarly unchanged. Those who took advantage of the services by attending classes, borrowing books from the library, and using the social parlor were from Yonkers' working class.[92] In 1894, 97 of the 209 Club members were factory workers. Another 24 were domestic workers. While 41 (19.6%) were listed as "at home," the remainder was divided among stenography, dressmaking, nursing, teaching, and the like.[93]

The women who ran the Woman's Institute and the Woman's Institute Club—donors and trustees who saw themselves as "bettering the conditions of the working girl"—continued to come from families of Yonkers' business and professional classes. The officers of the Institute, Mary Marshall Butler, Harriet Allen Butler, and Florence Parsons (ex officio the officers of the Club), were the same from 1894 to 1900.[94]

On the other hand a variety of new activities began to expand the scope of the Institute. One of these was an Employment Bureau under the leadership of Helen Baldwin, wife of William Delavan Baldwin, then a high official in Otis Brothers Elevator Company. Formed in 1892 prior to the move to the new building, the Employment Bureau was intended to "meet the need of providing employment for women in other than domestic service." It registered dressmakers, seamstresses and the like for a fee of fifty cents.[95] Initially, it was hardly a major contributor to the Yonkers job market, with 91 placements for the 35 women who registered in the year following the opening of the new building.[96] The vast majority of these jobs were temporary.

But the Employment Bureau was transformed by the depression, and its work opened up new directions not only for the Institute women, but for all of those concerned with the problem of poverty in Yonkers. The Mayor's Relief Committee, meeting at the Woman's Institute, recommended an adjunct to the work of the Employment Bureau, to cope with the hardships of the depression. The Institute accordingly opened a Free Employment Bureau which required no fee and, unlike the original Bureau, willingly placed women as domestics. In the first year, it received applications from 400 women. More than one hundred found permanent work as domestics, fifty more in miscellaneous "day work," and another fifty-three "were given sewing and cleaning."[97]

These services were not abandoned when the factories started up again: the Employment Bureau continued to serve more impoverished women who could not afford the fifty cent fee and who did not have a skill which took them out of the market as domestic servants. Between 1892 and 1900, of the 1,022 permanent placements, 495 were in domestic service. It is likely that a large proportion of the 1,042 additional placements in day work were also domestics. The annual report registered concern over the "applicants lack of training and realization of what skilled labor means."[98]

The major significance of the expansion of the Employment Bureau, however, was not an expanded capacity for providing employment to the poor but an enhanced ability to gather information on them. Rather than waiting for jobs to open up for the women who applied to the Bureau, Florence Parsons (General Secretary of the Woman's Institute) directed investigating visitors to the applicants' homes. The visitors gave "relief, advice, and sympathy . . . and work when possible," and gathered information on the home conditions of the families of more than a thousand applicants for work. Parsons emphasized, moreover, that this massive effort was not intended "to take the place of an Intelligence Office." The Employment Bureau's home visiting project became the model for further investigative campaigns sponsored by the Woman's Institute, including a massive tenement housing inspection.[99]

In order to carry out these projects, the Woman's Institute broadened its appeal to Yonkers women. Heretofore the women involved in the Institute had been either the working girls who joined the Woman's Institute Club, or the small group of wives and daughters of the Yonkers elite who directed it. Early in 1895, the Woman's Institute formed a "Civic League" as a "department of the Institute for the promotion of an interest in and study of civic affairs . . . and as an effort to arouse a more united and efficient public spirit among the women of Yonkers by means of active co-operation with the public authorities. . . ."[100] While the Civic League included many of the wives and daughters of the benefactors of the Woman's Institute, it provided a means to involve a new, larger group of middle-class Yonkers women: only about one quarter—24 of 102—of the members of the Civic League listed in 1900 were donors or wives of donors to the Building Fund between 1887 and 1894.[101]

While the working-class Woman's Institute Club had travel lectures and magic shows, the women of the Civic League heard talks on the Consumers' League, kindergarten work, milk inspection and working-class housing. The Civic League was much more than a self-education group, however. While membership remained relatively small, this group clearly had an effective influence on Yonkers decision-makers. It became involved in the whole range of Progressive reform movements, successfully lobbying City Council, the Board of Education, and various city agencies to secure the introduction of manual training, cooking classes and kindergartens in the local schools, to develop an "early closing movement" along lines pioneered by the Consumers' League, to improve conditions in the city jail, and to set aside and develop land for parks and playgrounds.

The Civic League used methods which might be expected of people with the resources available to its members. The School Visiting Committee, for example, made its debut in the Yonkers educational arena in 1897 by holding a tea at Round Oak, the Butler mansion, for the Board of Education and teachers. Close to the center of power, the women of the Civic League formed the most dynamic reform element not only in the Womans' Institute, but in Yonkers society as a whole in the 1890s.[102]

Mary Marshall Butler regarded the successful campaign for a Woman Sanitary Inspector as the "crowning achievement" of the Civic

League. The Free Employment Bureau's home visiting campaign provided the Civic League with a *modus operandi.* As in the earlier investigation, the gathering of information on the poor was central to the new task envisioned by the Civic League.

In 1896, the Civic League initiated a systematic tenement house inspection in conjunction with the Yonkers Board of Health:

> Reports on the sanitary condition of the houses as to plumbing, ventilation, cleanliness, &c., number of families, overcrowding and general hygienic conditions were to be made on forms supplied by the Board of Health and to be paid for at a small sum per house, while social statistics on cards, carefully prepared by the Secretary of the League, relating to the nationality, occupation, church connection, number in family, income, etc., should be collected for the League, the salary being guaranteed by few individuals who were willing to aid in this experiment.[103]

The Civic League's inspector was a Mrs. Pearce, who had worked with the New York Tenement House Commission. The Yonkers Board of Health authorized her activities and provided her with an official badge as "evidence of her authority." After inspecting 119 houses during a five-week period, Mrs. Pearce reported that "the conditions she discovered were fully as vile as any she had found in our adjoining city."[104]

Her successor, Miss Lena Leeds, held the position from April 1896 to June 1897. By the time of her resignation she had visited more than 1,000 families, "reporting nuisances, aiding the poor, finding employment. . . ."[105] She was succeeded by Mrs. Johanna von Wagner.

Von Wagner occupied the position through the years during which it was transformed into a government position. In October, she was appointed by the Board of Health as Sanitary Inspector (the appointments up to this time had been made by the Woman's Institute.) The Board, however, still did not provide a salary. Following a tour of Great Britain in 1899, during which she studied the activities of several cities' woman sanitary inspectors in several cities, Mary Marshall Butler argued that the Board should assume full funding for the position. Mrs. von Wagner assumed office under the Board of Health in February, 1900.[106]

The Woman Sanitary Inspector campaign branched into related projects. A nurse by training, Von Wagner included in her inspections not only the gathering of information, but "practical instruction of mothers" in regard to feeding babies, prevention of tuberculosis and general sanitary precautions, and care of the sick in their homes. These nursing duties, too time-consuming for the Inspector, were taken over in May 1899 by a Visiting Nurse, appointed by the Woman's Institute and paid for through special contribution.[107] The inspections also provided data for tenement housing exhibitions and for Ernest Bogart's study cited above. Mary Marshall Butler handed over to Bogart data on 1,394 families, or 6,519 individuals, living on sixteen streets in working-class neighborhoods, more than one sixth of the total population of Yonkers. While his main concerns were crowding and cleanliness in housing, he also obtained from the Civic League's inspectors information on the families' nationalities, occupations, incomes, and lengths of residence in Yonkers.[108]

Thus the Woman's Institute grew during the 1890s through its relief work connected with the Employment Bureau, through the Woman Health Inspector and the tenement housing campaign and, finally, through the visiting nursing program. These thrusts were closely related: they involved sending women from the Institute out into the homes of the poor in Yonkers rather than waiting for the workers to come into the Institute. The Free Employment Bureau provided the Institute women with their first experience of this method. As the decade progressed, the women of the Institute looked for ways to formalize the activities which grew out of the depression, to enhance their legitimacy, and to enlist public funds for their support. A model for the Woman's Institute campaigns gradually evolved. First, supported by private charitable funding, the Institute expanded its ability to contact and gather information on the poor. Then it secured some government involvement. After a period of joint cooperation, it pressed increasingly for government assumption of major responsibilities and funding. Official authorization, a first step, was replaced by official support and eventually the shedding of responsibility by the Woman's Institute.

By 1899, recognizing that they had turned in a substantially new direction, the women formed a Department of Philanthropy within the Institute. The Department was "the natural outgrowth of circumstances rather than a part of the original plan for Institute work. It developed so gradually and was so closely interwoven with other departments that it may be said to have reached years of maturity before receiving a name."[109]

The Department of Philanthropy became Yonkers' central coordinating agency for the provision of relief and the gathering of information on the poor, building on the position established by the Woman's Institute during the depression. Offering to coordinate a "central bureau of registration and investigation at the Institute," the Department quickly supplanted the Yonkers Charity Organization Society as the center of Yonkers relief efforts. In 1900 the C.O.S. officers, acknowledging that the Woman's Institute had "a well equipped corps of assistants" and a "large and comprehensive system and field of action," resolved to "suspend its work and refer all inquiries for relief to the Department for Philanthropic Work of the Woman's Institute."[110]

Though the goals of these two organizations sounded similar, the transfer of responsibility from one to the other marked a change in the Yonkers elite's organizations for dealing with the poor and unemployed. At the beginning of the decade, the Charity Organization Society, presided over by Norton P. Otis, coordinated the investigation of the poor. Otis was a co-owner of one of the largest companies operating in Yonkers, mayor from 1880 to 1882, and subsequently a New York State Assemblyman from the district.[111] By the end of the decade, the local male industrial elite, which took such an active personal interest in local philanthropy during the last decades of the nineteenth century, was turning the work over to women. And these women, through the Woman's Institute, pressed increasingly for salaried professionals to carry out the actual work of visiting and gathering information on the poor.

The charity organization movement had stressed the gathering and coordination of information in the provision of relief. The Woman's Institute campaigns took up where the C.O.S. left off, applying this principle to an broadened field of work. With investigation and intervention into the lives of the Yonkers poor becoming more extensive, the shift of institutional activity from men to women was not incidental. The local investigative campaigns were based, in part, upon an ideology of feminine domesticity. Mary Marshall Butler's idea for the Civic League came from a discussion of "the special role of women" at the National Convention of Good Government Clubs. She wanted to make Yonkers "feel the power of women along civic lines."[112] The official title of the new health inspector was "Woman Sanitary Inspector."[113] The designers of the tenement housing campaign, where one of the major innovations was to have a female rent collector noted the special role of women in overseeing the health and welfare of home and family:

> If social scientists generally admit that the home is the focal point in which the life of a city centres and the source to which the good and evil in a community, to a great extent may be traced, then, surely, whatever tends to promote the welfare of the family should be regarded as of the greatest moral and economic value to the city. . . . For these reasons cities in this country and in Great Britain employing the best methods of administration and taking the broadest view of the needs of all classes have recognized the absolute necessity of employing women inspectors qualified as teachers of household hygiene as indispensible to the best results of their Health Departments.[114]

The family and the home were seen as the basic building block of social stability. The threats posed by transient workers or homeless unemployed could be reduced if the family bonds among the poor were reinforced. Middle-class women, with their special knowledge of family and home, were seen as particularly suited to the work of shoring up family life among the poor.

The retreat of the male factory-owners and their associates from the field of local relief and charity organization was not, however, simply an acknowledgment of the special role of women in the family. Rather, it was part of the fundamental transformation in the capitalist order which occurred in the years around the turn of the century. At this time, the predominant American business enterprise became the large, nationally based corporation, rather than the locally based company.[115] The capitalists of Yonkers, prior to the 1890s, had been strongly rooted in the local community where they focused their charitable concerns. In this regard, the Smith, Waring, and Otis families were exemplary. The emergence of corporate capitalism removed the identification of the company from the community. Management of community stability, which had been largely in the hands of local male business leaders like William F. Cochran, William Allen Butler, Norton P. Otis, and John Oliver (all of whom were dead by the next severe unemployment crisis in 1907–1908), was handed over to women while a new generation of corporate leaders explored ways to manage labor on a more comprehensive scale than ever before.[116]

Notes

1. See Susan Levine, "'Honor Each Noble Maid': Women Workers and the Yonkers Carpet Weavers' Strike of 1885," *New York History* (April, 1981), 153–176.

2. On the reorganization of capitalist enterprise into the modern industrial corporation during this era, see Alfred D. Chandler, Jr., *The Visible Hand: The Managerial Revolution in American Business* (Cambridge: Harvard University Press, 1977).

3. This chapter should add another dimension to Katz' observation that charity organization was "a bureaucratic resolution of tension over sex roles among the well-to-do in the Gilded Age," and that "tensions over sex roles were acted out in local contests over the control of charity." *In the Shadow of the Poorhouse: A Social History of Welfare in America* (New York: Basic Books, 1986), 79. For a comparison of male- and female-dominated local charity organizations, see John T. Cumbler, "The Politics of Charity: Gender and Class in Late 19th Century Charity Policy," *Journal of Social History* 14, 1 (Fall, 1980), 99–112. On women and reform in this era, see Allen Davis, *Spearheads for Reform: The Social Settlements and the Progressive Movement, 1890–1914* (New York: Oxford University Press, 1967); Kathryn Kish Sklar, "Hull House in the 1890s: A Community of Women Reformers," *Signs: A Journal of Women in Culture and Society* 10, 4 (1985), 658–677; Lynn Gordon, "Women and the Anti-Child Labor Movement in Illinois, 1890–1920," *Social Service Review*, 51 (June, 1977), 228–248; Blanche Wiesen Cook, "Female Support Networks and Political Activism," in Nancy Cott and Elizabeth Pleck, *A Heritage of Her Own: Toward a New Social History of American Women* (New York: Simon and Schuster, 1979), 412–444.

4. The institutional emphasis on gathering and coordinating information, particularly on the working class and poor, is part of what Foucault calls the "movement. . . from a schema of exceptional discipline to one of a generalized surveillance," resting on "the gradual extension of the mechanisms of discipline. . . their spread throughout the whole social body, the formation of what might be called in general the disciplinary society." Michel Foucault, *Discipline and Punish: The Birth of the Prison* (tr. Alan Sheridan) (New York: Random House, 1979), 209. On C.O.S. information-gathering, see Katz, *In the Shadow*, 76–77.

5. Frank Dekker Watson, *The Charity Organization Movement in the United States* (New York: Macmillan, 1922), 248.

6. For an overview of Charity Organization Societies and relief during the depression, see Watson, 249–280 and Leah Hannah Feder, *Unemployment Relief in Periods of Depression* (New York: Russell Sage Foundation, 1936), 71–188. Also see William Trattner, *From Poor Law to Welfare State: A History of Social Welfare in America* (New York: Macmillan, 1974), 75–95; Clarke A. Chambers and Andrea Hinding, "Charity Workers, the Settlements, and the Poor," *Who Spoke for the Poor?* (New York: Family Service Association, 1968), passim; and Paul Boyer, *Urban Masses and Moral Order in America 1820–1920* (Cambridge: Harvard University Press, 1978), 143–161.

7. Charles D. Kellogg, quoted in Amos G. Warner, *American Charities: A Study in Philanthropy and Economics* (New York: Crowell, 1894), 379.

8. S. Humphreys Gurteen, *A Handbook of Charity Organization* (Buffalo N.Y., 1882), 30 quoted in Boyer, 149.

9. Watson, 32; see also Devine, *The Principles of Relief* (New York: Macmillan, 1904), 345–347 on C.O.S. investigation.

10. Warner, 372, 382, and Table XXXII, facing 372.

11. Warner, Table XXXII, facing 372.

12. Feder, 113.

13. Feder, 93.

14. Quoted in Watson, 271; also see Feder, 92–94.

15. Feder, 71–97.

16. Yonkers *Statesman*, Sept. 5, 1893, 3.

17. Watson, 265. This assessment is counter to the predominant historical opinion; e.g., "As elsewhere, in Boston, the Depression of 1893 exposed the bankruptcy of organized charity." Katz, *In the Shadow*, 80. "Its day had past," Katz writes of the New York C.O.S. in the depression of 1893." *In the Shadow*, 15[illegible].

18. U.S. Census, Compendium of the 11th Census (1890) Part I, Population, 566.

19. Ernest Bogart, "The Housing of the Working People of Yonkers," in *Economic Studies* 3, 5 (Oct., 1898), p. 290. Bogart, born in Yonkers, had recently completed a PhD. at the University of Halle, Germany, and was Assistant Professor of Economics and Social Science at Indiana University. He later taught at Princeton, and published several widely used texts on economics and economic history. *Who Was Who in America* Vol. 3, 1951–1960 (Chicago: Marquis, 1960), 86. Bogart's sample showed 32.25 percent of the adults in manufacturing.

20. Daniel Nelson, *Managers and Workers: Origins of the New Factory System in the United States, 1880–1920* (Madison: University of Wisconsin Press, 1975), 7; David B. Sicilia, "Technological Risk in Manufacturing, 1850–1880: Yonkers, New York, A Case Study," Unpublished paper, Brandeis University Department of the History of American Civilization, 2. Part of this paper was published as "Steam Power and the Progress of Industry," *Theory and Society* 15 (Jan.-Mar., 1986).

21. Sicilia, 2.

22. Sicilia, 2–4. See also, Charles E. Allison, *The History of Yonkers* (N.Y.: Wilbur B. Ketcham, 1896), Alvah P. French, *History of Westchester County, New York* (New York and Chicago: Lewis Historical Publishing Co., 1925), 564–567.

23. In 1890, 69.74 percent of Yonkers' population was of foreign parentage. Bogart, 274, 275; U.S. Census, Compendium of the 11th Census (1890), Part I, Population, 566, 718.

24. Bogart, 298, 280.

25. Bogart, 295.

26. Bogart, 293–294.

27. Bogart, 319.

28. *In Memoriam: William Francis Cochran* (Yonkers: 1902), 75–80. (Located in HRM). First National Bank of Yonkers officers are printed in frequent ads; see, e.g., Yonkers *Herald*, Sept. 14, 1894. On the Smith family and the Smith company in the nineteenth century, see Donald L. Grant, M.A. Thesis, Princeton, 1941. (A copy, located in the Hudson River Museum, is missing the title page). Grant had access to the now lost diary of Warren Smith and company letter book, 1867–1882.

29. Sicilia, 3; *Norton P. Otis: Memorial Addresses Delivered in the House of Representatives* (Washington: Govt. Printing Office, 1905), 29–32.

30. Sicilia, 4–5; *Yonkers Illustrated* (Yonkers: Yonkers Board of Trade, 1902), 43.

31. French, III, 34, 20, 129. The Butler family papers, 1816–1902, are located at the New York Historical Society.

32. Obituary, Yonkers *Statesman,* June 8, 1922, 1; John Craig Havemeyer, *Life, Letters and Addresses* (New York: Fleming, Revell Co., 1914). This brief outline of a Yonkers elite invites comparison to David Hammack's extensive analysis of New York City during the same time period. Yonkers being much smaller, the wealthiest were less divided. The vast majority were Protestant, and there is no evidence of a division among those identified as elites because of family, wealth, and "culture." While owners of local industry in New York City were usually not members of the elites identified by Hammack, they formed the core of the Yonkers elite. As we will see, New York City's emergence as national corporate headquarters helped to siphon local wealth from activities in smaller industrial cities like Yonkers. David C. Hammack, *Power and Society: Greater New York at the Turn of the Century* (New York: Russell Sage, 1982).

33. Fisher Baker, "Historical Review" Address to Conference on Charity Work, quoted in Yonkers *Statesman,* June 2, 1908, 6. Also see Charles E. Allison, *The History of Yonkers* (New York: Wilbur B. Ketcham, 1896), 337.

34. Susan Levine, "Honor Each Noble Maid": Women Workers and the Yonkers Carpet Weavers' Strike of 1885, *New York History* (April, 1981), 153–176, 174.

35. Yonkers *Statesman,* April 2, 1896, 1.

36. Yonkers *Statesman,* Sept. 5, 1896, 1.

37. Yonkers *Statesman,* Sept. 7, 1896, 1. The front page contained large pictures of Cochran and the planned building.

38. Yonkers *Statesman,* Sept. 7, 1896, 1.

39. Yonkers *Statesman,* Aug. 29, 1896, 1.

40. *Souvenir History of Yonkers* (Yonkers: Fiftieth Anniversery Celebration Committee, 1922), 35. HRM. That there must have been a large number of "self-supporting women" in Yonkers can be deduced from the marked imbalance between male and female populations. In 1890, there were 15,259 men and 16,774 women, but the imbalance was even greater in Ward 3, where women outnumbered men by almost twenty percent (5,502 to 4,644). U.S. Census, Compendium of the 11th Census (1890) Part I, Population, 566.

41. Woman's Institute *Annual Report,* 1900, 5. The unsorted papers of the Woman's Institute are located in the attic and basement of the Woman's Institute Building, 101 N. Broadway, Yonkers.

42. On the Association of Working Women's Societies, see Annie Marion MacLean, *Wage-Earning Women* (N.Y.: Macmillan, 1910).

43. Woman's Institute *Annual Report,* 1894, 17–21; *Yonkers Historical Bulletin* 29, 1 (Winter, 1982), 12.

44. Woman's Institute *Annual Report,* 1900, 5.

45. Yonkers *Statesman,* July 29, 1893, 1; July 31, 1893, 3. In 1890, there were 3803 operatives in the carpet mills, of a total number of 9,194 operatives in Yonkers. U.S. Census, Compendium of the 11th Census (1890) Vol. II, 1034–1037.

46. Bogart opposed the widespread practice of boarding on this basis: "inasmuch as the greatest evil of the workingman's lot is the unsteadiness of employment and income, the introduction of a new source of uncertainty can have only harmful results." Bogart, 337. He suggested as an alternative, smaller, cheaper apartments for workers' families, and the establishment of a lodging house for men without families. In seeking to reduce the practice of boarding with families and expand the practice of lodging, Bogart's reform

position was exactly the opposite of that which Mark Peel claims was the dominant reform position at the time. Mark Peel, "On the Margins: Lodgers and Boarders in Boston, 1860–1900: *Journal of American History* 72, 4 (March, 1986), 813–834, esp. 813–815.

47. Yonkers *Statesman,* July 28, 1893, 1.

48. Yonkers *Statesman,* July 29, 1893, 1.

49. The two local newspapers, the Democratic Yonkers *Herald* and the Republican Yonkers *Statesman* disagreed on the severity of hardship which the closures would entail. The *Herald* carried the headline on Friday morning, July 28.

50. Yonkers *Statesman,* July 31, 1893, 3.

51. Yonkers *Herald,* July 28, 1893, 1. The fiercely partisan Democratic *Herald* actually minimized the degree of hardship caused by the shutdown (under a Democratic President and Congress, attacked as responsible for the panic by the *Statesman*).

52. Yonkers *Statesman,* Sept. 1, 1893, 3.

53. Yonkers *Statesman,* Sept. 2, 1893, 3.

54. Yonkers *Statesman,* Sept. 8, 1893.

55. Yonkers *Herald,* Sept. 7, 1893, 1. A conference of the Knights of Labor, the New York State Federation of Labor, and an *ad hoc* New York City movement on behalf of the unemployed recommended such authorization to the Governor in January. Yonkers *Herald,* 1894, 2. See also Udo Sautter, "Government and Unemployment: The Use of Public Works before the New Deal," *Journal of American History* 73, 1 (June, 1986), 596.

56. Yonkers *Statesman,* Oct. 9, 1893; Oct. 21 1893, 3; Dec. 20, 1893, 3. It is hard to measure the relief effort against the population of Yonkers because of inconsistency in reporting. At times, it appears that the numbers refer to the unemployed themselves; but elsewhere numbers benefitting from relief efforts include dependents or refer to numbers of families, e.g. Yonkers *Statesman,* Jan. 10, 1894: "177 families supplied with food.

57. Yonkers *Statesman,* Sept. 18, 1.

58. Yonkers *Statesman,* Jan. 3, 1894; Yonkers *Herald,* Jan. 4, 1894.

59. Yonkers *Herald,* Jan. 11, 1894, 1; Jan 13, 1894, 1.

60. Yonkers *Statesman,* Feb. 7, 1894, 1.

61. Yonkers *Statesman,* March 29, 1894, 1.

62. See, e.g., Yonkers *Statesman,* March 17, 1896, 1; July 23, 1896, 3; Aug. 29, 1896, 1. The last of these announced the lay-off of 700 employees and the possibility of further reductions at Alexander Smith as the entire worsted spinning mill closed.

63. Yonkers *Statesman,* Jan. 6, 1894, 2.

64. Yonkers *Statesman,* July 31, 1893, 2.

65. Yonkers *Statesman,* Feb 10, 1894, 3.

66. Yonkers *Statesman,* Sept. 18, 1893, 3. Cornell had been President of Yonkers Gas Light Company since 1857, director of the First National Bank of Yonkers since 1856, and a trustee of the Yonkers Savings Bank. (Scrugham, mentioned above as president of Yonkers Gas Light, succeeded Cornell after his death in December, 1894. Yonkers *Herald,* Dec. 29, 1894, 1.

67. Yonkers *Statesman,* Sept. 18, 1893, 3.

68. Yonkers *Statesman,* July 6, 1893, 2.

69. Feder, 72–73.

70. Yonkers *Statesman,* July 31, 1893, 1.

71. Yonkers *Statesman,* Sept 12, 1893, 2; see also Feder, 94.

72. Yonkers *Statesman,* April 9, 1894, 3.

73. Yonkers *Statesman,* Aug 17, 1893, 1 and Aug 29, 1893, 3.

74. Yonkers *Statesman,* June 6, 1894, 3.

75. There was a labor paper called the Yonkers *Workman,* but I have been unable to locate any copies of it.

76. Yonkers *Herald,* July 31, 1893, 1; Aug. 22, 1893, 2; Aug. 31, 1893, 2; Sept. 7, 1893, 2.

77. Yonkers *Herald,* Aug 3, 1893, 1.

78. The *Herald* presented them as "a much better class socially and intellectually than the factory hands of the cotton and woolen mills of New England," in that they owned their own homes and had savings accounts in the local banks. At the same time, it claimed that a large proportion were single men and women with "no family ties to keep them in Yonkers," and that large numbers would leave during "a spell of protracted idleness." Yonkers *Herald,* July 28, 1893, 1.

79. Yonkers *Herald,* Sept. 20, 1893, 1.

80. Yonkers *Herald,* July 26, 1893, 1; July 27, 1893, 1.

81. Yonkers *Herald,* July 30, 1894, 2.

82. Yonkers *Statesman,* Dec 20, 1894, 2.

83. Feder, 83.

84. See Eric Monkkonen, *Police in Urban America, 1860–1920* (Cambridge: Cambridge University Press, 1981), passim.

85. U.S. Census, Compendium of the 11th Census, Part I, Vol. II, 608 and 12th Census Reports Vol. I, Part I, 800.

86. Yonkers *Statesman,* March 19, 1894, 3.

87. Yonkers, N.Y., *Annual Reports of the Several Departments of the City Government, 1899–1907* (Yonkers, 1900–1907), *NYPL Annex; Yonkers Police Blotters,* Nov. 16, 1867–Jan.6, 1907, New York Historical Society.

88. Yonkers *Herald,* Feb. 6, 1895, 1. Silkman was speaking at the Woman's Institute to a meeting of the Prison Association of New York.

89. Yonkers *Statesman,* Feb. 5, 1896, 2.

90. Yonkers *Herald,* June 10, 1895, 2. See also Sept. 29, 1894, 1; Nov. 22, 1894, 1; and Eric H. Monkkonen, ed., *Walking to Work: Tramps in America, 1790–1935* (Lincoln and London, Nebraska: University of Nebraska, 1984).

91. Woman's Institute *Annual Report,* 1900, 17.

92. Woman's Institute *Annual Report,* 1900, 10.

93. Woman's Institute *Annual Report,* 1900, 10. In 1900, 124 of 242 were factory workers, 21 were domestics, 50 stayed at home, and the remainder were distributed similar to 1894.

94. On the class background of members of Working Girls' Clubs, see Grace H.Dodge's introduction to Annie Marion MacLean, *Wage-Earning Women* (N.Y.: Macmillan, 1910), ix.

95. Woman's Institute *Annual Report,* 1900, 25. Other new activities included daily lunches, accredited University Extension courses, bathing facilities, and a Penny Provident Stamp Station. See Warner, 391, on stamp deposit funds set up by various charity organization societies.

96. Woman's Institute *Annual Report,* 1894, 13.

97. Woman's Institute *Annual Report,* 1894, 13. On employment bureaus for domestics, see David Katzman, *Seven Days a Week: Women and Domestic Service in Industrializing America* (Urbana: University of Illinois Press, 1981; New York: Oxford, 1978), 101–106.

98. Woman's Institute *Annual Report,* 1900, 26.

99. Woman's Institute *Annual Report,* 1900, 25–26.

100. Woman's Institute *Annual Report,* 1900, 30.

101. Woman's Institute *Annual Report,* 1900, 40; *Annual Report,* 1894, 19–21.

102. Woman's Institute *Annual Report,* 1900, 30–33.

103. Woman's Institute *Annual Report,* 1900, 34.

104. Woman's Institute *Annual Report,* 1900, 34; Yonkers *Statesman,* Feb. 19, 1896, 2.

105. Woman's Institute *Annual Report,* 1900, 34.

106. Woman's Institute *Annual Report,* 1900, 34–36.

107. Woman's Institute *Annual Report,* 1900, 35, 43.

108. Bogart, 283–285.

109. Woman's Institute *Annual Report,* 1900, 41.

110. Woman's Institute *Annual Report,* 1900, 42–43.

111. He was elected to the U.S. House of Representatives in 1902. *Norton P. Otis: Memorial Addresses Delivered in the House of Representatives* (Washington: Govt. Printing Office, 1905), 27–30.

112. Yonkers *Herald,* Feb. 23, 1895, 3.

113. Woman's Institute *Annual Report,* 1900, 35.

114. Woman's Institute *Annual Report,* 1900, 37, 36.

115. Chandler, *The Managerial Revolution,* passim.

116. Yonkers *Statesman,* Feb. 21, 1908, 5.

2

Yonkers, 1900–1913: Unemployment as a Community Problem

In the early years of the twentieth century, fluctuations in the demand for labor, both seasonal and cyclical, imposed unpredictable burdens on Yonkers' ad hoc mechanisms for providing relief. Institutional arrangements for dealing with the problem changed in undramatic ways. Yet a new configuration of forces set the parameters for perceptions, definitions, and ultimately policies. Underlying these was the changing relationship of the largest manufacturing establishments to the city and changing perceptions of the local community's boundaries. By examining these relationships and perceptions, we can begin to see how local forces intersected with larger, national trends to shape the emerging discourse on unemployment.

In the local social analyses at the turn of the century, the problem of unemployment was still largely undefined. Homeless tramps and vagrants exemplified extreme cases of the moral ailments which might strike families as well, but which had tenuous analytical connection to industrial and economic issues. Similarly, seasonal unemployment, a fact of life for many workers, was the occasion for pondering the moral shortcomings of the improvident worker who failed to lay away stores for the difficult seasons. In addition to tramps and improvident workers, the elements which made up the prevailing analyses of social problems included immigrants, speculators, trusts, and radicals. These only began, in these years, to coalesce around the problem of "unemployment." How did the people of Yonkers come to draw the relationships among these elements? Who defined the problems? What were the limits of their perceptual universe? Under what constraints did they formulate definitions?

In drawing the limits of articulate Yonkers' perceptual universe, we must consider not only how they saw what was around them, but also how they envisioned what *might be* around them, their possible futures. Positive scenarios included economic growth, prosperity and the amelioration of social problems through reconstruction of a more solidary community. The negative included economic stagnation and divisiveness caused by labor-management conflict, political radicalism, the influx of unassimilable populations, or some combination of the three.

The political economy of the factory-dominated city provided the constraining context within which the definition of unemployment was developed in Yonkers. A peculiar conjunction of forces shifted the local balance of power between labor and capital during these years. During most of the 1890s, all of Yonkers' major employers lived in the city and none had branches elsewhere. They played important roles in Yonkers organizations, and undertook massive philanthropic campaigns. They felt their interests bound up with the well-being of Yonkers, and successfully promulgated this identity among the Yonkers population.[1] Objectively, the relationship changed around the turn of the century, particularly with Otis and the sugar refineries becoming parts of national "trusts," but also with a third generation of the Smith family less involved with the mills and the community. Yet the carefully constructed perception of the identity of interests of the large manufacturers and the community did not fade quickly. Ironically, a new objective relationship—the fact that the large factories provided an increasing proportion of the city's employment—reinforced the old perception among Yonkers workers. The nineteenth century capital-labor relationship had been mutually bound by the borders of the city. Now, just as local labor became more exclusively dependent upon large capital for its livelihood, large capital increasingly forged structural connections beyond the local community. The well-being of the Yonkers working class became more dependent on the large factories, while factory owners became less dependent on Yonkers.

In good years, this imbalance went unchallenged; during "hard times" elites perceived threats, as the swelling ranks of Yonkers' unemployed workers read reports of militant workers and radical demonstrators elsewhere in the country. Yonkers reformers and city officials responded in the context of a city dominated by large manufacturers who jealously guarded their control over the employment relationship: they constructed definitions of unemployment which carefully avoided trespass on what the large factory-owners perceived as their own domains.

They did so by defining unemployment as a "community" problem—as opposed to one stemming from problems in the employment relationship. Reformers could thus enlist the aid of interested factory owners and managers, without confronting them in an adversarial position on the issue of the employment relationship, and even allowing for the possibility of owners' continuing their nineteenth century tradition of community philanthropy. Ira Katznelson has called attention to a peculiarly American phenomenon, the "radical separation in people's consciousness, speech, and activity of the politics of work from the politics of community."[2] In this case study, we confront an example of the ongoing construction of that separation and see its origins in Yonkers in the hegemony of capital.

At the turn of the century, Yonkers was showing many signs of the return of prosperity. Mayor Michael J. Walsh noted the progress in his annual message on December 3, 1901:

> It is with satisfaction that we witness the constant growth of the manufacturing industries of the city. The carpet, hat, and elevator works have all made large additions to their already large plants, and their prosperity, as thus indicated, speaks well for the future of Yonkers as a manufacturing center.[3]

Walsh's message was at odds with the decennial U.S. Census figures on the city as a whole. These showed that capitalization of Yonkers industries had remained stagnant during the previous decade (dropping from $13,153,308 in 1890 to $13,097,205 in 1900), and that total number of manufacturing wage-earners in the city had dropped from 10,443 in 1890 to 8,615 in 1900.[4] These gross figures, however, obscure the consolidation of economic power in the largest manufacturing establishments in the city. Through a series of business failures, takeovers, and mergers, the number of manufacturing firms in Yonkers had plunged from 628 in 1890 to 387 in 1900, while the labor force of the hand trades of the smaller establishments had experienced a net loss of almost two-thirds.[5] Although the larger manufacturing establishments had not yet made up the employment loss in hand trades by decade's end, they were in a better position than ever before to provide the growth and employment which Walsh predicted for the new century.

Between 1900 and 1910, as the number of manufacturing firms in Yonkers continued its plummet to 158, the number of wage-earners in Yonkers' manufacturing jumped to 12,711 and capitalization more than quadrupled.[6] The published census reports do not permit analysis of individual firms, but the New York State Industrial Directory for 1912 shows over 12,500 or about one out of every three Yonkers employees in the four largest industries (five companies).[7] As Walsh knew, the prosperity of most of the people of Yonkers continued to depend—or rather increasingly depended—upon the well being of her large manufacturers.

Economic consolidation and growth was set against several potentially troubling issues which clouded the otherwise rosy picture painted by Walsh in his mayoral message. Among these were the growth of slum neighborhoods in Yonkers, recently documented by Bogart's study, the influx of new immigrants, and the possibility of labor unrest. To those who wrote in the columns of the city's newspapers, the three problems seemed related.

Older Yonkers residents decried what they perceived as a flood of new immigration. Editorials and letters to the editor heaped scorn on the new arrivals. One correspondent recounted "a sight which caused me to quake for the future of our country:"

> A score or more of freshly-imported Italians, raggedly clothed . . . were wandering up [Broadway] . . . in quest of work. And I could not resist the thought that if immigration of such material was not checked, what an amount of trouble there should be in store for our Government.[8]

News articles reeked with contempt. One, on naturalization of aliens at the city clerk's office, bemoaned their "ignorance of the law and the language, and the spelling of their names," all of which "made the work of dealing with them tedious and difficult." Moreover, "they came in droves."[9]

The perceived problem was less with immigration in general than with immigration from Southern and Eastern Europe. Immigrants actually made up a slightly smaller proportion of Yonkers' population in 1900 than they had in 1890. Even by 1910, at 33.3 percent of the Yonkers population, they did not comprise the proportion they had in 1890. There was a dramatic change, however, in their countries of origin. Whereas in 1890, 3.5 percent of the Yonkers population came from Southern and Eastern Europe, by 1910, 17 percent—more than one half of the foreign born—did. The *Statesman* saw the trend early and warned of the "undesirable immigrants."

> German, English, Scotch, Scandinavians are, and always will be, welcome to come and stay. . . . But these desirable classes of immigrants are vastly outnumbered by the more undesirable classes of Italians, Hungarians, Poles, and Russians who overrun the labor market and accept wages which can not possibly maintain decent living . . . they herd themselves in parts of the cities and towns which they congest and turn to slums. They do not learn our language nor care to do so. The live commonly in physical squalor and debasement, shaming the sweet and cleanly life of American workingmen. . . . From their ranks are chiefly recruited the Socialists who in these times are so conspicuously in evidence in all our great centres of population.[10]

The editor had understandable problems with the Irish, who belonged ethnically with the Northern Europeans but economically with the others. But he laid out clearly what he perceived as the two major problems with the new immigrants: they lowered American standards of living, and they tended towards unAmerican radicalism.

Labor unrest formed a second cloud on the horizon. As Yonkersites looked around them, they expressed concern that strike-prone industrial relations were damaging the character of the American worker, and thus exacerbating the same problems seemingly created by Eastern and Southern European immigration.

> All over the country it is strike—strike—strike, everywhere. . . . The American workman was a man in whom his Nation took a pride because he was the Nation. He was a member of the church, he sent his children to the public schools, he enlisted in the militia and helped to enforce the public laws . . . he was a man who did some reading and some reasoning, he was economical and thrifty, he was a man with whom it was a pleasure to associate. . . . Is he that kind of man today?[11]

In a commentary on the 1903 Pennsylvania coal strike, the *Statesman* complained about the imagined effects on workers:

> As a consequence of being supported without work for weeks altogether, the miners are physically and mentally below par. . . . Discipline has been impaired; the habit of work is lost; it will take weeks and months to restore strength and system.[12]

Strikes were dangerous, in this view, in part because of the effect on the character of previously disciplined and hard-working laborers. This argument would resurface, in modified form, in the writings of the unemployment reformers a few years later.

Similar editorials and anti-strike news articles peppered the pages of the press during these years, but within Yonkers, labor conflict assumed a distinctive form. While there were major incidents in construction, on public works, and on the street railways, labor in Yonkers' major factories remained remarkably quiescent through the years which set record numbers of strikes in the United States., and which one historian has labelled the "age of industrial violence."[13]

Most of the labor movement in Yonkers outside of the building trades participated in the Yonkers Federation of Labor. Six local unions formed the Y.F.L. and applied for affiliation with the A.F. of L. in 1903.[14] Within a few years, it included fifteen or sixteen unions among bartenders, bakers, engineers, and clerks.[15] The leadership spoke a militant language, but from the record, appears to have made only sporadic advances in uniting large numbers of Yonkers workers in opposition to employers. In the major labor dispute of these years—the 1907 confrontation between the Street Railwaymen's Organization and the Yonkers Railroad Company—the community lined up behind the union. It had done so in the 1885 carpet strike, but against a very different adversary and for significantly different reasons. In the earlier strike, the issue had been one of solidarity against the exploitative labor practices of a major employer in the city.[16] No such strike or community mobilization occurred in the first fifteen years of the new century. The Yonkers Railroad played an important role as provider of streetcar transportation but was not a major employer. The poor service provided by the monopoly had been a sore point for a decade: "it requires no statement from me," Mayor John Peene had stated in his annual message of 1897, "to enlighten you as to the unsatisfactory service provided by the Yonkers Railroad Company."[17]

In October, 1907, two hundred trainmen walked off the job demanding union recognition and a wage increase to 25 cents an hour. President Maher of the Yonkers Railroad Company brought one hundred strike-breakers into Yonkers to restore service and asked Democratic Mayor Coyne for help in protecting them. Coyne responded abusively, "The condition in which we find ourselves with no cars running is very little worse than that which prevails during the period of so-called operation."[18] Other city officials responded similarly: police arrested strike-breakers for carrying guns; and Health Officer McCormick had

President Maher arraigned in court for using the Main Street car barn as a "boarding or lodging house" for scabs. Yonkers merchants refused to serve the strike-breakers, and the machinists union held a large benefit ball in support of the strikers. According to the *Herald*, "nearly every citizen in the city is in sympathy with the strikers and resents strongly the action of Maher in bringing the strike breakers here."[19] Attempts to run the cars met with violence on October 26, but Mayor Coyne resisted Maher's requests for the militia. Two days later, one hundred and fifty deputies to the sheriff were ordered sworn in by Governor Charles Evans Hughes. By October 28, with the intervention of Rev. James Freeman and Samuel Untermyer, the strikers and the company reached a temporary agreement, re-establishing the status quo, but promising a forum for workers' representatives on wage increases. The Company pleaded financial hardship in November and refused any wage increase. The men, fearing "hard times" in the wake of the October bank panic, did not resume the strike. Even without the increase, the Yonkers Railroad Company went into receivership in January.[20] When the Yonkers Federation of Labor hosted a massive parade during the following April, no other Yonkers employer was the target of the such bitter attacks as those heaped upon the trolley company.[21]

While the trolley strike provided the most significant show of working-class unity in Yonkers in this period, there were other strikes and organizing campaigns. A bricklayers' union dispute with the "boss masons" precipitated a major construction trades strike in 1903.[22] In the Spring of 1908 teachers organized and Bronx Valley sewer workers struck; in the summer of the same year the police organized and the lamplighters went on strike for recognition by the Welsbach Street Lighting Company.[23] In 1909, the Triangle Shirtwaist Company tried to escape the union organizing campaign in New York City by opening a non-union shop in Yonkers, precipitating protest and strike by a Yonkers Workmen's Circle, mass meetings, and appeals to the Yonkers Federation of Labor. But the Triangle Company was seen as an "outside" organization, trying to impose "the same 'sweating' conditions upon its employes here that it imposes upon its New York employes."[24] Organized labor consistently made demands upon smaller employers or public services and utilities in Yonkers, but left unchallenged the large factories at the core of the Yonkers economy.[25]

William Collins, an executive member of the Street Railway Men's Organization, confirmed this pattern. After serving on the executive for four years, Collins became President of the Yonkers Federation of Labor, a position he held when the New York State Factory Investigating Commission came to Yonkers in 1912. He estimated that there were about 6,000 members in the affiliated unions of the Yonkers Federation. He asserted that the "general conditions of labor in Yonkers . . . are, speaking generally, in very good condition." He acknowledged, however, that he was not in a position to assess the situation inside the major factories, as "organized labor does not exist in the factories." Trade unions overwhelmingly concentrated in the smaller establishments and construction industries, while the larger factories remained non-union.[26]

How did the large factory owners keep Yonkers workers quiescent in a period of major labor unrest? Did they have anything in common other than their economic dominance? We have only glimpses of the relations between labor and capital within these large establishments, but these provide clues.

The Alexander Smith Carpet Company, the largest employer in Yonkers, expanded considerably following the hard times of the mid–1890s without undergoing any major structural reorganization. Employing around 4,000 workers during the 1890s, Smith provided work for 7,318 by 1912.[27] Control of the company passed to a third generation with the deaths of William F. Cochran in 1902 and Warren Smith in 1903 but stayed firmly within the family network. (Cochran had been married to Eva Smith, daughter of Alexander and sister of Warren. Their son, Alexander Smith Cochran, became president in 1902 and was succeeded by his brother Gifford in 1914.)

At Alexander Smith, labor relations must be set against the strike of the 1880s and the paternalism of the 1890s. The family which owned Alexander Smith was the city's major philanthropist—and on a grand scale. In the early years of the twentieth century, in spite of plant expansion, there was no major technological or organizational change through which management might attempt to alter patterns of shop-floor control. Technological development in the carpet industry, according to its historians in 1941, had "since the early 1870s . . . related to refinements of existing apparatus, techniques, and processes rather than to the invention of new types of machinery.[28] At least two attempts to form a national "carpet trust" failed during the 1890s.[29]

By 1912 four mills, for tapestry, print, worsted, and moquette (or Axminster), sprawled along the valley of the Saw Mill River. About half of the employees were women. Even in immigrant-dominated Yonkers the carpet shop employees were disproportionately foreign-born, these overwhelmingly from Southern and Eastern Europe: 9 percent of all employees were Irish, 19 percent Slavs, 17 percent Polish and Russian, 4 percent Italian, and 10 percent immigrants from other countries. These percentages do not include children of immigrants, who must have made up much of the remainder.[30] The general superintendent dictated the hours of work according to production needs. Almost all of the women and probably half of the men were paid on a piece work basis, so a reduction in hours did not necessarily force management to announce pay cuts as well.[31] In fact, an order to reduce hours might be accompanied by the statement, "There will be no reduction in wages," which applied, of course, only to those paid by the day.[32] Hours were gradually reduced so that, after 1906, 54 hours was considered the full week.

Under persistent questioning from the Factory Investigating Commission in 1912 General Superintendent Reuben Borland testified that piecework pay for experienced women yielded about $8 a week, perhaps $9 for men. If this was accurate, then it was somewhat below the 1910 average for Yonkers wage earners.[33] William Collins, having worked at Alexander Smith six years before, claimed that they had "more or less of a speeding-up system," that is they would reduce the piece rates when employees worked faster. Superintendent Borland denied Collins' charge, however, and there is no way of testing its accuracy.[34]

Smith provided rewards for loyal employees, particularly those with long service. But these were never structured in a set of explicit rules or procedures to which the company would adhere. They were effected by confidential memo among managers and presented to employees as ad hoc gifts from an all-powerful corporation. In 1911, the carpet company instituted a system of semiannual bonuses which would be the hallmark of its paternalism over the next decades. In the first distribution on September 1, all employees of ten years received ten percent of their semi-annual pay as a bonus. In the second distribution, six months later, the bonus was expanded to pay five percent to employees with five years' experience.[35] The company announced and the local papers reported the bonuses with great fanfare, signifying that the distributions were unsolicited gifts from a benevolent company, not a part of the pay package which employees had any right to expect.[36] In the following year, Borland instructed the managers of the mills not to lay off "any hand who has worked for the company 20 years, whether their service be continuous or not, without consulting me."[37] Care was taken to distinguish between those laid off during slack times and those discharged for various disciplinary infractions. Borland instituted a four-tiered system whereby employees laid off could be rehired immediately. Those discharged were hirable after four weeks, three months, or never, depending upon the nature of the offence.[38] Alexander Smith management was at pains to appear benevolent, and even generous, but not without remaining in firm control of all aspects of its relations with employees. Before the Factory Investigating Commission, William Collins testified that the Yonkers Federation of Labor had "never . . . had the opportunity to get near the women at all" because there were "very strict rules about organizations in the carpet factory."[39] It took heavy prodding from the Commission for Borland to admit that the company would not permit unions in the carpet shops.[40]

As a dynamic modern corporation, Otis Elevator Company was a different kind of operation from the locally-based, family-owned Alexander Smith. The Otis Elevator Company underwent perhaps the most profound transformation of any of the major Yonkers industries in this period. Charles and Norton Otis had run Otis Brothers and Company in the early 1890s. In 1898, in a merger organized by Otis' William Delavan Baldwin, the Otis Brothers Elevator Company absorbed eight other elevator companies and became the Otis Elevator Company, with Norton Otis as Chairman of the Board and Baldwin as President. Fueled not only by the new corporate organization but also by rapid technological change, the growth of Otis was much more dynamic than that in the sugar, hat, and carpet industries of Yonkers. With the electrically-powered elevator still a recent development, Otis joined in 1892 with General Electric, Thompson-Houston Electric, and another local firm to manufacture electric elevator motors in a new building in Yonkers.[41] This operation became part of the 1898 merger. In 1900 Otis introduced the first escalators, and in 1902 the gearless traction electric elevator, which removed barriers of height and speed imposed by the older technology. The technological expansion fueled a dramatic expansion of the Yonkers plant.[42] In 1908, the new Otis *Indicator* boasted of new stock buildings, a forge-shop, electrical works, two mammoth machine shops, a power plant, testing towers and more in the expanded Yonkers works, all of which had been built in the past decade. North American—and European—urban development, which provided rapidly growing markets for the elevator manufacturer, drove the expansion in Yonkers. Otis was thus representative of the newest corporations whose advanced technology and corporate organization characterized the "second industrial revolution."[43]

Though evidence of labor relations in this period is fragmentary, we learn something from what is not there. The search for evidence of a labor policy or labor problems in the minutes of the Board of Directors or in the corporate communications reveals little. The overwhelming issues for the expanding company revolved around competitive salesmanship (including maneuvering around an anti-trust suit) and technological development.[44] The Otis *Indicator*, published from 1908 to 1913, aimed not at increasing productivity or loyalty of shop-floor operatives, as did other employee magazines of the period, but at coordinating middle-management.[45] A substantial portion of it was directed towards establishing uniform bureaucratic rules throughout the widely dispersed organization. Rules concerned problems of production, and not of labor. From the archives, it almost appears as if employees at Otis presented no problem for management, especially compared to the issues of developing technology and competitive salesmanship that did occupy the Board of Directors and filled the pages of the *Indicator*.

Nor did conditions at Otis trouble the visitors from the Factory Investigating Commission in 1912. Yonkers' building inspector, J. Sims Bartley, who had recommended safety-related changes in every other Yonkers factory he inspected in 1911, said that Otis was "in first class shape" and that there was "nothing wanting that I could see to improve on present conditions."[46] When the Commission called Martin Christopherson, Otis' Manager of Construction and Manufacture, it questioned him as an expert on elevators, not as a factory official (and he was the only Otis employee questioned.)[47]

Otis employees were overwhelmingly male, with a shop-force of 1140 men and 85 women in 1912.[48] A rough calculation based on the 1910 census of manufactures shows the average annual wage to have been around $690.[49] Otis instituted a benefit package for employees in 1913. The plan provided death benefits after ten years' service, disability benefits after twenty years regardless of age, and a pension for workers 60 years old and older who had worked for Otis for a minimum of 20 years. In a 1923 study of the benefits paid under the plan Vice President Abraham G. Mills noted that "the group that furnishes the majority of pension cases comprises the shop men, for the benefit of which group, indeed, in the first instance, . . . [the] pension system was inaugurated." Among the shop men, however, many continued to work into old age after "their efficiency has become impaired" at a reduced pay greater than what they would have collected as pension.[50]

The Otis plan differed from the Smith benefits in a way that exemplified the differences in the labor policies of older paternalistic companies and some of the new corporations. Otis laid out the terms of its benefits for all to see. There was no semiannual decision on the part of management as to what to pay, and no semiannual thanks from the rest of the city. The 1923 Mills study, reviewing the company's liabilities, concluded that it was "at least under a strong moral obligation," if not under direct legal obligation, to continue to pay pensions to employees who had been awarded them.[51] Otis' efforts to win employee loyalty—every bit as successful as those at Alexander Smith—were less arbitrary, less personal, and more bureaucratic.

Consolidation and growth in the hat industry arose directly from the business failures of the 1890s. In 1895, the Waring Hat Manufacturing Company, the largest in the industry in Yonkers, bought out the machinery and fixtures of one of its major rivals, the H.F. Flagg Company. Employing 1,700 workers (second only to Alexander Smith Carpets in Yonkers), Waring now had the capacity to turn out 15,000 fur and wool hats per day.[52] In 1907, the company expanded into a third plant, taking over the buildings of the Westchester Hat Company.[53] By 1912 Waring employed 2,437 workers, according to the *Industrial Directory*, and at times as many as 2,700.[54]

Waring's workers not only earned less than Otis' or Smith's in a week (with many of the women earning less than $7 a week, and men around $8), but were far more exposed to seasonal employment fluctuations.[55] General Superintendent William V. Campbell explained to the Commission investigators:

> The hat industry is not an industry that is usually running the year round; our business is done in seasons. There are times in the year when we possibly don't work 30 hours a week, which our books will show. . . .

Campbell claimed that the employees were "glad to be allowed to work sixty-six hours a week" during busy periods, to make up for lost time during the slack periods.[56] In fact, they needed to if they were to make a living.

Even with varying hours, the size of the workforce fluctuated tremendously, as well. As Campbell said, "at times I may have as high as 2,700 and at other times as low as sixteen or seventeen hundred."[57] The ample supply of labor in pre-War Yonkers gave Waring the flexibility it wanted. In 1908, treasurer Le Grand W. Ketchum explained how Waring did its hiring:

> There are always men looking for work. They hang around the factory doors when they are opened in the morning, hoping to be taken on. . . . Sometimes there are 20, sometimes 40: they are always men and usually foreigners. They have no trade as a rule, and when we need a man we pick one out of the crowd and start to train him in the work we wish him to do.[58]

Exposure to fur dust and mercury (used to treat rabbit skins) made the work at Waring more hazardous than that at the other shops. Without any (recent) monumental acts of civic philanthropy on the part of the owners, without a program of corporate welfare for its employees, with low pay and insecure and physically debilitating work, still, there was no labor trouble at Waring in the early years of the century.[59]

In 1893, Benjamin Howell's sugar company, which ran a small refinery at the foot of Main Street providing sugar and molasses for the local market, went out of business. The property was taken over by a group of local entrepreneurs and bankers incorporated as the National Sugar Refinery. Erecting a new plant, the National Sugar Refinery employed 175 men and turned out 2,000 barrels a day. The organizers were George and Albert Bunker, Benjamin Howell, Nathaniel Tooker and James N. Post.[60]

Responding to the promise of the Yonkers waterfront as a location for sugar refineries, Claus Spreckels (with John Mackay and John Mathews) opened a larger plant—the Federal Sugar Refinery—at the foot of Vark Street ten years later.[61] Spreckels was the leading sugar grower on the West Coast and in Hawaii, and Yonkers' Federal Refinery provided him with an East Coast outlet, an important weapon in his rivalry with H.O. Havemeyer's American Sugar Company, the sugar "trust" which dominated the industry. By 1907, however, Havemeyer too had moved into Yonkers by taking control of the

National Sugar Company, thus making Yonkers the local site of a nationwide sugar rivalry.[62]

Mayor Walsh projected in December, 1902 that the Federal Sugar Refining Company would soon employ 500 people.[63] By 1912, it employed 853. By that time, the National Refinery employed 541.[64] Refining sugar was a continuous process, and the mills ran 24 hours a day, in two twelve hour shifts, six days a week on a regular basis. When demand for sugar was high, men worked seven days (or eighty four hours) a week, the only major Yonkers industry with more than a 54 hour work week. Much of the work involved unskilled, physical labor. According to National's Warren Kipp, temperatures in the refinery were generally ninety degrees or more. Workers were generally Slavs, Poles and Hungarians and included no women in either of the two mills. At 19 cents per hour (or more than $13 per week) the pay was considerably better than the unskilled male laborers could make at the other Yonkers workplaces.[65]

There was no union at Kipp's National Refinery—he testified that "we pay no attention to [whether the factory labor is organized.]"[66] At the same time, the Federal Refinery workers were "organized thoroughly," according to Collins. But apparently they considered the refinery conditions nothing to complain about: Collins waxed enthusiastic about the management and pay: "It is the only organized sugar refinery in the Greater New York and it is the best sugar refinery in New York."[67] Questioned more closely by the Factory Investigating Commission's Mary Dreier, Collins explained the union's tolerance of the twelve-hour day:

> They do work twelve hours, but I would like to say this however in relation to the sugar refineries: That the Federal Sugar Refinery is an independent firm and of course it is competing with the trusts; the management itself is very generous; they have been willing to do anything that the organization believed it should do in justice to their business, and I believe they would have put in an eight-hour shift there if it was possible to compete with the trust; but under the conditions that prevail, they have to abide by these conditions, and that compels them to work the men for twelve hours.[68]

Collins' enthusiasm for the Federal refinery might be explained by the union man's opposition to the trusts. But Spreckels' Federal firm, as part of the Spreckels sugar empire, was not an independent Yonkers firm.

Yonkers' four major manufacturing industries, carpets, elevators, hats, and sugar, had a variety of corporate forms ranging from the family-owned Smith to the new corporate Otis. They had a variety of work-forces, from the skilled, male Otis to the unskilled male sugar refineries, to the significantly female Waring and Smith. And they all had different approaches to labor relations. Yet all were characterized by labor quiescence in the first decade and a half of the new century, a time of massive labor unrest around the country, and considerable challenge to Yonkers' own smaller utilities and public works contractors.

Yonkers was a city defined by its large manufacturing plants. They were the base upon which the community was built. So deeply were the employers' interests identified as the community's interests that Republican Mayor Sutherland saw improved living conditions in Yonkers not as an end in themselves but as an attraction for new industry:

> With our hospitals, the Woman's Institute and Hollywood Inn, institutions of a semi-public character but offering their advantages to all, our baths, parks, pavilion, and our excellent record for healthfulness and general progressiveness, we should present a favorable prospect to employers of intelligent labor seeking new locations.[69]

Democratic Mayor Coyne, who claimed to speak particularly for the interests of the Yonkers' workers, issued a variation on the same theme. Referring to the carpet, hat, elevator, and sugar industries in his Annual Message in 1905, he stated:

> It is not too much to say that upon their prosperity depends to a very great extent the prosperity of the city. I favor all proper concessions to our manufacturing interests, and would gladly second a movement to induce others to come to Yonkers.[70]

As we have seen, by 1912 the five largest firms employed more than one third of the total workforce in Yonkers. Yonkers citizens were dependant upon the well being of these major industries in a way that they were not on the smaller firms. The bankruptcy of the Yonkers Railroad Company did not threaten the livelihood of a large number of Yonkers residents. Its services could be replaced, and its laid off workers would not themselves create a glut on the Yonkers labor market. But threats to the major factories were on a different order.

Large manufacturers were hard to attract to Yonkers. If labor militancy made it difficult for them to operate, their expansion if not their existence would be imperilled, and it would be impossible to attract new industries.

This logic was spelled out clearly by the Alexander Smith Company in the course of hearings on the construction of a new street past its Elm Street mills.

> . . . anything which would tend to curtail the development of the business of the Company and prevent the extension of its works and the employment of additional hands would work to the detriment of the city.[71]

The Company noted, in addition, that if the city forced the abandoning of existing mills, the consequence would be unemployed mill workers. The company thus articulated the identity of workers' interests with its own.

During the 1890s the factory owners' had deliberately cultivated a sense of community built upon their benevolence, and the effects lingered into the new century. After William F. Cochran's death, his Hollywood Inn continued to thrive as a workingman's club, increasing membership even in the depression year of 1908.[72] Cochran's widow, Eva, made the final philanthropic initiative of the older generation by donating fifty thousand dollars for the preservation of Manor Hall, the seventeenth century Philipse family residence used until recently as quarters for the Yonkers city government. The growing city administration planned a new City Hall, leaving uncertain the fate of historic Manor Hall. Cochran's gift providing for its preservation tied the Alexander Smith heirs to the symbol of the City's past, reinforcing the identity of the city's heritage and the family's generosity.[73]

The older generation of factory owners in fact identified the well-being of the community with their own. At the 1893 founding meeting of the Yonkers Board of Trade William F. Cochran presided, appropriately, as owner of the city's largest industry. He complained,

> We have a large population who sleep here and do business elsewhere. It is to be regretted that they do not take a very deep interest in promoting the welfare of Yonkers. To make this movement successful, we shall have to depend largely upon those whose business interests are here.[74]

With Cochran on the Board's Executive were Yonkers' other major employers, Norton Otis, his Treasurer and General Manager, William

D. Baldwin, and President John T. Waring of the hat company. John Oliver of the *Statesman*, Thomas Cornell, President and Treasurer of the Yonkers Gas Light Company joined them, as did two bankers, a building supplier, and a real estate man.[75] In the new century, however, many of the owners of Yonkers industry had pressing interests beyond the community, and no longer concerned themselves so centrally with Yonkers: they did some of their business in Yonkers and slept and did other business elsewhere. In part reflecting these changes, the Board of Trade was moribund by 1908. When a new group of locally based merchants and employers took up the cause of local boosterism—in the new Chamber of Commerce—they no longer represented the city's dominant employers. James V. Lawrence, the building supplier from the original board now appropriately assumed the presidency. Four of the thirteen trustees and officers were builders or building suppliers, two were in real estate, and at least two more ran small businesses. Only two owner-managers took part: David Allen who ran the small Yonkers Foundry, and Federal Sugar's Louis Spreckels. Neither Smith nor Otis was represented.[76]

Yet the new Chamber promoted a similar message and issued a familiar complaint:

> Most other cities, having natural advantages offer many special inducements to bring the manufacturer to the town. On this most important subject Yonkers is in a deplorable condition, nothing whatever being done to induce others to come or to encourage those that are here to remain.[77]

They feared that Yonkers was not growing at the same rate as neighboring cities, and held out the promise of growth and prosperity in return for more concessions from the local population and government.[78]

The dominance of large local manufacturing employers, and the identification with the city of Yonkers which they cultivated until the turn of the century, even as they moved beyond the city in new patterns of corporate organization which made the city a less meaningful political-economic unit, provide the essential backdrop to local responses to the depression of 1907–1908.

A decade of growth and speculation led to a bank panic in New York in October, 1907.[79] Yonkers bankers were concerned, but could not predict at the end of the month, whether the run on New York's Knickerbocker Trust Company would extend to the Yonkers banks.[80]

Local industries were affected in fits and starts. Alexander Smith officials maintained their usual veil of secrecy and refused to be interviewed about the possibility of layoffs. "Other sources" at the company stated that "the mills have plenty of work ahead and will have to keep running continually for a year to keep up with orders."[81] In early December, however, Smith closed the entire spinning mill, laying off 500 employees for the month. Again, officials refused to comment or explain.[82] In November, Waring reduced its work week to five days but did not announce wholesale layoffs until the beginning of January, when the whole plant shut down for a week.[83] A reduction of orders led Otis to shorten its work day and to lay off employees in November. December brought a temporary surge at the elevator plant, returning many to work before a total shutdown for the first week of January.[84]

Yonkers responded slowly to the crisis of unemployment in 1907 as it had in 1893. At first there was denial. The post-Christmas edition of the *Herald* blared: "Yonkers Merchants Laugh At Hard Times With Fine Christmas Trade."[85] The new mayor, Dr. Nathan Warren, made no mention of unemployment in his first message to Common Council in January.[86] Charity Commissioner Fox was the first to indicate a general increase in hardship in the community. He reported that the number of applicants seeking relief from his office had surged in recent months, and that this was

> due to the shutting down of factories, the money stringency and general curtailment of help in all trades and occupations, which has all been brought about by the recent talk of panic. . . .[87]

Fox particularly noted the increase in the number of male applicants—usually a small minority at the local charity commissioner's office—and the number who applied repeatedly—again, usually only a small minority. He attributed the changes to the "prolonged scarcity of work" in the last months of the year.[88]

In the new year, the incoming Commissioner of Charities Frank P. Hickey confirmed Fox's report and sought extra appropriations for his office, claiming "unprecedented destitution" in the city. The *Herald* reported:

> Not in any one particular section . . . but in almost every district of Yonkers this condition of absolute poverty and distress is only painfully apparent. . . . All the charitable institutions are stormed with seekers of aid.[89]

Yonkers community leaders digested news of unemployment from around the country and began to search for their own solutions.[90] There was pressure for expansion of government public works. In New York City, workers' demonstrations demanded an end to delays in proceeding with subway construction contracts.[91] A delegation to President Roosevelt pressed a plan for work on harbors and rivers, funded by federal government appropriations.[92]

But in Yonkers, as elsewhere, there was a reluctance to extend government aid except under great pressure. The *Statesman* urged "those having incomes above the day laborer, mechanic and clerk" to "find out who is out of work and do something as neighbors for such families." What the unemployed did not need, it editorialized, was "wholesale demoralizing official and semi-official relief."[93] As conditions became harsher over the next month, the *Statesman* suggested the possibility of charitable hiring by employers. "Not for several winters," ran an editorial in the beginning of February, "have conditions been such as to produce the suffering there is among the poor today. . . . A line of benevolence that is often overlooked [is] the giving of work even though the product is not in immediate demand."[94]

Only a few days later, Alderman Nugent introduced a measure in Yonkers Common Council requesting $10,000 for public works for the city's unemployed.[95] There were precedents for the proposal: Common Council had first appropriated funds for stone-breaking during the winter of 1896–97 with $4,050. Mayor Peene spoke the following April of being "gratified to know that this practical method of giving honest but needy men work, instead of charity, has met with general approval by the people."[96] Similar appropriations were made each winter until 1900–1901 when Mayor Walsh cited "lack of funds" as the reason for ending the practice.[97]

As had the earlier measures, Nugent's proposal in 1908 provided funds for the purchase of "trap rock," and wages for the unemployed to break it, for paving outlying streets in the city. The Council approved the plan in mid-February, expecting to provide work for about 400 men.[98] On February 20, contracts were given out to private contractors with the expectation that each man employed would receive about $12 worth of work.[99]

But concern for the poor was still heavily laced with the Charity Organization caution about the moral effect of relief on the unemployed. As if stone-breaking for road work did not of itself provide enough work-discipline for the relief recipients, the stone provided was extraordinarily hard to break. By February 29, twenty-five of the men employed had quit work in protest. One stated to a Yonkers *Herald* reporter, "No man can break niggerhead [sic] with a hammer and I think giving us such stones to break in our position is an outrage."[100] Commissioner of Public Works Ferguson claimed that the stone was nothing but "a good hard quarry stone," confirming the suspicions of some about those seeking relief from the government. In the beginning of March, the *Statesman* reported 100 men at work.[101]

The question of immigration received renewed attention during the employment crisis, as policy makers and community leaders searched for solutions and scapegoats. In May, 1908, Yonkers Commissioner of Charities Hickey assessed the past winter's problems. He concluded that the increase in relief was caused "not so much by hard times as by increase in population." Most of the relief was distributed, he went on, among the "foreign residents," directly tying the increase in population to immigration.[102] In Yonkers, where the foreign residents and their children made up two thirds of the labor force, it made little sense to single out "immigrants" as the core of high unemployment: in any economic downturn, immigrants were bound to make up a significant proportion of those out of work. In fact, Hickey's report from two months earlier gave a more realistic picture. During March, of thirty new relief cases thirteen were U.S. citizens and seventeen were immigrants (and, aside from the Irish, all were of Southern and Eastern European origin.) At that time, Hickey acknowledged that "lack of employment was responsible for the conditions in a majority of these cases."[103]

Local authorities like Hickey drew their conclusions in large part from what they could see around them. While there was general economic depression throughout the country, its immediate effect in Yonkers were the line-ups of unemployed immigrants at factory gates and charities offices. The authorities called for more restrictive immigration, but even with no further immigration Yonkers would be left with masses of immigrants from the past twenty years. Such officials increasingly subscribed to an analysis which held the promise of removing some of the resident immigrants from the city. In the depths of the winter's unemployment, the Yonkers *Statesman* editorialized:

> It is true that our cities are filled with thousands of men who claim they are going hungry. They may be, but there is no need of it. The city may not be able to give them anything to do, but the country is crying aloud for laborers. . . . There is good food in the country districts, plenty of healthful work, and good wages.[104]

This analysis held a special promise for Yonkers because of its proximity to New York City, the gateway to the United States. Residents feared that, through ignorance or lack of resources, immigrants arriving in New York City failed to move to the parts of the State or the country where labor was needed. "The new arrival who wants to move on from New York is steered just as far as his cash will carry him," the *Herald* editorialized, but without any plan for distribution according to labor needs of the regions.[105] "Broadcasting the immigrant" away from the big cities, and in particular to the South and West, "where they are needed," would give them better economic and social opportunities and more assurance of Americanization.[106] "Why not," chorused the *Statesman*, "place large numbers of these immigrants upon our cheap farms?"[107] In a nation-wide depression, such exhortation was based much more on the experience of labor over-supply in the cities than it was on an accurate assessment in the countryside's labor needs.

Yonkers labor leaders responded to the employment crisis through perspectives likewise shaped by the local setting. Wary of displacement by recent immigrants, the Yonkers Federation of Labor passed a resolution

> asking certain information of the Reverend James E. Freeman concerning an employment bureau of St. Andrews Church, which it was said was furnishing a large number of aliens in factories in the lower part of the city, who are taking the places of Americans.[108]

Freeman refused to discuss the Federation's position that "giving employment to foreigners is detrimental to citizens." He acknowledged that he helped the unemployed find work, but denied running an employment agency and steered the Federation to St. Mary's Parish, which "was much more instrumental in bringing employment to foreigners."[109]

Later in the year, the Democratic Yonkers *Herald* campaigned against Republican Congressman Andrus, who allegedly "scourged the

Yonkers Workingmen for the benefit of imported labor."[110] "Men of families," it claimed,

> have been driven from their homes to seek employment elsewhere, owing to the fact that the scum of the earth has been allowed to come into the city and work under conditions which no bona fide respectable citizen of the city of County of Westchester could work under.[111]

The issue was the construction of the Bronx Valley Sewer which ran through Yonkers and of which Andrus was a Commissioner. Yonkers Federation of Labor organizer John T. Windell denounced the commission as "notoriously unfair to labor."

> While thousands of home workingmen have been walking the streets in these hard times, it has suffered imported scabs to be given the sewer jobs, thus taking bread from the mouths of local men and their families.[112]

As in the trolley strike, the scabs in the sewer construction dispute were identified as non-Yonkers immigrants brought in from outside the community.

Labor's localism was not merely anti-immigrant. When the City awarded a water department contract to a non-Yonkers firm, the Yonkers Federation of Labor demanded "work for home industries." President J.F. Hannigan, argued that such action

> practically takes money contributed by the taxpayers of this city out of circulation among our merchants and robs the working people of the city out of the chance to earn an honest dollar, thus perhaps making them objects of charity.[113]

Ultimately, he concluded, the cost to the city would exceed the small difference in contract prices. A large labor turnout at the February 7 meeting of the Board of Contract and Supply forced a revocation of the original contract, and an award to a local bidder.[114] Organized labor—like the city officials—formulated its solutions to the threat of unemployment from a localist perspective.

The employment situation in Yonkers improved temporarily during the summer of 1908. In June despite continuing irregular employment, the *Statesman* judged that "the situation in Yonkers may be said to be brighter than for some months past. . . ."[115] Otis resumed the full work week in July, but even then work was sporadic. At the end of

August, Superintendent Campbell Scott reported the lingering effects of the depression, with some departments back on short time, and only 1,100 of the full 1,650 employees at work.[116] Reviewing the year in December, the *Statesman* noted,

> probably not since 1893 has there been experienced in this city such a prolonged period of trade stagnation and business depression. Such a condition was especially manifested in the building trades. Most of the large factories have been running on shorter time and with a reduced force of employees.[117]

And there was another measure before Common Council, to provide an additional $20,000 for work relief for the coming year.[118]

One group which did not share the localist perspectives of business and labor in Yonkers was the constituency of the various progressive reform groups which rippled outward from the Woman's Institute in the pre-War years of the early twentieth century. They looked outward for ideas, and for organizational strength.[119] Yet because they worked in Yonkers, their reform strategies were shaped in part both by the localist tendencies of business and labor, and by the dominance of Yonkers manufacturers. In this setting, their distinctive reform agenda carefully defined unemployment relief to avoid issues of employment practices just as it defined public health to avoid issues of industrial hygiene.

In January, 1908 Mary Marshall Butler's Civic League invited Associate Director Anna Garlin Spencer of the New York School of Philanthropy to speak in Yonkers on "Applied Social Science: What is It." In her talk, Spencer explained, "We are not content with giving temporary relief to the poor. We grasp the subject in a large manner and make it a great social question."[120] A few months later, when Butler sought to reorganize the Woman's Institute Philanthropic Department (which had absorbed the C.O.S. in 1900) she invited others to make poverty in Yonkers "a great social question."

The depression of 1907–1908 precipitated the reorganization just as the depression of the 1890s had led an older generation of Yonkers industrialists to give over the work to the vibrant women reformers in the Woman's Institute. By the summer of 1908, Mary Marshall Butler and Florence Parsons sought a way to remove the still expanding work from the Woman's Institute Philanthropic Department and to re-establish an independent Charity Organization Society.[121] They supervised the transition with great flair, using the occasion to host a major conference of charity organization and social work leaders with national reputations.

The plan originated in the Philanthropic Department of the Woman's Institute in April, 1908 with invitations to a join a Conference Committee extended to Yonkers charity leaders.[122] Aside from Commissioner of Charities Hickey and Y.M.C.A. Secretary Haskett, most members of this Conference Committee were associated with churches, and none was an important Yonkers employer. The three-day General Conference on Charity Organization Work and Methods which they designed took place at the Woman's Institute Building in the beginning of June. "Industrial Relief" was one of two major topics. Participants heard discussion of woodyards, work-rooms for unskilled women, stone-breaking, road improvement, and vacant lot cultivation. Speakers included among others, Frederick Almy of the pioneering Buffalo Charity Organization Society, Francis H. McLean of the N.Y.C.O.S., a national authority on charity organization, Lawrence Veiller, prominent in N.Y. housing reform, and Homer Folks, Yonkers resident and secretary of the State Charities Aid Association.[123] The Conference consciously involved outside experts in touch with national developments at a critical juncture in the reorganization of Yonkers' attempts to deal with relief of the unemployed.

One week after the end of the conference, the trustees of the Woman's Institute passed a resolution, "in view of the increasing need of progressive Charity Organization work in the City of Yonkers," to reestablish the Yonkers Charity Organization Society. The resolution called upon the Conference Committee to reconvene to create a "Board separate from that of the Woman's Institute."[124] At Round Oak and the Woman's Institute, through December, 1908 Mary Marshall Butler presided over a series of meetings which established by-laws and officers of the new Society. The only additional participant in these meetings from outside the ranks of clergy and charity was the National Sugar Refinery's George Bunker, who had been an active contributor to the Woman's Institute. Thomas Ewing, Jr., who had married into the Smith-Cochran family, declined an invitation to sit on the Board of Directors. Mary Marshall Butler stepped into the vice-presidency of the new organization, while Rev. A.C. McMillan, president of the Yonkers Clerical Association, became president.[125] In June, 1909, the Yonkers Charity Organization Society was incorporated, and more than a year later, in January, 1911, the Woman's Institute Philanthropic Department transferred all of its general relief work to the new organization, along with money for the C.O.S. visitor's salary.[126]

Working on the principles developed by the charity organization movement in the late nineteenth century, the new C.O.S. aimed both to coordinate relief efforts within Yonkers and to standardize this work through coordination with other societies beyond the city. Thus, in designing the record-keeping, General Secretary Albert Jones wrote to Margaret Byington at the Russell Sage Foundation in New York City asking for standard case-work cards used by other local societies.[127] Before opening a relief work woodyard for Yonkers, Jones wrote for advice to William Nichols (among others) of the Brooklyn Bureau of Charities: Nichols had suggested the woodyard in his talk on Industrial Relief at the General Conference.[128]

Coordination within Yonkers developed as the C.O.S. took on the Woman's Institute visitor, Sophia Manck, and as churches gradually handed over their general relief efforts to the new organization.[129] The beginnings of centralization of relief put a burden on the organization at a time when the needs in Yonkers were again increasing. Once more, in the winter of 1910–1911, the C.O.S. noted that "work is very slack in our factories and many out-door industries are either irregular or discontinued."[130] But the major innovation of that season did not particularly target Yonkers families.

The C.O.S. woodyard, opening in March, 1911, was the first "industrial relief" effort of the C.O.S. not to do so. It ran on a ticket system: only those presenting tickets at the woodyard would be allowed in. The C.O.S. sold books of tickets to more prosperous Yonkers residents in the hopes that they would give them, rather than cash, to street beggars. A recipient would prove his deserving character by making his way to the woodyard on the public dock at the foot of Main Street, presenting the ticket, and chopping one-twelfth of a cord of wood in return for 35 cents (working three hours at 11 cents per hour).[131] The C.O.S. then sent a report to the purchaser of the ticket regarding the "action taken in the case." The C.O.S. also distributed tickets directly to applicants at its office.[132] In the first seven months of its existence, more than one third of the men who were given work there were not from Yonkers.[133]

Later, fear was expressed that the establishment of facilities like the woodyard actually increased the transient population of Yonkers. In 1919, C.O.S. General Secretary Mary Jolly Van Hook noted:

> In the year ending 1913, a great deal of work seems to have been done for homeless men and transients. It is interesting to note this as we are called upon now to do much less work for this class of people than at that time. It causes one to wonder if the woodyard and the missions . . . brought the class known as tramps to Yonkers in larger number than at present when there are no such institutions.[134]

Just as the Institute women spun off the new C.O.S. from its Philanthropic Department, other Institute projects became independent organizations in the new century. In 1903 Butler started a summer garden project for tenement children. In 1908, she and her "Fairview Garden School Association" approached the Russell Sage Foundation (not, significantly, local factory owners) to buy three and a half acres of Yonkers property for the project. By the 1910 season the Association provided plots for six hundred children.[135]

While the Civic League and Consumer's League remained under Institute auspices, many of the public health concerns which the Institute women articulated in the 1890s were now taken on by others. The visiting nurse, first engaged in 1897, was discontinued in 1914 due to lack of funds and her work transferred to the St. John's Visiting Nurse Association.[136] The Sanitary League took on other public health work at its inception in 1904.[137] Though public health and unemployment reform were distinct issues, the attitudes towards health reform were a closely related part of the ideological universe which shaped the options of those considering the problem of unemployment: a brief examination of these attitudes helps to shed light on their choices.

The Sanitary League focused its efforts on the problem of tuberculosis. In its first year, the League completed a massive study of the disease, successfully pressured the city of Yonkers for a dispensary and hospital for chronic cases, and obtained funds from Alexander Smith Cochran for a hospital for incipient cases. Further, it directly employed two visiting nurses to track down and follow up tuberculosis cases throughout the city. The Sanitary League was successful not only in institution building: it claimed responsibility for the reduction in the death rate from 22 per 10,000 to 12.5 per 10,000 between 1904 and 1912. Nevertheless, there was one glaring omission in its work: it steered a wide path around the factories of Yonkers. In view of what was known about the disease at the time, this was remarkable. The Massachusetts State Board of Health in 1895 listed defective workplace ventilation, inhalation of industrial dust, and overcrowding in workshops and factories among the most important causes of tuberculosis.[138] The Health Officer employed by the City of Yonkers acknowledged under questioning that "a large proportion of the cases [of tuberculosis] come from people employed indoors."[139] Yet, according to Dr. Samuel Getty, the Sanitary League's president, its inspectors and nurses "never made a direct attempt to go into the factory and they have never gone in."[140] The Sanitary League, like other progressive organizations in Yonkers, left the factories untouched. They marshalled impressive resources to deal with the problem of tuberculosis as long as it was defined as a community problem. Defined as an industrial problem, tuberculosis would have led them into interference with what the factory owners considered to be their own territory. And the factory owners were not only their direct benefactors; in a more global way, owners' interests were seen as those of the city.

In testimony before the New York State Factory Investigating Commission, Getty did say that he supported their proposed bills regulating sanitary conditions in factories. Responding to a Commissioner's question, he emphasized the importance of their enforcement being under State control: they would be, he said, "very much less" affected by local influence.[141]

Community problems in industrial Yonkers were amenable to reform at the turn of the century, and there was an active local constituency that pursued a variety of reform projects. But the projects were defined in such a way as to avoid interference in the way the dominant local factories were run. The Smith and Waring shops, the large factories owned by local families with no ties to larger corporations, guarded most jealously their control over the employer-employee relationship. Alexander Smith, in particular, maintained virtually total secrecy surrounding hiring, lay-offs, wage rates, and changes in hours. Officers rarely commented on conditions of trade or plans for expansion or contraction. Insofar as possible, they maintained a monopoly not only on decision-making about the wage-relationship, but on the information on which those decisions were based. The management of the new Otis corporation appeared less arbitrary and secretive and could afford to maintain a first-rate shop with high wages at a time when it was rapidly expanding beyond Yonkers. But it did little better in protecting its workers from the threat of unemployment.

Organized labor was a force to be dealt with in Yonkers, but not in the factories. The sole exception was a union among recent immigrants in one of the sugar refineries. Though local labor pressed for better wages and conditions on contract work, construction and public services it did very little to force the large factories owners on whom it depended most heavily for employment to grapple with the problem of unemployment.

Politicians and city officials, labor, and reformers left managing the factories to the factory managers. To deal with the problems of unemployment which swept Yonkers every winter and throughout the seasons in many years, they defined unemployment as a problem of the "community," that is, as a problem of relief, and not as a problem in the politics of work or economics. In times of crisis, they provided relief work either through the city or through a rehabilitated Charity Organization Society. But they also saw unemployment as a community problem in the sense of being a local problem. Pressure for immigration restriction, contracts for local companies, concessions to local employers, and appeals to move the unemployed elsewhere were all manifestations of this localist orientation. Factory owners encouraged localism, even as they themselves moved beyond the city.[142] Both aspects of "community" orientation were indications of the strength of factory owners relative to other local leaders.

Because the factories were so dominant locally at the turn of the century, the impetus for broader reform had to come from beyond the local setting.[143] Glimpses of such reform came from the hearings of the New York State Factory Investigating Commission, whose commissioners grilled Yonkers' large factory managers in ways that local officials never did. At the same time, New York City's metropolitan reformers prepared for what they hoped would be changes on a national scale in the organization of the labor market. We turn now to an examination of their work.

Notes

1. Stephan Thernstrom, and others, have noted the identification of nineteenth century elites with their communities. Thernstrom, *The Other Bostonians: Poverty and Progress in the American Metropolis 1880–1970* (Cambridge: Harvard University Press, 1973); see also Thomas Bender, *Community and Social Change in America* (Baltimore: Johns Hopkins University Press, 1978), 93.

2. Ira Katznelson, *City Trenches: Urban Politics and the Patterning of Class in the United States* (Chicago: University of Chicago, 1981), 6.

3. Yonkers, N.Y., Mayors' Annual Messages, 1897–1906, 29. (NYPL Annex)

4. The 1890 total employment is the sum of wage earners and piece-workers in Yonkers. U.S. Censes (Manufactures) 1890, 1900.

5. From 2706 to 939. U.S. Census, 1900, Manufactures, Vol. 7, ccxcvii, cclvi.

6. U.S. Censes (Manufactures) 1900, 1910.

7. U.S. Census, 1910 Populations, Vol.4, 287 shows the total working population of Yonkers to be 34,364. Two years later, the 1912 the New York State *Industrial Directory* 1912, 493, 494, shows a total of 12,607 working for the five largest companies. The first figure is based on people living in Yonkers, the second on people working in Yonkers. If a significant proportion of those employed in Yonkers mills did not live in the city, then my conclusion would be wrong, but it is my impression that most did.

8. Yonkers *Statesman* May 29, 1896, 2.

9. Yonkers *Statesman* April 24, 1896, 1.

10. Yonkers *Statesman* January 23, 1896, 2.

11. Yonkers *Statesman,* Mar. 10, 1903, 4.

12. Yonkers *Statesman,* Jan. 24, 1903, 2.

13. Record numbers of strikes occurred in 1901 and 1903. Bruno Ramirez, *When Workers Fight: The Politics of Industrial Relations in the Progressive Era* (Westport, CT: Greenwood, 1978), 9. Graham Adams, Jr. *The Age of Industrial Violence 1910–1915* (New York: Columbia University Press, 1966).

14. "Application for Certificate of Affiliation to the American Federation of Labor," Yonkers, March 8, 1903. There is no further record of the "Central Trade and Labor Assembly" which had applied for affiliation seven years earlier (May 26, 1896). Copies of these records were kindly supplied to me by Katharine Vogel of the George Meany Memorial Archives, A.F.L.-C.I.O., Washington, D.C.

15. There was also small socialist party, which had carried on weekly meetings in Getty Square. A report noted "the usual rally of Socialists . . .on Friday evening and the usual crowd was around them." *Statesman,* Sept. 19, 1896, 3.

16. The 1885 strike was led by the Knights of Labor, whose concern for community solidarity was an important organizing principle. Susan Levine, "'Honor Each Noble Maid': Women Workers and the Yonkers Carpet Weavers' Strike of 1885," *New York History* (April, 1981), 153–176.

17. John G. Peene, Annual Message, April 12, 1897, 26, in Yonkers Mayors' *Annual Messages.*

18. Yonkers *Herald,* Oct. 22, 1907, 1.

19. Yonkers *Herald,* Oct. 25, 1907, 4.

20. Yonkers *Herald,* Oct. 28, 1907, pp. 1–3; Oct.29, 1907, 1; Nov. 12, 1907, 1; January 18, 1908, 1.

21. 2,500 organized workers marched in a protest against the application of the Sherman Law to labor. Yonkers *Herald,* April 20, 1908, 1. The Yonkers *Statesman* estimated the same parade at 4,000, April 20, 1908, 6.

22. Yonkers *Statesman*, Mar. 17, 1903, 1, with succeeding articles through March and April, 1903.

23. Yonkers *Herald*, March 27, 1908, 1; May 3, 1908, 1; Yonkers *Statesman*, Aug.3, 1908, 1; Aug. 29, 1908, 1.

24. Yonkers *Herald*, Dec. 7, 1909, 1. See also Dec. 4, 9, 13. On the shirtwaist strike in New York City, see Nancy Schrom Dye, *As Equals and As Sisters: Feminism, Unionism, and the Women's Trade Union League of New York* (Columbia and London: University of Missouri Press, 1980), 88–96.

25. During the construction trades strike, union members who worked for the large Yonkers factories (e.g. carpenters at Otis) were not required or expected by the unions to go out. Yonkers *Statesman*, April 1, 1903, 1. Labor's focus on public service contracts in Yonkers invites questions of their relationship to urban reformers of the period. If discontent with urban services helped labor's community mobilization, as in the trolley strike, one might expect to find evidence of labor-reform alliances. I have found none in Yonkers, however.

26. N.Y. State Factory Investigating Commission (hereafter NYFIC), Second Report, Vol. 3 (Albany: J.B. Lyon, 1913), 748.

27. N.Y. State *Industrial Directory* (1912), 494.

28. Arthur Cole and Harold F. Williamson, *The American Carpet Manufacture: A History and an Analysis* (Cambridge: Harvard University Press, 1941), 130.

29. Cole and Williamson, *American Carpet Manufacture,* 207–208.

30. NYSFIC, 2nd Report, Vol. 3, 752, 755, 756. The proportion of women is confirmed by the 1910 census and the 1912 *Industrial Directory*. For a comparison to male/female ratios in the carpet industry nationally, see Cole and Williamson, *American Carpet Manufacture,* 167. An exhaustive physical description of the Carpet Mills Complex and a history of the company were recently prepared in an application to the National Register of Historic Places by Karen Morey Kennedy and kindly provided to me by Michael P. Rebic of the Yonkers Planning Bureau.

31. NYSFIC, 2nd Report, Vol. 3, 752,753.

32. *Rule Book: Rules and Men,* Alexander Smith Company Archives, Hudson River Museum, May 13, 1905.

33. At steady work, for 52 weeks, $9 would give a yearly income of $468, compared to the Yonkers average of $529.NYSFIC, 2nd Report, Vol. 3, 754; U.S. Census, 1910, Vol. 9 (Manufactures), 894, 895.

34. NYSFIC 2nd Report, Vol. 3, 749.

35. Yonkers *Statesman*, Feb. 1, 1921, 1 gives a retrospective summary of the bonus distributions over the years. Such summaries appeared with virtually every distribution.

36. NYSFIC 2nd Report, Vol. 3, 755.

37. August 21, 1912 entry in Rule Book, "Rules and Men" (1902–1931) in Alexander Smith Company Papers, Hudson River Museum.

38. March 12, 1907 entry in Rule Book, "Rules and Men" (1902–1931).

39. NYSFIC, 2nd Report, Vol. 3, 751.

40. NYSFIC, 2nd Report, Vol. 3, 759. The absence of organization at Smith Carpets is not unexpected, according to the general features of the carpet industry—especially Axminster carpets—outside of the Philadelphia region after 1900. They note the predominance of large plants with strong anti-union policies combined with welfare provisions to build loyalty. *American Carpet Manufacture,* 193.

41. Sicilia, "Technological Risk in Manufacturing," 3–4.

42. See Otis Elevator Company Annual Report, 1905, in Otis Elevator Unsorted Chronological Box #1, 1890–1914. United Technologies Archives.

43. Sicilia, 3,4; "The Story of the Yonkers Works" in *Yonkers Works Digest* 8,10 (Nov., 1949) and 8,11 (Dec., 1949), n.p.; The Otis *Indicator,* 1,1 (July, 1908), 2.

44. Minutes of the Board of Directors, Otis Elevator Company, in Unsorted Chronological Box #1, 1890–1914. United Technology Archives.

45. National Industrial Conference Board, *Employee Magazines in the United States* (New York: N.I.C.B., 1925), 3 and passim. Also see David Nye, *Image Worlds: Corporate Identities at General Electric, 1890–1930* (Cambridge, MA: MIT Press, 1985).

46. NYSFIC 2nd Report, Vol. 3, 743

47. NYSFIC 2nd Report, Vol. 3, 782–787.

48. N.Y. State *Industrial Directory* (1912), 494.

49. U.S. Census, 1910, Vol.9, 894–895. Otis is not separated as a firm, but must have dominated the 1,346 foundry and machine shop products wage-earners, who earned an aggregate of $924,953.

50. A.G. Mills, "The Otis Pension System as Investigated an Conducted With Costs, Actuarial and Actual," Typescript, 1924, 5, 7, 14, located in Box 1, File "Otis Elevator," Abraham Gilbert Mills Papers (NYPL).

51. A.G. Mills, "The Otis Pension System as Investigated an Conducted With Costs, Actuarial and Actual," Typescript, 1924, 1, located in Box 1, File "Otis Elevator," Abraham Gilbert Mills Papers.

52. Sicilia, "Technological Risk in Manufacturing," 2.

53. Yonkers *Herald*, Oct. 21, 1907, 1.

54. New York State *Industrial Directory* (1912), 494; NYSFIC, 764.

55. NYSFIC 2nd Report, Vol.3, 762, 765. Men received 15 and women 12.5 cents per hour, for a 54 hour week.

56. NYSFIC 2nd Report, Vol.3, 766, 767.

57. NYSFIC 2nd Report, Vol.3, 764.

58. Yonkers *Statesman*, June 24, 1908, 4.

59. Charles Allison, *The History of Yonkers* (New York: Wilbur B. Ketcham, 1896), 337 mentions the existence of a hatters' union in Yonkers, but even then, he wrote little on it because it kept no historical records.

60. Charles E. Allison, *The History of Yonkers* (N.Y.: Wilbur B. Ketcham, 1896), 354. Yonkers *Progress,* Nov., 1929, 13 (published by Yonkers Chamber of Commerce, located at Yonkers Planning Department); also see Yolanda Johnson, et al., *Yonkers Through the Years* (Yonkers: Yonkers Board of Education, 1962), 33–35.

61. Yonkers *Progress,* Nov., 1929, 15.

62. Alfred Chandler, Jr. *The Visible Hand: The Managerial Revolution in American Business* (Cambridge, MA: Belknap, 1977), 328; Yonkers *Herald*, Jan.7, 1908, 1.

63. Yonkers, N.Y., Mayors' Annual Messages, 1897–1906, December, 1902, 30–31.

64. N.Y. State *Industrial Directory* (1912), 493–494.

65. NYSFIC, 775–777; N.Y.S. *Industrial Directory*, 1912, ccxxiii. Frances Kellor (see Chapter 3 for identification) noted in 1915 that sugar refining employed the highest percentage of foreign-born workers of all industries in the United States. Kellor, *Out of Work: A Study of Unemployment* (New York: G. P. Putnam and Sons, 1915; reprint, New York: Arno, 1971), 112–113.

66. NYSFIC, 776.

67. NYSFIC, 748, 751.

68. NYSFIC, 750.

69. Mayor Sutherland's Annual Message, Dec. 4, 1900, 64 in *Yonkers Mayors' Annual Messages, 1897–1906.*

70. Mayor Coyne's Annual Message, 1905, 21, Yonkers Mayors' Annual Messages, 1897–1906.

71. Yonkers *Statesman*, July 9, 1908, 6.

72. Yonkers *Statesman*, Sept. 25, 1908, 4.

73. Yonkers *Statesman*, April 28, 1908, 1.

74. "Board of Trade: An Important Movement Begun Under Favorable Auspices," May 2, 1893, in "Board of Trade" bound typescript copies of articles in the *Statesman*, 1893–1908, located in the Yonkers Historical Society Room, Hudson River Museum.

75. The bankers were J. Harvey Bell, also involved in real estate, and William H. Doty. Frederic Shonnard was in real estate, James V. Lawrence in building supplies. Philip Verplanck and N.K. Martin had no occupations listed in the City Directory. "An Important Movement Begun Under Favorable Auspices," May 2, 1893, in "Board of Trade," (bound copies of reports of meetings sent to Yonkers *Statesman*), Yonkers Historical Society Collection, Hudson River Museum; Turner's *Second Annual Directory of the City of Yonkers* (1893–1894), Yonkers Historical Society Collection, Hudson River Museum.

76. "Chamber of Commerce Officers," March 3, 1909, "Chamber of Commerce, 1909-" (Bound copies of reports of meetings sent to Yonkers *Statesman*), Yonkers Historical Society Collection, Hudson River Museum; City Directory, 1909, Yonkers Historical Society Collection, Hudson River Museum.

77. "Chamber of Commerce on Water Tax," April 6, 1909; from "Chamber of Commerce, 1909-.

78. "Chamber of Commerce Men at Dinner," April 20, 1910, in "Chamber of Commerce, 1909-. In fact, although manufacturing employment did increase during these years, it did not keep up with Yonkers' mushrooming population growth. Either more Yonkers residents worked in jobs outside of the city, more residents worked in non-manufacturing jobs, workforce as a proportion of population shrank, or some combination of these.

79. See Ernest L. Bogart, *An Economic History of the United States* (New York: Longmans, Green and Company, 1922), 522–523; Leah Hannah Feder, *Unemployment Relief in Periods of Depression* (New York: Russell Sage, 1936), 189–217.

80. Yonkers *Herald*, Oct. 24, 1907, 1.

81. Yonkers *Herald*, Nov. 14, 1907, 1.

82. Yonkers *Herald*, Dec. 6, 1907, 1.

83. Yonkers *Herald*, Nov. 14, 1907, 1, and Jan. 7, 1908, 1.

84. Yonkers *Herald*, Dec. 10, 1907, Yonkers *Herald*, Jan. 7, 1908, 1.

85. Yonkers *Herald*, Dec. 26, 1907, 1.

86. Yonkers *Statesman*, Jan. 3, 1908, 5; Yonkers *Herald*, Jan. 3, 1908, 1.

87. Yonkers *Herald*, Dec. 21, 1907, 1.

88. Yonkers *Herald*, Dec. 21, 1907, 1.

89. Yonkers *Herald*, Feb. 21, 1908, 1.

90. See, e.g. "March of Unemployed: Thousands in Cincinnati Seeking Aid and Work," Yonkers *Statesman*, Jan. 10, 1908, 1.

91. Yonkers *Herald*, March 19, 1908, 7.

92. Yonkers *Herald*, April 9, 1908, 8.

93. Yonkers *Statesman*, Jan. 3, 1908, 4.

94. Yonkers *Statesman*, Feb. 1, 4.

95. Yonkers *Herald*, Feb. 4, 1908, 1, 4.

96. Mayor John Peene, April 12, 1897, 24–25 in Yonkers Mayors *Annual Messages, 1897–1906.*

97. Mayor Michael J. Walsh, Annual Message, Dec. 3, 1901, 22 in Yonkers Mayors, *Annual Messages.* See also Leah Hannah Feder, *Unemployment Relief,* 168–188. Feder (169) says "the depression of the nineties marked the first extensive use of work relief . . . as an unemployment relief measure." Yonkers was thus neither ahead of nor behind the national trend. The relief program was part of a second political agenda in Yonkers, where Republican sought to extend services to unimproved land in the Seventh Ward. Democrats opposed incurring expenses for the sparsely populated area. Republicans may have been tied to land development interests. See the above-cited annual messages, and that of Leslie Sutherland, December, 1898, 17, and Dec. 5, 1899, 11.

98. Yonkers *Statesman*, Feb. 11, 1908, 5; Yonkers *Herald*, Feb. 14, 4.

99. Yonkers *Statesman*, Feb. 20, 6.

100. Yonkers *Herald*, Feb. 29, 1908, 1.

101. Yonkers *Statesman*, Mar. 2, 4.

102. Yonkers *Statesman*, May 29, 1908, 5.

103. Yonkers *Statesman*, April 10, 1908, 1.

104. Yonkers *Statesman*, Jan. 29, 1908, 4.

105. Yonkers *Herald*, Jan. 7, 1908, 6.

106. Yonkers *Herald*, March 24, 1908, 2.

107. Yonkers *Statesman*, March 27, 1908, 4.

108. Yonkers *Herald*, March 5, 1908, 1.

109. Yonkers *Herald*, March 5, 1908, 1.

110. Yonkers *Herald*, Oct. 16, 1908, 4

111. Yonkers *Herald*, Oct. 21, 1908, 1.

112. Yonkers *Herald*, Oct. 22, 1908, 1.

113. Yonkers *Herald*, Feb. 6, 1908, 1; and Feb. 8, 1908, 1.

114. Yonkers *Herald*, Feb. 8, 1908, 1.

115. Yonkers *Statesman*, June 24, 1908, 4.

116. Yonkers *Herald*, July 11, 1908, 1.

117. Yonkers *Statesman*, Dec. 31, 1908, 5.

118. Yonkers *Statesman*, Dec. 31, 1908, 5.

119. This observation conforms to Robert Wiebe's analysis in *The Search for Order, 1877–1920* (New York: Hill and Wang, 1967), 164–176.

120. Yonkers *Herald*, Jan. 15, 1908, 4. On the New York School of Philanthropy, see Chapter 3, below.

121. Minutes of the meetings leading to the new C.O.S. are not very specific as to the reasons for Butler's desire for the new organization. A Yonkers *Statesman* report summarized: "Owing to increasing demands upon the time and resources of the Institute, it was deemed best to again revive the old society, but on a newer basis." Yonkers *Statesman*, Nov. 24, 1908, 4.

122. Minutes of the Trustees of the Woman's Institute, April 8, 1908, contained in a lined scrapbook entitled "Standard Compositions." The latter contains the records of the conferences and transition to the new C.O.S. It is located in the Chamber of Commerce Archives, Woman's Institute Building, Yonkers.

123. "Program of the Conference" in "Standard Compositions," Woman's Institute.

124. Minutes of the Trustees of the Woman's Institute, June 10, 1908, in "Standard Compositions" Woman's Institute.

125. Minutes of the Board of Directors of the Yonkers Charity Organization Society, Dec. 3, 1908, in "Standard Compositions," Woman's Institute.

126. Minutes of the Trustees of the Woman's Institute, Jan. 11, 1911, located in the Chamber of Commerce Archives, Woman's Institute Building, Yonkers.

127. Jones to Byington, Feb. 14, 1910, Box 4, Yonkers Family Service Society Papers. These unorganized papers (hereafter FSS) are currently located at the Yonkers Family Service Society, Yonkers.

128. Jones to Brooklyn Bureau of Charities, Jan. 14, 1911. Box 4, FSS.

129. C.O.S. Finance Committee Appeal to Henry Morris, Jan., 1911. Box 4, FSS.

130. C.O.S. Finance Committee Appeal to Henry Morris, Jan., 1911. Box 4, FSS.

131. The numbers are 29 of 85. Report of the Wood Yard of the Charity Organization Society, March 20, 1911 to October 14, 1911. File "Work of the C.O.S. 1909–1911," Box 4, FSS. This seems like a small number of men, for seven months, but the work must have been highly seasonal. A fund raising letter in April, 1911, sixteen days after it opened said it had already provided for 95 applicants, in this case, probably including men applying twice as two applicants.

132. Ralph Prime, Jr., Public Appeal Letter for Wood Yard support, April 10, 1911, File "Work of the C.O.S., 1909–1911," Box 4, FSS.

133. The numbers are 29 of 85. Report of the Wood Yard of the Charity Organization Society, March 20, 1911 to October 14, 1911. File "Work of the C.O.S. 1909–1911," Box 4, FSS. This seems like a small number of men, for seven months, but the work must have been highly seasonal. A fund raising letter in April, 1911, sixteen days after it opened said it had already provided for 95 applicants, in this case, probably including men applying twice as two applicants.

134. Mary Jolly Van Hook, Typescript history of Yonkers C.O.S., 1909–1919, 1, Box 4, FSS.

135. Fairview Garden School Reports to John Glenn, Russell Sage Foundation, Nov. 18, 1909; Sept. 30, 1910; 1911 Annual Report; Folder 170, Box 11, RSF Papers, Rockefeller Archives.

136. The Woman's Institute *Annual Report* 1914, 7 (located in the Yonkers Chamber of Commerce Offices, Woman's Institute Building).

137. NYSFIC, 769.

138. "Circular from the State Board of Health giving information and advice on the prevention of tuberculosis, January 1895," reprinted in Barbara Gutmann Rosenkrantz, *Public Health and the State: Changing Views In Massachusetts 1842–1936* (Cambridge: Harvard University Press, 1972), 216–219.

139. NYSFIC, 731.

140. NYSFIC, 769–772.

141. NYSFIC, 771.

142. On "community" orientation as political weakness in the twentieth century, see Thomas Bender, *Community and Social Change in America* (Baltimore: Johns Hopkins, 1978), 149.

143. Dr. Getty testified before the New York State Factory Investigating Commission that he supported their proposed bills regulating sanitary conditions in factories. Responding to a Commissioner's question, he emphasized the importance of their enforcement being under State control: they would be, he said, "very much less" affected by local influence. NYSFIC, 771.

3

Towards a New Understanding of Unemployment

The thinning ranks of philanthropically-committed local manufacturing owners might have created a crisis in local social management, if they had not been replaced by two new projects, one locally based, committed to problems of poverty within the community, and the other working on a regional and national level, committed to experimenting with stabilizing the labor market. The first group coalesced around the Yonkers Woman's Institute in the 1890s (chapter 1). While these women dealt with perceived problems of poverty, health, education, recreation, and relief, they shied away from direct criticism of the employment relationship (with the exception of child labor and women's hours of work.) They consistently avoided the issue of employment reform in Yonkers' large factories (chapter 2). The second group, confronting the "industrial" problems of employment, unemployment and labor markets, was based beyond Yonkers and looked for solutions beyond the local community.

The intellectual underpinnings of nineteenth century charity organization—which well supported the activities of the local nineteenth century factory owner/philanthropists—would not bear the weight of these two new thrusts, but did not have to. Metropolitan reform theorists based in Charity Organization Societies in the larger cities, in university departments of economics and social economy, and in new organizations with a nation-wide scope, such as the American Association for Labor Legislation, the Russell Sage Foundation, and the American Association of Societies for Organizing Charity, developed new theories of poverty and new recommendations to deal with it. Appropriate to the new situation, they promoted a bifurcation in the understanding of poverty, distinguishing between that due to individual incapacity—problems of "charity" which they left largely to the locals—and that due to unemployment and underemployment—problems of "industry" which demanded broader organization.[1]

Three interdependent trends characterized the evolving work of these reform theorists. First, they rejected the strictly localist orientation which had been fostered in earlier community efforts to deal with the poor. Gathering information on local working populations continued to be important for purposes of classification of the poor. And none of them wanted either dependent people or able unemployed workers wandering about the country looking for a livelihood. But the idea of broadly organized administrative distribution of labor—workers' geographic mobility directed by agencies at the state or national level—gained virtually universal currency among reform theorists. Second, unemployment became increasingly important in their analyses as the root cause of poverty. Earlier C.O.S. analysis had tended to search for causes of "lack of work" in poor morals, poor health, and poor habits; the new paradigm sought the roots of poor morals, poor health and poor habits and found them largely in unemployment. This theoretical reversal opened the possibility of the analytical distinction between the "reform of industry" for the prevention of unemployment and family social work to deal with the casualties of the industrial system. Third, painfully aware of their own relative lack of power and sensitive to the attack that their plans were utopian or unrealistic, reform theorists worked toward an analysis of unemployment which would appeal to business leaders with the power to shape employment policy and to influence state decision-making.

The trajectory developed by metropolitan reform theorists between 1900 and 1913 was directed to two constituencies. Local social workers and reformers responded in part because of their dependence for legitimacy upon their contact with the organizations headed by the metropolitan reform theorists. They could no longer depend on their ties with local elites to legitimate their activities. The second group—reform businessmen in firms increasingly organized as large corporations operating on a nation-wide scale—responded to these theories in the interests of industrial peace and labor efficiency. Our understanding of the receptiveness of these two constituencies depends in part on a serious consideration of the theories they embraced.

Many of the key metropolitan reform organizations responsible for these ideological developments—such as the *Survey*, the Russell Sage Foundation, the American Association for Labor Legislation (AALL), the influential New York C.O.S., and the National Association of Societies for Organizing Charities—were located in New York City.[2] So too were Columbia University's Department of Political Economy and the greatest concentration of headquarters of the new, large corporations with the resources and incentives for considering stabilized labor policies.[3] With important links to virtually all of these institutions, at the center of the early twentieth century ideological transition, stood Edward T. Devine.[4]

Born in rural Iowa in 1867, Devine attended Albion Seminary and Cornell College, traveled to Germany to study economics, and returned to the University of Pennsylvania's Wharton School of Finance and Economy. Upon graduation in 1895 he began twenty years as General Secretary of the New York Charity Organization Society.[5] In 1898, he founded the journal *Charities* which consolidated with the Chicago *Commons* to become *Charities and the Commons* in 1905, and in 1909 the *Survey*, the leading journal of social work and social reform in the early twentieth century. He was the founding director of the New York School of Philanthropy established to train workers for the N.Y.C.O.S. In 1905, he was appointed to the new Jacob H. Schiff Chair in Social Economy at Columbia University. To admirers, he was an important leader in the social welfare movement. To detractors, he was the head of the "charities trust."[6] In either case, he was in a good position to shape the new field.

During the first decade of the twentieth century, Devine's thinking changed significantly. His first major work, *Principles of Relief* (1904), was intended to guide the efforts of "those who look forward to active volunteer or professional service in any branch of social work." Its subject matter grew directly out of the Charity Organization Society paradigm: it aimed to define and separate the various classes of dependents according to the form of relief appropriate for them.[7] Devine claimed, nevertheless, that *Principles of Relief* represented a break with the past. Social work in 1904, he claimed, rested "upon such new premises," that it would "alienate, rather than attract, those who have been most completely identified with the traditional distribution of relief."[8] Among the new premises Devine advocated an approach based on reform of the "environment" rather than "character."

Shedding the morally loaded categories of "worthy" and "unworthy," Devine argued that every community had a "normal" standard of living. The social worker's task was to identify those families and individuals which did not achieve that standard and to bring them up to it either by "disciplinary or charitable measures." In addition, they were responsible for "securing the withdrawal from the industrial class of those who are unfit for a place in it." Social work thus aimed not to raise the standards of living of the entire working class, but to bring the subnormal up to the norm established by the particular community.[9]

Maintenance of the standard required that a husband would have an income adequate to support a wife at home and children at school.[10] Desertion, disease, accident, alcohol, shiftlessness and unemployment threatened steady, adequate wages. Devine's "environmentalism" did not lead him to reject intervention to reform the individual. Desertion or shiftlessness might be treated through a substantial term in a labor colony. Sometimes, Devine suggested, mental discipline would be improved by "actual deprivation for a time of the necessities of life."[11]

Shortly after the publication of *Principles of Relief*, in his inaugural address as Schiff Professor of Social Economy at Columbia, Devine defined the field of social economy in a way which revealed his sense of the relationship between individual and environmental causation of sub-standard conditions. "Social economy," he explained,

> finds its particular field in the study of those conditions, activities, and agencies which promote or hinder the making of every individual into an industrially efficient and hence independent human being, and in the relief of those who cannot by their own efforts realize the social standards of the community of which they are a part.[12]

Two implications of this formulation should be noted. First, "dependence" refers here to a condition of infirmity or pauperization, not workers' dependence on wages for a living.[13] Secondly, the statement reveals Devine's implicit assumption of socially "independent" individuals which he tried so hard explicitly to move beyond. It works plausibly for such issues as tenement reform, prescribing improved housing to reduce the numbers of "dependent" tubercular workers too weak to support their families, and a clean, restful hospital to heal the sick. But it makes no sense applied to the problems of seasonal unemployment or industrial depression: Devine assumed that the major reason for men or women being out of work was that they were "inefficient," that the problems stemmed from health, character, or habit.

Accordingly, Devine thought simple lack of employment was frequently overestimated.

> Lack of employment, which, at the time of application, is given in the great majority of instances as the reason for being in need, is usually found on inquiry to be due to some personal deficiency in the employee. . . . In a certain proportion of instances, however, by no means insignificant in the aggregate, destitution is due to lack of employment, which cannot properly be charged to any fault of the employee.[14]

Devine was ambivalent, but most of the analysis he presented drew on the work of his C.O.S. predecessor Francis McLean's "careful study of industrial displacement and unemployment" from the late 1890s. McLean had studied the records of families who applied to the NYCOS for aid and whose cause of need was assessed by C.O.S. investigators to be "lack of work."[15] McLean concluded that only 53.3% of 720 cases were genuinely destitute through lack of work. He identified personal problems as "the most probable exciting cause" in the other cases. The thrust of this study and of Devine's citation was to demonstrate that even the careful C.O.S. workers had vastly overestimated unemployment: "By this analysis," Devine wrote, "the percentage of cases credited to unemployment is reduced from 49 to 26.1 per cent [of the total]."[16]

The fear that premature aid might lead to character destruction and pauperization shaped Devine's 1904 proposals for solving the problem of lack of work. He quoted approvingly from N.Y.C.O.S. founder Josephine Shaw Lowell:

> When industry and trade are natural, the only safe course for the working people is to accommodate themselves to their circumstances, or to change them by their own action. The efforts of philanthropists to compensate, by artificial means, for irregularity of work or low wages can only result in mischief.[17]

His fear extended even to aid in the search for employment: Devine cautioned that charitable societies should help in finding employment for able relief applicants only as a last resort.[18] Devine assumed that in "normal" times there was plenty of work to be done and what was needed was "individual effort to find it. . . ."[19]

In 1906, two years after *Principles of Relief* the Charities Publication Committee induced the recently formed Russell Sage Foundation to fund a massive study of life in Pittsburgh focusing on the nature of employment in the steel industry and the conditions faced by workers and their families. The Russell Sage Foundation employed Devine's managing editor at *Charities and the Commons*, Paul Kellogg, to direct the Pittsburgh Survey and Devine was closely involved throughout the study. The results were first published in three special issues of *Charities and the Commons* in 1909 and subsequently in six volumes published by Russell Sage. They generated numerous public speeches, press releases and popular magazine articles. If the *Survey* had a major impact on the steel industry and on Progressive reform in general (as indicated in part by changing the name of *Charities and the Commons* to *The Survey*) it also had an impact on Devine. Specifically, it challenged the idea that able-bodied industrial workers were in any sense the "independent" entities Devine had imagined in *Principles of Relief*.[20]

Devine was also the principle investigator a smaller Russell Sage study on the feasibility of a privately financed employment bureau for New York City. Eventually bearing fruit as the National Employment Exchange, the bureau was to maintain contacts across the United States in an effort to distribute unemployed workers in New York City to areas which needed them.[21]

These two studies (the Pittsburgh Survey and the National Employment Exchange study) and a third on the Standard of Living (for the State Conference of Charities and Correction) put Devine into contact with "certain aspects of the lives of workingmen which do not necessarily and regularly enter into the experiences of the charitable societies."[22] And the problems of work, employment practices, and unemployment began to assume a more central role in his writing.[23]

Devine's change in orientation reflected the research on industry, work, and labor markets funded by the giant new philanthropies. The early research agenda of the Russell Sage Foundation, like that of the Rockefeller Foundation, dealt in much more depth with labor policies and the workplace than had its local charitable forerunners.[24] In January, 1908, Russell Sage took first steps toward the creation of a Department of Industrial Studies.[25] Its program brought concern with labor into focus, and opened the possibility of dealing with poverty on a national scale through employment reform and labor market management.[26]

The differences appear in Devine's 1909 volume, *Misery and its Causes*. First, he gave unemployment a higher profile than previously:

one (of six) chapters dealt exclusively with the problems of those who were "out of work." Secondly, he saw employment policies (and immigration policy) and the nature of the labor market as major and direct contributors to unemployment in "normal" times. Third, he used an investigation of 5000 applicants to the C.O.S. to demonstrate that unemployment was the single largest cause of misery, affecting 69.16 percent of the families in the study.

In his earlier work, cyclical depressions were the occasion for social workers to act on the problem of unemployment. For "normal" times, following Lowell's proscriptions, Devine had few suggestions. By 1909, Devine's position had reversed. Aside from a vague suggestion of "some insurance plan" to cover unemployment during depressions, Devine wrote simply that "prosperity is the only solution" for "sheer industrial contraction."[27] He devoted most of the chapter on unemployment to exploration of the causes and remedies for unemployment during "normal" times.

The problem of character receded almost entirely from Devine's analysis of the causes of unemployment. Casual labor, seasonal labor, unemployment due to the introduction of new machinery and new processes, concentration of industries in the cities (displacing rural labor) and immigration, now occupied the center of his analysis. "[I]n our generation," he wrote,

> we have seen these influences acting on an unprecedented scale, in every conceivable combination, and with disastrous consequences to large numbers of workingmen and their families.[28]

Devine included the employment exchange as a key part of the solution to unemployment. In a radical shift from his position in *Principles of Relief*, Devine wrote:

> . . . there is at present a maladjustment between work and workers, both within our own community and as between communities, and . . . there is a loss of time and serious hardship involved in the search for labor which might be obviated by the creation of an employment exchange, or work market. . . .[29]

With social work theorists like Devine focusing more on the problems of employment and unemployment, they turned naturally to the employer of labor.[30] While the nineteenth century capitalist had supplied the money for running the charity organization and the ideological model of independence and initiative toward which the applicants for relief were to aspire, now the employers' relationship to workers came under scrutiny.[31]

Achievement of a normal standard of living for all depended, in Devine's new formulation, upon wise management policies instituted by the economically powerful.

> Industrial training, steadiness in employment, capacity for team work, efficiency in management, prevention of waste, utilization of by-products, sound business methods, the discovery of a full market and the maintenance of stable relations between employer and workingmen are all favorable conditions for that adequate income on which normal family life depends.[32]

Devine's redefinition of the problem of relief sprang from his sense that dependence was a function of a larger economic system in which businessmen were the dominant force, but many businessmen were not living up to their responsibilities:

> Distress due to unemployment resulting directly from the faulty judgment and the reprehensible practices of financiers and other business men is a form of that maladjustment which I hold to be responsible for so large a part of our poverty.[33]

Devine's writings betrayed an accurate sense of the limitations of social workers' power in comparison to that of business elites. He called on the "men of wealth and influence" to take the "leadership which naturally belongs to them in dealing with congestion and overwork. . . . [T]hen we may safely leave to what are ordinarily called organized charities in the narrower sense all that remains of the problem of dependence."[34] Employers alone were in a position to reform the "system of casual, intermittent, and uncertain employment."[35]

Although Devine's reform analysis looked toward the powerful to institute change, for businessmen it offered little beyond a moral appeal: it did nothing to connect social problems directly to their major concerns. The businessmen themselves were not particularly interested—as employers—in the "subnormal" standards of living which were the consequence of irregular and insecure unemployment. Edward Devine's colleague, Henry Seager, considerably broadened the appeal of the social analysis of unemployment. But before we consider his contribution, developments in England must be brought into the picture. The work of William Beveridge, particularly, helped to transform the terms of the American debate on poverty and set unemployment and reform of "industry" at the center. The fact that Beveridge's recommendations were quickly implemented in England enhanced their appeal to American reformers.[36]

In 1905, leaving Toynbee Hall settlement where he had been immersed in the problems of unemployment, Beveridge at the age of twenty-six divided his time between reporting for the *Morning Post* and administering the recently passed Unemployed Workman's Act (1905) where he could test his early thinking. By 1907, exasperated by the workings of the Act, Beveridge had come to see the employment exchange as a the key solution to the problem of unemployment.[37] His pathbreaking study, *Unemployment: A Problem of Industry*, appeared in 1908. In it, he argued that the central problem in unemployment was the chronically underemployed casual laborer, whose situation was created by an unorganized labor market.

Beveridge formulated the problem in a way which would bring Devine's earlier work on the "normal" standard of living into clear relationship with the unemployment problem:

> The problem of unemployment lies . . . at the root of most other social problems. Society is built up on labour . . . its ideal unit is the household of man, wife and children maintained by the earnings of the first alone. . . . Reasonable security of employment for the bread-winner is the basis of all private duties and all sound social action.[38]

Beveridge argued that unemployment was due both to technological change, which rendered certain jobs and occupations obsolete, and to several kinds of fluctuation in industry. Reserves of labor (the unemployed) were necessary in order to meet changes in the demand for labor, thus a certain amount of unemployment could not be eliminated. His solutions aimed at reducing the unnecessarily large numbers of seasonally and sporadically unemployed which resulted from the "disorganization of the labor market." He suggested administrative mechanisms which would match the supply with the demand for labor and dovetail the available jobs. This would end unenderemployment by assuring all workers an income sufficient to support a healthy family. If, he proposed, after the organization of the labor market there were too many workers for the available part time jobs, then the surplus would have to be removed entirely from the labor market (perhaps through emigration to Canada, perhaps by institutionalization).[39] Either of these was preferable to a labor glut in which casual laborers could not maintain normal standards for their families. The "organized fluidity of labor" would thus be achieved through a national system of labor exchanges which constituted the core of Beveridge's "decasualization of labor."[40]

Beveridge's thought and social reform program helped to put labor exchanges at the top of the agenda for unemployment reform in England. He testified before the Royal Commission on the Reform of the Poor Laws, and exerted personal influence on Commissioners Sidney and Beatrice Webb. The result of his work was the British Labour Exchanges Act of 1909. As a member of the Board of Trade in 1909, he worked with Winston Churchill to develop the national system of labor exchanges which opened in 1910. By the end of 1912, Beveridge administered a system of 1000 local offices.[41]

Beveridge was a key theorist in a range of Liberal unemployment reformers including Percy Alden, C.G.B. Masterman, and John A. Hobson, but his work was picked up by the Americans in a way that the others' was not. Beveridge's book and the British labor exchanges had an immediate impact on Devine, William Leiserson, Francis Kellor, John Andrews and other influential American theorists.[42] In contrast, theorists like Isaac Max Rubinow, who did not put the organization of the labor market at the top of the list of unemployment reforms, were pushed aside, and found themselves largely outside of the mainstream of American reform organization on the topic.[43] One of the important beneficiaries of Beveridge's work was Henry Rogers Seager.

Seager's education frequently ran parallel to Devine's. Born in Lansing, Michigan, he too did undergraduate work in the mid-West, studied economics at Halle, Germany (one year after Devine) and returned to complete a doctorate at the University of Pennsylvania. He moved to Columbia University in 1902, where his position as Professor of Economics put him directly in touch with Devine.[44] And as unemployment became a more central concern for Devine, Seager's position as president of the American Association for Labor Legislation made him an important contact: Seager joined the Board of Directors of the *Survey*. Unlike Devine, whose reputation was established in the practical work of the C.O.S., Seager's was based on the university. By 1910, he had published two major texts in economics.[45] In that year at Devine's School of Philanthropy, he delivered a series of lectures on social insurance, published soon after in the same series as *Misery and Its Causes*. The resulting volume, *Social Insurance: a Program of*

Social Reform, was, according to Daniel Nelson, "the first important work on unemployment to appear in the United States."[46]

Seager's distinctive contribution resulted from his background in economics, combined with a strong moral aversion to the "tramps and vagrants," whom he nevertheless saw as victims of the economic system. The problem with unemployment, according to Seager, was that it demoralized its victims and their families, and thus contributed to the oversupply of the lowest type of workers, who in turn, threatened the standards of the better organized and more highly skilled workers as well. He relied on Devine's work both for the notion of the normal standard of living and in his advocacy of the labor exchange/labor colony combination as the first step in dealing with unemployment. Although he did not cite Beveridge, he used the Report of the Royal Commission on the Poor Laws, which relied on Beveridge, and the then unpublished work of William Leiserson, which rested squarely on Beveridge's *Unemployment: A Problem of Industry*.[47]

Social Insurance opened with an attack on "individualism," which Seager acknowledged as a fundamental but nevertheless outdated American attitude. "The simple creed of individualism is no longer adequate," Seager wrote, particularly in those sections of the country "in which the wage earner is the typical American citizen."[48] Urban industrial capitalism undermined the potential for social progress, because workers neither would nor could put away portions of their wages for the future. Their incentives for saving—the promise of owning their own homes and tools—were gone in the new urban, industrial landscape. Since they did not save, they could not provide for the emergencies of disease, accident, unemployment, premature death, and old age. These emergencies, Seager argued, occasioned a constant recruitment into "the mass of unorganized, unskilled workers whose lack of standards and unregulated competition oppose the progress of wage earners all along the line."[49] He estimated that half a million wage-earners were affected each year.

> These 500,000 persons, or many of them, are the recruits that prevent the army of standardless workers from growing smaller in this land of opportunity. And the presence of this army seems to me to constitute an insurmountable obstacle to the realization of the individualist's millennium. Skilled workers, by developing standards that they adhere to in good times and in bad and by organization, are able to advance their wages. . . . [Unskilled and unorganized workers, on the other hand] always live from hand to mouth. From their ranks employers can always recruit their labor force when those a little higher up in

> the labor scale strike to improve their condition. Unemployment finds them without savings, and soon reduces them to the position of social dependents."[50]

There were two parts to Seager's program of social reform: first, to make adequate plans of insurance against the five types of emergencies to which wage-earners were exposed and second, to remove the "lowest grade of workers, the tramps and casuals" from industrial competition and to put them in graded farm and industrial colonies.[51]

Subsequent chapters spelled out in more detail proposals for both preventing and insuring against industrial accidents, illness, premature death, unemployment, and old-age. In that devoted to unemployment, Seager saw the major problem as seasonal unemployment resulting from the "irregularity in the requirements of industry from month to month."[52] Casual labor, supporting industries which required "those who are in search of work to present themselves from time to time on the chance of securing it" added significantly to the problem by maintaining a reserve army of labor, all of which could never be employed. He advocated two steps to reduce unemployment. The first involved asking employers, employees and consumers to alter their economic activity so as to reduce variations in the demand for labor; the second involved a "thoroughgoing organization of the country's labor market that will be as effective in distributing the available labor force where it is most needed as our banks are in distributing capital where it is most required."[53] Seager referred to Devine's writing on labor exchanges and labor bureaus in *Misery and Its Causes*, and said he could "add little to his argument." He did, however, believe that the state—and not philanthropically funded efforts like the National Employment Exchange—would have to assume responsibility for labor distribution.

One of the major advantages of the employment exchange, in Seager's view, would be its ability to segregate unemployed workers into three types: the competent and industrious; the inefficient who were characteristically "unemployed during dull seasons;" and finally, "the class which, for physical or moral reasons, is incapable of doing steady work." Because of their effect on the labor market and on "standards" in general, Seager was particularly concerned with ascertaining the numbers of the last class, and with segregating them from other unemployed workers. He advocated that tramps and vagrants be confined to compulsory labor colonies not only as rehabilitation, but as deterrence—to reduce the attractiveness of the wandering way of life—and to segregate them from the worthy unemployed.[54]

After these preventative measures, Seager considered other means to "mitigate the present situation." Stopping short of compulsory state unemployment insurance for all because of the administrative difficulties, he nevertheless advocated consideration of state subsidies to unions for unemployment benefits (the "Ghent system"). He thought that relief work tended to pauperize, but supported state-subsidized training to the temporarily unemployed who were not covered by trade union insurance.[55]

Like Devine, Seager failed to build into his analysis serious consideration of cyclical unemployment, perhaps because the labor exchange/labor colony solution was so clearly unworkable under the circumstances of a general business depression.[56] He made no distinction among the various industrial dislocations and irregularities which led to unemployment. He categorized the types of unemployed (according to skill, character, and ability) rather than the types of unemployment (according to changes in the demand for labor.) Concern with the effects on other workers fueled his fear of the lowest group of desperate casual laborers. By accepting very low pay and by serving as strike-breakers they undercut the bargaining position of organized, skilled workers. Because they were desperate, they supported radical political movements.[57] Finally, they set a poor example for others in what Seager regarded from time to time as their choice of refusal to work. This, then, was where Seager's analysis went most clearly and importantly beyond that of Devine: unemployment threatened not only the unemployed, but the entire working class and indeed "social progress" itself. Such a threat justified the abandonment of a severely limited role for the state in mitigating the problem.

William Morris Leiserson advanced the discussion still further by translating Seager's threat to social progress into a threat to "industrial progress." He thus moved the discourse on unemployment an important step closer to one which was relevant to financial and industrial elites. Almost a generation younger than Seager and Devine, Leiserson was equally influential in shaping the new conception of unemployment in New York in the early twentieth century. Born in Estonia around 1883 he immigrated as a child with his mother, brothers and sister to the Lower East Side of New York City in 1890. He attended public school until the age of fourteen when he left to work in a shirtwaist factory. Thereafter he took advantage of the opportunities for self-education available in New York City: a boys' club at University Settlement, Cooper Union lectures, and the libraries. In 1904 he went to the University of Wisconsin, where he became a favored student of John R. Commons. He participated as a student on the staff of the Pittsburgh Survey in 1907–8 (where he very likely came into contact with Edward Devine). The following year he received a fellowship to do graduate studies at Columbia in New York (where he undoubtedly studied with Seager). In October of 1909, he was hired as Special Investigator for the New York State Commission on Employers' Liability and Unemployment (the Wainwright Commission). Leiserson wrote the Commission's report on unemployment and submitted it to Columbia as his doctoral dissertation. In the process, Leiserson achieved his position as a "pioneer student of the labor market in the United States."[58]

The impetus for the Wainwright Commission came from the social work community at the end of the Depression of 1907–1908. It was neither a spontaneous creation of the politicians themselves, nor the direct result of popular demonstrations, as were local emergency committees on unemployment in following years. Commission members openly expressed their considerable ignorance of the issues during hearings in January, 1910. The senators and assemblymen who made up the majority on the Commission were unfamiliar with the subject. (The governor's appointees—Henry Seager, Otto Eidlitz, Crystal Eastman, George W. Smith, and John Mitchell—were considerably more knowledgable.) Chairman Wainwright virtually apologized to Florence Kelley:

> A committee of some sort appeared before the Legislature last year, and asked for the appointment of a Commission to take up the subject of unemployment. . . . Here are we, people who knew very little about this problem, except in a vague way. . . .[59]

Later in the morning, the Commission confronted Frank J. Warne, a member of the "committee of some sort" which had asked for the Commission.[60] Warne tried repeatedly to have the Commission clarify the topics on which he was to speak, saying it was "absolutely impossible" for them to cover the "whole subject of unemployment." The Commission was unable to be specific. "Don't let us be too technical," said Wainwright, "you start in and tell us just what you think we ought to do."

Warne protested:

> . . . you are tackling a subject which has baffled the most astute statesmanship of modern Europe You are tackling a subject that is a conspicuous cause of this great social problem of poverty; in other words, this Commission has undertaken to attempt to solve one phase of the great problem which the Twentieth Century has set itself to do.

Wainwright replied, "We have not undertaken it; it has been fired at us."[61]

In this situation, the "experts" had a free rein in defining the problem and proposing solutions, but there was a minimum of political will available for pressing their proposals into legislation. Warne was correct, of course, in drawing attention to the magnitude of the problem. Even in the experts' hands, before the question of political will became paramount, the task was to scale this size down, to render it manageable. This was Leiserson's strength.

Leiserson's reform program juggled two goals which seemed at the time of his writing to be working at odds with each other. First, and most basic, he wanted to maintain "industrial progress." This goal was so universally accepted by Leiserson's audience that it was largely implicit. Without entering into a detailed analysis of what produced "industrial progress," Leiserson assumed that competition engaged industrialists in an unceasing drive towards greater efficiency. This led to new technology and new processes. Firms expanded and contracted in response to market conditions. Inefficient firms collapsed. New ventures started. Old firms relocated in response to new raw material and market conditions. Leiserson did not propose to restrict any of these phenomena, as they were the lifeblood of "industrial progress." Yet he saw that this ceaseless change produced a fluctuating demand for labor.

> A reserve of labor is needed to meet the fluctuating requirements of industry. There must be unemployed people ready to begin work when the busy seásons come, when employers want to extend their operations, when extra hands are needed anywhere.[62]

Unemployment was thus neither accidental nor occasional, but a necessary and permanent feature of the industrial landscape.[63]

Leiserson's second basic goal was to conserve the disciplined laboring capacity of the working class. Like Seager, he saw exposure to the debilitating insecurity of irregular employment as one of the greatest risks to workers.

> Just as vagrancy leads directly to crime, so unemployment leads directly to vagrancy. The most stringent measures need to be taken to prevent men from remaining for long in the ranks of the unemployed, lest they drop into vagrancy and crime.[64]

Cyclical unemployment, because its duration was longer than the savings of even thrifty families could tide over, had particularly devastating effects.[65] But seasonal and casual labor posed similar dangers. "It is the casual demand," Leiserson said, "which brings into existence the casual workers." And casual laborers soon lost their ability to work steadily.[66] Each instance of irregular unemployment, which posed a threat to virtually every working person, swelled the ranks of casual laborers or the destitute unemployed who became unable to work steadily, even when demand for labor increased.

Leiserson supported these assertions about the effects of unemployment with a study of 439 C.O.S. cases in which lack of work was seen as the cause of destitution.

> The effects of unemployment as gathered from the records in these cases illustrate very strongly what the most dangerous results of unemployment are. First, is the fact that when a man is thrown out of regular employment he is likely after a time to take any job that is offered. This draws him into the great group of irregular, casual laborers. . . . Secondly, the unemployed workman with a family to support is apt to resume work after a period of idleness at a wage lower than his real earning capacity. . . . Thirdly, the lower earning capacity of the men compels the women to go out to work, and that means several children neglected. . . . And fourthly the children neglected while they are under the legal working age, are sent to work as soon as the law allows.[67]

Unemployment and the fear of unemployment made laborers unfit for steady, disciplined work: they became casual laborers, of which there was always an oversupply, and worse yet, "tramps and vagrants" unwilling to work at all for their living. From time to time, the political threat of dissatisfied workers entered into Leiserson's argument, but this was secondary to the threat of a working class unwilling or unable to work.

Alice Willard Solenberger's study of records of one thousand homeless men in Chicago confirmed the Leiserson argument about the effects of unemployment. In her Russell Sage-sponsored work,

Solenberger pointed to the role of employment practices and working conditions in the creation of "tramps."[68] She also cited the "high speed pressure" of modern industry, the irregular character of work, and the living conditions in the large cities where casual laborers congregated during periods of unemployment as contributing to personal deterioration.[69]

Leiserson recognized that the very phenomena which made industrial progress possible were those which led to instability of employment, and thus the degeneration of the working class. But the downgrading of the quality of labor—as certain as the incidence of unemployment—was not only bad for the individual family, it was also bad for industrial progress. As a part of his study, Leiserson sent questionnaires to 723 employers throughout the State, asking, among other things, what kind of labor was scarce and what labor was over-supplied. He found that there was an oversupply of unskilled and inefficient labor coexisting with a scarcity of skilled and efficient labor.[70] In Leiserson's analysis, the problem with unemployment was its contribution to the scarcity of steady, efficient workers.

His reform proposals aimed to reconcile two previously conflicting goals: to maintain "industrial progress" without restricting the freedom of capital to hire and fire according to the demands of the market; and to preserve workers' capacity for labor by reducing the debilitating consequences of unemployment. With this formulation, Leiserson had arrived at an analysis of unemployment which had a direct relevance to the employers of labor.

Leiserson's most important proposal was that for centralized administration of the labor market through a network of public employment offices.

> We have been going on the theory that free competition will of itself adjust the supply of labor to the demand. That is, if there is a scarcity in one locality or in one industry, wages will go up and workmen will be attracted from other industries; if there is an oversupply in a city or industry, wages will drop and workers will leave the city or learn new trades. This has not worked out, however.[71]

Leiserson proposed a large and comprehensive system of agencies which was efficiently coordinated and thoroughly in touch with industrial conditions throughout the State to eliminate unnecessary unemployment.[72] For the "reserve of unemployed workers . . . necessary and inevitable in the ordinary course of industrial progress,"

Leiserson favored unemployment insurance, but it was to be considered only after the organization of the labor market through the employment bureau.[73]

Leiserson's report thus focused on the politically feasible and relatively simple introduction of a new state agency to solve a massive and far-reaching problem. Strict attention to sound administrative principles, not wholesale political or economic re-ordering, would produce the needed changes.[74] He did not challenge the rise and fall of industries and firms, the dislocations resulting from the competitive struggles of corporate capitalism; he did not meddle in any way with the free rein of capital to hire, fire and dislocate: most of this was necessary for "industrial progress." The report envisioned for the state a role of picking up the dislocated pieces, and reassembling them for hire with increased efficiency.

Leiserson recommended three measures in addition to the public employment offices: vocational guidance through a juvenile branch of the employment offices to work in cooperation with the schools; and the publication of a monthly labor market bulletin; and the planning of public works so that they would be carried out during seasons and years of high unemployment.[75]

The commission's work on unemployment was largely ignored when it was reported to the New York State Legislature in the halcyon days of 1911. Without the pressure of widespread, visible unemployment, the otherwise politically acceptable administrative proposals received no action. The report represented, nevertheless, the culmination of Progressive thought on unemployment before the depression of 1914–1915.

Devine, Seager and Leiserson had produced a succession of social analyses of unemployment within a relatively short span of years. Devine helped to define the move from individual to social causation and to develop the idea of the normal standard of living which became an important tool in measuring the impact of unemployment and campaigning for reform. Devine's responsiveness to the new work studies helped him to begin the integration of problems of work into problems of welfare. Seager demonstrated the social consequences of unemployment beyond the unemployed themselves. Unemployment, he argued, even if it directly affected only a minority of workers at any one time, continually undercut standards of living for the entire working class and thus made unrealizable the promise of general social uplift and progress. Leiserson made the most extensive empirical study and concluded that the unemployment which was in part a "necessary" result of industrial progress, in turn threatened that very progress by sapping the work-discipline of the working class. He thus completed the specification of unemployment as the key factor in poverty in such a way that it would appeal to businessmen of the time.

Interest in the new conception of unemployment was initially limited to a small circle of reformers. But when depression hit in 1914, the ideas explored in this chapter formed the foundation of a much wider public discussion. As a larger body of social "experts" gathered in New York City to deal with the crisis, they relied on the ideas and research of Devine, Seager, and Leiserson.[76] We turn now to their activities.

Notes

1. Few efforts have been made to trace the evolution and relation of American theories of poverty to theories of unemployment. Daniel Nelson sketches only briefly developments before 1910, *Unemployment Insurance: The American Experience, 1915–1935* (Madison: University of Wisconsin Press, 1969), 3–14. John Garraty's trans-Atlantic survey of thinking about unemployment spells out the connection between thought on poverty and unemployment most clearly in the work of the English Charles Booth, but neither sees a similar process in North America nor explains the change in terms of political economic developments, *Unemployment in History: Economic Throught and Public Policy* (New York: Harper and Row, 1978), 110–113. Alexander Keyssar, who has taken on the probably more difficult task of assessing the impact of unemployment on the unemployed, is less concerned with theoretical developments. While he brilliantly traces the social origins of unemployment in the nineteenth century to 1870, his close examination of 1870–1920 fails to yield changes in the patterns of unemployment which might help to explain the new theoretical developments, *Out of Work: the First Century of Unemployment in Massachusetts* (Cambridge: Cambridge University Press, 1986). See also Roy Lubove, *The Struggle For Social Security, 1900–1935* (Cambridge: Harvard University Press, 1968), 144–174.

2. These organizations had multiple ties to each other, through personnel, projects, and even shared office space. See John F. McClymer, *War and Welfare: Social Engineering in America, 1890–1925* (Westport: Greenwood Press, 1980), 1–69; and, e.g., Peter Romanofsky, *Social Service Organizations* (Westport: Greenwood Press, 1978), 798–799.

3. David Hammack, *Power and Society: Greater New York at the Turn of the Century* (New York: Russell Sage Foundation, 1982), 37–51; Roy Lubove, *The Professional Altruist* (Cambridge: Harvard University Press, 1965).

4. Devine, says Guy Alchon, was "at the very center of a new technocratic profession." *The Invisible Hand of Planning: Capitalism, Social Science and the State in the 1920s* (Princeton: Princeton University Press, 1985), 12.

5. My source actually lists the school as University of Pennsylvania's "Walton" School of Finance and Economy. W.D.P. Bliss, *Encyclopedia of Social Reform* (New York: Funk and Wagnalls, 1908) ; Edward T. Devine, "Organized Charity and Industry," Folder "Social Conditions," Box 160, Community Service Society Papers, Columbia University (hereafter CSS). The figure of twenty years at the C.O.S. I take from Devine's preface in *Social Work* (New York: Macmillan, 1922), vi.

6. See, e.g., Louis Weitz, *Out of a Job?* (New York: Peoples Educational Society, 1915), 43, copy located in Box 2, Folder "Unemployment, 1915," AALL Papers, LMDC.

7. Edward T. Devine, *Principles of Relief* (New York: Macmillan, 1904), 7.

8. Devine, *Principles of Relief,* 12.

9. Devine, *Principles of Relief,* 19, 38. On the historical background to the normal family standard, see Wally Seccombe, "Patriarchy Stabilized: the Construction of the Male Breadwinner Wage Norm in Nineteenth Century Britain," *Social History*, 11, 1 (Jan., 1986), 53–76.

10. Devine, *The Family and Social Work* (New York: Survey Associates, 1912), 59.

11. *Principles of Relief,* 179.

12. Devine, *Efficiency and Relief,* 18.

13. Workers' dependence on wages was soon recognized by reformers as the key problem in industrial society. See Henry Bruere's foreword to *How to Meet Hard Times* discussed below in Chapter 4.

14. Devine, *Principles of Relief,* 151.

15. "A Study of Industrial Development," n.d., Folder: Industrial Development Studies, Box 134, CSS.

16. Devine, *Principles of Relief,* 154; "A Study of Industrial Displacement," 11. McLean suggested the possibility of further investigation of the 58 cases as unemployed because of "seasonal dullness of trade," since "seasonal depressions come periodically and can be anticipated." The families, he implied, were probably "improvident" rather than "unemployed," since they should have anticipated the seasonal lay-off. On early studies of dependency, see Michael Katz, "Early Social Science and the Causes of Pauperism," in Katz, *Poverty and Policy in American History* (New York: Academic Press, 1983), 90–133.

17. Devine, *Principles of Relief,* 419.

18. Devine, *Principles of Relief,* 152.

19. Devine, *Principles of Relief,* 419.

20. *The Pittsburgh Survey*, Paul Kellogg, ed. (New York: Russell Sage, 1909–1914); John M. Glenn, Lilian Brandt, F. Emerson Andrews, *The Russell Sage Foundation 1907–1946* (New York: Russell Sage, 1947), 210–213; David Brody, *Steelworkers in America* (Cambridge: Harvard University Press, 1960), 159–164.

21. Unlike Jacob Schiff who made the initial proposal, Devine recommended that academics and workers join the men from "mercantile and industrial classes" on the Board of Directors, though he qualified himself, "The control should of course, remain with those who furnish the working funds." Devine, "Employment Bureau for the People of New York City" in Julia Johnsen, ed., *Selected Articles on Unemployment* (New York: H.W.Wilson Co., 1915), 161, reprinted from the *Annals of the American Academy* 33 (March, 1909), 225–238. Also see Paul T. Ringenbach, *Tramps and Reformers 1873–1916: The Discovery of Unemployment in New York City* (Westport CT: Greenwood Press, 1973), 146–148.

22. Devine, *Misery and its Causes* (New York: Macmillan, 1910), viii; the third study was Robert C. Chapin, *The Standard of Living Among Workingmen's Families in New York City* (New York: The Russell Sage Foundation, 1909).

23. Devine, *Misery and its Causes,* viii.

24. See Glenn, Brandt, and Andrews, 152–168. The Rockefeller Foundation hired Mackenzie King to direct work on industrial relations in the first year of its operation, but the initiative backfired with the storm over the 1914 Ludlow Massacre. Thereafter the Foundation withdrew from direct investigations and dealt with industrial relations only through grants to other organizations. Waldemar Nielsen, *The Big Foundations: A Twentieth Century Fund Study* (N.Y.: Columbia University Press, 1972), 53–54.

25. Alchon, 12–13.

26. A few years later when members of the U.S. Commission on Industrial Relations attacked the foundations' philanthropic activities as anti-democratic, Devine presented an extended defense. See his *Organized Charity and Industry* (New York: New York School of Philanthropy, n.d.), copy in "Social Conditions," Box 160, CSS Papers.

27. Devine, *Misery and its Causes,* 136–137, 142.

28. Devine, *Misery and its Causes,* 136.

29. Devine, *Misery and Its Causes,* 141.

30. See, e.g., Devine, *Misery and its Causes,* 130.

31. The charity organizations, of course, still relied for funding on the beneficence of the philanthropically-minded business elite. See Devine's defense of contributions from John D. Rockefeller, J.P. Morgan and Andrew Carnegie for submission to the U.S. Commission on Industrial Relations, in Devine, *Organized Charity and Industry* (New York: New York School of Philanthropy, 1915), 6,7 and passim. McClymer points out that not only the NYCOS but also the new "social experts" of the Russell Sage Foundation were dependent upon boards drawn from New York City's financial and philanthropic elites. McClymer, 53–54.

32. Devine, *The Family and Social Work,* 63.

33. Devine, *Misery and Its Causes,* 200.

34. Devine, *Social Forces,* 82.

35. Devine, *Misery and Its Causes,* 134.

36. William Beveridge, *Unemployment: A Problem of Industry* (London: Longmans, Green, 1909); Jose Harris, *Unemployment and Politics: A Study in English Social Policy 1886–1914* (Oxford: Clarendon Press, 1972); Jose Harris, *William Beveridge: A Biography* (Oxford: Clarendon Press, 1977); Derek Fraser, *The Evolution of the British Welfare State* (London: Macmillan, 1973), 135–163; Roy Lubove, *The Struggle for Social Security 1900–1935* (Cambridge: Harvard University Press, 1968), 149–153.

37. Harris, *William Beveridge,* 126.

38. Beveridge, 1.

39. Beveridge, 204–206. For a particularly harsh formulation of the process of decasualization of labor, see the quotations from Beveridge in Michael Freeden, *The New Liberalism: An Ideology of Social Reform* (Oxford: Clarendon, 1978), 184–185.

40. Beveridge, 201–208. See Freeden, 206–235. Incidentally, Beveridge's solution to the problem of underemployment is interesting in the context of recent employment trends and current "solutions" to the problem of unemployment which are its mirror image. Job-sharing, temporary, and part-time work (i.e. casual labor) are being suggested to alleviate the problems of unemployment, ostensibly created by too great a proportion of

the workforce working at secure and highly paid jobs. See, e.g. "Part-time work new labor trend," *New York Times* July 9, 1986, 1.

41. Lubove, 153.

42. Neither *Unemployment: a Problem of Industry* nor the British legislation had an immediate impact on the opening of new state agencies in North America, however, according to the dates provided in Udo Sautter, "North American Government Labor Agencies Before World War I: A Cure for Unemployment?" *Labor History* 24, 3 (Summer, 1983), 372, 383–384.

43. Sautter and Lubove have offered reasons for the attractiveness of the labor exchange, and thus Beveridge's work: they challenged least the laissez faire, anti-state predilections of American culture and seemed to involve much less state expenditure than other proposals. Sautter, "Labor Agencies," 371; Lubove, *Social Security*, 153–154. On Rubinow, see J. Lee Kreader, "Isaac Max Rubinow: Pioneering Specialist in Social Insurance," *Social Service Review*, 50,3 (September, 1976), 402–425. Rubinow's 1913 *Social Insurance* originated as lectures at Devine's New York School of Philanthropy. He shared with Devine and Seager membership on the American Association for Labor Legislation's Department on Social Insurance. Andrews to Rubinow, Feb. 10, 1913, Folder 16, Box 1, Rubinow Papers.

44. The first direct evidence I have found of their contact is not until 1906, though doubtless they were in touch earlier. Seager to E.R.A. Seligman, Jan.28, 1906, Seligman Papers, Columbia. Biographical information from *Who Was Who in America* Vol. 1, 1897–1942 (Chicago: Marquis Co., 1942); *Dictionary of American Biography* (N.Y.: Scribner's, 1935), Vol. 8, 531–532. On the AALL, see Daniel Nelson, *Unemployment Insurance: the American Experience* (Madison: University of Wisconsin Press, 1969), 13–27.

45. Henry Seager, *Introduction to Economics* (New York: Henry Holt, 1904) and *Economics: Briefer Course* (New York: Henry Holt, 1909).

46. Nelson, 11.

47. Seager, 89, 100. William Beveridge, *Unemployment: A Problem of Industry* (London: Longmans, Green, 1908). Leiserson was also heavily influenced by Charles Booth; see Garraty, *Unemployment in History*, 140.

48. Henry Seager, *Social Insurance: A Program of Social Reform* (New York: MacMillan, 1910), 5.

49. Henry Seager, *Social Insurance: A Program of Social Reform*, 8.

50. Henry Seager, *Social Insurance: A Program of Social Reform*, 18.

51. Henry Seager, *Social Insurance: A Program of Social Reform*, 20.

52. Henry Seager, *Social Insurance: A Program of Social Reform*, 89.

53. Henry Seager, *Social Insurance: A Program of Social Reform*, 92, 93.

54. Henry Seager, *Social Insurance: A Program of Social Reform*, 103. Orlando Lewis, secretary of the New York State Prison Association, was a leading advocate of labor colonies and contributed substantially to Seager's thinking on the subject. See Lewis, "Vagrancy in the United States," National Conference on Charities and Corrections *Proceedings*, 1907, 64; Ringenbach, *Tramps and Reformers*, 62. Several proposals to establish labor colonies in New York failed to get the necessary appropriations in the State Legislature. New York Commission on Employers' Liability and Other Matters, Third Report: Unemployment and Lack of Farm Labor, April 26, 1911, 187. John Mitchell articulated labor's objections: workingmen would not support, he said, "putting men under restraint if they are out of work" with "no crime against authority except they were

unemployed and compelled to beg. . . ." Third Report, 189. See also W.D.P. Bliss, *Encyclopedia of Social Reform*, 1246–1247.

55. Henry Seager, *Social Insurance: A Program of Social Reform*, 102–114.

56. Ironically but unsurprisingly, their remedies for unemployment in "normal times" did not receive much public attention until the numbers of the unemployed swelled in an industrial depression in 1914–1915. See chapter 4.

57. Henry Seager, *Social Insurance: A Program of Social Reform*, 84.

58. J. Michael Eisner, *William Morris Leiserson: A Biography* (Madison: University of Wisconsin, 1967), 6–21. Leiserson's dissertation was Appendix I to the Wainwright Commission's Third Report.

59. Commission on Employers' Liability and Other Matters, Third Report: Unemployment and Lack of Farm Labor, April 26, 1911, 167–168.

60. Warne was secretary of the New York State Immigration Commission and chairman of the Labor and Industry Committee of the Association of Neighborhood Workers. Third Report, 174.

61. Third Report, 174.

62. Third Report, Appendix I, 55.

63. Third Report, Appendix I, 28.

64. Third Report, Appendix I, 27, also see, e.g., 50, 54, 55, and Appendix VII.

65. Third Report, Appendix I, 43.

66. Third Report, Appendix 1, 50.

67. Third Report, Appendix VII, 150.

68. Alice Willard Solenberger, *One Thousand Homeless Men: A Study of Original Records* (New York: Russell Sage, 1911), 136.

69. On the other hand, Solenberger's work reveals the thin edge of the reintroduction of individual causation in its twentieth century guise—disease. "Industrial conditions alone cannot be held responsible for all the wandering about in search of work that is done by men who plead the lack of it in their own town as their excuse for starting out." Among one third of the "confirmed wanderers" (or tramps, 220 of her 1000 homeless men) she detected an "abnormal restlessness" which was the sole reason for tramping. (Others started out as itinerant laborers and became "confirmed wanderers.") Solenberger, 209–226. The boy who ran away had a "disease" which became chronic in some at maturity. Solenberger, 257. Casual labor as individual pathology reached its apotheosis a decade later in the work of Carleton H. Parker, *The Casual Laborer and Other Essays* (New York: Harcourt, Brace and Howe, 1920.) On unemployment as psychopathology, see also Estelle B. Freedman, "'Uncontrolled Desires': The Response to the Sexual Psychopath, 1920–1960," *Journal of American History*, 74, 1 (June, 1987), 88.

70. Third Report, Appendix 9, Table VI, 160.

71. Third Report, Appendix I, 52–53.

72. Third Report, Appendix I, 50.

73. Third Report, Appendix I, 66.

74. Also see William Leiserson, "Theory of Public Employment Offices and the Principles of their Practical Application," *Political Science Quarterly* 29 (March, 1914), reprinted in Julia Johnsen, ed., *Selected Articles on Unemployment* (New York: Wilson and Company, 1915), 110.

75. Third Report, Appendix I, 67–68. See also Udo Sautter, "Government and Unemployment: The Use of Public Works before the New Deal," *Journal of American History* 73, 1 (June, 1986), 59–86. Leiserson and the Commissioners followed Beveridge's gloomy assessment of the potential of modifying business cycles: "[Cyclical fluctuations] probably cannot be eliminated without an entire reconstruction of the industrial order. . . . Within the range of practical politics no cure for industrial fluctuation can be hoped for . . . Third Report, 7. A few years later Wesley C. Mitchell's *Business Cycles* (Berkeley: University of California Press, 1913) would challenge this view and gain an influential following in the 1920s.

76. I disagree here and in the following chapters with Ringenbach's claim that the Wainwright Commission report was forgotten by 1914, 155.

4

New York City, 1914–1917

The depression of 1914–1915 offered unemployment reformers their first chance to test the new conceptions in practice. In New York City, demonstrations and petitions by the unemployed, particularly those led by the I.W.W., created widespread concern beyond the usual reform constituency about the threat to social order which high levels of unemployment posed. The new mayor, John Purroy Mitchel, assumed office in the midst of the depression, and openly embraced the well-organized reform thinkers based in the social settlements, relief organizations and universities. Seizing the initiative, the reformers received the Mayor's backing. In their rhetoric, they initially subscribed to the notion that unemployment was a "problem of industry," not a "problem of relief." But they discovered that aspects of the Leiserson formulation were problematic as a guide to managing a cyclical unemployment crisis.

The new conception treated unemployment and the poverty it created as economic problems which demanded systemic solutions, as opposed to well-coordinated relief efforts aimed at individual moral reform. A second aspect of "the problem of industry" formulation was its geographic dimension. Relief had always been a "community" problem. Since industry was increasingly organized on a national level, unemployment as a "problem of industry" implied organization for solutions beyond the municipal level.

Ironically, the immediate problem faced in 1914–1915 was, in fact, precisely one of local "relief:" ensuring that unemployed New Yorkers would not freeze or starve. The crisis demanded action for which the long-range theoretical stance actually provided little guidance. During the acute phase of the depression, the reformers generally fell back, not without an ongoing tension, on their nineteenth century charity organization principles of relief—investigation, distinguishing worthy from unworthy poor, and the suppression of pauperism—to guide the programs.

Unemployment as "a problem of industry" acquired a third, implicit meaning in the context of American political ideology which did shape both activity during the crisis, and the theoretical revision in its wake. Here the "problem of industry" emphasized the central role of industrial leaders organized voluntarily outside of formal state institutions. To deal with the crisis, reformers (supported by the mayor) initiated a special citizens' committee explicitly designed to be dominated by businessmen guided by the expertise of the social service workers.[1] They saw winning the support of business leaders as crucial to the success of the reform project. Private interests invested with quasi-public authority apparently had more authority or more capacity to deal with acute social problems than did agencies of the state.

Shortly after his inauguration in January, 1914, Mayor John Purroy Mitchel convened hearings on the problem of unemployment in his offices.[2] Mitchel aimed to assess the extent of the problem and to begin to work out some immediate and long term plans. Of the seventeen people testifying, none was there in his or her capacity as a business manager. Members of the reform constituency, on the other hand, were heavily represented. There was testimony from Edward Devine of the Charity Organization Society, socialist Paul Kennaday, Professor Henry Seager of Columbia University, John B. Andrews of the American Association of Labor Legislation, and Frances Kellor of the North American Civic League for Immigrants.[3]

Henry Seager, who in addition to being an economics professor was also president of the American Association for Labor Legislation, represented the dominant "expert" opinion on unemployment at this time. Like others at the Mayor's hearing, one of his major concerns was the separation of the various categories of the unemployed. He was concerned with the "floating individuals in the community who do not really want to work and whose presence is an embarrassment when we try to do anything for those who do want work."[4] A moral hierarchy stood out clearly as he ranged through three categories, from those unemployed skilled workers who "would be in the same position as, perhaps, one of us would be if for some reason our income ceased and we had no accumulated property to fall back upon," through unemployed unskilled workers who would be suited to public relief work, to the "Weary Willie type," who did not really want to work at all. Seager emphasized the importance of segregating the three groups of the unemployed, and suggested the Municipal Employment Agency (set up temporarily under the Department of Licenses) and the Municipal Lodging House might be developed to serve that function. Once identified, the "Weary Willies" could be sent to a compulsory labor colony and "trained out of [their] constitutional dislike for work."[5]

Frances Kellor was equally emphatic on the importance of classification of the unemployed. Not only in her testimony at the mayor's hearing, but in a series of articles which appeared in the *Survey* during February, Kellor drew out the connection between segregation of the two groups of the unemployed, and the organization of the labor market. Only after the unemployable, "a problem of relief," had been separated from the employable, "an industrial matter" could efforts to organize the labor market through good employment agencies bear fruit.[6]

Other participants categorized on slightly different bases: City Coroner Timothy Healy put family men before single men for aid (with no mention of women), but the purpose was similar: segregation was necessary both so that relief measures would not encourage pauperism, and so that efficient organization of the labor market could proceed through the labor exchanges.[7] The concerns of the president of the A.A.L.L. exemplified the transitional nature of the dominant reform thought in the fall of 1914. Reformers acknowledged the existence of the many who were unemployed simply because there was no work; but they could not resist spending much of their efforts on the task of sorting and segregation.

A.A.L.L. thinking found a responsive ear in the Mitchel administration. When Secretary John B. Andrews suggested to Mayor Mitchel that he set up an Advisory Board on the problem of unemployment, Mitchel responded that he would take the question "under advisement with the Commissioner of Charities at once."[8] The advisory board, which did not materialize in full form until the depression deepened in the following fall, and the two city agencies mentioned by Seager (the Employment Bureau and the Lodging House) constituted the institutional core of the emergency program set up by the city.

On February 27, one month after his own unemployment hearings, the Mayor delivered the opening address of the first National Conference on Unemployment at City Hall. Organized by the A.A.L.L., the Conference attracted two hundred delegates representing governors and mayors of cities of the leading industrial states. Mitchel's opening was followed by an assessment of the extent of unemployment around the country. Many of the subsequent papers and discussions revolved around the A.A.L.L. remedies for unemployment and their European precedents.[9]

The first remedy was the "regularization of business." At this point "regularization" meant chiefly the leveling of seasonal fluctuation of employment: cyclical unemployment was hardly mentioned. The responsibility for "regularizing" lay with the employers themselves, who could be shown that it would be to their advantage. The second remedy was the establishment of a system of efficient public employment offices at the municipal and state levels, coordinated by the federal Department of Labor. The efforts to match "jobs without men and men without jobs" was a major theme of the conference, despite evidence presented of a net job shortage. Finally, the A.A.L.L. favored an "economical system of unemployment insurance."[10]

Mitchel's hearings, his participation in the Unemployment Conference, and his public statements of concern stimulated a flood of correspondence to his office on the subject of unemployment. Perhaps the greatest number of these letters came from the unemployed themselves who, upon hearing of the Mayor's concern, sought jobs from him. The Mayor's office referred the job seekers to Commissioner of Licenses George H. Bell, who was already organizing the Municipal Employment Agency.[11]

After the requests for jobs, the most persistent theme was the question of separating the worthy from the unworthy unemployed. Mitchel's correspondents agreed that the city had a responsibility to help many of the unemployed but, like Henry Seager and the nineteenth century Charity Organization movement, feared where this might lead. In a typical letter, John Franklin Crowell of Dow, Jones Publishers pressed Mitchel as to "what steps were being taken to distinguish between the vagrant, floating element of the unemployed which drifts into New York every winter, and the deserving poor and unemployed who are resident in the city and can give account of themselves as such."[12] Crowell expressed concern with the directionless mobility of the unemployed in nineteenth century localist terms: residents should come first in any relief program. Social thinkers more in harmony with twentieth century political economy sought policies not to stop worker mobility but to channel it in accordance with the fluctuating needs of capital.

Paul Kennaday, who wrote on behalf of the Socialist Party's Unemployment Conference, forwarded suggestions not much different from those advanced by the A.A.L.L. Beyond pressing for more liberal relief measures immediately, the Socialists endorsed the regularization of industrial employment, both by decasualization of labor and by the reduction of seasonal variation in certain industries, the expansion of public employment, particularly during periods of unemployment, a network of state labor exchanges, and more vigorous enforcement of protective labor legislation.[13]

One of the most remarkable letters came from H.F. Stimpson, a consulting engineer with thirty-two years of professional experience "including six years of intensive research into Business, or Applied Economics." He advertised himself as an expert in "economics, organization, administration, and efficiency." He had attended the National Conference on Unemployment and congratulated Mitchel for his participation. Mitchel's actions, he wrote, were "most gratifying to those who supported you last Fall because of their conviction that you had some high ideal as to the functions of popular government or, rather, the *management of popular affairs*." (Stimpson's emphasis)[14]

Stimpson noted the limitations of the presentations at the Conference, and was apparently (and justifiably) concerned that Mitchel's emergency programs would rely too heavily on them. There was an undue emphasis, he felt, on "getting the man and the job together," while "it did not seem to be realized that there were not enough jobs to go around. . . ."

Stimpson shared with Mitchel's advisors a faith that expert opinion could be applied successfully to the social and economic problems of the day. Like them he saw contemporary business leadership as occupying the crucial position to do something about the problem of unemployment. But he viewed the relationship between social experts and the business elite differently. Like the charity organization movement from which they developed, the latter relied upon the good will and leadership of the capitalist class for the success of their program, while Stimpson wrote as an adversary.

In a five page, single-spaced missive, Stimpson explained that wage earners were not being granted in wages the productivity increases due to them from the increased use of machinery. Nor, on the other hand, were businessmen reducing prices to reflect the lower cost of machine production. Workers, consequently, could not purchase the "outrageously inflated" and "unscientifically" valued commodities they produced. Employers gradually cut back production, increasing unemployment and decreasing workers' ability to buy. "The ugly fact is that the merchandizers or 'business men' who together constitute less than 15% of the community, are charging for the commodities or service which they supply, a fearful excess over the cost, to them, plus a normal compensation for their own services." Stimpson suggested that the city join in pressing the federal government to establish a scientific department to set once and for all, the values of different forms of power and skill, so that workers and consumers would be able to determine whether their wages and prices respectively were fair. The dissemination of these values would, Stimpson felt, permanently settle the wage question and the price question "on the basis of fact." This would solve the problem of underconsumption which in turn would solve the problem of unemployment. In closing, Stimpson suggested that the City warn businessmen that failure to reform would lead to "harsh treatment at the hands of an infuriated majority."[15]

Threats in various forms, in fact, formed the backdrop for most of the proposals heard by the Mayor through the conferences and correspondence of early 1914. A series of demonstrations by the unemployed in late February and March heightened public awareness. Although I.W.W. responsibility for these demonstrations was never proven, the press generally assumed it. Peter Speek's testimony to the U.S. Commission on Industrial Relations described a typical incident. Speek arrived to observe Bell's new Municipal Employment Exchange two days after its opening, on February 16 at 7:30 A.M. He later described the desperate scene. Of the two to three hundred unemployed men milling around trying to keep warm, he estimated that ten percent had adequate shoes; about half had rags and burlap wrapped around their feet. A request to form a line caused a panic and a rush, prompting the Exchange official to call the police to restore order. The crowd grew to an estimated five hundred. A man complained that the Exchange was deceiving the men, that there were no jobs, and that the officials were trying to freeze them to death by having them stand in one place in line. Finally, someone cried, "Brothers, let's go to City Hall!" and seventy to one-hundred marched off behind a Wobbly named Harry Klein to demand a meeting with Mitchel, who was out of town. The angry crowd dispersed but Speek warned that the incident demonstrated the volatility of New York City's unemployed.[16]

Later in February and in early March, I.W.W. member Frank Tannenbaum's leadership of "invasions" of churches with an "army of the unemployed" gained much wider publicity. Nightly meetings of homeless unemployed men in Rutgers Square led to four occasions where church officials granted permission for the men to use their buildings as shelter. On the fifth, church officials at St. Alphonsus Roman Catholic Church resisted, leading to a clash with police and arrests of the unemployed men.[17]

As the pitch of public discussion and debate rose, the Mayor's office itself found it difficult to keep up, taking one month to respond to an offer of help from the Clergymen's Committee on Unemployment, because, as the Mayor's secretary apologetically wrote, "it was received at the time when the agitation of the unemployed was at its height."[18] The *Survey*, normally a promoter of reform discussion and activity, commented at the end of March:

> With a new unemployment committee forming over night, a mass meeting or conference on the unemployed called daily, and with state and municipal plans changing every week, it is well nigh impossible to untangle the actual facts and the important occurrences in the unemployment situation in New York city during the past two months.[19]

New York City had become not only a center for the country's unemployed, but a center for the country's experts on unemployment.

The employment exchange occupied a central place in their thinking on unemployment.[20] It was a key institution in the organization of the labor market and thus in what reformers held to be the long-range solution to the unemployment problem. But it could also be set in place fairly quickly and plausibly provide some immediate benefits. This combination of long-term and short-term promise thrust the employment exchange to the forefront of municipal activity. One of the first measures Mitchel took, following his solicitation of opinions on unemployment, was the establishment of an experimental Municipal Employment Exchange on February 14, 1914. The *Survey* reported that it was "expected to overcome some of the present haphazard methods which Miss Kellor has pointed out." During the first month of its operation, the Municipal Exchange found temporary employment for 3,973 persons, and Mitchel requested that the Board of Aldermen make it permanent by ordinance.[21]

There was little further action for several months. Relief societies and the Municipal Lodging House continued to have much higher than normal numbers of applicants, but these rates attracted little attention except from those directly responsible for the institutions. Whatever the actual levels of unemployment during the summer of 1914, there was little of the public discussion which had occurred during the first months of the Mitchel administration, perhaps because I.W.W. activity had abated.

By September, however, the European war had disrupted international markets. As concern in the City quickly rose, the Board of Aldermen approved a more permanent Employment Bureau. Mitchel recruited Walter B. Sears, head of the State Free Employment Office in Boston, to organize and supervise it. Sears pressed vigorously for centralization of efforts to deal with unemployment within the city.

> I have repeatedly emphasized the importance of centralizing the demand for labor at the Government Bureau . . . as against the antiquated methods now practiced. We have in this city more than 1000 churches, each with their Committee on Unemployment, besides similar Committees from each local fraternal organization, more than 600 private employment agencies, and hundreds of other agencies, and well-educated, well-to-do and well-intentioned individuals, all endeavoring to assist the unemployed. This antequated [sic] policy results in confusion and duplication, to say nothing of the enormous waste of time and money, with a minimum of results.[22]

The Public Employment Bureau was not to supplant the private for-profit bureaus of which there were over 650 (and which had been subject to considerable criticism, investigation, and regulation).[23] Nor was it meant to replace the semi-philanthropic agencies run by charity organizations and churches. Rather, in addition to functioning as an agency in its own right, it would coordinate the others and act as an overarching clearinghouse for labor. There were several major problems, however, which stood between Sears and centralized management of the New York City labor market.

Superintendent Sears was cautious about the offer of "the closest cooperation" he received from Bailey B. Burritt, General Director of the Association for Improvement of the Condition of the Poor (A.I.C.P.). He was afraid that too close an association with the A.I.C.P. or the C.O.S. would damage the ability of the Public Employment Bureau to secure the patronage of major employers.

> Doubtless you appreciate the importance of keeping the office on a strictly business basis, and allay all suspicion on the part of the public, especially the employing public, that we are to run a charity bureau (caring only for the down and out) so to speak. After we are established, and have several thousand employers as patrons of the office, we shall then be able to care for a percentage of the handicapped, the same as we have done in Boston, and until such time, we must give the public to understand that it is to be a business proposition pure and simple, and not a charity in any sense of the word.[24]

Once his employment bureau was tainted by a reputation of catering to the marginally employable, Sears felt it would be difficult for him to attract employers seeking to hire more skilled or more reliable labor, and so he kept his distance from the swelling ranks of the relief societies.

Sears' second problem concerned the relationship between the local and national labor markets. Advocates of organization of the labor market emphasized the inadequacy of strictly local agencies. Their analysis was most pertinent to New York City which, as Frances Kellor wrote, was "the distributing point for the bulk of unskilled labor east of the Mississippi and for a considerable part of all unskilled labor."[25] Kellor's *Survey* articles proposed a network of employment exchanges to organize the national labor market. But her first caveat was that "unemployment must be dealt with beyond the municipal level." Here was the contradiction between the long-term and the short-term attractiveness of the employment bureau project and between its progressive and regressive dimensions. As long as it remained a strictly local project, it harkened back to nineteenth century efforts to deal locally with the local unemployed. In this form it could not become the organizing institution for a national labor market.[26]

Sears understood the resources with which he had to work, and that his effectiveness was limited, at best, to the local aspect of the problem. "Each locality should devote its energies to its own residents," Sears wrote in classically nineteenth century form. "I fully realize this policy may not be popular, but I am certain that it is the sensible thing to do." The Bureau gave preference to "permanent residents with dependents."[27]

Beyond these problems, there was the relatively small scale of his operation. Sears advocated measures to expand his offices and others which would reduce the pool of job-seekers needing them. He suggested that residents of cities be removed to farms in the countryside, that immigration be curtailed, and that prison labor be restricted. Further measures advocated by Sears for reducing unemployment included shortening the work day, extending vocational training and, not surprisingly, providing more money for public employment agencies.[28]

Despite Sears' best efforts, however, the first months of the employment bureau were not promising. Its opening day imbalance—2,500 job applicants and four employers seeking help—continued into the winter. In December, the *Survey* reported the placement of only 270 of the 9,565 bureau applicants.[29] Matching "job and man" only scratched the surface of the problem.

As winter approached, leaders both inside and outside the administration geared up for what they already foresaw as a most difficult season. In particular, the memory of the previous winter's demonstrations by the I.W.W. stimulated preventative measures. George William Douglas communicated the sense of foreboding in a November letter to members of the New York Federation of Churches:

> The problem of unemployment, and the consequent danger that the needy and unemployed may be misled and troubled by the I.W.W. and other agitators, is now, more than ever, presented to the minds and hearts of all serious citizens. . . . Miss Kellor and other experts are convinced that this winter there will be more of the I.W.W. agitation than ever before in the history of New York City.[30]

The relief agencies were ahead of the churches in their organizational efforts. The C.O.S. prepared an internal memorandum detailing sources of information on previous depressions, as it prepared for the winter. It mentioned as useful for planning Carlos Closson's work on 1893, Warner's *American Charities*, The *Survey*, and the Charities and Correction's Conference Proceedings. Not surprisingly, the precedents came from the relief agency constituency, and not from either governments or business. But over the next months, this constituency itself helped to place business in the forefront of New York City efforts.[31]

On September 17, the A.I.C.P. put forward a draft, probably written by Bailey Burritt, entitled "Tentative Plan Proposed to Meet Possible Unemployment Emergency Growing Out of the European Situation." Its seven points included exhortations to private employers to maintain their workforces, expansion of public works, development of the city and state employment bureaus, organization of data-collection and provision for an emergency relief fund. Its last suggestion was the creation of a citizens' committee "possibly appointed by Mayor" to raise funds and coordinate relief efforts.[32]

A week later, an informal conference was held to consider the proposal. Conferees included John Kingsbury of the Department of Public Charities, John Glenn of the Russell Sage Foundation, Edward Devine representing the N.Y. School of Philanthropy, and representatives of the C.O.S., the United Hebrew Charities, and the Brooklyn Bureau of Charities. Cornelius Bliss and Bailey Burritt represented the A.I.C.P. Each of the conferees reviewed the dramatically increased load of his respective organization over the past year. They moved the proposal for a citizens committee (from the September 17 Tentative Plan) to the head of the list, and constituted themselves as an informal committee with Bailey Burritt as secretary.[33]

When the committee met in conference five days later, it also included Homer Folks of the State Charities Aid Association, Mayor Mitchel, and City Chamberlain Henry Bruere. At this meeting Commissioner Kingsbury stated that he thought "it would be desirable to announce to the public the existence of some committee formed for the purpose of keeping in touch with the whole situation and of devising plans for meeting any emergencies" during the approaching winter. The others concurred, but Bruere suggested that the committee include "bankers, employers and others who would be definitely and vitally interested in the problem confronting the city this winter." Furthermore, he revived the idea that it be constituted as a "mayor's committee."[34]

A subcommittee planned the details. Three of the five members of this committee—Folks, Burritt, and Kingsbury—were able to discuss plans for the Mayor's Committee on Unemployment after they left the City for the suburbs in the evening, as they lived within a block of each other in Yonkers. The other two members of the subcommittee were Frank Persons of the C.O.S. and Henry Bruere.[35]

Bruere's influence was considerable: his suggestions on the role of businessmen in the City's efforts ultimately determined the shape of the committee. His personal history gave him a strong sense of the role which progressive businessmen might play in the reform process. As a student at the University of Chicago, Columbia, and Harvard, Bruere was immersed in the culture of the settlement house. He obtained employment as a welfare worker for International Harvester through Stanley McCormick, and the personal support of the McCormick family enabled him to establish and run an Institute for Harvester employees over the occasional objections of non-family executives.[36] Leaving

Chicago he became a central figure in efforts to reform city government through R. Fulton Cutting's Citizens' Union's "Bureau of City Betterment," which expanded and became an independent Bureau of Municipal Research with the support of Union Pacific's E.H. Harriman. As he remembered them later, these experiences schooled Bruere in methods of applying "the techniques of business management to public affairs and civic problems."[37] He remembered Harriman as advocating in government what he "had fostered in the Union Pacific."[38] Recruited by Mitchel for the largely ceremonial post of City Chamberlain, Bruere managed to become virtually an "assistant mayor," and, in the words of Frances Perkins, "probably the most useful person in the whole Mitchel administration."[39]

Bruere drafted the October 15 tentative proposal which formed the basis of the city's program for the winter. The Yonkers-dominated subcommittee approved it on October 26. With several stylistic modifications, it was published in November as "A Proposal In Reference to Unemployment in the Winter of 1914 for Consideration by His Honor, the Mayor of the City of New York."[40]

The proposal consisted of two parts: an extended introduction which defined a theoretical position on unemployment, and a "working plan." The central role of businessmen and bankers was highlighted throughout both parts. The introduction pointed to "the organizers and responsible managers of public and private business enterprises" as "the principal factors of unemployment." To interpret this as an accusation, however, would be to miss Bruere's point. The document was a call for business leadership and participation. It continued in italics:

> **The major element of the program suggested is the plan for dealing with the problem not as a problem of relief or one calling for philanthropic action, but as a problem of business and industry for consideration and action by those who are the dominant forces in our American industrial life.**[41]

The working plan was thoroughly consistent with the orientation outlined in the introduction. It called for representation of labor and city, state, and federal governments. But five out of the nine categories of representatives went to business. Similarly, four of the five proposed measures included a calling a "meeting of influential business men and bankers" to urge their cooperation; appointing a "permanent committee . . . to consist of men who are members of the group of greatest influence in our present economic system" to monitor employment opportunities and industrial conditions; forming a "sub-committee consisting of business men and social workers" to pursue the subject of labor exchanges; and constituting "subcommittees of different industries," in which executives would monitor their own industries. The fifth proposed measure—to ascertain facts on employment and unemployment—was the only one not specifically delegated to businessmen. (And eventually the chairman of this committee was Harry Thayer of A.T.&T. see below).

Bruere's Proposal took an extremely cautious stance towards unemployment insurance. In the introduction, he mentioned employment exchanges and unemployment insurance as "European expedients," which could be enacted by government agencies. These, he implied, were better than the "makeshifts" devised in the United States, but still did "not reckon with the principal factors of unemployment," i.e. managers of business enterprises. Confronting the unemployment question meant, above all, dealing with employment policies, and those who controlled employment policies were the corporate executives. Aside from being politically controversial, the question of unemployment insurance did not seem to bear directly on employment policies. In the recommendations which made up the last part of the Proposal, unemployment insurance received mention only as something to be "considered," while measures such as vocational education, labor exchanges and data collection were to be "pushed," "organized," "urged," and "compelled."

It was in these months, in fact, that John Andrews and the A.A.L.L. were working out a new position on unemployment insurance which could be reconciled with the business orientation expressed in the Bruere proposal. As this position developed, it held that unemployment insurance could function in much the same way as did workers' compensation, that is, as a government-sponsored incentive to responsible business practices. Industries with higher rates of layoffs and turnover would be compelled to pay heavier unemployment insurance premiums. The effectiveness of unemployment insurance would lie, not in providing money to the unemployed, but in preventing unemployment in the first place. But this view of unemployment insurance was not yet under broader public discussion, and there is no evidence that Bruere or other members of the subcommittee were aware of it at the time.[42]

In one respect the Proposal was not as business-dominated as the Mayor's Committee itself actually turned out to be. The Proposal suggested that the Mayor's Committee be organized under "an executive experienced in labor problems." To give a sense of the type of person it had in mind, it mentioned the names of Charles T. Neill, former U.S. commissioner of labor, and Mackenzie King, former commissioner of labor in Canada. Within a week of the subcommittee's approval of the Bruere proposal, on December 2, the *Evening Post* announced the formation of the Mayor's Committee with the headline, "Gary to Aid the City's Unemployed."[43] *The New Republic*, among others, questioned the appointment of Elbert Gary, Chairman of the Board of Directors of United States Steel, as chairman of the Mayor's Committee. "It must not be forgotten," ran the editorial, "that Judge Gary, however excellent his intentions, suffers from the defect that in these matters he belongs to the least enlightened class in the whole community."[44]

Bruere became the General Secretary of the Committee. Six subcommittees were chaired by Gary, Edward Devine, Henry Seager, Harry B. Thayer, Mrs. James Speyer, and William H. Truesdale. The approximately one hundred other members of the committee reflected a broad range of social outlooks, running from Rose Schneiderman of the Woman's Trade Union League, through more conservative unionists like John Mitchell, through church and social work activists like Charles Stelzle, Frances Kellor and John Kingsbury to businessmen like Oscar Straus of Macy's, George Perkins, and F.A. Vanderlip.[45] The top of the list of contributors to the Committee funds made the project look strikingly like a nineteenth century charity drive with the names of Astor, Harriman, Rockefeller, Carnegie, and Guggenheim.[46]

The first concrete actions taken by the Committee involved the assessment of the seriousness of the situation. Logically, it was the first task, in that organization of both the labor market and of effective emergency relief efforts required an understanding of who was unemployed, and what their employment prospects were. Thayer's Committee on Facts Regarding Existing Conditions of Unemployment was gathering information by mid-December.[47] It based its first report on two sources: the figures which showed increased loads of the relief societies (similar to those which had been presented to the Mayor in September by the members of the planning committee) and returns from questionnaires to 602 employers, representing about one eighth of those employed in trade and industry in New York City. The latter returns simply showed the difference between the number who had been employed during the corresponding week in December, 1913, and those currently employed. It was an admittedly rough way to estimate the total unemployment, particularly since unemployment during the winter of 1913–1914 had been high. Yet it represented an advance over the only previous statistics on unemployment which were based on trade union figures alone.[48] The Committee concluded that there had been an 8 percent increase in unemployment over the previous December. Factory employment had decreased 13.5 percent, while the number of factory employees on part time nearly trebled.

In the following months there were much more comprehensive attempts to assess the extent of unemployment. In January, the Committee requested that the Metropolitan Life Insurance Company conduct a survey of its industrial policy holders in New York City, to determine the extent of unemployment among them. Vice-President Haley Fiske of the Metropolitan, a member of the Mayor's Committee, made the arrangements. Metropolitan agents, who collected fees from most policy holders on a weekly basis, asked their clients about their employment status. For the purposes of this survey part-time work was considered as full-time. Results were classified by sex and by industry, and showed unemployment to stand at 18 percent, affecting 23.7 percent of the families surveyed.[49]

A second survey was carried out almost simultaneously under the auspices of the U.S. Bureau of Labor Statistics. Bailey Burritt, in preparing arguments for the unemployment subcommittee the previous fall, had written two letters to Royal Meeker, the U.S. Commissioner of Labor Statistics, on the need to organize more comprehensive statistics on unemployment.[50] But the Bureau of Labor Statistics simply did not have the money, mechanism, nor even the expertise, to conduct its own survey. It was not until late January that the Bureau completed arrangements with other agencies for its own survey. Meeker arranged with the Bureau of Immigration, the New York Police Department, and the New York Tenement House Commission to supply inspectors to canvass 104 representative city blocks, and 3703 additional individual tenement houses. Once the information was assembled, it was turned over to the Metropolitan Life Insurance statisticians for compilation and analysis. The Bureau of Labor Statistics participated only minimally in its own study—by paying the street carfare of the surveyors, and publishing the results. The B.L.S. survey found unemployment standing at 16.2 percent of all individuals. The Mayor's Committee report concluded that the two studies confirmed each other, despite this small difference.[51]

Resurveys were undertaken in August and September, again, under the direction of both the Metropolitan Life Insurance Company and the B.L.S. Though the resurveys differed from each other more than the February surveys, both showed improvement in the unemployment situation.[52]

The B.L.S., with a clear view of its own lack of resources, called upon the Metropolitan to conduct similar surveys in cities throughout the United States. According to its own publication, the B.L.S. employed the Metropolitan because the latter's results in New York City "tallied so closely" with those of the B.L.S. study. Not until 1930 did Royal Meeker refer to the "humiliation" in the B.L.S. asking help from a private company (without compensation) because the "lack of funds rendered the Federal officials helpless to obtain the required information."[53]

In spite of the new emphasis on unemployment as a problem of industry, and therefore on participation of business leaders and the collection of survey information, New York City did confront a crisis of unemployment whose immediate manifestations long range planning would do little to mitigate. Consequently, despite the misgivings of the charity organization experts, much of the Committee's practical work pointed backwards, toward emergency relief efforts, rather than forwards, towards organization of the labor market. The innovations in relief work were piecemeal and did not lead towards new ways of dealing with unemployment as might capitalist participation in administrative organization of the labor market. Nevertheless, a brief summary is in order.

The Committee provided relief work for 5,000 people a day through 22 workrooms, between the end of January and the middle of April. Women sewed women's and children's garments by hand, while men made fly traps for the health department, repaired furniture, and made rugs. They worked five days a week, from 10:00 to 3:00 in workrooms set up in churches, the Y.M.C.A., Y.W.C.A., the Children's Aid Society, and charitable societies. Men earned 50 cents a day with lunch; and women 60 cents, without, so they could return to their homes at lunch hour to cook for their children. As the report explained, "The payment made to the workers was in no sense regarded as a wage, but rather as a tide-over until real work opened up." Nor was anything made in the workrooms sold on the market. The Committee which aimed to treat the problem of unemployment as a problem of industry was very careful not to allow relief measures to be confused with business.[54] The same pay was awarded to girls who enrolled in vocational classes set up by the Committee "to capitalize" the girls' unemployed time. About 1,000 girls selected by philanthropic agencies as needing more training for successful vocational placement took part in this program.[55]

Considering the emphasis on unemployment as an industrial problem, comparatively few of the concrete programs of the Mayor's Committee dealt directly with the creation of jobs. Private employers were urged, by various avenues, to maintain their workforces.[56] Though the Committee did "not regard it as wise to urge new and special public undertakings to give employment," it did recommend the beginning of all projects for which appropriations had already been made, and which could be worked on during the winter.[57] Provision of public works stimulated fierce debate both inside and outside the administration in January 1915.[58] In fact, the subway and aqueduct construction which were already underway already employed 25,000 people in "two of the largest public works undertakings in the history . . . of the City of New York."[59] These projects dwarfed the new public works programs of snow-clearing, parks improvement (sponsored by the A.I.C.P.) and street-cleaning (organized by the police department). Though the Mayor's Committee made recommendations on planning public works for business depressions for the future, it did not list such works among its accomplishments during the winter of 1914–1915.[60]

Ironically, Frances Kellor, whose *Survey* articles the previous year had focused on the importance of organizing the national labor market, found her energies on the Committee directed towards the collection and distribution of bundles of clothing in "Bundle Day," on February 4, 1915. While the scale of this operation (over two million articles of clothing collected, sorted, repaired and distributed to some 300,000 people) set it apart from nineteenth century efforts, in conception it was among the more backward looking of the Committee's projects. (Joining Kellor on the Committee were Mrs. Astor, Mrs. Vanderbilt, and Mrs. Biddle.)[61]

The other major project which involved relief in kind was the provision of shelter to homeless men (and a few women) through expansion of the Municipal Lodging House. Unlike Bundle Day, reformers linked the Lodging House project to the larger task of organizing the labor market. As Henry Seager had suggested in January, 1914, a progressive Lodging House could sift the unemployed from the unemployable through social investigation, and send the former to the labor exchange and the latter to the labor colony or the hospital.

The Lodging House had never been called upon to perform a social service function other than providing shelter, bath, breakfast and supper for its inmates. From 1896, when the first provisions were made, until 1909, a building rented by the city had sufficed. In the latter year, the city constructed a six-story building, and claimed to have "the largest and best-equipped municipal lodging house in the world," accommodating somewhat more than 1,000 people per night.[62] By law, men could stay no more than three nights consecutively.

In the winter of 1913–1914, the number of applicants to the Lodging House increased dramatically. With up to approximately 2,000 per night, an overflow had to sleep "on the bare floors of boats moored at the dock at the foot of East 26th Street, on the floors of waiting rooms and even on the floors of the prison pen and the morgue."[63] In January, Commissioner of Charities Kingsbury expanded the capacity of the Municipal Lodging House by providing a 1,100 bed annex on the East 24th Street Recreation Pier. With extra army cots the Lodging House plus annex could now house around 2,700.[64] Arrangements were also made with the Commissioner of Immigration to accommodate at Ellis Island up to several hundred men who had stayed their legal limit at the Lodging House.[65] By the winter of 1914–1915, the physical capacity of the municipal lodging facilities seemed adequate to the demand.[66]

Little had been done, however, to convert it to a progressive sorting agency and adjunct to the labor exchange. In part, this was due to confusion about who the homeless were and which agencies were responsible for them. In an unpublished report for the Russell Sage Foundation Charles Barnes noted "more confused thinking on this question than on any other sociological problem."[67] The A.I.C.P. and the C.O.S., which had supported a Joint Application Bureau to deal with homeless men and women, were now in the process of turning over that work to the public charities. Many social workers thought that private charity organizations should be concerned with families, while the public should be responsible for the homeless, though there was no clear rationale for this division, and others advanced alternative divisions of labor.[68]

Charity Commissioner Kingsbury took up Seager's challenge. In fact, he made it into somewhat of a crusade, publishing articles, commissioning studies, and speaking at conferences, in addition to carrying out reforms at the Lodging House itself.[69] He aimed, in his own words, to turn it into "a great human repair shop."[70] At the same time that the Mayor's Committee was assembling, Kingsbury put together an Advisory Social Service Committee for the Lodging House. He invited prominent members of the New York social welfare community to join the committee. Kingsbury wrote to John Andrews, requesting that he assume the chairmanship:

> I am trying to broaden the work and increase the usefulness of the Municipal Lodging House. . . . It is obvious that if we merely house and feed these unfortunate men and women for three days, we have come far short of accepting the opportunity, and I may say, the responsibility, which has been afforded us.
>
> In order that we may adopt the most wise, efficient and humane policy in the treatment of these homeless men and women, and in order that we may make the best social use of the invaluable information secured through the channels of the Lodging House, I desire to have the counsel of men and women familiar with the problems of unemployment relief, immigration, labor conditions, etc. in working out a program and policy for the institution.[71]

The Social Service Advisory Committee did not include a strong business constituency like that which dominated the Mayor's Committee. Nor did the committee have an official connection with the Mayor's Committee on Unemployment. Yet, the fact that Kingsbury was Commissioner of Charities, that John Andrews accepted its chairmanship, and that Bailey Burritt was one of its most active members insured the necessary coordination with the Mayor's Committee.[72] Walter Lippmann, one of the few members not directly connected to private or public charitable organizations, objected when it appeared that the Advisory Committee might set its own course too independently:

> The one first [sic] thing I want to see done this winter is a centralization of responsibility, so that all the credit and all the criticism shall fall upon the Mayor's committee. I think we ought to subordinate ourselves to doing that phase of the work which was assigned to us; it has enough ramifications to keep us busy, and when we want money or legislation let's go to the Mayor's committee and ask for it.[73]

Kingsbury extended the accessibility of the Lodging House to homeless men by securing, with the help of the Mayor's Committee, an extension to the three day legal maximum stay. He justified both expansion and extension first on the basis of need, and second, by claiming that the most useful social service for the men could be provided only with a more extended stay.[74] The more men he could accommodate and the longer he could have them, the more chance he had to effect his vision of a "human repair shop," and Seager's of a sorting agency. Yet both these visions depended upon increased appropriation for staff, and this he had a harder time getting from the City government. "It is manifestly absurd," he wrote to the Aldermen, "to conduct so important an institution . . . with a Superintendent, an Inspector, and a few Hospital Helpers who must be recruited from the ranks of the applicants at the lodging house itself." Kingsbury was finding it difficult to separate employable from unemployable and to enforce work requirements with existing staff.[75] How could Kingsbury run his "human repair shop" with what Lippmann called an "absurd mass of rusty machinery?"[76]

Kingsbury explored his vision of a "well-regulated" municipal lodging house in an article published in April, 1914. He described an institution which, beyond temporarily housing the homeless, would serve as a "clearinghouse" separating the employable from the unemployable, steering the employable to jobs, and the unemployable to institutions where they would be rehabilitated. Each applicant would be examined, "physically, mentally, and socially."

> . . . it should be prepared to send to hospitals, to asylums, to farm colonies, or to workhouses, those physically, mentally, and morally unfit to engage in labor or to hold a job; it should be prepared to provide labor suited to the physical and mental capacity of those who are physically and mentally fit, and so far as possible to provide such labor *before* meals and lodgings are supplied. . . .[77]

Attached to the lodging house, there would be an industrial plant to supply work in a variety of occupations, an employment agency to direct the fit to jobs beyond, and a plain-clothes social police force to apprehend "mendicants, vagrants, tramps, and criminals who are apt to frequent free shelters not so protected." These officers would be responsible both for social investigation and for bringing vagrants before magistrates for commitment to the workhouse, where necessary. "Such a program of relief," Kingsbury concluded, ". . . vigorously enforced, surely would reduce Unemployment to its lowest denomination."[78]

The physical expansion of the Lodging House would be worse than useless, measured against Kingsbury's objectives set out in this article, if the larger program could not be put into effect. The Advisory Social Service Committee was designed in part to build the needed support for reform measures.[79] Its most important work was a major report published in September 1915 by the Department of Charities.[80] The report had three purposes. First, in its analysis of data gathered on 1500 Lodging House applicants from the prior year, it aimed to demonstrate the utility of the institution as a social laboratory for probing the causes of poverty and homelessness. Secondly, it aimed to show how Kingsbury's sorting and "human repair shop" objectives had been partially met by reforms already introduced. And finally, it was an argument for more resources being committed to the Lodging House, so that it could truly fulfill the promise which the reformers claimed for it.

Soon after he became Commissioner of Charities, Kingsbury oversaw the detailed study of 1500 applicants to the Lodging House. He turned over the still unpublished findings to the Advisory Committee at the time of its formation. Mary Van Kleeck responded with a devastating critique of the statistical work, concluding that "no mere editing of the present manuscript could make it of a kind which we would wish to see published." With characteristic clarity, she pointed out that "when efforts have been made to label each case with the primary cause of poverty, the result throws more light on the mental outlook of the interviewer than on the cause of poverty." She argued for a reworking of the data, in order to be able to comprehend the "interlocking of the various factors" which produced the conditions which led the applicants to the Lodging House.[81]

Van Kleeck's arguments were persuasive: the Committee obtained the cooperation of a class at the New York School of Philanthropy to reanalyze the data. This work was combined with portions of Charles Barnes' unpublished Russell Sage study, and with some work by the deputy superintendent of the Lodging House, William Alberti Whiting. A.A.L.L. staff member Robert Bertrand Brown wrote the final report.[82]

Published as "The Men We Lodge" in September, 1915, the report began with the results of a "census" of homeless men and women completed by the Mayor's Committee on the night of January 30. It included all the people living in lodging houses charging 25 cents or less per night, or sleeping in "shelters, employment agencies, back rooms of saloons, or found in unprotected places." Of the total (25,969) 19,417 were in cheap lodging houses, 1831 were in the Municipal Lodging House. The Ellis Island Immigrant Station, housing 628 on the night of the census, and the Staten Island Farm Colony, housing 269, served as temporary extensions to the Municipal Lodging House facilities.[83]

It went on to analyze the results of Kingsbury's data from the previous March. The introduction to this section claimed that this data would be analyzed in order to distinguish the unemployed from the unemployable, "two distinct though constantly merging groups." But it acknowledged that no adequate method had been perfected for separating the two.[84] The sections which followed were divided into "unemployed" and "unemployable." But, probably as a result of the Van Kleeck criticisms, no percentages or numbers were given which might have indicated the relative proportions of the entire group in each category. The section on the Unemployed did more to assemble evidence that there was in fact such a group, than to indicate what proportion of Lodging House applicants it represented. The evidence consisted of three parts: first, that approximately three out of four of the 417 who had arrived in New York within the past six months said they had come in search of work; second, that a number of employers said they would rehire the particular men laid off if work picked up; and that about nine out of ten of all the men examined were judged physically able to work. The Report pointed to the seasonal fluctuations in the demand for labor as additional evidence for the existence of this group.

Various factors underlying the unemployability of the second group were outlined. Included were physical handicaps, mental handicaps, alcohol, habitual idleness, lack of training, and old age. Consistent with the Van Kleeck criticism, no attempt was made to divide the entire group into these categories. Rather, the report emphasized their interlocking nature as they affected particular individuals:

> Perhaps in no single instance does any one of them appear alone. In many, several are found in various combinations. With the exception of old age, each of these factors augments and is augmented by the others, and all of them contribute jointly to the production of a group of dependents, more or less unemployable. . . .[85]

After the analysis of the data, the remainder of the report gave a picture of the facilities of the Lodging House and the services it provided. While not minimizing the importance of its provision for the physical needs of its applicants, it stressed throughout the need for expansion of its social service function. The argument was buttressed by citing the beneficial effects of the investigation completed in March, 1914, and of the presence of two "social investigators" provided by outside organizations during the winter of 1914–1915. The report pointed out that, despite important (and in many cases money-saving) referrals resulting from these investigations, the budget provided for no social investigators.[86] Staffing appropriations per lodger, the Report pointed out, had declined precipitously since the expansion of capacity and the increased use caused by the economic downturn.[87] Not only should social investigators be hired, the report argued, but pay should be increased for existing positions, in order to obtain better qualified staff. Finally, the report claimed a need for an industrial plant and an employment bureau "under the direction of the Municipal Employment Bureau and in immediate and intimate cooperation with the Social Service Department of the Lodging House."[88]

In fact, the Lodging House did maintain its own employment agency under the direction of Walter Sears from the beginning of March until the end of June, 1915. But the experiment was not what Kingsbury had hoped for, and consequently the Mayor's Committee reversed the Lodging House Report's recommendation. Employers seeking labor through the Lodging House generally paid substandard wages (from five to twelve dollars a month.) Out of desperation, lodgers took the work, but as the report acknowledged, this contributed to unstable work habits:

> Either the man secured better paying work, if competent, or was dismissed because of inefficiency or intemperance, a natural enough sequence following a low wage standard. The men were the natural victims of untoward economic conditions and were often under compulsion to accept anything that offered a living, however meagre.[89]

Rather than clarifying the employable/unemployable distinction, opening up the Lodging House to employers apparently blurred the lines with an additional, stigmatized segment of the labor supply willing to work for less than market wages. The Lodging House Employment Bureau actually increased the casual labor which reformers were trying to eliminate.

The coordinated but quasi-independent work of the Lodging House Advisory Committee found a parallel in the work of the Police

Department Committee on Distress and Unemployment. Police Commissioner Arthur Woods, a Mitchel appointee and friend of Henry Bruere who would figure prominently in national wartime and post-war labor market management efforts, appointed the Police Committee in November, 1914 and received its final *Report* almost a year later.[90] Unlike the Mayor's Committee and the Advisory Committee, the Police Committee was composed of City staff: police inspectors. The rationale for police involvement was their daily, intimate contact with the poor. The police committee distributed aid in the form of grocery and fuel tickets, ostensibly to "worthy families in need." Coordination with other social agencies was assured, as police notified the "Social Service Exchange," the clearinghouse of all social service agencies, after each distribution.[91]

This contact, however, can not have mitigated friction between the relief societies and police. Of the 791 families which the Police Committee continued to support (after the distribution of the initial relief tickets), 60 percent had been discontinued by the charity organization societies because of "bad record, drink, or unwillingness to follow the plan selected for them by the relief society." The police thus lifted from the charity societies the control over relief they used as a tool to reform the poor. Social reformers pointed out that police lacked the specialized social investigatory skills which the charity societies claimed as their territory.[92]

In addition to the distribution of relief tickets, the Police Committee distributed bundles of clothing and claimed to have found 2811 jobs for the unemployed. 263 of these were "temporary positions for men who were employed by the residents of various blocks to keep the sidewalks and areaways clean."[93]

Different methods notwithstanding, the Police Committee's final *Report* sounded much like the other committees of 1914–1915, referring to the "difficult task in social diagnosis" of separating the unemployed and the unemployable. Its moral hierarchy of categories for the unemployed began, like the others, with the single, mobile unemployed, the "large numbers of tramps, bums, pan-handlers, criminals, morons, imbeciles, degenerates and professional beggars who drift from one section of the country to another, continually trying to find a place to exist where the greatest personal comfort can be obtained with the least possible effort." Above these were those who, debilitated by "years of casual, seasonal employment in the lowest paid and least efficiently organized trades," had "drifted into a state of lethargy and complacency that deadens all their ambitions and atrophies their energies," i.e. the Weary Willies. At the top were the resident, unemployed family men who simply need a job, or money to tide them over until jobs were available. Like Henry Seager and the Mayor's Committee, the Police Committee looked toward the Municipal Lodging House and a State Colony for Vagrants to help with the task of segregation.[94]

By September, 1915, the worst of the unemployment crisis was over. The surveys by the Metropolitan Life Insurance Company and the B.L.S. documented the improvement.[95] The Mayor's Committee, freed from the task of organizing immediate relief programs, concentrated on conferences and studies, and then on assembling material for its substantial final report which appeared in January, 1916. The first part was a record of the events and programs of the first winter. The second part laid out a program for prevention and relief of unemployment, with steps which could be taken "now and in the immediate future" rather than by outlining any "ultimate solutions."[96]

The *Report*'s emphasis on stabilizing employment gave it a significantly different tone from the statements at the early hearings on unemployment. Practically devoid of the moralism of the schemes from one year previous, it divided labor into four classes (steady work, seasonally fluctuating work, casual labor, and the unemployable) in order to stabilize work opportunities through organization of the labor market. The indispensability of the employment exchange was argued for the first three of these four classes.

Nevertheless, in a cyclical depression, such as that which New York experienced during the winter of 1914–1915, the *Report* acknowledged that the employment bureau was powerless to create jobs. In order to prevent unemployment in such times, it advocated the long range planning of public works, over a period of seven to ten years, so that it could be intensified during periods of economic contraction. This proposal bore no relation to "relief or charity," the report emphasized. "No preference is to be given the 'unemployed' nor is there to be any departure in any respect from accustomed methods of hiring, supervision or discharge of workmen."[97] The Committee, of course, had been able to effect very little if anything in the way of action on this proposal during the previous winter.

The report was clear in pointing to private industrial management as the key to regularizing employment in industry.

> [The] tremendous fluctuations in employment can . . . be controlled by special effort. This is more particularly true in the more highly organized industries in which facilities exist for study of the conditions of manufacture, the state of the trade, and means of marketing the product.[98]

On the other hand the individual employee's responsibility clearly played a minor role in unemployment, according to the report. The *Report* also took a new turn when it considered how to induce industrial leaders to institute measures which would regularize employment. For the first time, a document generated by the Mayor's Committee suggested that legislation for unemployment insurance might help to pressure that regularization by penalizing firms which had high layoff and turnover rates.[99]

After summarizing measures for relief and unemployment insurance taken in Britain, Scandinavia, and Continental Europe, the final section of the *Report* proposed that the present committee be dissolved and that a new permanent committee be formed for study and action. It suggested a structure, including subcommittees on Investigations, Seasonality and Irregularity of Employment, Public Policy, Industrial Training and Vocational Guidance, and Relief and Emergency Employment. The new committee was appointed January 25, 1916.[100]

William D. Baldwin, president of the Otis Elevator Company, replaced Elbert Gary as chairman of the new committee. Of the twenty-three members of the new committee only ten had served on the first committee, and five of those, including all the representatives of organized labor, quit before the second committee dissolved. The Yonkers triumvirate of Folks-Burritt-Kingsbury was not directly in evidence (though perhaps the choice of Baldwin as chairman was a part of their legacy.) Edward Devine, Mary Van Kleeck and Lillian Wald constituted a strong core for the social work contingent which dominated the new committee. Herbert Croly replaced Walter Lippmann from the *New Republic*.[101]

The major task of the Baldwin Committee was to discuss and make recommendations "to deal constructively with the problem of unemployment and prepare against a recurrence of unemployment crises." Its work was contained in three reports, two specialized (on public expenditures during business depressions, and on decasualizing dock employment) and one comprehensive statement published in January, 1917 as *How to Meet Hard Times*.[102]

How to Meet Hard Times made recommendations which differed from those of the earlier reports in a number of ways. The domination of the committee by those in the social work camp may have played some role in this change. But probably more important was the fact that the committee was not acting in an environment of high unemployment. Nor, with the considerable change in personnel, did it feel constrained to build its theory in any way as a justification for the actions which had been taken during the crisis.

The Baldwin Committee started by distinguishing between "normal" and "abnormal" unemployment. The first comprised unemployment resulting from personal characteristics, seasonal changes in demand for labor, poor machinery for matching jobs with workers, and "industrial maladaptation," as opposed to unemployment arising from "general depression of enterprise" when there was broad unemployment across the occupational and industrial spectrum. While labor market disorganization and ignorance exacerbated both, the remedial measures demanded by the former were quite different from those which would ameliorate the latter.[103] *How to Meet Hard Times* specifically addressed cyclical unemployment which occurred during a "general depression." Already, this was a major advance over the first committee which, with a theoretical orientation shaped by Leiserson and Beveridge, disclaimed any solution for "abnormal" (or cyclical) unemployment.[104]

The analysis which followed from this distinction was based upon three premises. The first concerned an elaboration of the relationship between personal and "industrial" causes of unemployment. The efforts of the first committee had involved much talk and considerable action aimed at separating the different "classes" of the unemployed—the able and willing, able and unwilling, and unable to work, following Beveridge and Leiserson, who saw the sorting process as the first step in coping with unemployment. *How to Meet Hard Times*, geared as it was toward crisis years and not "normal" unemployment, assumed that *most* unemployment during a depression was a direct result of lack of work.

The second premise followed from the first: the major problem was how to maintain and to stimulate the demand for labor (not how to separate those who needed physical, moral, or mental rehabilitation from those who did not, nor how to match men with jobs, nor how to provide relief.) The Baldwin Committee stated explicitly, "the only cure for unemployment is employment."[105] Focusing on this problem, the Baldwin Committee arrived at its third premise, which involved its most significant departure from the thinking of the Gary Committee and from Leiserson's and Beveridge's earlier work.

How to Meet Hard Times saw that stabilizing the demand for labor was a problem largely beyond the reach of the individual firm. Though the report praised individual employers who took measures to avoid layoffs during slack times, it judged that their role (like the role of consumers) was secondary. It looked instead to businesses with monopolies or near monopolies ("big business"), combinations of employers, financial institutions, and governments to stabilize the business cycle, and thus the demand for labor.

> We have been more and more driven to the conclusion that the consumers['] and . . . employers['] . . . share in a community effort at stabilizing employment, are secondary in importance to the steadying effect . . . which can be produced through the power of the big financial and business interests. . . .[106]

Taken together, these three premises added up to an orientation quite different from anything previously suggested: that the vast majority of the unemployed in times of depression were victims of the "industrial" system, that there was something more to be done than providing relief and awaiting the end of the crisis, and that the responsibility for those actions rested with large organizations of industry, high finance, and governments. What this orientation had in common, however, with that of the Gary Committee, was the pre-eminent role the social workers gave to business leaders.

On this framework, the report constructed a multitude of proposals, with frequent references to the experience of the recent depression in New York. Though necessarily secondary in the larger plan to maintain demand, the report had some suggestions for measures which could be taken by consumers and individual employers. It recommended public education programs to combat the "psychosis" of trade depressions during which there was often unnecessary curtailment of consumer spending and production. It recalled approvingly the distribution of available work among as many workers as possible, as "by far the most potent influence in warding off distress" during the recent depression.[107]

But it emphasized the limitations of actions by individual employers. To overcome these, it proposed a corporatist "unemployment preparedness program" where employers' organizations in each industry would

> create standing committees . . . to define and assist in securing agreement among employers in their respective industries of a contingent labor policy which would be applicable to the special circumstances of each industry, industrially practicable and socially desirable.[108]

These committees, in turn, could be coordinated either through an agency of the city government or through the Chamber of Commerce or Merchants' Association. Remarkably, the Baldwin Committee saw little difference between setting industry-wide labor policies through government agencies or employers' associations. *How to Meet Hard Times* made only the most cursory bow toward organized labor's participation on these committees, but did call for a "recognition of a wider public interest in the labor policy of industrial groups." The mechanisms for insuring this recognition, however, remained extremely vague.[109]

The report reiterated John Shillady's recommendations for counter-cyclical spending on public works published the past November. It expressed hopes that the establishment of the Federal Reserve Board, and the exercise of its power would help to reduce fluctuations in the business cycle. Likewise, it sought foresight and awareness of responsibility to the public on the part of those in charge of major credit institutions. But other than stressing the important role the latter might play in averting panic, it did not offer concrete recommendations.

As did the Gary Committee, the Baldwin Committee saw the ability to assemble more complete information on the state of the labor market as one of the first steps in ameliorating the problem. It recommended increased appropriations for government agencies involved in gathering information, and focused on a system of public employment bureaus as key among these. In the eyes of the second committee, however, the value of the bureaus in combating cyclical unemployment lay more in their ability to monitor labor market changes, and less in their ability to match man (or woman) and job.

Another institution whose value the Baldwin Committee revised considerably was the Municipal Lodging House. Kingsbury's conception of the "human repair shop" had gained wide currency by this time.[110]

The committee's objections stemmed again from the belief that most of the unemployed during a period of crisis were willing and able to work. Those among the unemployed who were evicted from their homes or searching for work in new cities would have little need for a "human repair shop." Moreover, they would be stigmatized and offended by being forced to share an institution with those who did.

The report reviewed the various forms of relief given during the recent depression, from breadlines, through the Bundle Day, to the work relief projects, and made a series of critical recommendations for the future. It predicted that compulsory unemployment insurance would ultimately provide the crucial palliative for periods of depression. Other methods of relief received as much attention in *How to Meet Hard Times* as they did only because the committee had a clear understanding of the political barriers to establishing an insurance program. It noted the vehement opposition of organized labor (whose representatives, Frayne and Holland had withdrawn from the committee). Furthermore, it perceived the establishment of a more extensive system of public employment bureaus as a prerequisite for an insurance system.[111]

In one area alone, did the report attempt to deal with the problem of the unemployable—in a final chapter on policy on juvenile workers. It claimed that more supervision was needed over youth's occupational training and decision-making, in order that they would not become unemployable adults:

> The appalling number of work-shy and unemployable men of middle age, of vagrants who are the plague and despair of police authorities the country over, can only be explained by a lack of oversight in youth which has had fatal consequences so far as the careers of these unfortunates were concerned.[112]

It approved of the limited vocational education arrangements made during the depression, and recommended extensions of such efforts during periods of crisis in the future, in part to keep young people out of the labor market. Vocational training, it asserted, would enable public authorities to increase "oversight . . . over the school work, over the choice of a career and over everything in the home and personal life, including health. . . ."[113]

By the time the draft of *How to Meet Hard Times* was complete, in December, 1916, the committee was having difficulty maintaining funding. The war, and not unemployment, was the question of the day. Rather than continuing with a skeleton organization, Secretaries Shillady and Lasker recommended that the committee disband and refer its recommendations to various appropriate ongoing agencies.[114]

In retrospect, Henry Bruere considered the Mayor's Committees to be a failure:

> The only tangible activity that resulted from that committee, besides some studies of the casual employment on the docks and three other inquiries . . . was the opening up workshops.[115]

In March, 1915, John Haynes Holmes, writing in the *Survey*, blamed "the great American public," which was "still in the antediluvian economic era of regarding unemployment as an emergency to be tided over, and not as a permanent social ill to be cured and thus abolished."[116] But the significance for us of the winter of 1914–1915 in New York City lies not in the failure of a well-placed and influential urban reform community to shape solutions to the problems of unemployment.

It is rather the fact that the intensive concern about the problem—based on Leiserson's theories, the Wobblies' demonstrations, and the social workers' organizations—led to calls for more participation and more organization on the part of businessmen. In the rhetoric, from Devine to Bruere, in the organization of the emergency committees themselves, and in the reform measures proposed for future emergencies, the Mayors' Committees looked toward powerful businessmen rather than the authority of strong state agencies to deal with problems generated by the capitalist economy.

The formulation of the Bruere plan for the Mayor's Committee marked the crucial juncture in this respect. The self-appointed planning committee, consisting of officers of relief societies and the Commissioner of Public Charities—leaders of the New York social welfare community—formulated a plan for a responsive mayor for the upcoming winter's emergency, which conferred its responsibilities onto a new committee designed to be dominated by business interests. The social welfare leadership, having struggled over the past decade to establish a professional identity beyond the nineteenth century philanthropic elites, now called in a new corporate elite to spearhead employment reform. While such action seems ironic, it stemmed directly from the reform experts' social analysis.

Their understanding that unemployment was "a problem of industry" and not of relief led them to seek the involvement of the people, as

Bruere put it, "of the greatest influence in our economic system." Reformers like Bruere, who had some experience with capitalists who combined progressive ideals with considerable personal power, came to think that the most effective programs would be those which enlisted the support of those elements of capitalist leadership. Leaders of industry, far from feeling accused, were responsive to this call, because it put them in position to guard a privately controlled economy from too much interference from social workers, professors, and government officials. At the same time, it allowed them in concert to take the initiative in confronting the major social and economic threats posed by unemployment.

In the New York City unemployment program of 1914–1917, we can see two different pictures superimposed upon each other. One looks back to the late nineteenth century community mobilization portrayed in chapter 1, in which local elites organized and contributed to *ad hoc* relief efforts, with guidance from the ongoing charity organizations. The other, less clear before the Baldwin Committee report, looks forward to the rationalization of labor market inefficiencies both through state institutions (employment bureaus, education, and economic statistics) and through support of increased planning and coordination by business leaders on a regional and national scale.

Notes

1. For comments on the implications of Progressive reliance on business support, see Robert Wiebe, *The Search for Order, 1877–1920* (New York: Hill and Wang, 1967), 175.

2. Edwin Lewinson, *John Purroy Mitchel, Boy Mayor of New York* (N.Y.: Astra Books, 1965); On politics in Mitchel's last term, see Kenneth S. Chern, "The Politics of Patriotism: War, Ethnicity and the New York Mayoral Campaign, 1917," *New York Historical Society Quarterly* 63,4 (October, 1979).

3. Kellor was recorded in the minutes as "Florence Kellor." "Unemployment problem" conference minutes, Folder 8, MJP Subject File: Unemployment, 1914–1917, Mitchel Mayoral Papers (hereafter MMP).

4. "Proceedings of a Hearing on Unemployment, Jan. 29, 1914," 38, Folder 8, MJP Subject File: Unemployment, 1914–1917, MMP.

5. "Proceedings of a Hearing on Unemployment, January 29, 1914," 38–40, Folder 8, MJP Subject File: Unemployment 1914–1917, MMP.

6. Frances Kellor, "Unemployment: A Program for Relief" pamph. reprinted from the *Survey*, February 7, 14, 21, 1914, NYPL.

7. "Proceedings of a Hearing on Unemployment Held at the Mayor's Office, January 29, 1914" Typescript, Folder 8, MJP Subject File: Unemployment, MMP.

8. "Proceedings of a Hearing on Unemployment, January 29, 1914," 54, 56, Folder 8, MJP Subject File: Unemployment 1914–1917, MMP.

9. "First National Conference on Unemployment," *Survey* 31, 32 (March 7, 1914), 693.

10. "Organize to Fight Unemployment," Press Notice issued for release not earlier than Sunday morning February 22, 1914, by the American Association for Labor Legislation, Reel 70, AALL Papers; "First National Conference on Unemployment," *Survey* 31, 32 (March 7, 1914), 693.

11. See Folder 9, MJP Subject File Unemployment 1914–1917, MMP.

12. John Franklin Crowell to John Purroy Mitchel, March 18, 1914, Folder 10, MJP Subject File: Unemployment 1914–1917, MMP.

13. Paul Kennaday to John Purroy Mitchel, February 9, 1914, Folder 9, MJP Subject File: Unemployment 1914–1917, MMP. The Socialist Party, according to its N.Y. State Chairman, was "extremely derelict" in "not taking a strong hold of the unemployment situation and letting freaks to be the only ones to call public attention to it." H. Slobodin to J. Gerber, March 4, 1914, "1914 Unemployment Conference 21 January–22 February, 1914," Reel 8, Series V–147, Local New York Letter Books, 1907–1914, Socialist Party Papers, Tamiment Library.

14. H.F. Stimpson to John Purroy Mitchel, March 2, 1914 in Folder 10, MJP Subject File: Unemployment 1914–1917, MMP. All following Stimpson quotes are from this letter.

15. This engineers' interests were a precursor to the more publicized and less adversarial efforts of Herbert Hoover through the Federated American Engineering Societies and the Department of Commerce. See chapter 8 below.

16. Peter A. Speek, "Report on Investigation of Congestion of the Unemployed People in the City of New York, February, 1914," 11–15, Box 20, U.S. Commission on Industrial Relations, National Archives.

17. The story of Tannenbaum and the churches may be found in Ringenbach, 162–164; also in the *Survey* 31, 26 (March 28, 1914, 792–795; 32,4 (April 25, 1914), 94 and in the *Masses* (May, 1914).

18. Mayor's Executive Secretary to W.D.P. Bliss, March 17, 1914, Folder 9, Subject File: Unemployment 1914–1917, MMP.

19. "The Churches, the City and the 'Army of the Unemployed' in New York," *Survey* 31, 26 (March 28, 1914), 792.

20. On public employment offices, see Shelby M. Harrison, et al., *Public Employment Offices: Their Purpose, Structure and Methods* (New York: Russell Sage, 1924); and Udo Sautter, "North American Government Labor Agencies Before World War One: A Cure for Unemployment?" *Labor History* 24, 3 (Summer, 1983), 366–393.

21. J.P. Mitchel to the Board of Aldermen, March 24, 1914, MJP Subject File: Unemployment 1914–1917, MMP; also see *Survey* 31,21 (February 21, 1914), 633. These numbers are remarkable, if accurate, particularly in comparison to the record of the Municipal Exchange later the same year. See below.

22. Walter L. Sears, Press Release "Relative to the Unemployment Problem in the City of New York," December 12, 1914, Folder 11, MJP Subject File: Unemployment 1914–1917, MMP.

23. See J.R. Dowman, "Private Employment Agencies in New York City: Agencies Conducted For Profit," March 24, 1914. Folder: Private Employment Agencies in New York City, Box 14, U.S. Commission on Industrial Relations, National Archives.

24. Sears to Burritt, October 3, 1914, Folder 317–2, Box 47, Community Service Society Papers (hereafter CSS.)

25. Frances Kellor, "Unemployment: A Program for Relief" pamph. reprinted from the *Survey*, February 7, 14, 21, 1914 in N.Y.P.L.

26. See chapter 5 for more discussion of Kellor's national perspective.

27. Walter L. Sears, Press Release "Relative to the Unemployment Problem in the City of New York," December 12, 1914, Folder 11, MJP Subject File: Unemployment 1914–1917, MMP.

28. Walter Lincoln Sears, "Unemployment: Its Cause and Cure" pamph. n.p. February, 1915. NYPL.

29. *Survey* 33, 13, (December 26, 1914), 329.

30. George William Douglas to members of the New York Federations of Churches' Committee on Economic Conditions, Nov. 21, 1914, Folder 317–2, Box 47, CSS.

31. "Some Sources of Information," Folder: "Unemployment, 1914–1915," Box 181, CSS.

32. Folder 317, Box 47, CSS.

33. "An informal conference of representatives of public and private relief agencies, Sept. 23, 1914, Midday Club," and "Tentative Plan," Sept. 23, 1914, both in Folder 317–2, Box 47, CSS.

34. "Memorandum of a Conference held at the Midday Club, September 28, 1914," Folder 317–2, Box 47, CSS.

35. "A Tentative Proposal In Reference to Unemployment in the Winter of 1914," Prepared by Henry Bruere, October 15, 1914, Folder 317–2, Box 47, CSS. Burritt lived at 16 Prospect Drive, Folks at 14 Hawthorne Avenue. Kingsbury to Cruger, April 6, 1915, Box 5, Folder 4, MJP Subject File: National Conference of Charities and Correction, 1915–1917, MMP. Folks was, like Devine, a pivotal figure in the social welfare movement and was, also like Devine, accused of leading the "charities trust." Lee Frankel, quoted in Walter I. Trattner, *Homer Folks: Pioneer in Social Welfare* (N.Y.: Columbia University Press, 1968), 10. According to Trattner, Folks remained "within the right wing of the reform movement." Trattner, 151. Folks' relationship with Kingsbury began in 1907 when he recruited Kingsbury, a Columbia University student, to full-time work with the S.C.A.A. Trattner, 159. Kingsbury was General Director of the A.I.C.P before becoming Commissioner of Charities.

36. Frances Perkins, "Reminiscences," Columbia University Oral History Project, Book I, 243; Robert Ozanne, *A Century of Labor-Management Relations at McCormick and International Harvester* (Madison: University of Wisconsin Press, 1967), 41–43. Also see Gerd Korman, *Industrialization, Immigrants, and Americanizers: The View from Milwaukee, 1866–1921* (Madison, Wisconsin: State Historical Society, 1967), 85–109.

37. Henry Bruere, "Reminiscences," Columbia University Oral History Project, 1949, 41.

38. Bruere, "Reminiscences," 3–41.

39. Frances Perkins, "Reminiscences," Book I, 292.

40. "Report of Sub-Committee of Unemployment Conference, October 21, 1914" Folder 317, Box 47, CSS. Copies of the "Proposal" in the NYPL and Folder "N.Y. City, 1914–1915," Box 2, A.A.L.L. Papers, New York State School of Industrial Labor Relations (hereafter NYSSILR).

41. "A Proposal in Reference to Unemployment in the Winter of 1914, for Consideration by His Honor, The Mayor of the City of New York," Prepared by Henry Bruere, New York, November, 1914. (NYPL)

42. Compare the discussions of the first and second National Conferences on Unemployment in February and December of 1914. The A.A.L.L. Program for the Prevention of Unemployment was made public at the second. Henry Seager made no mention of the prevention aspect of unemployment insurance in his *Principles of Economics* (New York: Holt and Company, 1913), 609–612. See Roy Lubove, *The Struggle For Social Security, 1900–1935*, Cambridge: Harvard University Press, 1968, 144–174; Daniel Nelson, *Unemployment Insurance: the American Experience, 1915–1935* (Madison: University of Wisconsin Press, 1969), 15–17 and passim.

43. N.Y. *Evening Post*, December 2, 1914, 1–2. Also see N.Y. *Times*, December 3, 1914.

44. Editorial, *The New Republic*, 1, 10 (January 9, 1915), 3.

45. New York City Mayor's Committee on Unemployment, "By-Laws of Committee and Organization of Executive Committee and Sub-Committees, 1914–1915," pam. (NYPL). Ringenbach's claim that "radical and conservative labor leaders" were "conspicuously absent" (174) is not borne out by the composition of the Committee.

46. "Contributors to the Mayor's Committee on Unemployment" no date, Folder 11, MJP Subject File: Unemployment 1914–1917, MMP.

47. N.Y. City Mayor's Committee on Unemployment, "Abstract of the Preliminary Report of the Committee on Facts Regarding Existing Unemployment," pam. New York, January 15, 1915.

48. Abstract of the Preliminary Report, 8. New York and Massachusetts had collected figures on trade union membership in the past. Massachusetts, in addition, had collected annual data on employment from manufacturing establishments since 1886. Leah Hannah Feder, *Unemployment Relief in Periods of Depression* (New York: Russell Sage Foundation, 1936), 225.

49. N.Y. City Mayor's Committee on Unemployment, *Report*, (New York, 1916), 11–13. See also Fiske to Mitchel, February 2, 1915, MMP, Box 13, Folder 1; Metropolitan Life Insurance *Intelligencer*, March 20, 1915, Metropolitan Life Insurance Company Archives.

50. Bailey Burritt to Royal Meeker, September 10, 16, 1914, Folder 317, Box 47, CSS.

51. New York City Mayor's Committee on Unemployment *Report* (New York,1916), 14–19; Ethelbert Stewart to William B. Wilson, July 12, 1915, Folder 15/4, Box 5, General Subject Files, 1913–1921, General Records of the Department of Labor, Office of the Secretary, Record Group 174, National Archives.

52. N.Y. City Mayor's Committee on Unemployment, *Report*, (New York, 1916), 20–21.

53. U.S. Bureau of Labor Statistics, *Monthly Review*, 1,5 (November, 1915), 5. Royal Meeker, "The Dependability and Meaning of Unemployment and Employment Statistics in the United States," *Harvard Business Review* 8 (July,1930), 387, quoted in Feder, 231.

54. N.Y. City Mayor's Committee on Unemployment, *Report* (New York: 1916), 28–29.

55. N.Y. City Mayor's Committee on Unemployment, *Report* (New York: 1916), 30–31. Also see the N.Y. City Mayor's Sub-Committee on Unemployment Among Women, Reports on Emergency Workshops for Women and Trade Extension (Scholarship) Classes for Girls During Winter and Spring of 1915. Folder "N.Y.City 1914–1915," Box 2, A.A.L.L. Papers.

56. See Elbert Gary, Chairman, Mayor's Committee on Unemployment, "An Open Letter to Employers in and About the City of New York" n.d., in NYPL; William Breed, Merchants' Association of New York, to John B. Andrews, January 14, 1915, Reel 13, AALL.

57. Gary to Mitchel, January 7, 1915, Folder 11, MJP Subject File Unemployment, 1914–1917, MMP.

58. See *Survey*, January 30, 1915, 454; also, Folder 11, MJP Subject File Unemployment, 1914–1917, MMP; also Folder 1, Box 13; Andrews to Dingman, January 12, 1915, Reel 13, AALL.

59. Gary to Mitchel, January 7, 1915, MJP Subject File Unemployment, 1914–1917, MMP; also see Persons to Burritt, October 24, 1914 Folder 317–2, Box 47, CSS.

60. N.Y. City Mayor's Committee on Unemployment, *Report* (New York: 1916), 52–53; Feder, 282, 287–291.

61. N.Y. City Mayor's Committee on Unemployment, *Report* (New York: 1916), 32–33; N.Y. City Mayor's Committee on Unemployment, *Report of the Bundle Day Committee*, New York: March 10, 1915, 3. NYPL.

62. The capacity of the Lodging House varies in three accounts from 1915. Kingsbury to N.Y. Board of Aldermen, January 6, 1915 Reel 13, AALL Papers put the number at 900. The number was 1064 in "The Men We Lodge" and 1,218 in William Alberti Whiting, "What the City of New York Provides for the Homeless" New York, 1915, pam., n.p.

63. Kingsbury to Board of Aldermen, January 6, 1915, Reel 13, AALL Papers.

64. "The Men We Lodge," 23.

65. Whiting to Howe, January 30, 1915, Reel 13, AALL Papers; and N.Y. City Mayor's Committee on Unemployment, *Report* (New York: 1916), 34.

66. New York City Mayor's Committee on Unemployment, *Report* (New York, 1916), 34.

67. Charles Barnes, *The Homeless Man: A Study* (New York, 1915), 2 typescript in Folder 1579, Box 101, Mary Van Kleeck Papers.

68. See John A. Kingsbury, "Our Army of the Unemployed," *Review of Reviews* 49 (April, 1914), 433–439.

69. In addition to the studies and reports cited below, see "Rehabilitation of the Homeless Man," Fifteenth New York State Conference of Charities and Correction, *Proceedings* 1914, 36–37.

70. Foreword to Advisory Social Service Committee, "The Men We Lodge: A Report to the Honorable John A. Kingsbury" (New York: 1915), 4.

71. Kingsbury to Andrews, December 7, 1914, Reel 13, AALL Papers.

72. Andrews gave Burritt the task of developing a set of subcommittees and defining their functions. Burritt suggested an executive committee made up of himself, Kingsbury, Andrews, Frank Persons of the C.O.S., and D.J. McMahon of the Catholic Charities. Mary Van Kleeck of the Russell Sage Foundation, as chairperson of the Committee on Records and Research, successfully objected to her absence on the executive committee. Burritt

to Andrews, January 7, 1915 and Van Kleeck to Andrews, January 12, 1915. Reel 13, AALL Papers.

73. Lippmann to Andrews, January 5, 1915. Reel 13, AALL Papers.

74. N.Y. City Mayor's Committee on Unemployment, *Report* (New York: 1916), 36.

75. Kingsbury to Board of Aldermen, January 6, 1915, Reel 13, AALL Papers.

76. Lippmann to Andrews, January 5, 1915, Reel 13, AALL Papers.

77. John A. Kingsbury, "Our Army of the Unemployed," *Review of Reviews* 49 (April, 1914), 433–439, reprinted in Julia Johnsen, ed., *Selected Articles on Unemployment* (White Plains and New York: H.W. Wilson, 1915), 12.

78. Ibid., 13.

79. Walter Lippmann, understanding this purpose, suggested that the Committee hold public hearings on the function of the Lodging House, possibly inviting Theodore Roosevelt. Lippmann to Andrews, January 5, 1915, Reel 13, AALL Papers.

80. Advisory Social Service Committee, "The Men We Lodge," (New York, 1915).

81. Van Kleeck to Andrews, January 6, 1915, Reel 13, AALL Papers.

82. Advisory Social Service Committee, "The Men We Lodge," (New York, 1915), 5 and Van Kleeck to Devine, March 2, 1915, Reel 13, AALL Papers.

83. N.Y. City Mayor's Committee on Unemployment, *Report* (New York: 1916), 23–24, 34–35.

84. "The Men," 11.

85. "The Men," 17.

86. "The Men," 26, 28, 31.

87. "The Men," 32–33.

88. "The Men," 37.

89. N.Y. City Mayor's Committee on Unemployment, *Report* (New York: 1916), 35.

90. New York City Police Department, "Report of the Police Department Committee on Distress and Unemployment," n.p., Folder New York City, 1914–, Box 2, A.A.L.L. Papers, NYSSILR. Bruere, "Reminiscences," 88. On Bruere's later career, see chapters 6, 7, 8.

91. "Report of the Police Department Committee," n.p. On the social service function of urban police more characteristic of the nineteenth century, see Eric Monkkonen, *Police in Urban America, 1860–1920* (Cambridge: Cambridge University Press, 1981).

92. John B. Andrews to J. W. Magruder, Baltimore Federated Charities, January 16, 1915, Reel 13, A.A.L.L. Papers: ". . . very little importance has, I believe, been attached to [the Police Census of New York's unemployed]; most people have found that the police are not the people to make such an investigation and that their results are, in their very nature, usually untrustworthy."

93. "Report of the Police Department Committee," n.p.

94. "Report of the Police Department Committee," n.p.

95. Schneider and Deutsch, 205; N.Y. City Mayor's Committee *Report*, 21.

96. N.Y. City Mayor's Committee on Unemployment, *Report* (New York: 1916), 44

97. N.Y. City Mayor's Committee on Unemployment, *Report* (New York: 1916), 54. See Udo Sautter, "Government and Unemployment: the Use of Public Works Before the New Deal," *Journal of American History* 73,1 (June, 1986), esp. 60–64.

98. N.Y. City Mayor's Committee on Unemployment, *Report* (New York: 1916), 62.

99. N.Y. City Mayor's Committee on Unemployment, *Report* (New York: 1916), 68.

100. N.Y. City Mayor's Committee on Unemployment, *Report* (New York: 1916), 91–95; Gary to Mitchel, January 7, 1916, MJP Departmental Correspondence Received: Mayor's Committee on Unemployment 1914–1916, MMP.

101. Baldwin to Mitchel, January 31, 1916, MJP Folder 1, Box 13, MMP; Mayor's Committee on Unemployment of the City of New York, *How To Meet Hard Times* (New York, 1917), 2.

102. N.Y. City Mayor's Committee on Unemployment, *How to Meet Hard Times: A Program for the Prevention and Relief of Abnormal Unemployment*, January, 1917.

103. *How to Meet Hard Times*, 7, 39

104. See chapter 3.

105. *How to Meet Hard Times,* 12.

106. *How to Meet Hard Times,* 28.

107. *How to Meet Hard Times,* 24.

108. *How to Meet Hard Times,* 26.

109. *How to Meet Hard Times,* 27.

110. The Committee on Unemployment of the Conference of Mayors of New York State (1916) endorsed the development of a state system of municipal lodging houses "not as a more or less temporary stopping place for those who can't and won't work, but as a human repair shop or clearing house." Quoted in *How to Meet Hard Times,* 111.

111. *How to Meet Hard Times,* 121.

112. *How to Meet Hard Times,* 113.

113. *How to Meet Hard Times*, 116.

114. "Report of the Secretaries on the Continuance of the Mayor's Committee," December 1, 1916, Folder 1073, Box 67, Mary Van Kleeck Papers.

115. Bruere, "Reminiscences," 122.

116. *Survey*, 33, 23 (March 6, 1915), 634.

5

Organizing the National Labor Market, 1914–1918

As we have seen in chapters 3 and 4, theorists working during the first decade and a half of the twentieth century attempted to separate the problems of relief from the problems of employment. While they envisioned solutions to the former continuing to rest largely on local voluntary agencies (albeit coordinated beyond the local level through voluntary conferences and federations), solutions to the latter, they claimed, rested on corporate and financial managers and on state officials who could implement solutions on a broad regional or national level. If relief and poverty were still local problems, the industrial problem of unemployment demanded national organization.[1]

Between 1914 and 1918, depression, a surge in union organizing and worker militance, and the production demands of war, brought the problems of employment to the forefront of the national consciousness and gave reformers unprecedented opportunities to build new institutions for bringing order to the labor market. Their proposals were mediated not only through escalating conflicts between labor and capital but also through a shifting configuration of politics and administration within the American state. The recent literature has been unanimous in its assessment of the impact of the decentralized state and the ideology of voluntarism in the Wilson era. It has also attended to the blurry lines between private power and public authority, particularly in the emergency war boards. Finally it has called for sensitivity in analyzing intrastate power conflicts.[2] These issues were crucial in shaping the implementation of a revised Seager/Leiserson employment reform program. This chapter will trace the outlines of the state response, in both New York State and the nation.

Initially, both in New York and at the federal level, the employment reform program was aided by the existence of commissions investigating industrial relations. The New York State Factory

Investigating Commission (1911–1915) and the United States Commission on Industrial Relations (1912–1915), both initiated before the depression, helped to focus attention on the "maladjustment" of labor markets as unemployment deepened in 1914. Both completed their work under Democratic administrations not unfriendly towards labor. But they merely set the stage for programs to deal with wartime "maladjustment." Federal and state officials dealing with labor market disorganization in the context of pressure for wartime production were able to mobilize unprecedented resources for a national labor stabilization program: labor shortage impaired "national efficiency" more immediately and more visibly than did labor surplus.

In 1914 Frances Kellor wrote several influential articles and a new edition of her *Out of Work* appeared in the following year. She, as much as anyone, rested her analysis on the geographic dimension of the unemployment problem and urged national, as opposed to local or community solutions. A strong advocate of labor exchanges, she saw their value as distributors of surplus labor. Answering her own title in "Is Unemployment a Municipal Problem?" she wrote:

> Unemployment is not a municipal problem. It is essentially an industrial problem to be solved by industrial methods. But the fact that industries locate in cities and cities are the reserve centers for labor and distributing points places the city in a curious position.[3]

While the city—and particularly New York City—functioned as a labor reserve for the nation, it was traditionally asked to cope with the problem of unemployment through its own resources. The problem could be dealt with, she argued, only by seeing the municipal problem as it fit into the national industrial system. New York City supplied workers to the nation, but was asked to cope as a city with the problems of the unemployed in a disorganized national labor market.

Her articles published in the *Survey* reiterated the calls for separation of unemployed and unemployable and the organization of a national system of labor exchanges.[4] In an age of "efficiency and economy and business management," she complained, "one of the most vital elements in production is ignored. There is no organization of our labor market. We have no record of our labor movement and no place to obtain one."[5]

Wandering workers were particularly disturbing to Kellor. "Nowhere else in the world is there so much ground covered in the blind pursuit of work as there is in these United States," she wrote in the new edition of *Out of Work*. The casual worker and the migratory laborer were "prominent among the unemployed" no matter what other types were added from time to time.[6] Following Leiserson's analysis, she expressed concern that casual labor would lead to demoralization and vagrancy with the price paid both by industry and the community.

> The cost [of unemployment] to industry in the waste of men through lost time and maladjustment and deterioration, in the loss of skill and the cost of supervision are beyond calculation at this time. To communities the cost is not less. . . .[7]

In chapters on women, children, and immigrants, she repeatedly returned to the theme of directionless migration. Seasonal industries were "creating a vagrant type of working women"; migratory immigrants slid downward in an "industrial descent," and families disintegrated as a result of the disorganized labor market, the burden of which was borne directly by workers.

Solving the unemployment problem hinged on organizing the national labor market and reorganizing business in such a way as to "put the burden of the transfer of laborers from workshop to workshop on the industry," and to "make industry so responsible that it may not close its doors without a moment's notice at its own sweet will, without considering its workers."[8]

Much of this was familiar to readers of Seager and Leiserson. The emphasis on cities, however, as nodes of reserve labor for the nation and on the consequent indispensability of a national organization of the labor market was new. "Only a nation-wide system can deal with conditions in labor and industry not bounded by city or state lines."[9] She proposed a Federal Bureau of Distribution which would provide labor exchanges in reserve cities and regulate all labor exchanges doing interstate business.[10]

Kellor's organization, the North American Civic League for Immigrants, drafted three bills embodying these measures and presented them to the new U.S. Department of Labor.[11] In April, 1914 Progressive Congressman Victor Murdock took up the fight in Congress, sponsoring a bill to create a Bureau of Employment in the Department of Labor. Introducing the bill he gave the rationale for federal action:

> The problem is essentially a national one. The nation has become one market and one workshop. This is the answer to the question why cities and states (and many have attempted the problem) have not attained the success in solving it they set out upon. The effectual unit is the nation and nothing less.[12]

The *New Republic* echoed, in support of the Murdock bill, "Unemployment . . . cannot be dealt with by local effort alone. The essential machinery even for a beginning is a national organization of the labor market."[13]

The House Committee on Labor, to which the bill was immediately referred, heard similar testimony from the National Liberal Immigration League.[14] Dr. Bela Sekely, field representative of the League, highlighted the importance of a system to organize the labor market and to transfer workers around the country in response to the demand for labor, "a principle cause of unemployment being that workmen are often without the means to travel to a place where employment awaits them. . . ."[15] Sekely coupled his recommendations for shifting labor around the country "wherever it is needed and whenever it is needed" with advocacy of industrial employment policies which would reduce turnover and promote steady employment.[16] Maximum mobility would thus be combined with maximum stability. Through the summer and early fall, the House Labor Committee delayed action on the Murdock Bill because the U.S. Commission on Industrial Relations (CIR) was examining unemployment and labor exchanges, promising "wider investigation and more expert opinion."[17]

Testimony before the CIR reflected similar concerns with labor distribution. Labor representatives J. A. Walker of the Illinois Federation of Labor and John Mitchell of the United Mine Workers spoke in favor of federal systems. Miles M. Dawson, Secretary of the upcoming International Conference on Social Insurance, opposed "dealing with unemployment in the limits of single communities . . . as it does not provide for sufficient mobility of labor."[18] Even Charles Blatchly of the A.I.C.P. and N.Y.C.O.S.' Joint Application Bureau, whose major concern was the separation of employable from unemployable, advocated a system which would keep employable workers mobile on a national scale. His difficulties with the marginal or "nearly employable" class led Blatchly to advocate industrial colonies with a passbook system to help regulate movement. "Every applicant should be required to have some sort of a 'work book' . . . so that, when a man is discharged, the employer is required by law to state his record in the work book or passport." Because of workers' mobility, Blatchly insisted, such a plan could be operated, "only by a national system."[19]

At this point, the only agency at the federal level which dealt with labor distribution was the Distribution Branch of the Division of Information within the Immigration Bureau of the U.S. Department of Labor. The Branch was represented at the CIR hearings by Inspector C.L. Green who explained its purpose as "to get people from the congested centers into the rural districts. . . ."[20] Originally established in 1907 to distribute immigrants, the Division of Information broadened its mandate to include U.S. citizens as well soon after incorporation in the new Department of Labor in 1913.[21] It called its publicity for Midwest harvest hands, "the beginning . . . of an effective national system for handling the perplexing problem of seasonal employment."[22] In 1915, it operated eighteen branches with 22 subbranches around the country. Though its administrative mechanisms were weak (William Leiserson called it a "joke") it handled steadily increasing numbers of calls for workers, and became the nucleus of the wartime United States Employment Service.[23] Most importantly, it actively shared in the vision of wide-ranging administrative direction of workers' geographic mobility. Secretary of Labor Wilson contemplated "labor vacations" organized by his department, where he would transport industrial workers by rail at reduced rates to agricultural regions for the harvest, while the factories enjoyed a seasonal slowdown. The Commissioner General of Immigration wanted the federal government to "supervise the conveyance to particular localities in the various States . . . all seekers after opportunity for employment. . . . These seekers after opportunities," he went on, "might be turned over when destination is reached . . . to the State or municipal agency."[24]

The Department of Labor also attempted to begin coordination of local, state, and national efforts to manage the labor market through a conference in San Francisco in August, 1915. It was announced as the beginning of a "unified system . . . as widespread within national boundaries as the Department of Labor can extend it, as complete in its local organization as State and municipal offices can construct it, and as efficient, extensively and intensively, as all three in cooperation can make it."[25] Charles B. Barnes, on the Conference's standing committee, oversaw the first experimental cooperative effort in New York.[26]

A competing body of public officials was already in existence, however. In 1913, William Leiserson had called a conference which initiated the American Association of Public Employment Offices (AAPEO). Its members gathered annually in order to standardize administrative procedures and facilitate coordination. Charles Barnes served as President of the AAPEO, but otherwise there was noticeable lack of overlap between the Association and the Department of Labor efforts apparently working toward the same end. Royal Meeker of the Bureau of Labor Statistics participated in the AAPEO, but there was no representation from the Bureau of Immigration. In 1916 the Bureau of Labor Statistics issued the proceedings of the three previous AAPEO annual meetings in its *Bulletin* with the judgment that the publication "brings us a long step nearer to a national system of employment offices."[27]

In September, 1914, the second AAPEO convention discussed preliminary recommendations by the CIR of a national system of labor exchanges. Walter Lincoln Sears, superintendent of the New York City Public Employment Bureau, commented typically that the whole employment problem was "mainly one of practical, prudent distribution." He suggested a bulletin of employment opportunities "similar to the Weather Bureau map" to direct workers to locations where they would be needed.[28]

William Leiserson was ubiquitous in these discussions. Now head of the Wisconsin State Employment Bureau, he was instrumental in organizing the AAPEO, served as its Secretary-Treasurer, and acted as consultant in the organization of Sears' municipal employment agency in New York City. (His absence from the Department of Labor efforts was thus significant.) He not only gave extended testimony to the CIR, but served as Assistant Director and as such was largely responsible for its recommendations dealing with unemployment.[29] In all of these settings, Leiserson echoed his position in the Wainwright Commission report, emphasizing the political feasibility of employment bureaus and the importance of developing uniform administrative detail as the next pressing task. He opposed any further comprehensive study of the question: "If you want to make a report on it, get Mr. W. H. Beveridge's book or get my report and that will be as good as you can get. . . ."[30]

> We have reached the point in dealing with unemployment where the theoretical questions have been solved and the principles of practical administration must

> now be emphasized. . . . We [must] begin at once to study the detailed problems of administration and to train men who will be able effectively to administer the remedies.[31]

The treatment of unemployment in the *Final Report* of the CIR rested directly on Seager's and Leiserson's earlier work. It summarized the effects as:

> a. actual loss of earnings . . .
> b. the depression of the wage level . . .
> c. waste in expenditure, due to irregularity of family income.
> d. deleterious effects upon the worker, such as demoralization, worry, loss of skill, irregularity of habits, etc.
> e. the gradual loss of economic status by workers who are thrown out of employment and the inevitable drift of a large proportion into the class ordinarily known as "casual laborers," the constant recruiting of the large army of dependents and delinquents who compose the unemployables, and the general loss of national efficiency that so great a number of incapacable citizens must entail.
> f. the existence of a supply of casual laborers and irregularly employed women and children, upon which parasitic industries, unable to exist unless they pay wages below the standard of decent subsistence, are called into being.[32]

The CIR's major advancement over the Seager/Leiserson analysis was its addition of the problem of labor turnover, defined even more explicitly than unemployment in terms of a geographic mobility. Industries which carelessly hired and fired workers contributed to unnecessary mobility. Preventing turnover, like preventing unemployment, demanded stabilization and rationalization of employment policies, as well as creating employment conditions attractive enough to make workers want to remain with the firm. In the absence of such policies, increasing segments of labor joined the "shiftless" or "floating workers" who regularly quit jobs out of habit or wanderlust. The CIR's *Final Report* pointed out how current employment practices led to degeneration of work habits and work discipline.[33]

Sumner Slichter, an economist in the research division of the CIR, was largely responsible for the conclusions on turnover. In 1914 he investigated 105 factories and mines with a total of 226,038 workers, and found nearly 100 percent turnover during the course of the year. His study complemented the work of Magnus Alexander and the New York State Factory Investigating Commission (see below) completed in the same year. With wartime labor shortages, interest in the problem of turnover mushroomed, and in 1919, Slichter's work was published in what John R. Commons called "the first comprehensive treatment of labor turnover."[34] *The Turnover of Factory Labor* argued that the "instability of labor" was due more to turnover than "to fluctuations in the volume of work."[35]

Turnover became one of the central issues for the new employment management movement, many of whose proponents envisioned labor stabilization through reform of industrial practices without any expansion of state institutions.[36] Turnover, like unemployment, apparently contributed to the degeneration of labor at a time when many perceived a need for increased skill, discipline and will-power. The problem was posed in terms of the unity of interests of capital and labor: an upgraded labor force protected from the devastation of unemployment and frequent changes of jobs would better serve the needs of capital for disciplined, loyal and committed workers. As Boyd Fisher of the Detroit Executive's Club put it,

> Turnover of labor is a special phase of the problem of inefficient labor. . . . The reduction of turnover is only the first step in a process of education and of economic pressure to elevate the standards of workmen. They aim not only to keep workmen but to develop them. And they are prepared to go as far, even, as the workmen's own home-life to solve their problem.[37]

E.M. Hopkins, an early leader of the Boston Employment Managers Association, was even more explicit. "It is coming to be understood," he would write in 1917, "that the opportunity for increased dividends and for advantage over competitive concerns, lies largely in the relationship which can be established with the men and women who make up the productive labor force."[38]

Reformers less directly connected with industry used reports of high turnover to reinforce arguments originally formulated for the unemployment question. Peter Speek, in a study for the CIR, called for the "regulation of labor conditions in unskilled industries, especially in those of seasonal character," in order to stop the increase in casual laborers, who roam "restlessly over all the country, from north to south, from coast to coast, back and forth. . . ."[39] Henry Seager, similarly concerned with workers' undirected geographic mobility, argued that turnover could be reduced through employment bureaus and unemployment insurance: "American employers complain that wage-earners are becoming less and less steady and reliable, more and more prone to shift from job to job and from place to place." He advocated unemployment insurance and a national system of employment bureaus as instruments "to detect the restless . . . type of worker, and put pressure upon him to reform his ways before he degenerates into a chronic vagrant."[40]

If Leiserson's contribution to the CIR was supplemented by the work of Slichter, it was also marked by a sharp rivalry with fellow John R. Commons student John Andrews (Secretary of the American Association for Labor Legislation), ironic in part because of the similarity of their views. In December, 1914, *The New Republic* published as Part 2 of the issue, Andrews' authoritative "A National System of Labor Exchanges." Andrews noted the opening of the New York City municipal exchange, the provision for a New York State employment bureau, and called for "forging into the chain the necessary third link, a federal system of public labor bureaus."[41] Like Leiserson, he acknowledged that additional provisions like unemployment insurance would eventually be necessary, but that the national system was necessary in order to generate "comprehensive, conscientiously collected information." He restated many of Leiserson's own arguments. But Congress had already adjourned (in October), allowing the Murdock bill to die in committee. Andrews chastised Congress and the Commission on Industrial Relations for delay in preparing new legislation.[42] Nor, Andrews found out, would the next session of Congress be able to act on unemployment recommendations from the CIR.[43]

Leiserson took Andrews' comments on the Commission as a direct attack on himself, and wrote defensively,

> . . . the CIR has not delayed unnecessarily its recommendations on unemployment as charged by the secretary of the American Association for Labor Legislation. We want to make an honest study and we are going to be sure that no joke like the Division of Information of the U.S. Immigration Bureau or the ordinary state employment office law will be put on the statute books through our efforts.[44]

The Leiserson-Andrews relationship, strained earlier, now became bitter. In January, Andrews complained to Commons of Leiserson's "disagreeable attacks" upon him. Leiserson was "underhanded", "daring and vicious," according to Andrews, and he countered by sending a series of letters defending himself to individuals influential in the unemployment reform movement.[45]

All of this is not to say that delay in establishing mechanisms to regulate a national labor market was due simply to internecine struggles within the reform movement. The proposition that unemployment and worker mobility were national problems because they were consequences of industrial policies of companies organized on a national basis was revolutionary. It attacked head-on the traditional notion, descended from the Elizabethan Poor Law, that the local community bore responsibility for maintaining those unable to support themselves.[46] The institutional framework which would sustain such a solution had to be created from the ground up, despite the enthusiasm mobilized during the depression of 1914–1915. Administrators actually grappling with the crisis of unemployment generally tried to narrow the geographic definition of the problem, not to expand it. As Elbert Gary wrote to Mayor Mitchel in the midst of the crisis,

> New York will have enough to do to take care of its own distressed and cannot now assist those from other communities in need of help, indeed there is not work here for all of our own men. *Every community should meet its own responsibilities.* Your committee urges that the authorities of other states and other cities in this state be notified not to encourage the unemployed of their communities to come to New York.[47]

Despite the agitation for employment exchanges, labor surpluses did not generate the political will to shift workers around the country for the jobs there were: the dominant response—outside the reform organizations—involved attempts to keep workers in their own communities. The dominant prescription for political stability in periods of unemployment still involved simple reduction of geographic mobility.[48] Not until the wartime labor shortages would efforts to administer the national labor market by directing workers around the country bear fruit.

In many cases the same reformers who were working on the national level mounted similar pressure in New York State. There, because of a somewhat different constellation of political forces, their ideas led more quickly to an institutional expression of the reform agenda. Broadly analogous to the CIR at the federal level, the New York State Factory Investigating Commission (NYSFIC) completed a no less massive investigation of its own. Created by the State Legislature in the wake of the Triangle Shirtwaist Factory fire in 1911, the Commission worked at first on issues directly related to the health and safety of workers in New York State's factories.[49] Labor advocates Robert Wagner and Alfred E. Smith served as Chairman and Vice-Chairman, respectively. In the election of 1912, Progressive Party strength forced both Democrats and Republicans to endorse labor/reform positions. Progressive inroads into Republican strength left Democratic majorities in the State legislature, with Wagner and Smith in control of the State Senate and Assembly respectively. In this legislative climate, the Commission enjoyed consistent success in pushing through health and safety bills, extending its own life, and expanding the scope of its investigations and recommendations.[50]

In twenty-five major bills in 1913, the Commission essentially oversaw the rewriting of the State labor code. Prior to the passage of this legislation, the Commission noted the inadequacy and backwardness of the New York State labor law: its "theory of factory legislation" the Commissioners believed to be "entirely erroneous" and "at variance with the systems in use in Wisconsin and in those European countries where the administration of labor laws has been a decided success."[51] In order to deal with the problems, New York State required a systematic overhaul of the entire Department of Labor. The NYSFIC recommended the establishment of an Industrial Commission which would have statutory power to make rules and regulations governing working conditions in the State. The reorganization would obviate the necessity of the entire legislature considering each specific factory regulation.[52] Frances Perkins, then investigator for the Commission, credited Assistant Counsel Bernard Shientag with the development of administrative law for New York labor problems. "Years later," Perkins recalled at the end of her career,

> . . . I realized how absolutely important it is to have the details of the regulations made by an administrative body that can change them . . . as new necessities arise.[53]

AALL reformers in New York were quick to see the importance of the new arrangements and formed a new "Citizens' Committee on the Administration of Labor Laws," which would seek not "more laws on the statute books," but "the more efficient enforcement" of laws already in place. Henry Seager noted that "recent developments in New York State make the present a peculiarly propitious time to concentrate on this subject."[54]

Nor did the NYSFIC itself minimize the importance of the successful passage of the 1913 legislative package. A subsequent report remarked:

> The enactment of these laws marked a new era in labor legislation in the State of New York. It placed the State of New York in the lead in legislation for the protection of wage earners.[55]

The rationale which underlay the Commission's work was that which had been articulated by Henry Seager in *Social Insurance*:

> The State is bound to do everything in its power to preserve the health of the workers who contribute so materially to its economic wealth and its industrial prosperity. Aside from the humanitarian aspect of the situation, economic considerations demand from the State the careful supervision and protection of its workers. Failure to perform this obligation will produce serious results in the workers of the future.[56]

The broad concern with the welfare of the worker as an industrial resource led the NYSFIC beyond issues of worker safety and health in industry to problems in mercantile establishments, child labor, compulsory education and women's work. Finally it centered on the problems of wages and hours and irregular employment.

> . . . what is the use of demanding safe and sanitary factories, if the men who work in them cannot earn enough to support their families in health and comfort? It seems rather futile to protect a girl from the evil effects of fatigue and overtime, if her wages for the hours prescribed will not enable her to live decently and have proper clothing.[57]

A supportive legislature at first gave free rein to the NYSFIC in these areas. In 1914, much of the Commission's work centered on a massive examination of the need for minimum wage legislation, including an investigation of the cost of living in various parts of New York.[58] The wage studies emphasized the importance of considering the annual earnings of workers who spent considerable periods of time each year unemployed. In this way, the problem of the minimum wage was consciously merged into the problem of unemployment: seasonal and irregular employment had profound effects on the ability of workers to pay for the basic necessities of life. The onset of depression and the American Association for Labor Legislation's new concern with the problem of unemployment reinforced this trend in NYSFIC work. Irene

Osgood Andrews, wife of John Andrews, completed a major study for the Commission on "The Relation of Irregular Employment to the Living Wage for Women."[59]

A living wage, she argued, demanded not only a minimum rate of pay, but also regularity of employment. She examined unsatisfactory conditions in a number of "disorganized" industries and concluded that the surplus pool of workers had to be reduced, wages high enough to support women throughout the year had to be guaranteed, or unemployment insurance was necessary. She did not see organizing the mobility of women workers on a state or national level as a major solution:

> Women workers . . . as a class are especially immobile. The majority of women workers are young and many of them live with their families. Numbers of the older women are struggling to support their children or to help in maintaining the family life. In any case, it is very difficult for them to move from town to town to secure work, and in the case of the younger girls, at least, it is obviously highly undesirable for them to leave the shelter and protection of their families.[60]

Andrews' approach to women workers differed significantly from the approaches of employment reformers to male workers. A central reform project for male workers, as we have seen, was to construct state institutions to manage mobility. The same reformers, without denying the economic importance of women's work, accepted and promoted the family as the woman's primary responsibility (in the case of older workers) and protection (in the case of younger) and thus never sought to organize or promote their mobility, except in the context of the recently immigrated family.

The Commission also took note of the pervasive effect of unemployment upon wage levels of all workers. Labor economist Don D. Lescohier explained in testimony:

> As soon as [the employee] is out of work . . . he is at a great disadvantage [in bargaining with the employer]. It makes a great deal of difference to him whether he gets a job or not, but if there are other men whom the employer may hire it makes little difference to the employer whether he hires this particular man or not. The net result of these facts is that the laborers in general are all the time at a relative disadvantage as compared with employers in general in bargaining over wages, and the employing classes are always able to force the mass of the laborers to accept a wage which is less than the employers could

> pay, and which is only as high as it is necessary for them to pay in order to keep the laborers alive.[61]

The NYSFIC proposed, among other things, vocational education, labor exchanges and more studies of the feasibility of social insurance to deal with the problems.[62] Its studies also helped to define and publicize the problem of labor turnover, and were cited in the CIR final report.[63]

The second thrust of the NYSFIC was thus much more comprehensive than the first, but as the Commission moved from a direct concern with factory conditions and Labor Department reorganization to the larger problems of unemployment, employment instability, turnover, and the minimum wage, it met with less immediate success, in part because Commissioner Samuel Gompers, who carried the weight of organized labor, opposed the whole concept of a legislated minimum wage for women; and in part because of the weakening of the Democrat's reform coalition in the Legislature.[64]

Mistrusting both organized labor and the impact of employer groups through the courts, the New York-based leadership of the AALL moved to safeguard the new labor legislation by forming a "Committee on Labor Legislation and the Constitutional Convention of the State of New York." Chaired by Henry Seager, the Committee submitted amendment proposals which would not only guarantee the constitutionality of recent labor legislation but also pave the way for various forms of social insurance, including unemployment insurance.[65]

Despite their appeals to industry and calls for the recognition of the unity of interests between employers and employees, the reformers' success at the state level was threatening to many employers. The new State agencies and the new labor code brought forth a new organization of New York manufacturers, seeking to minimize the cost to themselves of state intervention in labor issues.

> Associated Industries is organized to obtain a just and reasonable interpretation of the Laws affecting industry and labor which now are a part of the laws of New York; to do a constructive work in the enactment of new laws which are just and wholesome for manufacturer, merchant, real estate owner and workman; to cooperate with the State Industrial Board and any other legislative or constructive body with the end in view of bettering conditions for workman and employer without unreasonable expense and in the most practical manner.[66]

A year later, Associated Industries joined with the N.Y. State Manufacturers Association to form a new Associated Manufacturers and

Merchants of New York State. "With unity and harmony," its bulletin declared, "the world is our oyster."[67]

Unlike contemporary social reformers and the officials of the new State agencies, the Associated Industries' "unity and harmony" did not refer to that between employers and employees. Over the years its monthly bulletin, *The Monitor*, reprinted relevant reports from around the State, offering acerbic editorial comments on various labor reform proposals aimed at the problem of unemployment. An AFL investigation of a shorter work day as a solution to technological unemployment was ridiculed, as was AALL advocacy of unemployment insurance.[68] The smaller, often locally based companies of the Associated Manufacturers and Merchants feared that they would bear directly the costs of reform implemented through expanded state institutions and regulations. The alternatives for stabilizing labor markets, specifically the personnel management movement, were not yet apparent to these employers.

By 1915 when the NYSFIC ended, it had had a profound impact, both structural and ideological, on the Department of Labor. Structurally, the Department was now headed by a five-member Industrial Commission advised by an Industrial Council composed of five employers' and five employees' representatives.[69] The Industrial Commission was responsible for formulating an industrial code, enforcing labor and workers' compensation law, administering the compensation fund, and running a new State Employment Bureau. It absorbed the office of the State Fire Marshall (responsible for industrial fire safety inspections) and controlled the Bureaus of Mediation and Arbitration and of Labor Statistics and Information.[70]

New publications reflected the expansion of the Labor Department's work. It began an official monthly Bulletin detailing the work of the Industrial Commission beginning in October, 1915, a second monthly bulletin entitled *The Labor Market*, beginning at the same time, and a series of special bulletins on particular subjects (including three numbers on unemployment in its first two years) starting in 1914. Though some of employers challenged the new requirement to supply employment data to the Industrial Commission's Bureau of Statistics, *The Monitor* provided space for Chief Statistician Leonard Hatch to explain the need. Hatch outlined the importance of detailed information and pointed out that manufacturers might themselves find this information useful as a gauge of business activity.[71]

Throughout the new structures and their publications ran the idea that the State's role was to insure harmony between labor and capital by promoting mutual respect, and particularly through conservation of the worker as an industrial resource. Marion K. Clark, head of the Commission's Bureau of Industries and Immigration proclaimed,

> efficiency can only be scientifically developed and increased by the conservation of health, energy and increasing intelligence of the industrial army. . . . The state, the corporation, and the individual employer owe a moral obligation to the immigrant population. The welfare of both the state and the employer is bound up in the welfare of the industrial worker.[72]

Clark endorsed both Taylorism and company welfare work in the same paragraph, as promoting industrial efficiency. "New York State," claimed the Industrial Commission's *Annual Report*, "has placed itself in the very forefront of progressive industrial states . . ." and it predicted that "capital and labor will be brought closer together and that there will be a more sympathetic recognition of the rights and obligations of each."[73]

The new State Employment Bureau rested on similar ideas. Under laws passed in April, 1914 branches opened in Brooklyn, Syracuse, Rochester, Buffalo, and Albany throughout 1915 with advisory committees of local employers and employees.[74] Charles B. Barnes, successively investigator for the Wainwright Commission, the Russell Sage Foundation, and the U.S. Commission on Industrial Relations, was appointed director.[75] In the case of the Employment Bureau, harmonizing interests of workers and employers further meant eliminating the waste and discontent stemming from unemployment by moving workers to where employers needed them. Commissioner Lynch predicted optimistically in July that the Bureau would be able to "prepare and put into effect the remedy [for unemployment]."[76] "In time," Barnes wrote, "it is hoped that the Bureau may become a central point of information where laborers in one seasonal industry which is about to end can learn of the opening up of other industries where their services will be required."[77]

Strapped by inadequate funding, Barnes hoped to induce municipal authorities to contribute facilities for local branch offices.[78] While he intensified the Bureau's coverage of the State, he also advocated coordination of the labor market on a national scale. The purpose was not to increase worker mobility, but to direct it. His recent study for

Russell Sage noted that "at present the homeless men are simply being shifted from one city or section to another." He reported that the principal request of most homeless applicants to local Charity Organization Societies was money for transportation. But these men's mobility was not governed by an accurate sense of the needs of the job market, and the local C.O.S.s, according to Barnes' survey, wanted federal intervention to help order the chaos.[79] By 1916, when production for the war started to tighten labor markets, he noted the "great shifting of labor" and the need for a network of state exchanges to direct worker mobility.[80]

On the other hand, Barnes did not want his agency swamped by the homeless unemployed. Unlike Blatchly's Joint Application Bureau, the National Employment Exchange, and the Alliance Employment Bureau, Barnes hoped as far as possible to avoid the marginal laborer. "It is not our intention," he stated, "to 'reclaim' shiftless and careless workingmen, who tramp around looking for any old job." Beyond dovetailing seasonal jobs, Barnes sought in terms ringing of Beveridge and Leiserson, "the elimination of 'casuals,' men who take odd jobs only for two or three days or until they accumulate a few dollars."[81] Barnes wanted unemployables directed to agricultural labor colonies.[82]

In this project, he was disappointed. In 1911, the Legislature had passed a bill establishing a State Industrial Farm Colony "for the detention, humane discipline, instruction and reformation of male adults committed thereto as tramps or vagrants."[83] Purchase of land for the colony was delayed until January, 1913. Further appropriations were not forthcoming, however, and by the time of the depression, plans had reached a standstill.[84] Through 1914 and 1915, a small nucleus of employment reformers continued to press unsuccessfully for establishment of the colony. Charles Blatchly, expecting to renew the campaign for the colony, wrote to John Andrews: "I have probably had as much to do with the establishment of the Farm Colony for the Care of Tramps and Vagrants as any other single person."[85] Andrews supported this work. But despite the appearance of activity towards selecting Colony personnel by the State Civil Service Commission in February, 1915, it was never established: separation of the unemployed from the unemployable vanished as an issue in the tightening labor markets.[86]

In 1915 the reform program of bringing order to a disorganized labor market seemed to be taking root in New York State as a result of the initial successes of the NYSFIC program and the subsequent broadening of its mandate. State agencies gathered and published information on the labor market on a monthly basis, and an expanding system of public employment exchanges operated under the direction of a nationally respected administrator. As the war in Europe began to have an impact on New York's labor markets, these early initiatives provided the groundwork for new institutional and ideological developments under very different conditions.[87] The pre-war reforms, it quickly became apparent, were entirely insufficient to coordinate industrial production in general and the labor market specifically, for wartime purposes. If unemployment virtually vanished as a public policy concern, it now appeared that pre-war reformers had only barely glimpsed the problem of labor turnover and labor distribution problems. The New York State Industrial Commission identified the problem in 1917:

> At every turn of the program to speed up industry and to increase our output of war supplies, the question arises as to procuring an adequate supply of labor. . . . Not only military service, but also the practical stoppage of immigration have combined to make the labor supply greatly unsettled. . . . The question we are faced with seems to be one rather of poor distribution of labor than of an actual shortage.[88]

The Commission report blamed both employees, who shifted "from place to place, seeking the additional cent an hour or a bonus," and employers, who depended "on 'scamping' or the stealing of labor from one another through newspaper advertising and the sending out of labor scouts armed with glowing promises." It saw a "great waste in man power result[ing] from this crude method of shifting men from one plant to another, as well as adding to the instability of the labor market."[89] Officials at both the state and national levels recognized that these problems demanded more elaborate institutional structures than propaganda campaigns, and they turned to Leiserson's language and program to respond to this new aspect of "labor market disorganization."

The relationship of the business community to the wartime organization of the labor market was complex. Employers were disturbed by the high quit rate of workers because of its impact on production and on worker discipline.[90] Some took the opportunity to enter the expanding advisory and administrative bodies convened to coordinate production for the war. The relatively underdeveloped institutions of the American state provided a gap into which representatives from this community readily stepped. Writing about the Council of National Defense and its Advisory Commission, Robert Cuff has observed,

> . . . both the initiative for an organizational response to war and the talent necessary to supervise the administrative results derived from private institutions. This development was largely inevitable in light of the institutional pattern of prewar America, for neither the state's regulatory agencies nor the military services could match the technical and bureaucratic experience and managerial expertise to be found in private hands.[91]

At the national level, the National Civic Federation established a Committee of 100 to work with Wilson's Council of National Defense in the "mobilization and conservation of the nation's industrial resources." V. Everit Macy, now NCF President, outlined three tasks of the committee: "to ensure the preservation of harmonious relations between employers and employes . . .; arranging matters so that skilled mechanics will be kept at the work bench; and providing for the comfort of employes . . . [to maximize production]." He described these as "industrial problems presented by the freedom allowed to capital and labor."[92]

But businessmen entering the government were generally interested in insuring the temporary and limited nature of state economic intervention. Thus their agenda differed from that of the pre-war reformers who enlisted in the same bodies. In regards to labor, they sought to limit the labor mobility which seemed responsible for firms bidding against each other to maintain their workforces, while keeping the mechanisms for such control as much as possible in their own hands. They supported bonuses and welfare measures as ways "to attach the workers to the enterprise in these days of shifting labor."[93] Likewise, the U.S. Chamber of Commerce supported government plans to train personnel managers in the interests of reducing turnover and preventing labor conflict.[94] But without direct management of the labor market beyond the level of the firm, there was no way for employers to guarantee that they would not continue to bid up the bonuses and benefits in the competition for scarce labor. Thus, they lent support to temporary expansion of the employment service and to wage rates set by temporary government agencies.[95] But when they approached the federal government, ambivalent businessmen met a confusing, and often conflicting array of agencies and bureaus, each jockeying for position under new circumstances. In labor issues as elsewhere in the Wilson war administration, the lines defining public authority were shifting and blurred.

The CND Advisory Commission included, under the chairmanship of Samuel Gompers, a Committee on Labor the limits of whose power were unclear.[96] Temporary boards, such as the Emergency Fleet Corporation, the Aircraft Production Board guarded jurisdiction over their own labor policies, while entire labor divisions were created within the U.S. Shipping Board, the Fuel Administration, and the War Industries Board.[97] Rather than concentrating power within the Department of Labor, federal efforts to resolve labor difficulties consisted initially of a series of decentralized labor adjustment boards whose success was predicated on voluntary compliance by labor and management. The labor adjustment boards were neither able to coordinate policies beyond a single industry, nor designed to deal with the problems of turnover and labor shortage, nor, ultimately, even able to enforce settlements between hostile parties in their designated industries.[98] In the fall and winter of 1917, increasing strike activity, fuel shortages, a widespread breakdown in railroad transportation, and escalating criticism of the government's ability to manage the war, all helped to generate the will to centralize agencies for controlling and directing labor. Debates about the form of such centralization ensued.

Assistant Secretary of Labor Louis Post led the resistance to proposals for an emergency war labor board independent of the Department.[99] According to Post, much of the labor problem was due to "a condition of labor maladjustment" which could be sorted out by a comprehensive employment service operating at the national level under the jurisdiction of the Department of Labor.[100] "[The nucleus of] a national system, thoughtfully planned and efficiently managed . . .," Post wrote to President Wilson, "is already in successful operation in the Department of Labor, where the function of labor distribution properly and lawfully belongs."[101] The Labor Department's ability to deal with the distribution of labor thus formed the basis of its appeal for a massive increase in funding. Inadequate funding, not a need for reorganization, was the problem according to Post. In fact, despite handling more requests for labor than ever, the Department's U.S. Employment Service functioned in an *ad hoc* manner during the early months of U.S. involvement in the war, publicizing war camp construction, supervising a Public Service Reserve through "decentralized methods" allowing "a maximum of administrative freedom," and organizing crop harvests.[102]

While both the U.S. Chamber of Commerce and the AFL supported expanded funding for the U.S.E.S. within the Department of Labor, Congress was less enthusiastic and cut a $750,000 budget request to $250,000.[103] In December, President Wilson made available $825,000 from his Emergency Fund for labor distribution (at a time when the entire Department of Labor had a mere $250,000 for the subsequent six months of the fiscal year.)[104] Shortly thereafter, the U.S.E.S. was reorganized and removed from the Department's Bureau of Immigration.[105] This reorganization coincided with President Wilson's formal resolution of the debate over centralization of federal labor administration. On January 4, 1918 he created a War Labor Administration, with William B. Wilson as administrator with power to select an advisory council to determine the scope of its activities.[106]

In New York State, despite the recent expansion of the Department of Labor's Industrial Commission, wartime attempts to deal with labor market disturbances were characterized by an admixture of private power and public authority not unlike that occurring at the federal level. Employment Bureau Director Barnes could track disturbing changes in labor market activity in late 1917 through his branch offices. He remarked on the "unrest in the labor field" expressed not only in strikes but in high rates of turnover:

> . . . a considerable number of men are applying for work who report that they have just left a local job or have come from another section where there was plenty of employment. This unrest is largely due to the unsettled state of the wage scale. . . .[107]

While Barnes blamed private labor agencies for encouraging the wasteful and unnecessary search for higher wages, the Industrial Commission also pointed to the practices of employers. Barnes prescribed standardization of wages and more labor market coordination as antidotes. The apparent labor shortage among skilled workers, he thought, could be filled through training of the semi-skilled and unskilled.[108]

The first expansion in New York labor market management came in September, 1917. The New York City Mayor's Committee on National Defense, with help from the State Council of Defense, expanded the purview of the State Employment Bureau by establishing an employment clearinghouse to link the more than one hundred non-commercial labor agencies in Greater New York. Charles B. Barnes administered the clearinghouse, planned by a committee under the chairmanship of Henry Seager, who called its establishment "a long step toward a much needed reform."[109] The goal was to integrate the separate offices so that labor surpluses in one office could be transferred immediately to cover needs reported in others. Barnes outlined an elaborate paper shuffle involving the collection and re-distribution of all unfilled orders for labor after the offices closed each evening. Copies of all of these would be maintained at the central clearinghouse until any individual office reported by telephone that it had filled the position. In addition to coordinating labor within Greater New York, Barnes also expected the clearinghouse to coordinate labor among the fourteen Industrial Districts of the state and also to direct all recruiting for shipment out of the state.

Barnes envisioned the records at the clearinghouse as "a veritable pulse of the flow of labor from hour to hour," and the clearinghouse itself as "the brain that directs the whole process." It is doubtful, however, that the clearinghouse ever reached the level of coordination which Barnes envisioned. As he himself pointed out, it was to serve a population of five million in Greater New York, with "the largest floating labor pool in the country" and the office was already plagued by "lack of space and personnel."[110] Barnes acknowledged, in an address to the Industrial Commission's Safety Congress in December, that "the pressure of work on our limited force . . . does not allow the registering of each worker who comes to us unless there is a job ready waiting to which he can be sent."[111]

Aside from the attempts at a clearinghouse, the State Employment Bureau was not enlarged over the next months. A slight reduction in applications for workers led Barnes to reiterate that the problems in the labor market were fundamentally unrest, turnover, and distribution, and not the overall shortage as believed by some. "It is time for more sanity . . . regarding the present labor conditions," he wrote in December, and he called for well-coordinated technical training of unskilled men "before we consider the use of large numbers of untrained women."[112]

In Spring, 1918, activity did start to expand dramatically and the Employment Bureau acknowledged a real shortage of labor.[113] By this time, however, the federal program under the War Labor Administration (WLA) was under way. In January, the WLA had called a War Labor Conference, which in turn called for a National War Labor Board. On

April 8, 1918 President Wilson proclaimed the NWLB, headed, significantly, by two men who had battled with eachother over the U.S. Commission on Industrial Relations, Frank Walsh and William Howard Taft.[114] Its major function was "to settle by mediation and conciliation controversies arising between employers and workers in fields of production necessary for the effective conduct of the war."[115] This agency, however, did little to meet the concerns about labor "unrest" and the uncoordinated labor market and, according to Robert Cuff, "simply added another independent agency that complicated further the burden of overall coordination."[116]

The creation of an agency with a broader mandate for directing wartime labor policies including managing the labor market did not occur until May, with Secretary of Labor William B. Wilson's announcement of the War Labor Policies Board (WLPB) headed by Felix Frankfurter.[117] Frankfurter outlined one of its major tasks as stopping "the grave abuses of labor turnover, resulting in inefficiency and discontinuity of employment . . . by creating stabilizing conditions."[118] Secretary Wilson noted the "increasing shortage of unskilled labor for war projects," and the "haphazard" arrangements through which labor was recruited. High turnover alarmed him, not only because of the "loss of war efficiency," but also because of "its effect upon the morale of workers in the restlessness which it produces and even encourages."[119] Accordingly, the responsibility for the U.S.E.S. was now placed with the WLPB.

In June, the WLPB drew up a set of nine resolutions for compulsory centralization of all war labor recruitment under the United States Employment Service. In this major escalation of attempts to coordinate a national labor market, the WLPB tried to limit the distance traveled by workers to their new jobs and established local community boards to "secure local quotas." But the attempt to stabilize the labor market went far beyond the simple localist doctrine of having industries employ workers from their own communities. The first principle was to assign workers to priority industries as identified by the War Industries Board. Then, *wherever possible*, they were to come from the nearby locations. The concept was unambiguously one of a national labor market under the guidance and control of a federal agency with the power to recommend suspension of war contracts and even to "shut . . . off raw material from a recalcitrant industry" (though voluntary cooperation was emphasized.) The WLPB joined with Secretary Wilson in urging

Woodrow Wilson to announce the new policy in a presidential proclamation.[120] On June 17, 1918, Woodrow Wilson spoke of labor being "induced to move fruitlessly from one place to another, congesting the railways and losing both time and money," and announced the new recruiting program which would begin August 1.[121]

Initially, the U.S.E.S. was to assume complete control over recruitment of unskilled labor in firms with more than one hundred employees; subsequently it would extend its control to skilled labor as well. WLPB directive established thirteen federal districts, each under a U.S.E.S. superintendent. Under them, state directors had full responsibility for intra-state labor movement. New York State was itself divided into fourteen districts or "communities" each of which was to be under the control of a Community War Labor Board.[122] In June, The U.S.E.S. absorbed the machinery of the New York State Employment Bureau and began a program of expansion which would lead to the creation of many new branches and a vastly increased administrative capacity. Henry Sayer, the supervising Commissioner in New York, became the Federal Director of Employment for New York State, while Charles B. Barnes became Superintendent of the Federal Employment Service.[123] Meanwhile, in another attempt to direct the activity of workers, a New York State "anti-loafing" statute took effect in July, requiring all healthy 18–50 year olds to be employed in a useful occupation.[124]

A week after the presidential proclamation, the U.S. Chamber of Commerce sent a bulletin to all its members explaining the history and new function of the U.S.E.S: "The Employment Service is not a new form of the old agency. It is a new and distinct service which undertakes functions of great importance to all employers and with which they should cooperate during the war." The circular explained the local advisory councils "composed equally of representatives of employers and of workers" as necessary to insure public trust.[125] Some employers, however, remained suspicious of the agency, blaming the WLPB for wage increases and objecting to the WLPB's recognition of the AFL as the representative of workers.[126]

Frankfurter tried to put the WLPB activities in a favorable light for the Chamber of Commerce. In a speech to its Industrial Relations Committee, Frankfurter outlined the major accomplishments of the first four months of the War Labor Policies Board, highlighting the work of the U.S. Employment Service in recruiting workers for war industries:

"for the first time in the history of this nation the placement, the recruiting, the distribution of workers is in process of being governed by national necessity and not by the varying and competitive urgencies of hundreds of thousands of competitive individuals. . . ." Secondly, he explained the activities of the WLPB in respect to wages. Frankfurter credited the WLPB with aiding the establishment of "uniformly satisfactory conditions of work so that by the personal choice of men and women the devastating thing called labor turnover might be eliminated." The WLPB had tried to standardize wages at an attractive level in pursuing this goal. Finally, Frankfurter defended the WLPB's consultation with the American Federation of Labor (as well as the National Industrial Conference Board.) AFL representation, he argued, did not comprise an "endorsement of unionism" but was simply the fairest way to achieve the input of . . . labor."[127]

If some Chamber of Commerce members thought the U.S.E.S. was extending state control of the labor market too far, the American Association for Labor Legislation thought that it did not go far enough. Delighted with the recognition and publicity being given to the problem of "maladjustment," and to the need for a comprehensive, national system of labor distribution, the AALL reminded that it had been calling for such a system for four years. Like Barnes, it argued that the "chaos in the labor market" was due less to labor shortage, than to uncoordinated labor distribution. But it was concerned that the U.S.E.S. was only an emergency measure and feared its dismantling after the war. The AALL called for legislation "to put such service on an adequate PERMANENT basis," to insure "the continued stabilization of the labor supply to meet the growing industrial requirements of the future" and to deal with "the ever-recurring problem of unemployment."[128] Its fears, of course, were ultimately justified.

The U.S.E.S., which had placed only 51,183 workers in January, 1918, placed 455,931 in October.[129] To what extent this increase in administrative capacity, along with the wage program of the WLPB and the state anti-loafing laws, contributed to a reduction in labor turnover and stabilization of the labor markets at the national level is difficult to assess. Vastly enlarged national administrative mechanisms to direct labor to where it was needed had been achieved, but had come with a new understanding that stabilizing labor markets demanded not only an employment service, separation of the employable from the unemployable (a non-issue in the tight war-time labor market), and dissemination of labor market information, but also agencies which could intervene and rule on wages, hours, union recognition and virtually all aspects of the employment relationship.

If employers had reservations about state employment agencies, they were much less willing to surrender jurisdiction over employment practices to state agencies beyond their control. Wartime skirmishes over labor stabilization thus educated all the players as to what was at stake. Workers' militant workplace activity during the war had forced new levels of government involvement in managing industrial relations. Business resisted the benefits this conferred on organized labor within the AFL, and poised for the struggle for retrenchment after the Armistice. And they searched for new means to reach the goal of stabilized labor, which might remain more under their own control.[130] But before turning to post-war reaction, we go back to the situation in Yonkers from 1914 to 1918, to examine the impact of state and national developments on the local community.

Notes

1. Following Seager and Leiserson, they recognized the connection between the industrial problem and the relief problem (in that they saw "unemployables" largely as "casualties" of the industrial system). The reform agenda included provisions to distinguish between the two. However, as the unemployment crisis of 1914–15 gave way to the pressure of production for war, this became less of an issue.

2. Robert Cuff, "The Politics of Labor Administration During World War I," *Labor History* 21, 4 (Fall, 1980), 546–569; David Kennedy *Over Here: The First World War and American Society* (New York: Oxford University Press, 1980); Valerie Jean Conner, *The National War Labor Board: Stability, Social Justice and the Voluntary State in World War I* (Chapel Hill: University of North Carolina Press, 1983); Bruce Bustard, "The Human Factor: Labor Administration and Industrial Manpower Mobilization During the First World War," PhD. diss., University of Iowa, 1984; Melvyn Dubofsky, "Abortive Reform: The Wilson Administration and Organized Labor, 1913–1920," in James Cronin and Carmen Sirianni, eds., *Work, Community, and Power: The Experience of Labor in Europe and America, 1900–1925* (Philadelphia: Temple University Press, 1983), 197–220; Stephen Skowronek, *Building a New American State: The Expansion of National Administrative Capacities* (Cambridge: Cambridge University Press, 1982). On pre-war employment bureaus, see Udo Sautter, "North American Government Labor Agencies Before World War One: A Cure for Unemployment?" *Labor History* 24, 3 (Summer, 1983), 366–393.

3. Frances A. Kellor, "Is Unemployment a Municipal Problem?" *National Municipal Review*, 3 (April, 1914), 366–370.

4. Frances a. Kellor, "The Crying Need for Connecting Up the Man and the Job," *Survey* 31, 19 (Feb. 7, 1914), 541–542; "Organizing to Fight Unemployment Effectively, *Survey* 31, 20 (Feb. 14, 1914), 611; "The Way Out of the Unemployment Situation," *Survey* 31, 21 (Feb. 21, 1914), 638–639.

5. Frances Kellor, "The Crying Need for Connecting Up the Man and the Job," *Survey* 31, 19 (Feb. 7, 1914), 542.

6. Frances A. Kellor, *Out of Work: A Study of Unemployment* (N.Y.: G.P. Putnam's Sons, 1915 (reprint N.Y.: Arno Press, 1971)), 17–18.

7. Kellor, *Out of Work*, 31.

8. Kellor, "The Way Out," 638–639.

9. Kellor, *Out of Work*, 352.

10. Kellor, "Is Unemployment a Municipal Problem?", 366–370.

11. *Survey* 31, 23 (March 7, 1914), 694.

12. Victor Murdock, "For a Bureau of Employment," *Congressional Record* 51, Appendix (May 1, 1914), 413–416, reprinted in Julia Johnsen, ed., *Selected Articles on Unemployment* (White Plains and N.Y., N.Y.: H.W. Wilson, 1915), 98.

13. *The New Republic* 1, 7 (December 19, 1914), 4.

14. Founded in 1906, the National Liberal Immigration League stood for "distribution and education, not restriction." Dr. Bela Sekely, "Minimizing Unemployment: A Plan for the Organization of the Labor Market: Statement to the Committee on Labor of the House of Representatives," (N.Y.: National Liberal Immigration League, April, 1916, pam. NYPL); John B. Andrews, "A National System of Labor Exchanges," *The New Republic*, 1, 8 (Dec. 26, 1914), part 2, 7.

15. Sekely also echoed the Leiserson admonition: "The great danger of unemployment is this: that the unemployed is liable to become an unemployable." Sekely, "Minimizing Unemployment," 5.

16. Sekely, "Minimizing Unemployment," 13.

17. John B. Andrews, "A National System of Labor Exchanges," *The New Republic*, 1, 8 (Dec. 26, 1914), Part 2, 7.

18. "Notes of a Meeting of the Unemployment Conference," Feb. 27, 1914, Folder: Perlman, Box 20, U.S. CIR Papers, National Archives.

19. Other testimony suggested that men who drank and applied for relief should be forced to work for nothing, "so that the opportunity for abuse might be avoided." U.S. Commission on Industrial Relations, "Topical Analysis of Testimony at Public Hearings on Employment Offices and Unemployment, N.Y. City, May 18–20, 1914," 5, Box 14, Records of the U.S. Commission on Industrial Relations (hereafter CIR). On the CIR, see Graham Adams, *The Age of Industrial Violence, 1910–1915: The Activities and Findings of the United States Commission on Industrial Relations* (New York: Columbia University Press, 1966).

20. U.S. CIR, "Topical Analysis," 71. William Leiserson called the Distribution Branch a "joke." See below.

21. U.S. Dept. of Labor, *Annual Report*, 1914, 49.

22. U.S. Dept. of Labor, *Annual Report*, 1914, 51.

23. U.S. Department of Labor, *Annual Report*, 1915, 35–36. See below for Leiserson quote. On the problems of government employment bureaus, see Henry G. Hodges, "Progress of the Public Employment Bureaus," *Annals of the American Academy of Political and Social Science* 64 (Jan., 1917), 91–102.

24. U.S. Department of Labor, *Annual Report*, 1915, 39, 70.

25. U.S. Department of Labor *Annual Report*, 1915, 32.

26. U.S. Department of Labor *Annual Report*, 1916, 57–58. In the same year the Department supported the Nolan-Phelan Bill to establish an independent Bureau of Employment outside of its Bureau of Immigration to reflect its expanded function. U.S. Department of Labor *Annual Report*, 1916, 71.

27. U.S. Department of Labor, Bureau of Labor Statistics, *Bulletin* 192 (Washington: GPO, 1916), 6. On Leiserson's role, see AAPEO *Proceedings*, 1913, 8.

28. *The Survey*, 33, 2 (Oct. 10, 1914), 49.

29. Ringenbach claims that the Leiserson's Wainwright Commission report had no impact on activity during 1914–1915. Leiserson, himself, in a plea for more state activity, claimed that the report had been filed away and not acted upon. But we should not take his assessment at face value. Leiserson's authority in the field was itself established through the report. Ringenbach, *Tramps and Reformers 1873–1916: The Discovery of Unemployment in New York* (Westport, CT: Greenwood Press, 1973), 155. *The Survey* 31, 23 (March 7, 1914), 694; 33, 2 (Oct. 10, 1914), 48; CIR, *Final Report and Testimony* (Washington: Government Printing Office, 1916), 344–357.

30. CIR, *Final Report*, 350.

31. Leiserson, "A Federal Labor Reserve Board for the unemployed," *Annals of the American Academy of Political and Social Science* 69 (Jan., 1917), 116.

32. CIR *Final Report* (Chicago: Barnard and Miller, 1915), 165–6. Note: this edition was published prior to the GPO edition of 1916.

33. CIR *Final Report*, 166–170.

34. Sumner Slichter, *The Turnover of Factory Labor* (New York: Appleton, 1919), (with an introduction by John R. Commons), 20; Graham Adams, *The Age of Industrial Violence*, 206n; Sanford Jacoby, *Employing Bureaucracy*, 115–126. Magnus Alexander's essay on turnover, "Waste in the Hiring and Firing" first published in 1914, was republished for different audiences. See, e.g. *Annals of the American Academy*, 65 (May, 1916). John R. Commons, introduction to Slichter, *Turnover*, vii. A covering letter by labor economist L.C. Marshall (head of the CND's Industrial Service Section) to Secretary of Labor William B. Wilson, enclosing Slichter's work, expressed a different attitude toward the flow of turnover studies: "Here is the third of the reports on Labor Turnover. Surely there is still room in the wastebasket." Folder 20/542, Box 88, Chief Clerk's Files, R.G. 174, General Records of the Dept. of Labor 1907–1942, National Archives; Bustard, "The Human Factor," 114.

35. Slichter, *Turnover*, 85.

36. See Sanford M. Jacoby, *Employing Bureaucracy: Managers, Unions, and the Transformation of Work in American Industry, 1900–1945* (New York: Columbia University Press), 1985. For the early concerns and language of the movement, see "Proceedings of the Employment Managers' Conference Held at Minneapolis, January, 1916," U.S. Bureau of Labor Statistics, *Bulletin* 196 (May, 1916).

37. Fisher, "How to Reduce Labor Turnover," *Annals of the American Academy* 71 (May, 1917), 15. A curious variant on the concern with turnover as geographic mobility was Fisher's report that the Saxon Motor Company of Detroit effected "remarkable" turnover reductions largely through "preferring men who live within walking distance of the plant." Fisher, "How to Reduce," 19.

38. E.M. Hopkins, "Advantages of Centralized Employment," *Annals of the American Academy* 71 (May, 1917), 2. On E.M. Hopkins, see also Jacoby, *Employing Bureaucracy*, 91, 124. Jacoby perceptively challenges reformers' assertions of the high direct cost of turnover to industry, *Employing Bureaucracy*, 121–126.

39. Peter Speek, "The Psychology of Floating Workers," *Annals of the American Academy* 69 (Jan., 1917), 77, 78. The article was the result of an investigation for the CIR in 1913–1915.

40. *Survey* 33, 21 (Feb. 20, 1915), 554.

41. John B. Andrews, "A National System of Labor Exchanges," *The New Republic*, 1, 8 (Dec. 26, 1914), Part 2, 1–8.

42. The congressional committee had not reported on the Murdock Bill, ostensibly to allow the Commission to develop more extensive proposals on the basis of its investigations. Andrews, "A National System," 7.

43. Andrews to Clayton, Jan. 7, 1915; Clayton to Andrews, Jan. 9, 1915, Reel 13, AALL Papers.

44. Leiserson to C. Henderson, Jan. 2, 1915, Reel 13, AALL Papers. Henderson wrote to Andrews saying that he did not understand the attack, asking for an explanation, and noting that it would be "very serious to lose the cooperation of the Industrial Commission," as "they have a very strong influence at Washington." C. Henderson to J. Andrews, Jan. 6, 1915.

45. Andrews to Commons, Jan. 13, 1915; Andrews to McCarthy, Jan. 27, 1915; Andrews to MacKenzie, Jan. 27, 1915, Reel 13, AALL Papers.

46. See Clarke A. Chambers, "Towards a Redefinition of Welfare History," *Journal of American History* 73, 2 (September, 1986), 421.

47. Gary to Mitchel, Jan. 7, 1915, Folder 11, Box MJP Subject File: Unemployment 1914–1917, MMP. Also see remarks by Walter Lincoln Sears in chapter 4, "New York City, 1914–1915," above.

48. For another example, see Commission of Immigration and Housing of California, "Report on Relief of Destitute Unemployed," June 25, 1915, 5–6, in Folder 1915, Box 2, AALL Papers.

49. New York State Factory Investigating Commission (hereafter NYSFIC) Preliminary Report (New York: 1912), 11–14; New York State Laws of 1911, Chapter 561. The most comprehensive secondary work on the NYSFIC is Thomas Kerr IV, "The New York Factory Investigating Commission and the Progressives," D.S. Sc. Thesis, Syracuse University, 1965.

50. NYSFIC, Fourth Report, Vol. I (Albany: J.B. Lyon, 1915), 5–7.

51. NYSFIC, Second Report, Vol.I (Albany: J.B. Lyon, 1913), 29. Wisconsin Industrial Commissioner John R. Commons worked with the NYSFIC in drafting its proposals. NYSFIC Preliminary Report (Albany: J.B.Lyon, 1912), 23.

52. NYSFIC, Second Report, Vol.I (Albany: J.B.Lyon), 26–52. The New York Association for Labor Legislation (whose executive included Henry Seager, John Fitch, I.M. Rubinow, and V. Everit Macy) endorsed the proposal, with modifications. NYSFIC, 2nd Report, Vol.II (Albany, N.Y.: J.B. Lyon), 1301–1308.

53. Frances Perkins, *Reminiscences*, Columbia University Oral History Project, Vol.1, 170–172. See also 137–143, which includes her account of and reactions to the Triangle Shirtwaist fire.

54. H. Seager to I.M. Rubinow, June 2, 1915, Folder 16, Box 1, Rubinow Papers, NYSSILR.

55. NYSFIC Fourth Report (Albany: J.B. Lyon, 1915), 7.

56. NYSFIC Preliminary Report (Albany: J.B. Lyon, 1912), 18.

57. NYSFIC Fourth Report, Vol.II(Albany: J.B. Lyons, 1915), 1.

58. Kerr, 116; NYSFIC Fourth Report, Vol.I (Albany: J.B.Lyon, 1915), 17–22. Mary van Kleeck worked on one of these reports, on women in the millinery trade. She had recently completed similar studies of women in bookbinding and artificial flower-making for the Russell Sage Foundation.

59. NYSFIC Fourth Report, Vol.II (Albany: J.B. Lyon, 1915), 497–635.

60. NYSFIC Fourth Report, Vol.II (Albany: J.B. Lyon, 1915), 508.

61. NYSFIC Fourth Report, Vol.I (Albany: J.B. Lyon, 1915), 461.

62. NYSFIC Fourth Report, Vol.I (Albany: J.B. Lyon), 50.

63. Sanford Jacoby, *Employing Bureaucracy*, 115–126.

64. Kerr, 96–119. On the controversy over support for a minimum wage for women, see Nancy Schrom Dye, *As Equals and As Sisters: Feminism, the Labor Movement, and the Women's Trade Union League of New York* (Columbia: University of Missouri Press, 1980), 146–148. The British background is outlined in Wally Seccombe, "Patriarchy Stabilized: the Construction of the Male Breadwinner Wage Norm in Nineteenth Century Britain," *Social History*, 11, 1 (Jan., 1986), 53–76.

65. "Constitutional Amendments Relating to Labor Legislation and Brief in their Defense, submitted to the Constitutional Convention of the State of New York, Jan. 9, 1915," Reel 70, AALL Papers.

66. *The Monitor* 1, 1 (June, 1914), 1. The NYSSILR has a set of *Monitors* from this era.

67. *The Monitor* 2, 1 (June, 1915).

68. *The Monitor* 2, 7 (Dec., 1915), 35.

69. N.Y. State Department of Labor Industrial Commission *Annual Report* 1915, 20–21.

70. N.Y. State Dept. of Labor, *Report of the Industrial Commission* (1915), 11; Yonkers *Statesman*, Sept. 4, 1915, 2. On worker's compensation in New York, see Robert Asher, "Failure and Fulfillment: Agitation for Employers' Liability Legislation and the Origins of Workmen's Compensation in New York State, 1876–1910," *Labor History* 24, 2 (Spring, 1983), 198–222. A summary of structural changes in the Department of Labor is contained in Christos A. Vavura, "New York State Department of Labor: a Century of Evolution," pam., n.d., in N.Y. State Dept. of Labor Library.

71. Hatch referred to recommendations of the Wainwright Commission as the original stimulus towards the gathering of labor market statistics in New York State.*The Monitor* 2, 3 (Aug. 1915), 41–42.

72. N.Y. State Department of Labor, *Report of the Industrial Commission* (1915), 343, 344.

73. N.Y. State Department of Labor Industrial Commission *Annual Report* 1915, 20–21.

74. William D. Baldwin served as an employers' representative for the Brooklyn office. N.Y. State Department of Labor, *Report of the Industrial Commission* (1915), 257–262. See also Charles Barnes, "Director Barnes Explains Working of New State Bureau of employment," *The Monitor* 1, 13, June, 1915, 4–6.

75. *The Survey* 33, 8 (Nov. 21, 1914), 192.

76. New York Associated Industries *Monitor*, 1, 2 (July, 1914), 1. At the same time, Lynch saw "the principle and contributory cause of the serious situation" to be "ninety-five years of [immigration of] . . . feeble-minded, insane, epileptic, diseased and

generally unfit." N.Y. State Dept. of Labor, *Annual Report*, 1914, 277–278. *The Monitor* was not overtly unsupportive of the State Employment Bureau, and provided room for Barnes to make his case.*The Monitor* 2, 1 (June, 1915).

77. N.Y. State Department of Labor, *Report of the Industrial Commission* (1915), 264.

78. N.Y. State Industrial Commission, *Bulletin* 1, 3 (Dec., 1915), frontispiece.

79. Charles B. Barnes, "The Homeless Man: A Study in New York City," unpublished typescript, 1915, 26–28, located in Folder 1579, Box 101, Mary van Kleeck (hereafter MVK) Papers.

80. N.Y. State Dept. of Labor, *Report of the Industrial Commission* (1916), 165.

81. *The Monitor*, 1, 9 (Feb., 1915), 36.

82. *The Monitor*, 1, 9 (Feb., 1915), 36.

83. David Schneider and Albert Deutsch, *The History of Public Welfare in New York State, 1867–1940* (Chicago: University of Chicago Press, 1941), 177. On the background of labor colonies, see Percy Alden, "Labor Colonies," in W.D.P. Bliss, *Encyclopedia of Social Reform* (N.Y.: Funk and Wagnalls, 1908), 678–685.

84. William P. Capes, Untitled, undated typescript, 7 in Folder 7, Box 16, CSS Papers.

85. Blatchly to J. Andrews, Jan. 5, 1915; see also J. Shillady to H. Seager, Feb. 2, 1915, Reel 13, AALL Papers.

86. Andrews to S. Untermyer, Orlando Lewis, Michael Drummond, and J.J. O'Keefe, Feb. 15, 1915; Orlando Lewis to J. Andrews, Feb. 16, 1915, Reel 13, AALL Papers. Orlando Lewis was the General Secretary of the New York State Prison Association.

87. In June, 1916, Barnes noted "the complete reversal of the demand and supply of labor in the last twelve months." N.Y. State Industrial Commission *Bulletin* 1,9 (June, 1916), frontispiece.

88. New York State Department of Labor, Industrial Commission *AR*, 1917, 13.

89. New York State Department of Labor, Industrial Commission *AR*, 1917, 231, 209.

90. "Stabilizing Industrial Employment: Reducing the Labor Turnover," the entire May, 1917 issue of *The Annals*, was dominated by the writing of employers and employment managers. *The Annals of the American Academy*, 71 (May, 1917).

91. Robert D. Cuff, "The Cooperative Impulse and War: The Origins of the Council of National Defense and Advisory Commission," in Jerry Israel, ed., *Building the Organizational Society: Essays on Associational Activities in Modern America* (New York: Free Press, 1972), 234. Also see Valerie Jean Conner, *The National War Labor Board*, viii.

92. Yonkers *Herald*, March 6, 1917, 1. Macy had input into the CND from another direction, as a member of the executive of the Advisory Commission's Committee on Labor, whose overriding purposes were "the conservation and welfare of workers," and to prevent "interruption of industry" through employment problems. Council of National Defense Advisory Commission, "Committee On Labor," (Washington: GPO, 1917), 3, 7.

93. New York *Times* editorial, quoted in AALL Press Release: "Forestalling 'Social Justice,'" April 10, 1918, on Reel 17, AALL Papers.

94. See, e.g. Committee on Industrial Relations of the Chamber of Commerce of the United States, "Employment Managers Training Under Government Auspices," April, 1918, NYPL; Bustard, 204–207; and Sanford Jacoby, *Employing Bureaucracy: Managers, Unions and the Transformation of Work in American Industry, 1900–1945* (New York: Columbia, 1985), 144–147.

95. Earl Dean Howard of the Chamber of Commerce suggested a system of a standard maximum wage: "A standard maximum rate at which unskilled labor could be hired would prevent [employers'] bidding [against eachother] and presumably stop excessive turnover." Howard to Felix Frankfurter, Aug 16, 1918, Folder: Chamber of Commerce of the U.S., Entry 2, Correspondence of the Chairman and Executive Secretary, RG 1, WLPB, National Archives.

96. Council of National Defense Advisory Commission, "Committee on Labor" (Washington: GPO, 1917). Also see Easley to W.B.Wilson, Jan. 22, 1918, quoted in Cuff, "The Politics of Labor Administration," 568.

97. Robert Cuff, "The Politics of Labor Administration," 548, 551.

98. This perspective on federal government activity is drawn from Bustard, Chapters 4 and 5. For the local impact of the wartime crises, see my chapter 6.

99. This argument is drawn from Cuff, "The Politics of Labor Administration." The job fell to Post because Wilson was out of Washington as a member of the Mediation Commission, Cuff, 553.

100. Louis Post, "Special Report of the Assistant Secretary to The Secretary of Labor . . .," Dec. 31, 1917, quoted in Cuff, "The Politics of Labor Administration," 555.

101. Post to Woodrow Wilson, Dec. 26, 1917, quoted in Cuff, "The Politics of Labor Administration," 557.

102. It also conducted studies of Black migration from the South and women as war workers. U.S. Department of Labor *Annual Report*, 1917, 66–79. The 1916 *Report* was the first to refer to an "Employment Service;" 1917 the first to refer to the U.S. Employment Service, even though legislation establishing an independent agency had not yet been passed.

103. U.S. Dept. of Labor *Annual Report*, 1917, 89–90; 1918, 206–207.

104. Post, "Special Report of the Assistant Secretary . . ." quoted in Cuff, "The Politics of Labor Administration," 556; Bustard, "The Human Factor," 114–116.

105. U.S. Dept. of Labor *Annual Report*, 1918, 206–207.

106. Bustard, 109–127; Cuff, "The Politics of Labor Administration," 546–569.

107. N.Y. State Industrial Commission, *Industrial Bulletin*, 3, 1 (Oct., 1917), frontispiece.

108. N.Y. State Industrial Commission, *Industrial Bulletin*, 3, 1 (Oct., 1917), frontispiece; and N.Y. State Industrial Commission, *Industrial Bulletin*, 3, 2 (Nov., 1917), frontispiece.

109. Seager was chairman of a subcommittee on industry and employment of the Mayor's Committee on National Defense, N.Y. State Industrial Commission, *Industrial Bulletin*, 2, 12 (Sept. 1917), 258; N.Y. State Industrial Commission, *Industrial Bulletin, 3,2* (Nov. 1917), frontispiece.

110. Charles B. Barnes, "State Clearance Division for New York" (unpublished typescript, n.d.) Folder 774, Box 43, MVK Papers.

111. N.Y. State Industrial Commission, *Industrial Bulletin*, 3, 3 (Dec. 1917), 71.

112. N.Y. State Industrial Commission, *Industrial Bulletin*, 3, 3 (Dec. 1917), frontispiece, 71.

113. N.Y. State Industrial Commission, *Industrial Bulletin*, 3, 8 (May 1918), frontispiece.

114. Taft, as President, had called for the creation of the Commission, but became disillusioned with it as Frank Walsh, as Chairman led it on a course Taft considered too radical. See Conner, *The National War Labor Board*, 19–20.

115. "Proclamation of the President of the United States" in U.S. Dept. of Labor, "National War Labor Program" n.d., in Folder: War Labor Board, W.W.I, Box 8, Frances Perkins Papers, Columbia University; Bustard, 124–127.

116. Cuff, "The Politics of Labor Administration," 560.

117. "The War Labor Policies Board—What It Is and What It Stands for in the New Era of Humanity," U.S. Employment Service *Bulletin*, 1, 40 (Nov. 7, 1918), 13. Cuff cautions against overdrawing the innovation of the WLPB, seeing it rather as "a minimum gesture toward coordination of policy. "The Politics of Labor Administration, 564–567. He does not examine its role in the expansion of the employment service. The recent historiography, in general, seems to downplay the WLPB. Bustard, Chapter 6, offers the fullest treatment. On the interagency rivalry between the NWLB and the WLPB, see Conner, 32–33.

118. "The War Labor Policies Board—What It Is and What It Stands for in the New Era of Humanity," U.S. Employment Service *Bulletin*, 1, 40 (Nov. 7, 1918), 13. On WLPB attempts to create uniform wage standards, see Bustard, 138–151.

119. Secretary Wilson to President Wilson, June 15, 1918, reprinted in U.S. Dept. of Labor, "National Labor Recruiting Program" n.d., in Folder: War Labor Board, W.W.I, Box 8, Frances Perkins Papers, Columbia University.

120. U.S. Dept. of Labor, "National Labor Recruiting Program" n.d., in Folder: War Labor Board, W.W.I, Box 8, Frances Perkins Papers, Columbia University. The U.S.E.S. actually grew out of the earlier efforts of the Division of Information of the Bureau of Immigration beginning in 1907. In 1914, the Department of Labor established a U.S.E.S. which worked on an ad hoc basis during special emergencies. The War Labor Policies Board directive fundamentally changed the scale of operation of the Service. See Edward T. Devine, "The Attack on the Federal Employment Service," *Survey* 41, 19 (Feb. 8, 1919), 662–663.

121. Presidential Proclamation, June 17, 1918, in U.S. Dept. of Labor, "National Labor Recruiting Program" n.d., in Folder: War Labor Board, W.W.I, Box 8, Frances Perkins Papers, Columbia University.

122. Yonkers *Herald*, Aug.1, 1918, 2; Aug. 6, 1918, 1. Bustard, 136–138. At the community level, quasi-public mechanisms for coordinating industry got under way at the same time as the labor administration mechanisms. In July, William Fellowes Morgan of the New York Merchants Association appointed W. D. Baldwin and William Campbell of Waring to the Regional Industrial Commission for Metropolitan New York, at the request of the War Industries Board. Yonkers *Herald*, July 8, 1918, 1.

123. New York State Department of Labor, Industrial Commission *AR*, 1918, 189; F. Frankfurter to Henry Bruere, Sept. 25, 1918 Folder: Henry Bruere, Entry 2, Correspondence of Chairman and Executive Secretary, RG 1, WLPB Papers, National Archives. Bruere replaced Sayer as the Director of Employment for New York State. Inexplicably, the Department of Labor reported the absorption to have taken place in January, 1918. U.S. Dept. of Labor, *Annual Report*, 1918, 201.

124. The Compulsory Labor Act did not include any additional machinery to allocate available workers. Newspaper reports did not specify males or females, but the law must have referred to males, as there was no special exception noted for women engaged in unpaid childcare or housework. Yonkers *Herald*, June 1, 1918, 4. See also David Kennedy *Over Here*, 269, on a federal "work or fight" order.

125. Chamber of Commerce of the U.S.A, "War Bulletin No. 37: Distribution of Unskilled Labor," June 24, 1918, Folder: Chamber of Commerce of U.S., Correspondence of Chairman and Executive Secretary, Entry 2, R.G. 1, National Labor Policies Board, National Archives.

126. William Chenery to F. Frankfurter, Sept. 28, 1918, Folder: Chamber of Commerce of U.S., Correspondence of Chairman and Executive Secretary, Entry 2, R.G. 1, National Labor Policies Board, National Archives. They had reason to be suspicious: according to Melvyn Dubofsky, "Union advances could be seen wherever the federal government intervened directly and regularly." Dubofsky, "Abortive Reform," 211.

127. These quotations come from William L. Chenery's notes of the address and not directly from Frankfurter. William L. Chenery, "A statement to be read by Professor Earl Dean Howard before the Directors at a meeting of the Chamber of Commerce of the United States, intended to express the sense of Mr. Frankfurter's talk before the Industrial Relations Committee of that body on Sept. 30, 1917 [sic, though it must have been 1918.] Folder: Chamber of Commerce of U.S., Correspondence of Chairman and Executive Secretary, Entry 2, R.G. 1, WLPB, National Archives.

128. This was a call for support for the Robinson-Keating bill which dealt with a federal employment service. AALL, "Labor Shortage or Labor Placement?" *Labor Laws in War Time: Special Bulletin*, 3 (Jan. 1918), Reel 70, AALL Papers.

129. Darrell Hevenor Smith, *The United States Employment Service: Its History, Activities, and Organization* (Baltimore: Johns Hopkins, 1923), 42.

130. See Melvyn Dubofsky, "Abortive Reform," 197–220.

6

The End of Localism in Yonkers, 1914–1918

"Xville, suddenly, was lifted out of its provincialism. That is probably the greatest social value of the war."

—Charles F. Weller[1]

Between 1914 and 1918, Yonkers workers felt the outside world impinge on their own in unmistakable ways. They felt the impact in various aspects of their lives. An editorial in the Yonkers *Herald* remarked ambivalently on the "passing away" of the "old-fashioned household":

> Railroads and trolley lines, the telegraph and telephone have begotten restlessness, and we have become gadabouts. The county line has ceased to be the limit of vision. We lead broader, swifter, perhaps more fruitful lives than ever could be embraced in the narrow confines of the old-time household.[2]

But technological change was only one source of the enlarged vision. The rapid vicissitudes of the national political economy profoundly and directly affected life in Yonkers during these years. Depression, war in Europe, mobilization, and demobilization in rapid succession disrupted labor markets and hastened the destruction of the localist orientation whose foundations had eroded, but which had nevertheless remained in place since the 1890s.

The first part of this chapter will examine the beginnings of the breakdown in the localist orientation before the U.S. entry into the war. It focuses on the activities of the Charity Organization Society which found itself forced to look outside of Yonkers in order to maintain its own legitimacy and authority. In the absence of a local manufacturing elite actively involved in philanthropy, the C.O.S. looked towards the metropolitan reform organizations and so became a conduit for the new ideas about poverty and unemployment to enter the city.

The second part of the chapter examines the more concerted assault upon the localist ideology which occurred with entry into the war. Severe shocks disrupted the national political economy. Nationally orchestrated propaganda campaigns replaced the theme of sacrifice for the sake of the city with sacrifice for the nation.

The breakdown of the localist ideology created new problems in the distribution of labor. Over the past decades, localism had moderated broader market forces in the distribution of labor. It held that workers should seek work first in their own communities, that their own communities had some obligation—at least moreso than other communities—to help them in hard times, and in return, that workers should aid continued local capital investment by accepting employment conditions with a minimum of protest. The localist model was actually increasingly unrealistic and problematic, both because class solidarity often superseded "community" solidarity and because workers—with or without their families—moved so frequently from town to town. As we have seen in the chapters on the 1890s and 1900s, a growing awareness of these phenomena led late-nineteenth century reformers and many employers to articulate the case for localism yet more forcibly. Understanding the dangers of an unregulated national labor market, their first reaction to mobile workers was to attempt to restrict mobility. Given slow and unreliable channels of communication, families and individuals wandering around the country in search of work threatened to bring on social chaos if not political revolution.

Between 1914 and 1918, with the breakdown of the ideology of localism, a reform alternative for moderating a chaotic national labor market gained currency: organization of the market through state administration. It promised geographic mobility without chaos. But the establishment of an effective administrative process demanded considerable political will. Despite the urging of reformers, elected officials, as it turned out, were most willing to spend money on labor market administration during the wartime labor shortage when a disorganized labor market impaired the war effort (and capital accumulation.) With the end of war and the threat of labor surplus and high unemployment, they reverted to the simpler solution of propaganda campaigns to reassert the ideology of localism.

The severe but relatively brief depression of 1913–1915 led Yonkers citizens concerned with the problems of unemployment and poverty increasingly to seek help from interested outsiders. Their contact brought the ideas of the metropolitan reformers into the city so that in the spasmodic changes in demand for labor in subsequent years, Yonkers residents were already familiar with the idea of administrative organization of the labor market.

Unemployment in Yonkers in 1914 occurred on the scale of 1893 and 1908, reflecting conditions in the State as a whole.[3] "Probably never before in the city's history has there been such a general lack of prosperity as has been felt in Yonkers during the year 1914," judged the Yonkers *Statesman* in its year-end review:

> Not even in 1893 was there such widespread distress. During the last two or three months, the resources of the Commissioner of Charities and of the different charitable agencies have been strained to the utmost in the effort to care for those who are in need.[4]

Not only had local factories shortened hours and cut back staffs, but construction slackened, and the city almost completely ceased its public works projects.

Alexander Smith began its cutbacks in January with an unanticipated and unexplained ten percent wage reduction. With "the usual reticence being preserved that is characteristic of the company," officials refused to speak to the press. President Gifford Cochran, at the Racquet and Tennis Club in New York City, would not be interrupted to comment because "he was engaged in watching a championship tennis match at the time."[5] The Yonkers St. Vincent De Paul Society noted that high levels of unemployment in February, combined with an unusually cold winter caused "extraordinary distress and suffering throughout the city."[6] A succession of snow-storms in late February, brought a respite of sorts, with the opportunity for publicly funded snow-shoveling for many of the unemployed. The City, in a variant on the older rock-breaking policy, hired more than 900 men to shovel snow, and estimated that about $20,000 would be spent on the task by winters' end, most of this having "gone into the pockets of men who have been unemployed—some of them for several months."[7] In March, the Yonkers C.O.S. appointed an Industrial Committee "to arrange a system of work for the unemployed," but no further record of its work has survived.[8]

Spring brought an easing both of the weather and of the unemployment crisis. By summer, the large factories were working at close to normal levels. Alexander Smith closed for two weeks in July for its annual summer stock-taking, and reopened with 7,000 full-time hands on July 13.[9] Waring was gradually rebuilding its shop force by rehiring old hands laid off during the winter. By mid-July, it had 1800 employees at work.[10] But Yonkers had hardly taken a deep breath of recovery when news of war in Europe rocked the labor markets again.

Supplies of raw materials and capital, labor and product markets would all be affected. But whether the war would bring panic or prosperity, labor shortage or mill-shutdowns, was not immediately apparent. Mill superintendents, queried by reporters, could not predict the effects of war on local employment.[11] The wartime shut-down of the stream of immigration promised a constriction of labor markets which would benefit the bargaining power of American labor.[12] Mass emigration to belligerent countries even seemed a possibility: a reporter calculated 2100 local Austrian employees, about the same number of Russians, and 150 Magyar workers who might leave if volunteers were summoned.[13] On July 31, local papers announced the closing of the New York Stock Exchange to forestall panic; but a month later the *Herald* assessed the closure as a healthy prevention of speculation.[14] It did not take long for local citizens to start to calculate the benefits to the United States, generally, and Yonkers specifically, of the disruption of European production. "It is the time," the *Herald* editorialized, "for American capital to give an impetus to trade such as it has never witnessed before."[15]

In fact, the local effects of the European war were different in the different industries. The sugar refineries, whose raw materials originated in the Americas, did a booming business supplying sugar to the British whose other sources were disrupted.[16] At the same time, the carpet mills went on half-time early in August. Officials made no comment but the papers reported that shortages of imported wool and dyes were responsible.[17] Felt throughout the city, the Smith reduction compounded the problem of rising food prices:

> Charitable workers here agree that if the half-time operation is prolonged . . . many people will feel the pinch of hard times severely. At best this summer has been a hard time for the poor. Work has not been too plentiful or steady, and the advancing cost of living has made the situation worse.[18]

By August 22, Smith had begun buying domestic wool, but according to reports, the shortage of dyes, largely supplied by Germany, left the mill on half-time. When the carpet mills resumed full-time in

November, the *Statesman* again noted that "officials in the Company, in accordance with their usual policy, are silent on its affairs when newspapers ask them questions," and speculated that the half-time had been "due in part also to the general industrial and business situation."[19] Along with the carpet-workers, employees who worked on city contracts were hard hit: on August 10, Comptroller Miller advised the Yonkers Board of Estimate that local bonds could not be sold, bringing to a halt public works which employed hundreds of unskilled laborers.[20]

Depressed conditions continued in Yonkers for about a year after the onset of war. The Otis shops were on reduced time, temporarily resuming full-time in September, 1914.[21] A New York City superintendent reported simply that "people are not putting in new elevators this year."[22] Reduced hours persisted at Smith, Otis and Waring through the first several months of 1915.[23] Even in the following September, the Charity Organization Society was taking on new families because of the poor employment situation.[24]

But the worst conditions in Yonkers probably took place during the winter of 1914–1915, when seasonal unemployment compounded the war-related unemployment and rising prices. At the end of December, Mrs. Hiram W. Taylor, meeting with twenty prominent Yonkers women on the subject of relief, stated

> . . . Just now it is not a question of finding employment for the poor; there is no employment. Most of our factories are working half-time, and it is our duty to care for those who are falling in the struggle.[25]

Few of those concerned were so willing to focus specifically on relief as the most important problem: Charity Organization movement principles remained too prominent in the local thinking. The C.O.S. principles insured that the effects on the individual character of any relief project—including relief work—would be the central concern. Such concern was evident in the calls for public works: "Pauperization is always to be guarded against," a *Statesman* editorial warned.[26] A few days later, another argued:

> What could be more wasteful than to support in idleness, by charity, people who are willing and able to work . . .? Just to put the streets of American cities in as good condition as the streets of Berlin would give employment to an army.[27]

It was concerned about getting full return for any relief dollars, but more importantly about the character of the recipients. The editor looked, furthermore to the individual worker to save and plan for hard times in order to provide a cushion for the hardship of lean seasons and years: "During [good times] . . . let workers be economical, save their money, start little sidelines of business or buy a piece of ground. . . . Then hard times won't bring so much unemployment."[28]

In the partisan political newspapers, there was also still a desire to make political hay out of the unemployment situation: the Underwood tariff, heavy local government spending, and the passage of workman's compensation were all mentioned as political causes of unemployment.[29] Such accusations surfaced in the course of election campaigns or during debates over legislation: in these unemployment was essentially a weapon in a fight about other issues. But other discussion went beyond both the political accusations and the individual moral concerns of the Charity Organization principles, and was much more significant as an indication of the changes in local thought on the problem of unemployment at this time.

Evidence of the impact of the more recent writings of Devine, Seager, Leiserson, and Kellor comes from the pages of the local newspapers which reported conferences and meetings from New York City and around the state and which occasionally reprinted condensed versions of papers presented by authorities in the charity organization/social work field. One of the most important developments was the acknowledgement that unemployment was beyond the control of the individual worker. "As long as the corporate industry exists, we are sure to have unemployment . . ." a local editor concluded.[30] Yonkers citizens read that "a permanent settlement to the unemployment problem is impossible" and that "in the business world are forces which prevent all the people from getting enough work."[31]

This recasting of the problem demanded a new kind of examination of the contours of unemployment. These analyses introduced the term "labor market" into the local discourse. Following the thought of Frances Kellor and Henry Seager, organizing the labor market implicitly meant locating more precisely the employable participants, and segregating more definitively the others. "The first step," reported the *Statesman* on a New York City meeting called to deal with the problem, "is the separation of the employables and unemployables."[32] In the Yonkers papers in these years, the unemployable included a broad range of "the hopelessly incapable, the dishonest, the criminals, beggars, vagrants, bodily unfit and the intemperate. . . ." Moreover, the same article continued, the "unemployable rightly . . . form a problem in the field of the charity worker rather than that in the student of the labor market."[33]

According to the *Statesman*'s report of another meeting, secretaries of New York charitable agencies assembled in Utica resolved that

> The problem of the casual and seasonal worker and hobo is yearly becoming a more serious and difficult one [complicating the employment problem] by jeopardizing the chances for employment of the men who are honestly seeking jobs.[34]

Discussion of the separation of the unemployable from the unemployed led generally to renewed advocacy of the State farm colony for vagrants, for which land had been bought but no additional funding appropriated. "Use the farm colony," was the message in a February, 1915 report from Charles Blatchly, superintendent of New York City's Joint Application Bureau of the C.O.S. and A.I.C.P.; "the problem of the tramp is becoming steadily more burdensome, menacing and expensive."[35] The unemployable clearly received much of the moral disapprobation which had been reserved for the "unworthy poor" of earlier years, but the new theoretical context, the problem of organizing the labor market, was not an insignificant innovation.

Yonkers resident John Kingsbury reflected the transition from moral, charity organization concerns, to those of the labor market. Kingsbury was Commissioner of New York City's Department of Public Charities in the John Purroy Mitchel administration. As such, he was responsible for New York City's Municipal Lodging House, which provided shelter for homeless men. (See Chapter 4.) He wrote an influential article in the *Review of Reviews*, published in April, 1914 as "Our Army of the Unemployed," in which he invoked the words of Buffalo C.O.S. pioneer, Frederic C. Almy: "Relief, like cocaine, relieves pain, but it creates an appetite."[36] Also like cocaine, Kingsbury argued, relief should be administered only on the advice of experts. Kingsbury rested his argument about homelessness and proposed lodging house reform on the distinction between the problem of relief and the problem of industry.

The Yonkers *Statesman* carried an editorial based on the Kingsbury article in mid-April. It highlighted the sections dealing with organization of the labor market, both through labor exchanges and through incentives to industry to minimize seasonal variations in employment:

> **The solution, declares Mr. Kingsbury, lies not in soup houses, bread lines, and free beds, but in a system of cooperation between those parts of the country which need men and those which have more men than they need. The minimizing of seasonal variations in industry, already worked out in some lines, must be encouraged.[37]**

In a similar vein, a November *Statesman* article condensed Ida Tarbell's *American Magazine* piece advocating employment bureaus, cooperation between city and country labor markets, and prevention of "closing down of factories and shops in critical times. . . ."[38] Similar editorials appeared in January, 1915.[39]

Through reports of meetings and digests of articles and conference sessions, Yonkers readers became familiar with the new discourse on unemployment and poverty. Personal ties between Yonkers residents like John Kingsbury and Homer Folks, and charity officials in New York City and New York State contributed to the spread of the new ideas in Yonkers, but more formal links developed through new local and state organizations were perhaps even more important. The links between these organizations formed the channels through which were transmitted not only the new ideas but also the information crucial to "organization of the labor market" beyond the local level.

The recently reconstituted Yonkers Charity Organization Society was—or more accurately, attempted to make itself—the nucleus of the local network of information on unemployment and poverty. The task involved not only coordinating various groups and agencies within Yonkers (including reining in such initiatives as Mrs. Hiram Taylor's), but also making contact with the state organizations which sought to operationalize the concept of the labor exchange or state employment bureau. The Yonkers C.O.S. occupied, with other groups and individuals working in this period, a transitional moment. Most of its efforts were based on the old Charity Organization principles, but its officers also groped towards new understandings of the problems they confronted.

In January, 1915, the C.O.S. visitor, Mary Jolly Van Hook, became General Secretary, a position occupied by Albert Jones since the reorganization in 1909.[40] During the four years of her tenure, she strenuously attempted to centralize charity efforts in Yonkers under her own direction, while coordinating with outside groups. But Van Hook's legitimacy in making herself the center of such efforts in Yonkers could not be built on her own stature in the community. Unlike Mary Marshall Butler or Florence Parsons, Van Hook came from outside of Yonkers and was hired for her experience in relief work in Harrisburg, Pennsylvania, and New York City.[41] Nor could she make appeals to a unified social elite such as that which supported the old C.O.S. under Norton P. Otis in the 1880s or the Mayor's Emergency Committee in the 1890s. Mary Jolly Van Hook looked repeatedly outside of Yonkers to those who might recognize her legitimacy, rather than mobilizing members of the Yonkers elites, who were either less interested, or committed elsewhere. Those to whom she did appeal were basically leaders of other charity and social work organizations. Others in Yonkers, even those who directly challenged Van Hook, did the same. Consequently Yonkers organizations became increasingly integrated with those outside of Yonkers, despite the failure of increased coordination among Yonkers agencies themselves. The new pattern of coordination reflected the abdication of the Yonkers elites from sustained interest in the local community. If they had been present as a more unified social body, social workers would have been less pressed to seek resources and legitimacy from their professional colleagues outside of Yonkers.

An appeal to Alexander Smith Cochran for a contribution to the C.O.S. reveals the new relationship of his family to Yonkers charity. Bailey B. Burritt, a Yonkers C.O.S. director (see below), prepared a draft of an appeal letter which recalled Cochran's mother's (Eva Cochran) generosity and noted the Cochran family connection to the high unemployment among carpet mill operatives during the past winter.[42] Burritt sent it to sugar refiner Warren Kipp, now President of the C.O.S., who discussed it with director George Bunker (also connected with National Sugar, and the only other one directly involved with a Yonkers factory). Bunker, in turn, suggested that Kipp "take the matter up with Mr. Eugene Clark . . . who is also close to Mr. Cochran, and he would be able to give us ideas of the proper approach to the gentleman in question."[43] A final draft, addressed to Cochran at the Ritz-Carlton Hotel in New York City, deleted the references to his mother and toned down those to Yonkers unemployment. Such gingerly treatment reveals the distance the charity organization directors, themselves members of Yonkers' fractured industrial elite, felt from Cochran.

Van Hook began her work optimistically in January, 1915, by inviting several charity leaders in Yonkers to a meeting to discuss the establishment of "a Central Exchange" which would act as an information repository on all families helped by any agency in Yonkers, and to which all agencies could refer in their investigations.[44] Other agencies were reluctant, however, and Van Hook made little headway.[45] In July she wrote to Fred Hall, Associate Director of the Charity Organization Department at the Russell Sage Foundation in New York:

> I am afraid there is an unusual degree of jealousy, and rather a consuming dislike of co-operation of the kind that Charity Organization Societies advocate, though each agency vociferously claims to co-operate.[46]

She referred elliptically to "other matters to be adjusted" some of which had been the subject of an earlier letter to the Foundation, and which she thought would require "some radical steps . . . perhaps . . . by a committee representing the leading agencies of Yonkers." She closed with an apology for "a rather free exposure of the skeleton in our closet" and a request for more suggestions about how to gain cooperation of other local agencies.[47]

City Judge Joseph Beall was cool to Van Hook's advances. "If people unfortunately come to Court," he wrote her, "for some other cause and we incidently find that they are poor I would rather be hesitant about compiling information on that subject and furnishing it to any organization for . . . I doubt our power and the propriety of doing it."[48]

Van Hook had additional problems with the Commissioner of Charities, Alfred Fox, whom she felt was distributing relief liberally and even lavishly (at the height of the unemployment crisis) without sufficient investigation. Her response in this instance was to contact Edward Devine in New York to complain of Fox's methods. Devine responded politely that Van Hook seek the advice of County Superintendent of the Poor, Everit Macy. "I do not know that he has any real authority over the distribution of relief by the Commissioner in Yonkers," cautioned Devine, "but I rather think that he might have some influence."[49] Van Hook remained unsatisfied with Fox. At the end of his tenure in 1917, Van Hook wrote to Margaret Byington at the American Association of Societies for Organizing Charity, "we are particularly hopeful that [the] new appointment will result in better cooperation. . . ." And in order to ensure such cooperation, Van Hook asked Byington to send the new Charities Commissioner literature which would help him "to do his work according to approved methods," and send the bill to her.[50]

Van Hook plowed on with her efforts and in October, 1915, mounted a display of fourteen charts showing the C.O.S. work. It included an explanation of the idea of the Social Service Exchange, and pushed "the value of cooperation" among social agencies.[51] Van Hook used publicity generated by the display to explore new ways of making contacts with other Yonkers organizations. When Fred Hall, at Russell Sage, wrote her about newspaper reports of the display, she responded, "If you are able to get clippings from some New York agency about us, without doubt that agency could furnish me with the material we need to have concerning other Yonkers organizations. . . ." Van Hook was now going through New York City to find information on Yonkers.[52]

While generally supportive, Hall leveled a methodological criticism of the display. The same problems which troubled Van Kleeck about the Kingsbury's 1914 Lodging House survey (see Chapter 4) troubled Hall about Van Hook's display. "I think any presentation is unfortunate," he wrote, "that assigns one disability as the most serious handicap or as 'the primary cause of maladjustment' to each family." And he referred her to Devine's tables in ***Misery and Its Causes*** as the way a display might present "all of the disabilities noted in all families."[53] Van Hook accepted the criticism, and promised to bring Yonkers C.O.S. practice into line.[54]

Van Hook's continuing efforts to coordinate Yonkers' charitable agencies under the C.O.S. eventually took form in a Social Service Exchange. Unable to enlist other agencies' active support for the venture, the C.O.S. sponsored the exchange itself, hoping to attract interest and use gradually. Van Hook also began publication of a Yonkers "Social Service Bulletin," in which news of the various Yonkers agencies was reported. In the first number of the Bulletin, Van Hook noted that the Social Service Exchange was "being maintained temporarily by the Charity Organization Society until such time as the social workers of the community may unite in its support."[55] Increased coordination did not come until the departure of Van Hook in 1919.

Van Hook acted as channel for the dominant ideas about poverty and unemployment to enter Yonkers, but she was not alone within the C.O.S. In 1913, the Board of Directors, reflecting the C.O.S.'

non-localist orientation, invited Bailey B. Burritt, general director of the New York A.I.C.P., to join its ranks. Burritt responded:

> I cannot help but think that the Board of Directors of the Charity Organization in Yonkers have been unwise in electing to membership in that Board, a person so engrossed in his work in New York City as I am and relatively so little known among people of means and influence in Yonkers.[56]

Connections with "people of means and influence in Yonkers" were less important to the new C.O.S. than connections with social work circles in New York City. Three years later, in 1916, Burritt became chairman of the Society's Finance Committee, though initially he protested in the same vein as he had the first appointment:

> If the work is done successfully, it ought to be headed by a Yonkers business man who knows Yonkers people. I know really very few Yonkers people, and certainly not well enough to do the job of acting as chairman of the Finance Committee successfully.[57]

Burritt became Treasurer in 1918 and occupied the position until 1940.[58]

Burritt served as an "insider" on the Yonkers Board. When Mary Jolly Van Hook's troubles in coordinating the organizations in Yonkers raised some doubts among the New York City social workers, Francis McLean, now General Secretary of the American Association of Societies for Organizing Charity, was able to write "confidentially" to Burritt, inquiring about "the condition of the Yonkers Charity Organization Society and of Mrs. Van Hook's connection with it."[59] Burritt reassured McLean as to Van Hook's methods and initiative, while acknowledging her "well-recognized limitations." According to Burritt, the problem lay not in Van Hook, but in the fact that "Yonkers, like so many places near New York, has not a well-developed civic sense."[60] Though the Yonkers C.O.S. did not formally join the Association until 1917, McLean, Margaret Byington, and others from the American Association of Societies for Organizing Charity continued to offer suggestions and supervision over the following years.[61]

In addition to her contact with metropolitan reformers, Van Hook also served as the first Yonkers contact with formal efforts to organize the labor market beyond the local level. As we saw in Chapter 5, two independent systems were competing in New York State by 1915: the State's Employment Bureau under Charles B. Barnes, and the federal

Distribution Branch of the U.S. Immigration Service.[62] In the summer of 1915, as the State Employment Bureau was getting under way, Mary Van Hook initiated contact with the U.S. Department of Labor in Washington, asking for literature "pertaining to opportunities for those out of employment or who should be moved from a congested city environment to other districts."[63] The Department of Labor referred her inquiry to the Distribution Branch of the U.S. Immigration Service, located close to Yonkers (and Ellis Island) at the U.S. Barge Office at Battery Park, New York City. Van Hook made no specific reference to immigrants, explaining:

> This is a very congested district, and many of the shops work so irregularly that it is exceedingly probable a large number of persons can be induced to leave the city for work on farms and small communities if there is any degree of certainty of the work continuing.[64]

The Distribution Branch willingly handled her requests, supplying bulletins of positions available around the country, and application forms for the unemployed. The latter concluded by asking "the number of cows you can milk," presumably an index of usefulness on farms, where the Service was hoping to place most immigrants.[65] The Service noted that there was steady demand for "men with farming experience and females desiring domestic work."[66] Van Hook reported "quite a number of persons" interested in applying and forwarded several applications immediately.[67]

A year later, Van Hook received a notice from Frederick Howe, Commissioner of Immigration, announcing that the federal Immigration Service was expanding its distribution efforts by organizing an Employment Service for New York State. (There was still no reference to Barnes' agencies.) The target for Howe's Ellis Island office was to establish a clearinghouse of information for the towns within a radius of one hundred miles from New York.[68] Howe also contacted the mayor, and asked for other Yonkers agencies concerned with the problems of unemployment and labor distribution. Van Hook responded enthusiastically, once again using the opportunity provided by contact with an outside organization to enhance the position of the C.O.S. within Yonkers. She offered to have the Employment Service use the C.O.S. office as its local headquarters and to provide a desk, clerical services, and perhaps the use of a telephone.[69] Van Hook then used the authority she gained as the Service's contact in Yonkers to request employment information from the local factories. She promised that the information would be useful not only to the federal agency, but to the local C.O.S. in finding positions for the unemployed.[70]

Van Hook's response to Howe is interesting further as a revelation of the extent to which the new thinking on unemployment had infused the operation of the Yonkers C.O.S.. Van Hook wrote that, aside from those with physical or mental handicaps, "all our clients may be permanently relieved when their labor problems are thoroughly adjusted."[71] This statement is particularly striking because Yonkers unemployment was not very high at that time.[72] In the space of two years, involuntary unemployment and underemployment had come to occupy a central theoretical position in the local understanding of poverty.[73] Within two more years the Yonkers C.O.S. would go on record as favoring "the establishment of a government provision that will insure work to every idle man."[74]

Well before U.S. entry into the war, then, the new thinking on unemployment and poverty made its way into Yonkers and helped to forge the first tenuous links of organization between the city, and federal and state agencies attempting to bring about regional or nationwide integration of the labor market. As much as they can be pinpointed, the agents of local change were charity organization officers who were responding to a changing social structure in the city, in particular to the demise of active elite participation in local philanthropy. With entry into the war, the pace stepped up.

Four conditions furthered the wartime demise of localism in Yonkers: conscription and enlistment of local men; booming industry as a result of wartime contracts for local factories; periodic shortages, most notably the fuel shortage in January-February, 1918; and the demand for contributions to Liberty Loans and other fund-raising efforts. The first two conditions produced a virtually unprecedented shortage of labor during the war. Workers quitting jobs in search of higher pay made employers extremely responsive to the demands of labor, triggering the state to enter experiments with regulation of labor movement. The latter two conditions generated a sense among Yonkers residents that their own personal sacrifices were contributions to the national cause. Such sacrifice, combined with concerted efforts to stimulate wartime nationalism, resulted in a new prevailing ideology in which the welfare of the nation largely eclipsed the welfare of community as the basis of appeals for labor discipline and political consensus.[75]

On the heels of the declaration of war, Yonkers industries shifted gears and turned towards military production. The sugar refineries continued to run at capacity supplying sugar to Europe until a shortage of raw sugar led to a shut-down in October, 1917.[76] In addition to elevators for army and navy bases, Otis retooled for the manufacture of gun parts and other war machinery. Smith virtually eliminated its production of carpets and revamped the entire plant for the supply of blankets and tent duck to the armed forces. Waring shifted into production of hats for the military, turning out one and a half million by the end of the war.[77] In its year-end review of 1917, the *Herald* noted the "prosperity of the city's chief industries, which have never known such rush, working day and night on armament contracts."[78]

Enlistment and conscription exacerbated the labor shortage brought on by the war-time demands on local industries and the closing off of European immigration. The Wilson administration saw the link between military mobilization and the distribution of labor in industry, and sought to dovetail the two tasks, so that conscription did not unduly dislocate industrial production. Wilson wrote in the Spring of 1917 that the idea of the draft

> is not only the drawing of men into the military sevice of the Government, but the virtual assigning of men to the necessary labor of the country. Its central idea was to disturb the industrial and social structure of the country just as little as possible.[79]

Initially hopeful of minimal disruption in the local labor market, the Yonkers Chamber of Commerce endorsed Wilson's plan of selective conscription.[80]

Even if selection were made on the basis of industrial need, the massive shift to wartime production was itself bound to cause dislocation. In Yonkers, as it happened, in spite of the fact that the factories shifted to the production of war-related goods, local draft boards granted very few individual exemptions on the basis of industrial need.[81] Neither in mobilization, nor, as we will see in Chapter 7, in demobilization, was the draft integrated into an overall labor allocation policy.

In some ways, conscription was an ad hoc affair. There was no mechanism other than public opinion to get potential draftees to register (though a nationally orchestrated propaganda campaign insured that this would be effective.)[82] Three local draft boards, composed of Yonkers "men whose time was otherwise occupied with affairs of business" volunteered under the terms of the Selective Service Act.[83] There were three registration days, embracing a widening circle of the male population. On June 5, 1917, all men between the ages of twenty-one and thirty were registered—a total of 8,862 when the day was over—while the local unit of the National Guard patrolled the streets to head off opposition or disorder.[84] A follow-up registration for those having a twenty-first birthday since the first date was held on August 12. Approximately 500 Yonkers men had voluntarily enlisted by that time, and the draft boards were having difficulty filling their quotas after exemptions were given for those with dependents and physical disabilities.[85] A month later, the ages were expanded to demand registration by all those between nineteen and forty-five. 1,839 were finally drafted from the city.[86] But the draftees represented only a fraction of those who joined the armed forces. Tabulations made by the City after the war was over indicated that 6,909,—7 percent of the total Yonkers population—enlisted at one time or another during the war.[87]

Information on the pool of workers available for the military and industry collected through selective service registration was supplemented by a special "military census." As in the Progressive campaigns of the late 1890s, women were given the task of making the house-to-house survey to gather the data. During June, 1917, volunteers from twenty-five women's organizations headed by the Woman's Suffrage Party canvassed the city's population, with questionnaires for all people between sixteen and fifty. By the end of the month, they had information on 54,000 residents.[88]

Of the city's major factories, Otis was most directly affected by the labor shortage perhaps because, aside from the refineries, its workforce was most overwhelmingly male. 450 of its employees joined or were drafted while 357 left Alexander Smith and 134 left Waring.[89] But the labor shortage had a ripple effect. With work readily available for all, poorly paid workers—male and female—freely left their jobs in search of more money. The *Herald* noted in February, 1918 that "many of the carpet shops workers have left town to accept more remunerative work elsewhere."[90] When schools opened in September, 1918, Superintendent Gorton (also Chairman of one of the draft boards) remarked on the difficulty of finding replacements for resigning teachers, many of whom were "attracted to more profitable fields."[91] The Commissioner of Public Works reported that sixty percent of his workforce had "quit for more profitable employment elsewhere," where they could make twice as much as the city paid.[92] Turnover became a problem locally just as it did throughout the country.[93]

With the labor shortage, Yonkers workers expressed dissatisfaction with the conditions of their employment by leaving for better jobs. But they also became more willing to make demands through union organization and strikes.[94] Owners met both these individual and collective expressions with pay increases, bonuses, and welfare measures which they could easily afford in the war-time rush of industry. When pay raises were not accompanied by the threat of union organizing or strike, they generally reflected a firm's bid to retain scarce workers. In 1917, Smith workers received a ten percent raise followed soon after by another four to ten percent increase in addition to their semi-annual bonuses.[95] In February, 1918, the labor shortage prompted another ten percent raise, while the bonuses were extended to workers with three years' service, and six months later to those with two.[96]

The bonus system spread to other Yonkers firms. Arlington Chemical Company's one hundred employees received a bonus of ten percent of their annual wages in January, 1917; 1,400 Otis Elevator employees and 400 at Habirshaw enjoyed one soon after.[97] The Otis bonus followed on the heels of rumors of a threatened strike at Otis, though Works Manager Edward Fitch denied any connection.[98] Waring provided free life insurance for all employees and reduced the work week by more than four hours without a pay reduction.[99]

During the first summer of the war, there were local strikes among workers at the Schneider Celluloid Factory, among the building trades, and once again on the street railways.[100] Nor did the Otis workers remain as content as Fitch would have them. Machinists joined a union in large numbers during an organizing campaign in August and struck a year later, receiving within a day the pay increase they demanded.[101] Apparently the bonus system which had worked well for Smith was not sufficient to meet workers' wartime expectations: they objected to the fact that the bonuses did not constitute promises of a permanent pay increase.[102] The effect of the tight labor market on wages and bonuses in Yonkers reflected the national condition. Having increased annually more than five percent per year since the outbreak of war in Europe, real wages jumped twelve percent in 1918.[103]

If workers benefitted from the constriction of the labor markets, they were also called upon repeatedly to make sacrifices; and the campaigns promoting sacrifice—in the national interest—were a major stimulus towards the expansion of the local consciousness to the national borders. One of the greatest of these surrounded the coal shortage of January-February, 1918. In an unusually cold winter, the Hudson and the Port of New York were frozen for much of the two months. The nation's rail transportation system was clogged with war-related shipments, and some ships lay idle for want of coal.[104] In Yonkers the Smith shops were closed for two weeks in January, as were the schools, because of the coal shortage. While Congressional Republicans charged that the shortage was due to massive incompetence on the part of the administration, Wilson's Fuel Administrator Harry Garfield ordered all factories closed from January 18 to January 22 in order to free the bottlenecks. All retail stores using coal were required to close for the period as well.[105] The Yonkers *Herald* editorial asked: "Do You Love America? . . . If we love America we will stand up now like real Americans under the first trial of any importance in which personal sacrifice enters that we have had in years."[106] Sacrificing to conserve fuel was a part of being a "good citizen."[107] About ten percent of the Otis workforce continued to work on ordnance contracts, but otherwise the industrial shutdown was complete in Yonkers.[108] On January 23, the factories reopened with a full workforce (except at the refineries, where raw materials were lacking). The government ordered a continuation of "fuelless Mondays" (also called Garfield Mondays) with factory closings, but there were no more extended orders for closings.

The coal shortage persisted in Yonkers, however. Editorials and articles noted the gloominess of the business district on Mondays, and the necessity for continued sacrifice for the national cause. By mid-February, with local coal shortages seemingly more severe than warranted by the national situation, a local Citizens' Committee including the Mayor William Wallin went to Washington to meet with Garfield to protest the situation. The meeting resulted in 5000 tons of coal directed towards Yonkers by boat.[109] There was no further discussion of a shortage. The sacrifices caused by the fuel shortages were added to dietary restrictions, and helped to generate a solidary sense of contribution to the national war effort—the language of sacrifice was the language of loyalty and nationalism.

Fund-raising efforts similarly directly linked personal sacrifice to the national cause. Fundraisers based their campaigns upon appeals to loyalty in a virtually uninterrupted series of drives during 1918. These involved not only mobilizing central coordinating committees, but also scores of volunteers, parades, mass meetings, speeches, posters, and full-page newspaper ads.[110] A parade and "Monster Armory Meeting" for the non-sectarian Catholic War Fund was hardly over when the city geared up for a Liberty Loan Bond Drive.[111] The embarrassingly poor attendance at a "Labor Night" rally in the loan campaign produced charges of labor's disloyalty. Local union leaders countered that the small attendance "did not represent the attitude of the toilers by any means" and pressed their members even harder for loan subscriptions to prove it.[112] Meanwhile, on April 26, 1918, headlines blared, "This is Liberty Day, When Your Liberty Bond is Your Certificate of Patriotism."[113] And management staged a parade of the entire 1700 person Otis workforce, headed by Baldwin and Fitch, "to stir up patriotism."[114] One week after the close of the Liberty Loan campaign, 12,000 Yonkersites paraded to open the drive for Red Cross funds.[115] Similar loyalty drives followed for War Savings Stamps and a Fourth Liberty Loan. The drives continued to aim at workers in factories, in part because they were conveniently organized and assembled as a captive audience. But the loyalty messages to workers in factories went beyond pleas for financial sacrifice for the bond drives.

Messages to produce more for the war fit well in the factory setting. Yonkers' Four Minute Men delivered patriotic exhortations on factory lunchbreaks to produce more, give more, and protest less. The war-time sacrifice campaigns thus provided employers concerned with productivity and labor loyalty with a ready vehicle for pursuing their own ends. On the political front, the pacifism of the Socialist Party, growing in strength in 1917 despite the split over the issue of the war in the previous year, offered employers an opportunity to brand all labor agitation and union militance as disloyalty.[116]

These Yonkers events mirrored activities in communities throughout the United States, not because there were widespread, spontaneous local forces generating such campaigns, but because they were orchestrated by the federal government and coordinated by George Creel's Committee on Public Information. Creel was a reform muckraker whose Progressive crusades in Kansas City and Denver had attracted national attention. The Creel committee developed the advertising campaigns and publicity, intervening in the public schools, distributing 75 million pamphlets and circulating six-thousand press releases.[117] 75,000 Four Minute Men, selected locally and approved by at least "three prominent citizens—bankers, professional or business men," carried messages to communities like Yonkers across the country. With the cooperation of Samuel Gompers, the Committee for Public Information funded the American Alliance for Labor and Democracy, and charged it with "the special responsibility of keeping labor industrious, patriotic, and quiet."[118]

The campaign for the loyalty of labor was closely related to the campaign for the loyalty of the immigrant. In cities like Yonkers, the workers and the foreigners were, to a large degree, one in the same. Not surprisingly, threats of wartime labor unrest seemed more ominous when immigrants made up a large portion of the workforce. Anti-immigrant fears flared when a small strike in the neighboring village of Hastings coincided with the declaration of war. On April 6, 1917 the strike by a dozen "foreigners" at a chemical plant precipitated an investigation by the Westchester County Sheriff: citizens feared they might incite a strike among the 3,500 workers at the nearby National Conduit and Cable Factory, which had government contracts for manufacturing ammunition (and which had had a violent strike the year before.) Headlines blared that they "Feared Foreigners Would Destroy Hastings Plant," though the sheriff judged "that the people of the village were unduly excited" considering the conditions he found.[119] When workers at National Conduit and Cable did strike two months later, they found soldiers from the National Guard already on duty.[120]

The war added rapidly changing layers of meaning onto anti-foreign sentiments in Yonkers. Exclusionist's fear of foreigners had existed for at least a decade side-by-side with the campaign for assimilation in Yonkers. While the exclusionist thrust had dominated at the end of the 1890s, the Progressive campaigns of the Yonkers Civic League—aiming at education and assimilation—had gained ascendency by 1914. Now the war heightened fears, increased the urgency of Americanization, and changed the relationship between the two approaches to immigrants. The most obvious anti-foreign sentiment was directed toward German- and Austrian-born immigrants.[121] While German-born residents assembled to swear resolutions of fealty and the local Slovak National Alliance held a patriotic mass meeting at Philipsburgh Hall, federal secret agents rounded up German and Austrian reservists.[122] German-born residents were soon being hauled before judges on charges that they had uttered anti-American sentiments, some as innocuous as a belief that the Allies would lose the war.[123] On April 30, 1918, enemy aliens, i.e. Germans and Austrians without naturalization papers, were forbidden from entering the waterfront neighborhoods of Yonkers, by virtue of a federal war zone decree.[124]

These measures were both cause and effect of tension as the nation mobilized for war. The federal propaganda campaigns, aimed as they were at public sentiment, had whipped up a virulent xenophobia which, like the campaigns for national sacrifice, helped to relocate the boundaries of consciousness from community to nation. The Americanization campaign, directed at a broad group of immigrants and essentially liberal in origins, was subject to the same influences.

Gerd Korman locates the origins of the organized Americanization movement in the 1908 formation of the North American Civic League for Immigrants, whose goals were "to protect, to disperse, and especially to educate the immigrant."[125] At the outbreak of war, Frances Kellor led the New York branch in a split (precipitated by anti-union activities of the League) to form the Committee for Immigrants in America. Kellor and the Committee became central in the war-time Americanization campaign. Their activities included the creation and funding of the Division of Immigrant Education in the United States Bureau of Education, the formation of an Immigration Committee in the United States Chamber of Commerce, and a National Americanization Committee which successfully promoted July Fourth as a day for mass naturalization celebrations. But war had an impact on Kellor's liberalism, and the tone and impact of the Americanization project changed. Her message became more strident, playing on the fear of unassimilated foreigners, and she explicitly endorsed the coercive power of employers in forcing their captive immigrant employee audiences into Americanization classes.[126] In the heat of war, the language of liberal Americanizers changed: U.S. Commissioner of Education Philander Claxton appointed a National Committee of One Hundred to lead an "America First" campaign, to teach immigrants "English and Patriotism."[127] "100 percent Americanism" aimed to eliminate any vestiges of Old World culture among immigrants.[128] These coordinated activities effectively filtered into smaller cities like Yonkers reinforcing a consciousness which was both nationalist and assimilationist at the expense of localism.

The *Statesman* responded to Kellor's 1915 National Americanization Committee campaign, calling for a new national symbolism around the Fourth of July. It suggested the new name, "Americanization Day":

> We should look forward, and not back, even on the Nation's birthday and improve its opportunities to make all our people foreign born and native genuinely American in feeling, ideas, and convictions.[129]

By 1918, Yonkers was ready to celebrate July 4 in just this way. In June "practically every social and fraternal organization in the city" sent representatives to a planning meeting for a July 4th "Loyalty Parade" in which foreign-born citizens would have an opportunity "to demonstrate their individual loyalty to the United States." The parade attracted 10,000 marchers "of many nations."[130]

Similarly, the Yonkers Chamber of Commerce followed the lead of the U.S. Chamber. It formed an Americanization Committee, under William Palmer East, and obtained lists of all non-English speaking workers at the sugar refineries and the Waring Hat Manufacturing plant. Kellor's understanding that the employer occupied a uniquely powerful position in respect to immigrant laborers appears to have been understood by the Yonkers Americanizers as well. The Chamber's Americanization Committee offered "its large amount of data . . . [to] any agency that desires to use it in connection with the Americanization problem," and promoted English language classes in the factories themselves.[131]

At a meeting called by Mayor Wallin in September, a National Americanization Committee spokesman urged Yonkers officials and organizations to make use of federal government resources for Americanization.[132] After the Armistice a local council on Americanizing began work with the Federal Bureau of Labor and Employment, stating its rationale directly: "In a city where 65 percent of the population are foreigners, it is essential that the American population should take the necessary steps toward homogeneity."[133]

Americanization activities of national organizations and the federal government complemented the State program, which was stepped up after the entry into the war. The New York State Industrial Commission's Bureau of Industries and Immigration initiated "an intensive campaign among the alien residents of New York State"

> to enlighten them as to their status in the war crisis and also to allay any possible feeling of unrest that might have been aroused by irresponsible and reckless agitators.[134]

The Bureau used mass meetings at factories where immigrant workers predominated and reported "a better feeling among the foreign born employees" where such meetings were held.

The State Bureau of Industries and Immigration also expanded its "alien industrial education" program with the appointment of Winthrop Talbot to "consult with employers with regard to installing classes in English in their factories and industrial plants."[135] Both the medium of Americanism—nationally, or at least extra-locally coordinated organizations—and its message—nationalist assimilation—contributed to the demise of Yonkers localism, whose material base had already disappeared.

During the war, then, the ideology of localism apparently received a death blow both from material forces stemming from wartime production demands and from concerted ideological assaults which aimed at establishing the primacy of nationalism. How successful were the reformers who pushed for state administration to bring order to a labor market no longer moderated by localism? In the last chapter we traced developments at the state and national levels. Here we look at Yonkers itself.

The foundations of industrial coordination had seemingly been laid before U.S. entry into the war with the Mayor Lennon's appointment of an all-male local War Advisory Committee which included ex-mayors, bankers, newspaper publishers and factory-owners. Alexander Smith Cochran headed the Committee, which also included mining magnate William Boyce Thompson, A.B. Waring, Louis Spreckels, and Edward Fitch (of Otis). The committee would mainly be concerned, Mayor Lennon stated, with "organizing the available quota to furnish towards the military and naval forces of the country" and supplying "the necessary equipment."[136] But this committee actually did nothing to coordinate the local labor market. More than a year later, in the summer of 1918, Mayor Wallin made the first efforts. When the Compulsory Labor Act was announced, he forwarded a request to the State Industrial Commission (in the process of being absorbed by the U.S.E.S.) to establish a branch of the employment bureau in Yonkers to help with the distribution of labor.[137] The *Herald* expressed support for efforts to coordinate the labor market, accepting the arguments of Frankfurter, Seager and Barnes.

> **such action by the government was necessitated by the fact that the chaos that exists at present in labor circles had a detrimental effect upon the progress of war work in this country. The workers [were] lured from plant to plant by an almost universal practice of labor stealing and poaching.[138]**

The report concluded, like Barnes, that the apparent labor shortage was actually a consequence of the "pirating" of unskilled labor.[139]

On August 1, when the system was supposed to begin operation, there was no Community War Labor Board for the Westchester-Dutchess-Putnam Counties district (in which Yonkers was the largest city.) The sole public mechanism for the coordination of labor was the Public Labor Employment Bureau branch (requested by Wallin in June) staffed by one person, Louis Mittler, in a City Hall office.[140] Five days later, employers in the district met to choose their representative to the Board, finally settling on Frank M. Ward, superintendent of the Yonkers Otis works under Edward Fitch.[141] After another week, the Yonkers Federation of Labor chose William McGeory as the labor representative and not until the end of the month did the Board receive its full complement of members with Henry Sayer's appointment of Yonkers contractor George T. Kelly.[142] Yonkers citizens thus dominated the Westchester-Dutchess-Putnam Counties Community Labor Board.

With the end of the war in sight, in mid-October, the local office was just getting under way. Yet assessments of its activities were not strictly bound by the purposes of the war. As the *Herald* reported, "this branch of the Government Service is becoming very important inasmuch as it will have entire control of the employing of all labor skilled and unskilled, mechanical, professional and clerical, etc. . . ."[143] Local residents were already anticipating the labor market disruption which would accompany the return of the troops and cessation of war contracts.

While the administrative apparatus for coordinating labor for the pursuit of war ends grew haltingly, the welfare of those spinning in the gears of a frenzied wartime labor machine was left to voluntary organizations. Women's organizations took on some of the tasks. The Y.W.C.A., for example organized an exchange to direct wives of enlisted men towards paid employment.[144]

Despite a tight labor market, the Charity Organization Society felt continued demands, noting the "greatly increased cost of living" and the temporary periods of unemployment caused by "adjustments which have been made in certain industries in Yonkers."[145] With war-related fundraising occupying centerstage, organizations like the C.O.S. were pushed to the side and found it as difficult as ever to meet expenses. In summer 1918, Burritt wrote to William Boyce Thompson the Society was "confronted with a considerable deficit and without resources to complete the year's work. . . ."[146]

The war exacerbated problems not only of finance, but also of identity for the C.O.S. Mary Van Hook's repeated failures to unite the social agencies of Yonkers under the C.O.S. reflected the predicament of other local Charity Organization Societies. In a memo to members of the executive committee of the American Association for Organizing Charity (a simplification in name of the American Association of Societies for Organizing Charity) General Secretary Francis McLean wrote that he wished to "withdraw us from any false positions we may be occupying as sole community organizers, positions already heavily assailed and justly so."[147]

> I cannot see but that community organization in the social field is now no more an exclusive possession of our societies than it is of other agencies . . . we will no longer assume to be the organizer of all movements, the coordinator of all activities.[148]

He surmised that organization and coordination would take place at a faster pace because of the war and local Councils of Defense, but that Charity Organization Societies could no longer hope to fulfill this role.

What remained, then, as a special task for the C.O.S., in a field where numerous other social service groups distinguished themselves either by their target populations (such as child welfare) or by problem (such as tuberculosis)? McLean suggested that work with families be made the centerpiece of C.O.S. activity, that "especially in the smaller city societies . . . disorganized family life is really becoming more and more the working basis of our day to day activities."[149]

Well before the war, national conferences, organizations, publications and foundations provided a well-developed network for disseminating new ideas about poverty and unemployment. Urban centers, of which New York City was probably the most important, provided modal points for these networks. Besides being the locus of the Russell Sage Foundation, the New York School of Philanthropy, the American Association of Societies for Organizing Charity, and the

Survey, New York City also had during the depression of 1914–15, as we have seen in Chapter 4, a reform administration ready to support and experiment with the new ideas.

But the ideas quickly spread from New York City to smaller locations such as Yonkers. The speed of their spread after 1914 came in part because of what was happening to the local social structure in smaller cities. The unified leadership which had taken on local philanthropy as a major project in the late nineteenth century was cracking or disintegrated. The new middle-class social workers and charity organization workers might look to the remnants of the local factory owners for contributions from time to time. But the elites were neither unified enough nor interested enough to provide the ongoing source of legitimacy and authority needed by the voluntary agencies to initiate and sustain the large community projects which they felt were needed. So their directors—like Mary Jolly Van Hook—were driven to their colleagues in the metropolitan centers, and men and women like Francis McLean, Edward Devine, Mary Richmond, and Fred Hall had direct channels of influence in the smaller local centers.

Metropolitan reformers offered, in turn, an alternative to the reliance on localism for problems of unemployment and poverty. In these years marked by dramatic economic reversals, as local citizens became increasingly aware of their vulnerability to national and international political economic trends, such solutions to labor problems became increasingly attractive. But replacing the idea of localism with the idea of administratively managed labor markets was apparently easier than actually creating the necessary administrative mechanism. In spite of all the forces working against localism, it would enjoy a resurgence after the war.

Notes

1. Charles F. Weller, "Permanent Values in War Camp Community Services," *Survey* 41, 10 (Dec. 7, 1918), 297. Weller worked with the War Department's Commission on Training Camp Activities.

2. Yonkers *Herald*, Sept. 8, 1914, 4.

3. The Yonkers *Statesman* published State Department of Labor figures, based on trade union unemployment in the State, showing higher unemployment (16.13%) in 1913 than any year since 1896, except for 1908 (22%). Yonkers *Statesman*, Jan. 2, 1914, 6.

These figures were subsequently criticized for their accuracy, but nevertheless provide a relative index of unemployment fluctuation.

4. Yonkers *Statesman*, Dec. 31, 1914, "Happenings of the Year," 1.

5. Yonkers *Herald*, Jan.23, 1914, 1.

6. Yonkers *Statesman*, Feb. 18, 1913, 2.

7. Yonkers *Statesman*, February 28, 1914, 4. The same kind of hiring was going on in New York City, where 50,000 cleared the streets. See the Yonkers *Statesman*, March 3, 1914, 1.

8. C.O.S. Board of Directors' Minutes, March 13, 1914, in Notebook, located in Box 2, Yonkers FSS papers.

9. Yonkers *Herald*, July 1, 1914, 1 and July 11, 1914, 1.

10. Yonkers *Herald*, July 16, 1914, 1.

11. Yonkers *Herald*, July 31, 1914, 1.

12. Immigration averaged more than one million people per year prior to 1914. See Maurine Weiner Greenwald, *Women, War and Work: the Impact of World War I on Women Workers in the United States* (Westport, CT: Greenwood Press, 1980), 15.

13. Yonkers *Herald*, July 31, 1914, 1; Aug. 1, 1914, 1

14. One and a half months later, it was still closed. *Yonkers Herald, July 31, 1914, 1* and Sept. 10, 1914, 4.

15. Yonkers *Herald*, Aug. 11, 1914, 4.

16. Yonkers *Herald*, Aug. 7, 1914, 1.

17. Yonkers *Herald*, Aug.6, 1914, 1; Yonkers *Statesman*, Aug.7, 1914, 4.

18. Yonkers *Statesman*, Aug. 13, 1914, 4.

19. Yonkers *Herald*, Aug. 22, 1914, 1; Yonkers *Statesman*, Nov. 5, 1914, 4. A 41 page, undated and unsigned "Report On Business Conditions Resulting from the War" based on research conducted by the National Civic Federation with a questionnaire dated October 20, 1914, notes: "Yonkers, with its textile industry has been considerably embarrassed by the shortage of materials and the carpet mills in that city are operating on half time only." Folder "Unemployment, 1914–1915," Box 181, CSS Papers.

20. Yonkers *Statesman*, Aug. 10, 1914, 1; Yonkers *Statesman*, Dec. 31, 1914, "Happenings of the Year," 1.

21. Yonkers *Statesman*, Dec. 31, 1914, "Happenings of the Year," 1.

22. From an A.I.C.P. study of the war's effects on employment in New York City, September, 1914, Folder 317–2, Box 47, CSS. Superintendent Kinzel was in charge of Otis' Eleventh Avenue and 26th St. shops. "Nearly half of our force of 125 are laid off while the other half are only working seven hours a day." This was probably the installation and maintenance crew.

23. Yonkers *Statesman*, Dec. 31, 1915, "Happenings of the Year," 1.

24. Yonkers *Statesman*, Sept. 11, 1915, 1; C.S. McClellan Jr. to Van Hook, Sept. 2, 1915, Correspondence, Box 4, Yonkers FSS Papers.

25. Yonkers *Statesman*, Dec. 31, 1914, 1.

26. Yonkers *Statesman*, Jan. 12, 1915, 4.

27. Yonkers *Statesman*, Jan. 16, 1915, 4.

28. Yonkers *Statesman*, Jan. 27, 1915, 4.

29. See e.g. Yonkers *Statesman*, April 8, 1914, 2; Yonkers *Statesman*, Oct. 5, 4.

30. Yonkers *Statesman*, Jan. 27, 1915, 4.

31. Frederic J. Haskin "Charity Gives Aid For the Idle," Chicago *News*, reprinted in the Yonkers *Statesman*, May 6, 1914, 2.

32. Yonkers *Statesman*, Jan. 13, 1915, 1

33. Frederic J. Haskin "Charity Gives Aid For the Idle," Chicago *News*, reprinted in the Yonkers *Statesman*, May 6, 1914, 2.

34. Yonkers *Statesman*, Jan. 13, 1915, 1.

35. Yonkers *Statesman*, Feb. 2, 1915, 1.

36. John A. Kingsbury, "Our Army of the Unemployed," *Review of Reviews* 49 (April, 1914) 433–439. Reprinted in Johnsen, 5–15.

37. Yonkers *Statesman*, April 17, 1914, 4.

38. Yonkers *Statesman*, Nov. 25, 1914, 4. See also Ida Tarbell, "The Golden Rule in Business" *American Magazine* 78 December, 1914, 24–29, reprinted in Johnsen, 16–25.

39. Yonkers *Statesman*, Jan. 12, 1915, 4.

40. See Chapter 2.

41. Draft of letter from Bailey B. Burritt to Alexander Cochrane [sic], May 4, 1915, Box 4, Yonkers FSS Papers.

42. Bailey B. Burritt to Alexander Cochrane [sic], May 4, 1915, Box 4, Yonkers FSS Papers.

43. Warren A. Kipp to Bailey B. Burritt, May 7, 1915, Box 4, Yonkers FSS Papers.

44. M.J. Van Hook to Mrs. Frederick G. Mahlmann, Jan. 26, 1915, Box 4, Yonkers FSS Papers. The initiative was based on the idea explained in Edward T. Devine, "The Confidential Exchange," *The Survey*, December 7, 1912.

45. See Rosalie Greenblat to M.J. Van Hook, Feb. 6, 1915, Box 4, Yonkers FSS Papers. No other record of a Social Service Exchange in these years has surfaced.

46. M.J. Van Hook to Fred S. Hall, July 22, 1915, Box 4, Yonkers FSS Papers.

47. M.J. Van Hook to Fred S. Hall, July 22, 1915, Box 4, Yonkers FSS Papers.

48. Joseph Beall to M.J. Van Hook, Nov. 23, 1915, Box 4, Yonkers FSS Papers.

49. E.T. Devine to M.J. Van Hook, Feb. 17, 1915, Box 4, Yonkers FSS Papers. The basis of Macy's influence in this case is hard to analyze, since he was at the same time an active member of the local social reform constituency and the national business elite. A resident of Westchester and recipient of a large inheritance, Macy managed his business interests while taking an active role in Westchester social reform. During the war he became President of the National Civic Federation (see Chapter 5.) "Macy: His Work," Yonkers *Statesman*, Oct. 20, 1922, 13.

50. M.J. Van Hook to M. Byington, Dec. 27, 1917, Box 4, Yonkers FSS Papers.

51. M.J. Van Hook to Fred Hall, Oct. 27, 1915, Box 4, Yonkers FSS Papers.

52. M.J. Van Hook to Fred Hall, Nov. 5, 1915, Box 4, Yonkers FSS Papers.

53. Fred Hall to M.J. Van Hook, Nov. 6, 1915, Box 4, Yonkers FSS Papers.

54. M.J. Van Hook to Fred Hall, Nov. 8, 1915, Box 4, Yonkers FSS Papers.

55. *The Social Service Bulletin* (Published by the Yonkers C.O.S.) 1,1 (1917), 4.

56. Bailey Burritt to C.N. Arbuckle, Nov. 24, 1913, Box 4, Yonkers FSS Papers.

57. B.B. Burritt to W.A. Kipp, Nov. 20, 1916, Box 4, Yonkers FSS Papers.

58. B.B. Burritt to W.A. Kipp, May 21, 1917, Box 4, Yonkers FSS Papers."Society Officers" Box 1, Yonkers FSS Papers; also "History of Yonkers COS, 1909–1919," compiled by M.J. Van Hook from Annual Reports, in Box 4, Yonkers FSS Papers.

59. F.H. McLean to B.B. Burritt, April 26, 1916, Box 4, Yonkers FSS Papers.

60. B.B. Burritt to F.H. McLean, April 29, 1916, Box 4, Yonkers FSS Papers.

61. M. Byington to M.J. Van Hook, March 19, 1917. Also see, e.g., F.H. McLean to B.B. Burritt, May 1, 1916; M. Byington to B.B. Burritt, June 2, 1916; T. Jacobson to M.J. Van Hook, July 17, 1916; F.H. McLean to M.J. Van Hook, June 25, 1918; all in Box 4, Yonkers FSS Papers.

62. See Chapter 5. On the State Employment Bureau, see also *Survey*, 33,8 (Nov. 21, 1914), 192. The first state office opened in January, 1915 and by the end of the year, there were branches in Albany, Brooklyn, Buffalo, Rochester, and Syracuse. New York State Industrial Commission, *Bulletin*, 1,3 (Dec., 1915), inside front cover. On the Distribution Branch as the origin of the U.S.E.S., see Darrell Hevenor Smith, *The United States Employment Service: Its History, Activities and Organization* (Baltimore: Johns Hopkins University Press, 1923), 1; Udo Sautter, "North American Government Labor Agencies Before World War One: A Cure for Unemployment?" *Labor History* 24, 3 (Summer, 1983), 385.

63. M.J. Van Hook to Department of Labor, June 29, 1915, Box 4, Yonkers FSS Papers.

64. M.J. Van Hook to U.S. Immigration Service, July 12, 1915, Box 4, Yonkers FSS Papers.

65. "Application for Employment, U.S. Department of Labor, Bureau of Immigration, Division of Information," in Box 4, Yonkers FSS Papers.

66. Immigration Service to Charity Organization Society, July 13, 1915, Box 4, Yonkers FSS Papers.

67. M.J. Van Hook to U.S. Immigration Service, July 12, 1915 and August 17, 1915, Box 4, Yonkers FSS Papers.

68. Howe to C.O.S., Yonkers, July 10, 1916, Box 4, Yonkers FSS Papers.

69. M.J. Van Hook to F. Howe, July 13, 1916, Box 4, Yonkers FSS Papers.

70. M.J. Van Hook to Waring Hat Company, Nov. 20, 1916; and "Application for Employees, U.S. Department of Labor Employment Service," filled out by Otis Elevator, Dec. 9, 1916, Box 4, Yonkers FSS Papers.

71. M.J. Van Hook to F. Howe, July 13, 1916, Box 4, Yonkers FSS Papers.

72. Warren Kipp wrote to the Editor of the Yonkers, "during the current year . . . there has been no unemployment situation." *Herald*, July 14, 1916, Box 4, Yonkers FSS Papers.

73. Two years earlier, Van Hook had written: "Several years ago my observation led me to conclude that a great deal of effort to rehabilitate impoverished families was wasted. That the steady improvement of health conditions, the continued elimination of causes for accident, and the decreasing opportunity for exploiting labor were not resulting in such rapid improvement of social conditions as we were justified in expecting. In a continuous search for underlying causes, I have repeatedly found the failure of a family to respond to improved conditions is due to their mental inability to realize the situation." M.J. Van Hook to J.J. Frawley, April 24, 1914, Box 4, Yonkers FSS Papers.

74. Yonkers C.O.S., "If I Refer A Family in Distress to the Charity Organization Society, What Happens?" pamphlet, n.d., 9, Box 4, Yonkers FSS Papers (located in 1918 correspondence.)

75. On wartime labor policies, see Bruce Bustard, "The Human Factor: Labor Administration and Industrial Manpower Mobilization During the First World War," PhD. Diss., University of Iowa, 1984.

76. Yonkers *Herald*, Oct. 22, 1917, 1.

77. Yonkers Honor Roll Committee, *Yonkers in the World War* (Norwood, MA: Plimpton Press, 1922), 63–65; Yonkers *Herald*, July 2, 1917, 1.

78. Yonkers *Herald*, Dec. 31, 1917.

79. Wilson to Mrs. George W. Bass, May 5, 1917, quoted in Kennedy, *Over Here: The First World War and American Society* (New York: Oxford University Press, 1980), 148.

80. Yonkers *Herald*, April 18, 1917, 1.

81. Yonkers Mayor's Honor Roll Committee, *Yonkers in the World War* (Norwood, MA: Plimpton Press, 1922), 30–32; On non-exemptions for Smith workers, see Yonkers *Herald*, Sept. 24, 1917, 1.

82. Kennedy, *Over Here*, 151.

83. *Yonkers in the World War*, 30.

84. Yonkers *Herald*, June 5, 1917, 1; June 6, 1917, 1.

85. Yonkers *Herald*, Aug. 4, 1917, 1; Aug. 16, 1917, 1.

86. Yonkers *Herald*, June 5, 1917, 1; *Yonkers in the World War*, 30–31.

87. Yonkers Mayor's Honor Roll Committee, *Yonkers in the World War*, (Norwood, MA: Plimpton Press, 1922), vi.

88. Yonkers *Herald*, June 9, 1917, 1; June 29, 1917, 1; *Yonkers in the World War*, 46.

89. *Yonkers in the World War*, 63–65.

90. Yonkers *Herald*, Feb. 25, 1.

91. By May, 1918, 12 or 13 teachers had resigned. Yonkers *Herald*, May 9, 1918; Yonkers *Herald*, Sept. 6, 1918, 1.

92. Yonkers *Herald*, Aug. 17, 1918, 1.

93. On turnover among women during the war, see Greenwald, 38.

94. In this regard, Yonkers conformed to the national pattern. 1917 saw a record number of strikes in the United States and the war caused a spectacular growth in A.F. of L. membership. During the course of the war, there were more than 6,000 strikes in the U.S.. Kennedy, *Over Here*, 258, 262; Greenwald, *Women, War and Work*, 39; Bustard, *The Human Factor* 71–72, 100, 132, 171–175..

95. Yonkers *Herald*, Dec. 31, 1917, 1.

96. Yonkers *Herald*, Feb. 25, 1918, 1. The August bonus was almost twice the sum of the next largest previous distribution. Yonkers *Herald*, Aug. 1, 1918, 1.

97. Yonkers *Herald*, Jan. 6, 1917, 1; March 2, 1917, 1, March 3, 1917, 1.

98. Yonkers *Herald*, March 2, 1917, 1.

99. Yonkers *Herald*, Sept. 28, 1918, 1.

100. Yonkers *Herald*, June 22, 1917, 1; July 2, 1917, 1; July 5, 1917, 1.

101. Yonkers *Herald*, Aug. 25, 1917, 1; Sept. 24, 1918, 1.

102. Another successful war-time strike involved 650 men in the building trades. Yonkers *Herald*, Apr. 1, 1918, 1; Apr. 10, 1918, 1.

103. Greenwald, 32, citing Paul H. Douglas, *Real Wages in the United States 1890–1926* (New York, 1930), 178.

104. David M. Kennedy, *Over Here: The First World War and American Society* (New York: Oxford University Press, 1980), 123–125.

105. The text of the U.S. Fuel Administration order to shut factories is printed in Yonkers *Herald*, Jan. 18, 1918, 4. On Garfield's approach to the crisis, see Robert Cuff, "Harry Garfield, the Fuel Administration, and the Search for a Cooperative Order During World War I," *American Quarterly*, 30, 1 (Spring, 1978), 39–53.

106. Yonkers *Herald*, Jan. 18, 1918, 4

107. Yonkers *Herald*, Jan 28, 1918, 4.

108. Yonkers *Herald*, Jan. 18, 1918, 1; Jan. 19, 1918, 1.

109. Yonkers *Herald*, Feb. 8, 1; Feb. 11, 1.

110. Secretary of the Treasury William Gibbs McAdoo encouraged these campaigns linking loyalty to the purchase of Liberty Bonds. For the effects on the nation, see David M. Kennedy, *Over Here*, 105–106.

111. Although he took no part in the ceremonies, Alexander Smith Cochran did send $25,000 to the fund drive in Yonkers. $137,000 was raised altogether, with thousand dollar contributions from W.B. Thompson, the National Sugar Refinery and two thousand from John Andrus. Yonkers *Herald*, Mar. 25, 1918, 1; Mar. 26, 1918, 1.

112. Yonkers *Herald*, Apr. 23, 1918, 1; May 2, 1918, 4.

113. Yonkers *Herald*, April 26, 1918, 1.

114. Yonkers *Herald*, May 2, 1918, 1.

115. Yonkers *Herald*, May 18, 1918, 1; May 20, 1918, 1.

116. Kennedy, *Over Here*, 70.

117. Greenwald, *Women, War and Work*, 32–35; Kennedy, *Over Here*, 59–75.

118. Mock and Larson, *Works That Won the War*, 190–191, quoted in Kennedy, 72. In Gompers' own version of the formation of the AALD, the idea initiated with himself. Nevertheless, "as of course, was necessary under war emergencies, I first submitted this proposition to the Advisory Commission and Council of National Defense and to George Creel. . . . The plan was approved. Samuel Gompers, *Seventy Years of Life and Labor* (New York: E. P. Dutton, 1925), II, 381.

119. Yonkers *Herald*, April 6, 1917, 1.

120. Yonkers *Herald*, June 30, 1917, 1. A walkout by machinists demanding a 48 hour week and 15 to 25% pay raise soon spread to 2,500 of the workers, though those in the ammunition division stayed on the job.Yonkers *Herald*, July 7, 1917, 1; July 11, 1917, 1. Secretary of War Baker fueled just such local fears when he called for increased industrial vigilance among Home Guards: "the greatest danger is from within the plants." Yonkers *Herald*, Feb. 28, 1918, 4.

121. Kennedy, 67–68.

122. These events occurred on Feb. 14, Feb. 6, and Mar.10, 1917, respectively. Yonkers Mayor's Honor Roll Committee, *Yonkers in the World War*, (Norwood, MA: Plimpton Press, 1922), 69.

123. Yonkers *Herald*, June 20, 1918, 1.

124. Yonkers *Herald*, April 30, 1918, 1.

125. Gerd Korman, *Industrialization, Immigrants and Americanizers: The View From Milwaukee, 1866–1921* (Madison: State Historical Society, 1967), 139.

126. Kennedy, *Over Here*, 67; Korman, *Industrialization, Immigrants and Americanizers*, 149–153. One of Korman's more interesting theses involves the attraction of the factory setting for social reformers, in part because of the potential of utilizing the coercive power wielded by employers. Korman, 10–11. On the employers' interest in Americanization, see "Big Business and the Alien," *Survey* 41, 19 (Feb. 22, 1919) 732.

127. Yonkers *Herald*, Feb. 9, 1918, 4.

128. Kennedy, *Over Here*, 67.

129. Yonkers *Statesman*, July 3, 1915, 4.

130. Yonkers *Herald*, June 15, 1918, 1; July 5, 1918, 1.

131. Yonkers Chamber of Commerce Annual Report, Mar. 1, 1917, typescript, 2; Minutes, Dec. 6, 1917, Yonkers Chamber of Commerce Papers.

132. Yonkers *Herald*, Sept. 28, 1918, 1.

133. Yonkers *Herald*, Feb. 14, 1919, 6.

134. N.Y. State Industrial Commission *Bulletin*, 2, 11 (Aug., 1917), 233.

135. N.Y. State Industrial Commission *Bulletin*, 2, 11 (Aug., 1917), 233. Talbot was the author of a "Handbook of Americanization," a "Bibliography of Helpful Relations Between Employer and Employee," and "Human Engineering," among other works. His subsequent Americanization debacle in Milwaukee is told in Korman, *Industrialization, Immigrants, and Americanizers*, 186–190. It is unclear from the New York State Industrial Commission *Bulletins* whether he had similar problems with the New York State mandate.

136. Yonkers *Herald*, March 26, 1917, 1.

137. Yonkers *Herald*, June 1, 1918, 4; June 29, 1918, 1.

138. Yonkers *Herald*, Aug. 1, 1918, 2.

139. Such thinking was the mirror image of the notion that employment bureaus would solve the problem of unemployment during a labor glut.

140. Yonkers *Herald*, Aug. 1, 1918, 2.

141. Yonkers *Herald*, Aug. 6, 1918, 1; Aug. 9, 1918, 1.

142. Yonkers *Herald*, Aug. 30, 1918, 1.

143. Yonkers *Herald*, Oct. 19, 1918, 4.

144. Yonkers Mayors' Committee, *Yonkers in the World War*, 49.

145. W. Kipp to B. Burritt "Draft of A Possible Letter to the *Statesman*," Dec. 14, 1917, Box 4, Yonkers FSS Papers. Barnes noted the problem of state-wide unemployment in January and February, 1918, largely as a result of the factory closures resulting from lack of fuel. N.Y. State Industrial Commission, *Industrial Bulletin* 3, 5, (Feb. 1918), frontispiece.

146. B. Burritt to W. B. Thompson, June 18, 1918, Box 4, Yonkers FSS Papers.

147. F.H. McLean, "Enlarged Future Program of Our Movement and Name of the Association," May 14, 1918, 3 in Box 4, Yonkers FSS Papers.

148. F.H. McLean, "Enlarged Future Program of Our Movement and Name of the Association," May 14, 1918, 1 in Box 4, Yonkers FSS Papers.

149. F.H. McLean, "Enlarged Future Program of Our Movement and Name of the Association," May 14, 1918, 1,2 in Box 4, Yonkers FSS Papers.

7

The Aftermath of War: Prevention of Unemployment as Patriotic Duty

Even before the Armistice, proponents of two competing visions of post-war reconstruction vied with each other. On one hand were those who sought rapid dismantling of wartime administrative institutions in an attempt to reconstruct the *status quo ante*. While wartime constraints had been necessary, they argued, American prosperity would reach full bloom only with a minimum of government intervention and regulation. Frank A. Vanderlip of the National City Bank articulated this point of view at the Conference of the Academy of Political Science on Labor Reconstruction in December, 1918:

> . . . we must now return to our former individualism. For my part I hope that return will be prompt and complete. The sooner we return to the old order the sooner the restrictions are removed, the sooner we will be prepared to start on what will be a long, hard race.[1]

The opposing view sought to consolidate the apparent wartime gains in centralized administrative direction and regulation which had been urged by Progressives in the pre-war years. At the same time, it sought to rejuvenate American democracy by channeling the wartime social involvement of a mobilized citizenry into permanent institutional forms. Proponents of this view often invoked the threat of potentially explosive social and political problems in the absence of such institutions. John Willis Slaughter offered a succinct version of this perspective in his January, 1919 appeal to the Rockefeller Foundation for funding to help extend the life of the Community Councils of National Defense as permanent institutions:

> A period of profound unrest is doubtedly [sic] approaching, a reflection of European movements that see all of life in terms of the class war and have a tendency to mob action of a violent type. There is reason to believe that

> Community Council organization will diminish these tendencies and render them devoid of danger by establishing the hold upon each citizen of a community organization of which he is thus made a conscious part; by bringing to bear through channels of established availability the best leadership; by supplementing the work of the United States Employment Service in a way to make the census of opportunities of employment systematic and continuous for the whole city; by helping to settle minor labor disputes and by helping to find homes for workers; by providing a medium of discussion and "letting off steam," thus avoiding spasmodic mob action, and by concerted efforts to maintain the people's morale.[2]

Employment problems and unemployment remained at the center of these debates.[3]

On the day that the Armistice was confirmed to the public in New York City, the staff of the *Survey* convened a conference of thirty-five to forty executives of nationally based social agencies to plan their strategies for the coming demobilization and reconstruction. As Progressive proponents of the second view outlined above, their discussions revolved around preventing social disruption from the rapid demobilization of war industries and troops, but even more centrally, around the consolidation of what they saw as political and administrative progress achieved during the war. "How," asked Paul Kellogg, "was the fresh interest and patriotic activity . . . of unnumbered laymen to be permanently enlisted in the public service?" Julia Lathrop, president of the National Conference of Social Work, singled out the United States Employment Service from all the war-time administrative innovations as an institution which "should grow to be a strong, constructive force—a sort of shock absorber for problems of industrial employment."[4]

The *Survey* conference empowered the chair to appoint a planning committee to organize a larger meeting of national executives to consider with more planning the problems of demobilization. The resulting Conference on Demobilization and the Responsibilities of Organized Social Agencies met in New York on November 29 and 30. Of several conferences on demobilization which took place at this time, none attracted figures more central to the planning of post-war labor policies.[5] Frank Walsh, co-chair of the National War Labor Board, Felix Frankfurter, chairman of the War Labor Policies Board, and Henry Bruere, who had replaced Henry Sayer as U.S.E.S. Director of Labor for New York State addressed the participants.[6]

Within the W.L.P.B., economist Walton H. Hamilton had been working on reconstruction labor plans with three colleagues. At the conference, he presented the results of what Bruce Bustard considers "the government's most significant investigations into labor questions."[7] He listed the dangers of a glut in the labor market which would follow a poorly planned demobilization. Laborers would be forced "by unemployment and starvation to bid against each other" lowering standards of living and working conditions. Lower wages would mean lowered family standards, including "a decrease in health and physical efficiency" and "denial to children of opportunities for education and development." The labor market glut and resulting unemployment and lower wages would take away workers' purchasing power, and, he argued, "if the buying power of laborers . . . is seriously impaired, the profits of employers are seriously threatened," posing "a serious threat to the maintenance of production" and possibly a depression. Finally, he warned of "serious industrial disturbances" including strikes and industrial wars of men with "knowledge of military tactics and who have been taught to kill."[8]

To avoid a labor glut Hamilton advocated, in addition to a well-planned demobilization, government policies which would help to stimulate the expansion of industry and thus the demand for labor (including government measures to reduce capital investment risk), and a program of public works tailored to provide "buffer employment" during the period of adjustment. He presented an elaborate "demobilization chart" to illustrate the flow of workers into the labor market and into industry. He wanted "a well-thought out and consistent policy," warning that "a timid, hesitating policy of control will merely muddle" the situation.[9]

Organized labor spoke in very similar terms about the problems and the promise of the future. At the Senate Committee on Education and Labor's hearings on labor and reconstruction, Samuel Gompers testified, "the people will not again stand for a condition as there was in 1893."[10] The New York State Federation of Labor noted the "enormous dislocation of occupations" involved in engaging in war and warned of "an aftermath of social peril that can be averted only by meeting the . . . peace problems in the same big, provident American way that conquered the sudden and huge problems of war."[11]

The Federation's "program of reconstruction" emphasized the problem of employment. "We know that there is plenty and more than plenty of work for all. The flaw is in its distribution." The Federation called for an improved state employment service with federal aid "on a permanent and adequate basis and supplied with a revolving fund to provide transportation for workers directed to distant jobs." The program also called both for minimum wage levels "based upon family and not upon individual standards," and for "equal pay . . . [for] men and women who perform equivalent work."[12]

When Bruere explained the problems of demobilization in New York, the lack of administrative direction became clear. It affected both war industry workers and returning soldiers and sailors. Bruere despaired that demobilization of war industries was "guided almost entirely by the exigencies of the actual economic situation" and was taking place "without any concerted action between government and industry."[13] Despite Barnes' earlier efforts within Greater New York, projected "clearinghouse" mechanisms of the U.S.E.S. were almost non-existent. In their absence, officials at the New York state level of the U.S. Employment Service called a meeting in Rochester to confer with representatives from private industry. They called for more advance warning of cancellation of war contracts and "more consideration of labor problems in this stoppage of the war industries." Bruere noted that major disaster had been avoided only because the war industries had not been "dismantled so rapidly as yet as to bring about a serious congestion of the labor market."[14]

The U.S.E.S. did promise to notify local representatives "at the earliest possible moment" of cancellations of war contracts at plants in their vicinity. Further, it instructed the representatives to obtain personal information from workers at those plants, to contact the local Chambers of Commerce about prospective jobs, and to "avoid sensational stories of immediate discharges through the local press."[15] But Bruere conceded (in the form of praise for local officials) that interaction between the national authority and the local employment service rested "almost entirely on local initiative and capacity."[16]

If the mechanisms for coordinating demobilization of war industries were weak, those for the demobilization of the army were practically non-existent. Despite Frankfurter's urging, demobilization was proceeding by military units, and not in terms of industrial needs. Bruere found it impossible to devise a centrally directed plan for absorbing discharged soldiers into "civil pursuits" as long as whole military units were being disbanded simultaneously.[17]

The U.S. Employment Service itself now emphasized the importance of local activities in placing returning soldiers. The chairman urged state directors of the Service to "impress and impose the task of finding occupations as a 'community responsibility.'" According to Graham Taylor, the U.S.E.S. officials "seemed silently to concede that their 840 employment offices and their 1,600 community labor boards are not of themselves adequate to cope with [the problem.]" The possibility of enlisting local draft boards to help relocate the men under their jurisdiction had been rejected by the general staff of the army. Alternatively, voluntary groups at the local level, including personnel from the disbanded draft boards and local defense councils, sought jobs for discharged men.[18]

In the face of the weak mechanisms for broad coordination of the national labor market, Bruere's strategy in New York State conformed to the U.S.E.S. policy of building up local voluntary resources for job-finding. In New York City, he convened representatives of welfare organizations in a "United Council" for re-employment. (See below.) Further, he initiated a city-wide advertising campaign "to mobilize sentiment behind a practical plan for finding a job for every mustered-out man." Only in the beginning of December did he begin to have the constituents of a Community War Labor Board, the critical local unit of the U.S.E.S. This structure, consisting of the Presidents of the Merchants' Association and the Brooklyn and New York Chambers of Commerce "with an equal number of workers" soon gave way to an organization completely dominated by employers.[19]

Weak administrative structures, lack of cooperation between the Department of Labor and the army, and continuing reliance on exhortation and voluntarism did not produce the political crisis in the months after the armistice which some of the planners predicted. While there was undoubtedly significant unemployment among discharged soldiers, the situation was made less explosive by delays in the transatlantic return of men from Europe. When the U.S.E.S. reported rapidly increasing unemployment in January and February, the Department of War allowed men who were out of work to delay their discharges until they found jobs.[20]

But Progressives, eager to consolidate what they saw as war-time gains in centralized administrative planning of social and industrial policy, eagerly pointed out programs which they could claim as successes, in the hopes that they might be sustained as permanent features of the post-war social landscape. We should understand Bruere's assessment to Frankfurter in this light. In spite of the administrative problems in New York, Bruere reported optimistically,

"Our internal organization is gradually getting into better condition, and in a week or two we shall be riding along smoothly to whatever ultimate destiny is in store for the Employment Service." He concluded:

> It will be many months before the personnel and program of the Service are satisfactorily adjusted to the opportunities before it, and before the workers and employers acquire the habit of adequately utilizing the Service, but I believe we are headed in the right direction. . . .[21]

Others were more glowing: Assistant Director-General Nathan S. Smyth of the U.S.E.S. stated at the American Academy of Political Science Conference on "Labor Reconstruction" early in December that "the Employment Service is now so thoroughly organized and has the backing of the government to such an extent" that he felt "very optimistic" about the future. He noted the cooperation of the War Department and of 80,000 local councils of defense "which have been instructed to cooperate with the Employment Service in organizing central bureaus for returning soldiers."[22]

The U.S. Employment Service's own publicity organ, not surprisingly, portrayed the agency as a major success. It claimed that its Bureaus for Returning Soldiers, Sailors and War Workers in every city and town in the United States would "unify all national and community efforts." In fact coordination was minimal, and the same *Bulletin* offered the rationale: "Since most soldiers are expected to go to their home communities—and should be encouraged to do so—the task of aiding them in finding work is primarily a community responsibility, and the local bureaus enable its discharge."[23] Basically the local bureaus were expected to coordinate any local agencies dealing with the employment problem, so that there would not be overlap. Local employers, urged the *Bulletin*, "should be urged as a patriotic duty to register their opportunities for employment at the central bureau. . . ."[24]

But as the U.S.E.S. was delivering these promising statements about itself, Wilson was dealing with the consequences of a Republican Congressional victory in the November, 1918 elections. He was now reluctant to entrust comprehensive planning for reconstruction to an independent Reconstruction Commission for fear that it would be subject to the direction of the new Congress. For their part, Republicans were eager to see the quickest possible dismantling of the wartime bodies and the resumption of business-as-usual. Nor, in particular, did they welcome an expanded role for the state in labor market administration.[25]

In March, the Republican Congress cut off funding for the United States Employment Service on the grounds that the service was a wartime emergency measure, without legal authority for operating after the war was over.[26] Wilson, controlling some discretionary funds sufficient to maintain a vastly scaled down service, wrote, ". . . to my great grief I see no escape from disbandment. I hope that it will be possible to keep a skeleton organization." Fifty-six offices remained after the reorganization. Progressives, unhappy at the disbanding of the federal service, looked to voluntary organizations and state governments to step in to help with the distribution of labor. The *Survey* opined, "States and cities and private organizations, it is quite conceivable, may resume responsibility for bureaus which have been taken over by the United States Employment Service during the last year or so, or may assume it for new bureaus which have become indispensable."[27]

In fact, other organizations did spring into the void, but the potential of their work was quite different from the potential of a nationally coordinated and funded service. They had to rely chiefly on public opinion for their efficacy, and in the absence of national coordinating machinery, their approach was both localist and voluntarist. The Council of National Defense formed an Emergency Committee under the direction of Arthur Woods (as Assistant Secretary of War) to locate employment for returning soldiers and sailors. Woods' operation, which continued until mid–1920, became the Service and Information Branch of the War Plans Division of the Department of War.[28] At Woods' request, the United States Chamber of Commerce recommended that "local commercial bodies either establish soldier placement divisions or lend definite cooperation and assistance to any existing agencies as are found to be able to handle the situation." The Chamber noted that the action came in the wake of the "crippling" of the Employment Service of the United States Department of Labor.[29]

The U.S. Chamber outlined the principles to be followed by the local Chambers: "Proper distribution demands that first and foremost every community should care for its own." "'Local jobs for local men,'" its press release stated, "should be the slogan used with and by the employers." It called upon "public opinion of the business men of that community" to force reluctant employers to rehire returning servicemen. In the event of delays in rehiring, business men were urged to help with the provision for the "immediate needs" of the unemployed, not only out of patriotism, but also "so that the returned soldier shall feel friendly to the business element." Employer initiative, self-interest, and localism were thus the cornerstones of the U.S. Chamber of Commerce policies.[30]

The dismantling of the U.S.E.S. had a ripple effect at the state level. But the Democratic administration of recently elected Alfred E. Smith controlled New York State politics and offered some contrast to the federal situation. Smith recruited Abraham Elkus (of the Factory Investigating Commission) to be chairman of a State Reconstruction Commission packed with Progressive volunteers.[31] The Commission submitted a report on "A Permanent Unemployment Program," in June, 1919.[32] Recalling the conclusions of the Wainwright Commission, the new report put the administrative distribution of labor through a well-funded Employment Bureau at the top of its list of recommendations.[33]

Smith also appointed reformer Frances Perkins to the five member New York State Industrial Commission. Perkins' background as secretary of the National Consumers' League, secretary of the Committee on Safety organized after the Triangle Waist Company fire, and Director of Inspections of the New York Factory Investigating Commission sparked opposition from state employers' groups who lobbied unsuccessfully against her confirmation by the Republican-dominated state Senate.[34] Perkins replaced the retiring Louis Wiard, an active member of the Associated Merchants and Manufacturers of New York, and thus significantly altered the political balance on the Commission.[35] According to Perkins, Smith appointed her because the Industrial Commission was "in a terrible condition. . . . We've got to make it over," he told her, "we've got to turn it inside out and get it to be a good department."[36] She agreed that the Commission was totally disorganized. She recalled later that it "hardly functioned at all, except that it put a rubber stamp on certain workmen's compensation settlements."[37] With her history of Progressive social activism, Perkins felt herself as an anomaly on the Commission. But Smith reassured her that social workers would have to take an active role in government "if you girls are going to get what you want through legislation."[38]

Industrial safety was Perkins' chief area of experience and interest. But her high valuation of the potential of enlightened employment practices supplemented and stimulated by protective legislation, provided her with a perspective from which to view the problem of unemployment and labor market management.[39] She placed her hopes on enlightened employers who would reduce unnecessary turnover, on a placement bureau which had the mechanism to forecast fluctuations in the demand for labor, and on vocational training for both children and adults.[40] In spite of the opposition of the organized employers, Perkins claimed not to "represent any class or group of interests." She claimed to come to the Commission with a

> disinterested desire to modify industrial conditions in such a way as to meet the changing needs of a great industrial community of a great industrial State, where even people who are not directly members of the employing class or of the employee class are nevertheless dependent upon healthy industry and satisfied labor for their own peace and prosperity.[41]

While the U.S.E.S. shrivelled, the New York State Employment Bureau expanded dramatically. Localism and voluntarism—often substitutes for centralized state administration—continued to be vitally important in New York State efforts. But there were also successes in the centralized administration of New York's labor market.

During the war, the U.S.E.S. had taken over the offices of the New York State Employment Bureau. When the funding cut-off forced their closure on March 22 Governor Smith requested and received an emergency appropriation of $50,000 to keep the offices open until June 30. Smith's message, quoting directly from his Reconstruction Commission's preliminary report, noted that the displacement of civilians was "assuming serious proportions," and that the "prevailing atmosphere of social unrest" was giving "the current unemployment problem a significance even more serious than it would ordinarily possess."[42] The U.S.E.S. offices in New York City remained open, while the State opened offices in Binghamton, Elmira, Schenectady, Utica, Watertown, Jamestown, Yonkers and Newburgh.[43]

Immediately following the armistice, the State Employment Bureau, functioning within the U.S.E.S., had acted largely in the spirit of the directives from Woods and the U.S. Chamber, i.e., putting a premium on localism and cooperation with voluntary agencies. Upstate, it helped to organize local reemployment committees with chambers of commerce and local welfare organizations. In Greater New York City, as we have seen, Bruere had enlisted the State Employment Bureau in a United Council for Reemployment, which included representatives from the

U.S.E.S. and the large welfare organizations such as the War Camp Community Service, the Y.M. and Y.W.C.A., the Red Cross, and the Jewish Welfare Board.[44]

In Greater New York where the United Council concentrated its work, the large employers of the Merchants' Association also responded to the calls from Woods and the U.S. Chamber to take the initiative.[45] The Merchants' Association helped to form an Employers' Council for Soldier Re-Employment, consisting of eighty of the most important employers' associations in the City. This organization then swallowed the United Council to form the new Re-Employment Committee of New York City for Soldiers, Sailors and Marines, the manager of which was the Executive Secretary of the Merchants' Association. Its Re-Employment Bureau began work on April 24, 1919.[46]

By that date, employment in the state had reached its lowest point since the end of the war and there were still no signs of industrial expansion. By summer, however, factories were actively hiring and continued to expand their workforces at a rapid rate until Spring, 1920.[47] At the same time, the Legislature put the State Employment Bureau on a permanent basis with a $275,000 appropriation, making possible several new offices upstate and in New York City.[48] Reports of the Industrial Commission for 1919 and 1920 documented the dramatic growth in the services of the Employment Bureau. In November, 1919, mechanisms for coordination of the labor market throughout the state were put in place, with a weekly "clearance" bulletin, through which each local office circulated its specific labor shortages and surpluses to all the others.[49] With increased demand for labor and increased funding for the State labor bureau, it seemed in 1919 as though the goal of coordinated administrative distribution of labor might at least reach fruition at the State, if not at the federal level. In the judgment of Smith's Reconstruction Commission, the State Employment Bureau had been placed "for the first time upon a basis in some degree commensurate with the size of the problem to be solved."[50]

But as the labor distribution machinery took shape, we gain an opportunity to see more clearly what was involved. In his July, 1919 report to the Industrial Commission, Employment Bureau Director David S. Flynn denied that there ever was a post-war unemployment problem.

> **We could not agree with the repeated [theories, prognostications and guesses of those in the United Council] that there was a serious condition of unemployment in the State and careful investigation in all the industrial communities of the State confirmed this opinion.[51]**

Figures collected from the employment offices around the State from December, 1918 to June 1919 appeared to support Flynn's judgment. A total of 83,493 workers sought employment in the offices, while employers came to the Bureau with 105,780 job openings. Furthermore, conditions varied to such an extent that the number of job openings at some offices was more than double the number of job applicants.[52] Because we know that soldiers were being demobilized during precisely these months, that the war industry contracts were being terminated and workers laid off, and that employment in New York State factories dropped precipitously in January and February and did not start to rise again until June, these numbers pose a historical problem.[53]

In July, 1919 Commissioner Henry D. Sayer, who oversaw the Employment Bureau stated that in his opinion, while there was "no acute problem of unemployment at this time," there was a constant problem of distribution of workers. He anticipated, moreover, an "acute shortage of labor within the next few months."[54] Although less dramatic than those for the first seven months of Bureau operation, figures published for July, 1919 through June, 1920 seem again to substantiate Sayer's judgment, with 300,572 jobless workers against 332,147 open jobs.[55]

There was a discrepancy, then, between widespread expression of fear of discontent and revolutionary activity from unemployed veterans and war industry workers on the one hand, and the apparent oversupply of jobs on the other. If "distribution" *was* the problem, then a central theme of the Devine-Seager-Leiserson formulation would be vindicated. A closer examination of Flynn's analysis gives us a more accurate picture of what was going on. In his July 1920 report, Flynn noted the changes which had occurred since the war.

> **The necessity which led employers, during the war period, to accept with forbearance the partly trained stenographer and clerk, largely disappeared during the past year, and applications for help were coupled with refusals to consider any but competent workers. On the other hand, the partly trained worker, only with reluctance, would consider employment corresponding to their experience, and, as a result, large numbers of such applicants suffered long periods of unemployment.[56]**

Just as wartime clerical workers resisted downgrading in a slack postwar labor market, so too were unskilled construction and building laborers unwilling to "accept the conditions met with on the farm as to hours and wages." "As a result," Flynn surmised, "a very great section of this class of labor became casual workers." Likewise, women who worked in the factories during the war, "having been drawn from domestic service, refused absolutely to consider this occupation."[57] As a result, substantially less than two-thirds of the job openings reported to the Bureau were actually filled.[58]

The Bureau operated with a language which seemed to make "workers seeking employment" functionally equivalent to "workers called for by employers," as in this message from David Flynn:

> There is a direct advantage to a man when he is placed again upon a payroll and there is direct advantage to the employer when his production is continued or augmented by the addition of an efficient worker. There is direct advantage to the State in that the spectre of unemployment is laid and the concomitant evils of unrest, poverty, hunger, illness and disease are removed.[59]

But the market in labor never really functioned with such balance. Nor, in fact, did the New York State Employment Bureau. As the institutional expression of Leiserson's theories, it existed to organize and distribute labor to meet the needs of capital, and not vice versa. When workers' aspirations outpaced the slots made available by employers, officials at the Bureau worked hard to demonstrate to them the "realities" of the market. And though Flynn had trouble with the women workers, who "resisted more firmly than did the men, the altered conditions," he ended with optimism, noting that workers were adjusting their expectations: "reconciliation to the changed conditions became more general toward the end of the year."[60]

The Progressive promise, such as it was, of well-funded state machinery for stabilized industrial relations and the administrative distribution of labor were not to be realized, even in New York State. Employment dropped off precipitously during the late summer of 1920; Smith was defeated in the fall elections; and Perkins was not reappointed by Republican Governor Nathan Miller who entered office with a promise of retrenchment in government.[61]

A closer look at Yonkers during these years reveals continuing fear of unemployment among returning servicemen at least through the summer of 1919. While federal and state agencies were far less important in actually locating jobs for these men than were voluntary agencies operating in the city, they did nevertheless have a local impact as stimulants of the chorus of advertising and exhortation. The new campaign bore considerable relationship to the wartime message of sacrifice for the benefit of the nation, but went through three overlapping incarnations. At first, it aimed to deal with the problem of potential discontent among unemployed returning soldiers. Second, it was used to counter the renewed labor militancy which hit local industries in a wave of "strike fever" in the summer of 1919. Third, it took on a life of its own in the nationally orchestrated Red Scare later in the year and into 1920. Insuring employment for returning soldiers, dampening labor protest, and guarding against Bolshevism were thus three trajectories of a larger stabilization project which relied for the most part upon public opinion for its success.[62]

Almost immediately after the armistice the Yonkers Community War Labor Board received a telegram from Henry Bruere, Federal Director of Labor for New York State. "It is of the utmost importance," the telegram read, "that the transition from a war to a peace footing shall be effected as rapidly as this can be accomplished without serious detriment to the interests of employers and employes alike." The Board arranged for a meeting with the major Yonkers manufacturers who were urged, in addition, to send their labor requirements directly to the U.S. Employment Service so that the latter could begin the task of distributing returning labor.[63]

Celebrations for returning soldiers were laced with concerns about where these young men would find employment. Fear lurked around the edges of the concern: all acknowledged the "bitterness and discontent" which would follow the idleness of returned servicemen.[64] Local newspapers helped to put on the pressure for jobs for returning servicemen. "Are Men Returning From the Service Securing Their Former Positions?" asked a *Herald* editorial in January, 1919:

> Are former employers seeing to it that they do? . . . For one reason or another, none defensible, there are cases when the returned soldier is being turned down, turned away in fact. . . .[65]

The *Herald* noted the presence of employment offices "all over the country—one of them here," but felt that the pressure of public opinion should be mobilized to help guarantee job placements:

> . . . there should be some way of identifying those who spurn to do the right thing with their men. . . . A little publicity given the names of those who may be fretful about "disorganizing their present force" might be satisfactory. In any even the returning troops are more than entitled to full consideration.[66]

"Disorganizing their present force" referred, of course, to laying off the women hired when men were recruited into the armed forces.

The federal government aided directly in focusing the pressure of local public opinion. The newspapers ran full-page ads placed by the Department of War. In the center of the page was a message from Assistant Secretary of War Arthur Woods: "Our work of getting positions for discharged soldiers and sailors has gotten away to a good start . . .," it proclaimed, with seventy to eighty percent of the veterans having access to their old jobs. Woods promised recognition to employers who pledged re-employment of discharged servicemen, and the borders of the advertisement were lined with complying industries and retailers in Yonkers.[67] Elsewhere, Woods urged not only filling existing positions with veterans, but also an expansion of investment and employment in general, to "spruce up for reconstruction." He presented the argument that timely expansion—before prices for labor and materials rose further—made sense from a business standpoint.[68]

In March, 1919, Mayor Wallin travelled to Washington, D.C. to attend a conference on unemployment for mayors and governors. There he heard similar arguments from the Department of Labor, which urged immediate expenditure on public works and roads. But he returned to Yonkers with the report that because of the high cost of materials, states and cities were not undertaking new public projects. On this point he was probably wrong, but on the more general point, that the conference produced no concrete aid to cities and states, he was right.[69]

In contrast to the federal propaganda presence in Yonkers, federal help in administration of the local labor market was virtually non-existent. Even before the closure of the U.S. Employment Service office, its work was hardly significant; voluntary organizations shouldered most of the work. The local War Camp Community Service, a new organization with headquarters at the Hollywood Inn, attempted to register all returning soldiers and direct them towards jobs in the city. Originally, it was billed as operating in cooperation with the U.S.E.S.[70] But in fact, as the U.S. Employment Agency acknowledged, "practically all the cases of employing service men in Yonkers were . . . handled through War Camp Community Service."[71] Other voluntary organizations joined in the efforts. On May 4, churches staged an "Employment Sunday" when every congregation would "devote its energies to personal activity and influence on behalf of all the unemployed men from service."[72] The Y.M.C.A., whose rooms and hallways were filled with returning soldiers, hung out a red, white and blue sign on the front of its building promising "Three Months Complimentary Membership Including Employment Bureau Privileges."[73] On request of the U.S. Commissioner of Education, Saunders Trade School began a job-training program in which veterans were given instruction to "enable them to follow some definite vocation."[74]

In March, 1919, less than six months after it opened, the Yonkers Branch of the U.S.E.S., whose work had been cut back eighty percent, was threatened with closure because of the Congressional cutbacks. Interim financing for the Yonkers office was provided not by Smith's emergency state appropriation but by "a firm of New York bankers" in order to keep the office open until the next session of Congress.[75] A *Herald* editorial slammed the Congressional action, and noted that the Service would now have to operate out of 56 offices nationwide, rather than the earlier 750. It noted the still serious unemployment situation and the fact that the area of labor surplus appeared to be increasing.[76] On July 1, after less than a year of operation, the office at 10 Main Street closed, but Yonkers branch personnel were rehired for a reduced service run by the State Employment Bureau.[77]

Federal government efforts to deal with problems in the local labor markets continued to rely on voluntary organizations after the demand for labor started to increase in late 1919. Arthur Woods' Service and Information Branch sent Lieutenant Fred W. Caswell to Yonkers to help the American Red Cross set up a Service Men's Welfare Committee whose purpose was "to discourage the floater, who goes from one job to another, and to encourage men who do not want to remain in the city to go to their own homes and to permanent employment."[78]

Mobilization of public opinion through a massive propaganda campaign may have been necessary, in part, because of the inadequacy of more direct and substantial intervention in the employment crisis.[79] With little local emergency public works investment, and the weakening of the meagre wartime labor distribution mechanisms, the administration's post-war public opinion campaign was the centerpiece of its efforts to deal with the political threat of unemployed veterans.

On the basis of nationalist enthusiasms fanned during the war, it promoted the continued activities of voluntary organizations, the retirement of women workers from the wage labor force, and the hiring of veterans by private industry. But by the summer of 1919, as employment began to pick up, the political threat posed by unemployed veterans blended seamlessly into the threat of militant strike activity.

With the cost of living soaring and the demand for labor beginning to increase, the summer after the armistice brought chaos to industrial relations in Yonkers. The city whose workers had placidly accepted with thanks the factory-owners' paternalism before the war now erupted in a rash of strikes which included not only the traditional targets, but the largest factories as well. While their demands grew in part out of the necessity with keeping abreast of skyrocketing inflation, their tactics also reflected the complete breakdown of the localist ideology which had contributed to labor peace in the early years of the century. The breakdown occurred despite new raises and bonuses given by employers. By June, 1919, Smith, Waring, and Federal had all raised wages another ten percent.[80] When Smith distributed its semi-annual bonus that August, workers with as little as one year's experience found that they were included. For the first time, a majority of employees benefitted.[81] Smith also instituted an eight-hour day while assuring the public that the action was not a response to workers' demands.[82]

On top of its ten percent raise and its recently instituted wartime measures, Waring now announced its own bonus program on August 14. Unlike Smith, Waring gave five percent of the annual wage to the entire force of 1600 to 1800 workers.[83] But the bonus announcement came too late for Waring: United Hatters' Union organizers were meeting with considerable success in the Waring plants. The day before the announcement, a small number of strikers had already walked off the job demanding raises.[84] The company struggled, initially unsuccessfully, to contain the union and the strike through discharges of union members. On August 26, three hundred new members walked out after company refusals to reinstate thirty-seven of their co-workers.[85] The union clearly gained strength from its ability to place striking workers at other nearby hat factories at union wages, and from the "sympathy of the police and the greater number of Yonkers citizens."[86] Speculation about a forced shut-down of the plant took place at a meeting of 600 strikers on August 27.[87] But the fact that the union was unsuccessful in calling out any of the 800 female employees stalled the prospects of a closing.[88]

Waring management then took the offensive, hiring out-of-town strike-breakers and renting McCann's Hall itself, so that the strikers were forced to meet in the much smaller Socialists' Hall, holding only one-hundred.[89] The presence of scabs exacerbated tensions, and violence erupted on September 5. A number of incidents occurred on succeeding days, for which strikers were eventually convicted and fined, but there was no break in the Waring offensive, and strikers, with no strike-pay, began to drift back to work. By September 25, the Hatter's Union organizers having left town, the Yonkers *Herald* declared that the "Hatter's Strike Was A Failure." Hundreds of former employees sought work at Waring but found their positions taken.[90]

Threats of union organization on the Yonkers trolleys prompted new benefits at the Yonkers Railroad Company. The trolleymen received a ten percent wage increase, followed less than a week later by an additional fifteen percent. The Company was now a subsidiary of New York's Interborough Rapid Transit whose workers were out on strike and calling for sympathy actions from Yonkers; stern warnings against joining the Amalgamated Transit Workers Union accompanied the announcements of increased wages.[91]

The troublesome National Conduit and Cable Company in neighboring Hastings also had a summer of labor strife ending in increased wages and increased paternalism. Though there was no union, National employees demanding a pay increase walked out in June and successfully closed the plant for three weeks. On July 14, the works reopened under protection from the Westchester County sheriff, and 500 of the 2000 employees returned. Towards the end of July, the company brought in scabs by train from New York City. On July 28, 1919, they were met at the station by "almost 2,000, including hundreds of women sympathizers of the striking foreigners." Many of the women carried babies and, according to a newspaper report, "gave the authorities as much trouble as the men." The police, assisted by the wartime Yonkers Home Guard, were unable to contain the crowd and three people were badly hurt in the confrontation.[92] On August 4, the strikers accepted a compromise of three cents an hour increase (they had demanded thirteen), with another increase in September "if the production warrants it."[93] National management did not wait until September, however, to begin a major new employee welfare program. Less than two weeks after the settlement of the strike it announced the purchase of a "moving picture machine" and weekly movies for the employees. Furthermore, there would be weekly dances for employees in one of the unused factory buildings and an expanded athletic program, adding factory football and basketball teams to the already existing baseball team.[94] The following winter, National announced a housing program whereby it would build 200 detached bungalows for its workers in Hastings.[95]

At the height of the Waring strike violence (and the same day that troops were called to deal with the Boston police strike), unorganized workers at the National Refinery walked out, demanding an eight-hour day and twenty cents an hour raise while Federal Refinery's three hundred cooperage employees left work.[96] The next week, three hundred Yonkers teamsters and chauffeurs walked out, gaining a three-dollar a week increase.[97] A smaller strike by journeymen barbers rounded out the summer of 1919's labor relations picture but was by no means an end of the confrontations.[98]

In 1920, the journeymen barbers were out again, and so were painters.[99] Yonkers resident Francis H. Sisson, Vice-President of Guaranty Trust Company in New York, denounced "strike fever" to no avail.[100] The most significant strike of the year took place among machinists at Otis, where they staged the first extended walkout against the company since its formation. On August 20, three to four hundred walked off demanding a pay raise and reinstatement of the discharged secretary of the local union.[101] At first officials regarded the strike "lightly." A reporter was impressed with "the order" of the men on strike and the "absence of the atmosphere of unrest so peculiar to a congregation of strikers."[102] But within a few days, the strike became much more bitter. By August 25, there were 700 men out, and there were strikes underway at other Otis operations in New York City, New Haven, Connecticut and Harrison, New Jersey. In early September, violence erupted as strikers attacked a scab on his way home from work, and Fitch requested police protection for the remainder of the strike-breakers.[103] At this point, the strike faded from the local headlines for unknown reasons, and the outcome remains unclear.[104]

Responses to labor militancy in the 1919–1920 thus included pay increases and bonuses, company welfare measures, and worker "representation" plans in order to head off disputes, unionization and strikes, as well as more traditional tactics to break strikes once in progress. State machinery to help resolve strikes, like the state machinery to help deal with post-war unemployment, was hardly in evidence in the city. The appeal to loyalty and nationalism also played a significant role but assumed a life of its own.

In Yonkers, anti-Communism was not a major force during the War. Leaders sought labor peace in order to fight German autocracy, not radical socialism. William Boyce Thompson, mining magnate and Yonkers resident, helped to sustain this orientation locally even after the Bolshevik victory in Russia. He returned from an assignment as commander of the American Red Cross mission to Russia in early 1918 with glowing words about the "remarkable program of the Russian democracy."

> The formation of the present Russian Government is a direct outcome of the intense desire of the great mass of the Russian people for unrestricted and unthreatened liberty, for peace, and for the distribution of land. . . .[105]

In addition to giving one million dollars to the Bolshevik Party to aid the spread of its doctrines in Germany and Austria, Thompson gave active support through speeches, both in Washington and Yonkers, front-page news in the Yonkers papers.[106]

The situation changed dramatically in Spring, 1919, with uprisings in Bavaria and Hungary, the creation of the Third International, the Seattle General Strike, and a series of bombings around the country.[107] With the end of the war and the possibility of the spread of communism, anti-communism drew deeply from the well of xenophobic nationalism whipped up during the war. Fully under way by mid–1919, the Red Scare offered a potent weapon in the battle against both labor militancy and political radicalization of unemployed veterans.

Veterans organizations began forming in Yonkers in Spring, 1919. One of the first, the F.I.F. Club, organized in March and heard speeches on the dangers of Bolshevism. One speaker, linking the danger of Bolshevism explicitly to the problem of unemployment, warned the young veterans that the Bolshevik government was worse than the war-machine which they had just defeated. Another counselled:

> There are many of you boys now out of work, many of you just discharged from the army and navy. Do not be discouraged . . . but just keep on trying. If anyone comes up to you and tries to sow the seed of dissension among you, knock him down and keep yourselves apart from the Bolshevik. . . .[108]

F.I.F. speakers took part in a meeting to lay the groundwork for a city-wide veterans' organization later that week. One of the central goals of the new organization was to maintain political orthodoxy:

> **With such organizations in the various cities and towns of the United States, the chances for the spread of Bolshevism and anarchy in this country would be greatly minimized.[109]**

On March 24, the Yonkers Veteran's Association announced its existence with an advertisement under a large American flag.[110]

"Bolshevik" quickly became a catchword for accusing any dissenter in any situation. When violence erupted over a fare-dispute on the troubled Yonkers Railroad Company, Mayor Wallin denounced the outbreak as "forms of Bolshevism."[111] In June, Yonkers' high school graduation ceremonies centered around a warning about the dangers of Bolshevism.[112] When Chauncy Loundes telephoned Yonkers police headquarters to say that a red banner was flying above the American flag at a neighbor's residence, two policemen were dispatched "post-haste." (They found no red flag.)[113] At the strike at Hastings' National Conduit and Cable, Sheriff Nossiter now "found evidence of a Russian society" and said that it was "this element that is behind the trouble" despite previous reports emphasizing the multi-national nature of the strike committee.[114]

Locally, the Red Scare reached a peak in January, 1920. Attorney-General A. Mitchell Palmer's raids hit Yonkers at the beginning of the month. Accompanied by Yonkers police, U.S. agents toured "homes, clubs and saloons where Communists having sympathy for the soviet form of government were thought to congregate." They found nobody to arrest until January 6, when three men were taken on deportation warrants.[115] During the following week, news from around the State served to whip up support for the raids. Arthur Woods, who had gained a public name through his action for the unemployed, now decried "American-born Bolshevists," as the head of the National Americanism Commission of the American Legion in New York City.[116] State Senator Clayton Lusk claimed that there were more than 20,000 alien enemies in the Communist Party of New York State "organized for the overthrow of the Government by force and violence," while the New York State Assembly suspended its five Socialist Assemblymen.[117] Ralph Easley of the National Civic Federation compiled a blacklist of "American Bolsheviki" which included Yonkers' William Boyce Thompson.[118] The *Statesman* called these "extraordinary times" which justified limitations on both free speech and the right to strike. "Before the Reds came," ran an editorial with considerable historical myopia, "no one ever questioned workmen's right to strike in a body." Now, it argued, the State's need for protection against Bolsheviks justified such limitations.[119] On January 12, in a second sweep for Reds in Yonkers, forty men in five cars and a van failed to come up with any arrests.[120]

Despite the hopes of Progressives that wartime institutions would be extended after the armistice to provide peace-time social engineering, "reconstruction" became retrenchment. The Smith administration delayed the process in New York State until 1920, enabling the State Employment Bureau to function through the immediate post-war employment readjustments. Although the Bureau catered to their needs, employers nevertheless opposed continued funding, as they perceived dangers to themselves in an expanded role for the state in employment affairs. They preferred local and/or voluntary mechanisms directly under their own control.

Reformers' appeals to extend the life of the wartime labor market machinery in the interest of combatting radicalism and social unrest backfired. Such appeals, in the wake of the wartime nationalist propaganda, ultimately lent support to easier and more direct ways of dealing with the threats posed by radicalism.[121]

The wartime propaganda developed initially to urge sacrifice for the national cause had been instrumental in breaking down localism. Now it was used to mute worker militance and combat radical politics. Furthermore, national propaganda was enlisted to stabilize the national labor market by urging a return to local "community" responsibility for employment problems. It seemed that the dangers of mobile, displaced, discharged soldiers and a rapidly changing national labor market might be defused by local veterans' clubs, Y.M.C.A.s, and the efforts of local businessmen, all supported by a vigorous national propaganda campaign urging rapid resettlement and a recreation of the bonds of local loyalty.

While this formula for muting class conflict bore some relationship to that of the 1890s, its proponents were operating in the context of a substantially different political economy. New contradictions became apparent as Herbert Hoover, with the aid of Arthur Woods, tried to apply the formula in the unemployment crisis of 1921.

Notes

1. John A. Fitch, "Labor Reconstruction: the Conference of the Academy of Political Science," *Survey* 41, 11 (Dec. 14, 1918), 335.

2. John Willis Slaughter to Starr Murphy, Jan. 31, 1919, Folder 168, Box 19, R.G. 2, Rockefeller Family Papers. Murphy eventually recommended that Rockefeller not support Slaughter's project, only because a similar but competing scheme, that of the War Camp Community Service, was a more "vigorous" organization. See Starr Murphy to J.D. Rockefeller, April 4, 1919, R.G. 2, Box 19, Folder 168, Rockefeller Family Papers; and Charles F. Weller, "Permanent Values in War Camp Community Services," *Survey* 41, 10 (Dec. 7, 1918), 297.

3. See Bruce Bustard, "The Human Factor: Labor Administration and Industrial Manpower Mobilization During the First World War," PhD. Diss., University of Iowa, 1984, 249–283.

4. Paul Kellogg, "The Conference on Demobilization," *Survey* 41, 10 (Dec. 7, 1918), 287.

5. Bustard, "The Human Factor," 262; Clarke Chambers, *Seedtime of Reform: American Social Service and Social Action, 1918–1933* (Minneapolis: University of Minnesota Press, 1963), 21–22.

6. Paul Kellogg, "The Conference on Demobilization," *Survey* 41, 10 (Dec. 7, 1918), 287.

7. John A. Fitch, "Gains to Be Consolidated in War-Time Industrial Relations," *Survey* 41, 10 (Dec. 7, 1918), 315. Hamilton worked with Harold Moulton, George Arnold and George Bell, all of the WLPB, on reconstruction labor questions. Bustard, "The Human Factor," 257–260.

8. Walton H. Hamilton, "When Labor Comes to Market," *Survey* 41, 11 (Dec. 14, 1918), 425.

9. Walton H. Hamilton, "When Labor Comes to Market," *Survey* 41, 11 (Dec. 14, 1918), 425–428. 100,000 copies of the chart were distributed to city, county, state and federal officials and politicians by the Union League Club of Chicago. *Survey* 41, 21 (Feb. 22, 1919), 730. Walton's comments echo a letter from his boss, Felix Frankfurter to Lieutenant Colonel John J. Coss, Nov. 19, 1918: "Demobilization should be in terms of industrial needs. . . . A hap-hazard discharge of men and cancellation of contracts will not give the men and materials in the order in which they are needed to hasten the resumption of ordinary business. . . . The rate of demobilization must be limited to the capacity of industry to reabsorb men. . . . There are abundant reasons for thinking that unless extreme care is taken the labor market will be glutted. . . . Many thoughtful persons even insist that there is a possibility of 'Bolshevism' if the process is not kept well in hand. Frankfurter to Coss, Nov. 19, 1918, WLPB, R. G. 1, Correspondence of Chairman and Executive Secretary, Folder: Reconstruction Correspondence, November, 1918, National Archives.

10. Yonkers *Herald*, Jan. 4, 1919, 1.

11. Yonkers *Herald*, Jan. 22, 1919, 5.

12. It did not call for unemployment insurance. *Survey* 41, 18 (Feb. 1, 1919), 642.

13. Bruno Lasker, "The Carrying Forward of War-time Industrial Standards," *Survey* 41, 10 (Dec. 7, 1918), 309.

14. Bruno Lasker, "The Carrying Forward of War-time Industrial Standards," *Survey* 41, 10 (Dec. 7, 1918), 309.

15. "Suggested telegram to be sent to local representatives of the U.S. Employment Service Concerning demobilization of war workers." n.d., War Labor Policies Board, R.G. 1, Correspondence of Chairman and Executive Secretary, Entry 2, Folder: Demobilization, National Archives.

16. Bruno Lasker, "The Carrying Forward of War-Time Industrial Standards," *Survey* 41, 10 (Dec. 7, 1918), 309.

17. Bruno Lasker, "The Carrying Forward of War-Time Industrial Standards," *Survey* 41, 10 (Dec. 7, 1918), 309; Graham Taylor, Demobilization and Reemployment, *Survey* 41, 11 (Dec. 14, 1918), 342–343.

18. Graham Taylor, "Demobilization and Reemployment," *Survey* 41, 11 (Dec. 14, 1918), 342–343.

19. Bruere to Frankfurter, Dec. 3, 1918, WLPB, R.G. 1, Correspondence of Chairman and Executive Secretary, Entry 2, Folder: Henry Bruere, National Archives. Bruere wrote this letter reporting his activities in order to broach the topic of his own resignation from the Service.

20. In the beginning of December U.S.E.S. centers reported only 12,000 unemployed. By the beginning of February, there were 262,000, New York being among the hardest hit. Officials concurred that there would be a critical period over the following months. *Survey* 41, 19, (Feb. 8, 1919), 664.

21. Bruere to Frankfurter, Dec. 3, 1918, WLPB, R.G. 1, Correspondence of Chairman and Executive Secretary, Entry 2, Folder: Henry Bruere, National Archives. Bruere wrote this letter reporting his activities in order to broach the topic of his own resignation from the Service.

22. John A. Fitch, "Labor Reconstruction: The Conference of the Academy of Political Science," *Survey* 41, 11 (Dec. 14, 1918), 336.

23. *U.S. Employment Service Bulletin* 1,43 (Dec. 10, 1918), 1.

24. *U.S. Employment Service Bulletin* 1,43 (Dec. 10, 1918), 3.

25. David M. Kennedy, *Over Here: The First World War and American Society* (New York: Oxford University Press, 1980), 249–251; Bustard, "The Human Factor," 260–262, 266–268. As further explanation for the rapidity of the war agency dismantling, Bustard notes that "the war had not really brought the dramatic institutional changes which the would-be 'planners' believed it had. (266).

26. Republican opposition to the U.S.E.S. may have come in part from employers' suspicions that U.S.E.S. employees were utilizing "their official positions to further the cause of unionism." *Industry* (Jan. 1, 1919). Edward Devine accused "certain employers" who benefitted from "idle men before their gates clamoring for jobs" of resisting the distribution of surplus labor to where it was needed. Edward T. Devine, "The Attack on the Federal Employment Service," *Survey* 41, 19 (Feb. 8, 1919), 662–663. See also Darrell Hevenor Smith, *The United States Employment Service: Its History, Activities and Organization* (Baltimore: Johns Hopkins University Press, 1923), 45; Bustard, "The Human Factor," 269–271.

27. *Survey* 41, 25 (March 22, 1919), 894.

28. Mathew C. Smith to American Legion Headquarters, et al., June 26, 1920, Folder: Unemployment, Committee on Community, Civic and Emergency Measures, Box 666, Commerce Papers, Herbert Hoover Papers (hereafter CP-HHP.)

29. Press Bulletin of the Chamber of Commerce of the United States, March 24, 1919, Folder: Unemployment 1916–1919, Box 2, AALL Papers, NYSSILR.

30. Press Bulletin of the Chamber of Commerce of the United States, March 24, 1919, Folder: Unemployment 1916–1919, Box 2, AALL Papers, NYSSILR. The New York State Chamber of Commerce, fearing "syndicalists, I.W.W.'s and other revolutionary or anarchistic bodies" urged, in similar tones, a conciliatory approach towards workers and the establishment of "representative committees in which differences and disputes can be ironed out." New York State Chamber of Commerce, "Report on Industrial Relations," Dec. 5, 1918, in Folder 166, Box 19, R.G. 2F, Rockefeller Archives.

31. *Survey*, 41, 19 (Feb. 8, 1919), 664–665.

32. "Report of Governor Smith's Reconstruction Commission on A Permanent Unemployment Program," June 17, 1919, (Albany: J.B.Lyon, 1919), copy in Folder: Unemployment, Cities, New York, Misc., Box 628, CP-HHP.

33. "A Permanent Unemployment Program," 4.

34. *Survey* 41, 22, (March 1, 1919), 803; N.Y. State Industrial Commission, *Industrial Bulletin* 4, 6 (March, 1919), 113.

35. N.Y. State Industrial Commission, *Industrial Bulletin* 4, 4 (Jan., 1919), 187.

36. Frances Perkins, "Reminiscences," Vol. 1, 431, Columbia University Oral History Project, Columbia University Archives (hereafter Perkins, OH).

37. Perkins, OH, Vol. 2, 12.

38. Perkins, OH, Vol. 1, 443.

39. On enlightened employers, e.g. "There were very good people in the Merchants' Association. They were not money grubbers. . . . We could get the Merchants' Association to agree with us about many social projects;" and on the National Civic Federation, "I've always thought that although they were laughed at a lot, to a certain extent they did do good. They introduced the idea . . . that there was some relation between production and a contented or satisfied personnel." Perkins, OH, Vol. 2, 91–94; and Vol. 1, 323.

40. "New York. Notes on Unemployment," Speeches and Articles, 1919 ? [sic], Box 42, Frances Perkins Papers, Columbia University.

41. N.Y. State Industrial Commission, *Industrial Bulletin* 4, 6 (March, 1919), 113.

42. "Aid for State Employment Bureaus: Message of Governor Alfred E. Smith, asking that Fifty Thousand Dollars be Appropriated," March 20, 1919, Copy in Folder: Unemployment, Cities, New York—Misc., Box 628, CP-HHP.

43. New York State Department of Labor, Industrial Commission *AR*, 1919, 219.

44. New York State Department of Labor, Industrial Commission *AR*, 1919, 216–218.

45. Whatever success Barnes had had with his Greater New York clearinghouse system, it was no longer in evidence by this time.

46. New York State Department of Labor, Industrial Commission *AR*, 1919, 217; N.Y. Merchants Association, *Yearbook*, 1919, 77.

47. "Index of Employment in Factories in New York State, 1914–1923," N.Y. State Industrial Commission, *The Industrial Bulletin* 3, 5 (Feb., 1924), 121.

48. New York State Department of Labor, Industrial Commission *AR*, 1919, 220; N.Y. State Industrial Commission, *Industrial Bulletin* 4, 10 (July, 1919), 187.

49. New York State Department of Labor, Industrial Commission *AR*, 1920, 181.

50. "A Permanent Unemployment Program," 6.

51. New York State Department of Labor, Industrial Commission *AR*, 1919, 218.

52. New York State Department of Labor, Industrial Commission *AR*, 1919, 225.

53. "Index of employment in Factories in New York State, 1914–1923," N.Y. State Industrial Commission, *Industrial Bulletin* 3, 5 (Feb., 1924), 121.

54. N.Y. State Industrial Commission, *Industrial Bulletin* 4, 10 (July, 1919), 187.

55. New York State Department of Labor, Industrial Commission *AR*, 1920, 190.

56. New York State Department of Labor, Industrial Commission *AR*, 1920, 181.

57. New York State Department of Labor, Industrial Commission *AR*, 1920, 180–181.

58. New York State Department of Labor, Industrial Commission *AR*, 1920, 190.

59. New York State Department of Labor, Industrial Commission *AR*, 1920, 182.

60. New York State Department of Labor, Industrial Commission *AR*, 1920, 180–181.

61. See chapter 8.

62. David Kennedy concludes that whipping up a diffuse nationalistic fervor to accomplish wartime ends was more acceptable in the American political ideology than more sharply focused administrative edicts based on "unilateral exercise of government power." In the emergency of war, Kennedy argues, the latter would have been more appropriate, and might have avoided the excesses of zealotry which nationalistic fear-mongering aroused after the war. Kennedy, *Over Here*, 142–143. On the functions of the ideology of voluntarism see also Robert D. Cuff, "Herbert Hoover, The Ideology of Voluntarism and War Organization During the Great War," *Journal of American History*, 64 (1977), 358–372.

63. Yonkers *Herald*, Nov. 14, 1918, 1.

64. Yonkers *Herald*, Aug. 13, 1919, 4.

65. Yonkers *Herald*, Jan. 3, 1919, 4.

66. Yonkers *Herald*, Jan. 3, 1919, 4. Also see May 23, 1919, 8.

67. E.g. Yonkers *Herald*, Aug. 12, 1919, 7.

68. Yonkers *Herald*, Aug. 13, 1919, 4.

69. Yonkers *Herald*, March 11, 1919, 1. The Department of Labor message was a reprise of a War Labor Policies Board address to governors in December, United States Employment Service *Bulletin* Dec. 17, 1918, 3. On the March conference, see John A. Fitch, "Unrest as the Governors See It," *Survey* 41, 24, 858–860. Fitch pointed out that nearly every governor "told of the plans . . . for road-building and public construction of various sorts in order to provide work for returning soldiers and others." He estimated from their remarks that there would be over half a billion dollars to be used in road construction in the next three years. Otto Mallery reported the "breaking of all public works records in 1919." Mallery, "Reviving Private Industry Through Public Works," typescript of an address to the International Association of Public Employment Services, Buffalo, N.Y., Sept. 8, 1921, in Folder: Unemployment 1920–1922, Box 2, AALL Papers.

70. Yonkers *Herald*, Jan. 14, 1919, 2. The War Camp Community Service, with units in 312 communities, was established in an attempt to provide community contacts and services for army camp residents, to substitute for "brothel and saloon." The idea was that the town's "best citizens" and particularly the women "of culture and resource" would extend themselves to resident soldiers, thus demonstrating that, in America "class distinctions are unimportant." At the time of the Armistice, the War Labor Policies Board requested the W.C.C.S. to establish industrial community services in a number of factory cities. Charles F. Weller, "Permanent Values in War Camp Community Services," *Survey* 41, 10 (Dec. 7, 1918), 295–297.

71. Yonkers Mayor's Committee, *Yonkers in the World War*, 29.

72. Yonkers *Herald*, May 2, 1919, 10.

73. The Y.M.C.A. Constitution of 1918 directed the Employment Committee to help solve economic and vocational problems relating to employment by keeping records of employers and employees. Yonkers Y.M.C.A. Constitution and By-Laws, 1918, 12. Yonkers Y.M.C.A. Papers. Yonkers *Herald*, Jan 9, 1919, 5.

74. Yonkers *Herald*, Jan. 3, 1919, 1.

75. Yonkers *Herald*, Mar. 17, 1919, 1; March 24, 1919, 1.

76. Yonkers *Herald*, May 29, 1919, 6.

77. Yonkers *Herald*, July 1, 1919.

78. Yonkers *Statesman*, June 3, 1920, 6. On Woods and Caswell in the ensuing years, see chapter 8.

79. This is an extension of Kennedy's lucid observation on the Wilson Administration's mode of operation in wartime.

80. Yonkers *Herald*, June 25, 1919, 1.

81. Yonkers *Herald*, Aug. 1, 1919, 1.

82. Yonkers *Herald*, Sept. 4, 1919, 1.

83. Yonkers *Herald*, Aug. 14, 1914, 1.

84. Yonkers *Herald*, Aug. 15, 1919, 1.

85. Yonkers *Herald*, Aug. 26, 1919, 1.

86. Organizer H.J. Glover promised that striking men with dependents would be placed in factories with higher wages than Waring. He cited the fact that "there are no hatters out of jobs" as the reason for his being able to do this. Three days later, an arrangement had been made for five hatters per day to be hired at Plants and Co. in nearby Peekskill. Yonkers *Herald*, Aug. 26, 1919, 1; Aug. 29, 1919, 1.

87. Yonkers *Herald*, Aug. 27, 1919, 1.

88. Yonkers *Herald*, Aug. 29, 1919, 1.

89. Yonkers *Herald*, Sept. 2, 1919, 1.

90. Yonkers *Herald*, Sept. 3, 12, 13, 18, 25, 26, 1919, 1.

91. Yonkers *Herald*, Aug. 14, 1919, 1; Aug. 16, 1919, 1; Aug. 20, 1919, 1.

92. Yonkers *Herald*, July 28, 1919, 1.

93. Yonkers *Herald*, Aug. 4, 1919, 1.

94. Yonkers *Herald*, Aug. 16, 1919, 3.

95. The article claimed that only one third of National Conduit and Cable Company employees lived in Hastings. Yonkers *Statesman*, Mar. 15, 1920, 1.

96. Yonkers *Herald*, Sept. 10, 1919, 1; Sept. 11, 1919, 1; Sept. 15, 1919, 1.

97. Yonkers *Herald*, Sept. 16, 1919, 1; Sept. 22, 1919, 1.

98. The demands were granted after one day. Yonkers *Herald*, July 16, 1919, 1.

99. Yonkers *Statesman*, April 1, 1920, 6; May 20, 1920, 1.

100. Yonkers *Statesman*, May 19, 1920.

101. Yonkers *Statesman*, Aug. 20, 1920, 1.

102. Yonkers *Statesman*, Aug. 20, 1920, 1.

103. Yonkers *Statesman*, Aug. 25, 1920, 1; Aug. 28, 1920, 1; Sept. 9, 1920, 1; Sept. 10, 1920, 1.

104. Neither the *Statesman* nor the *Herald* has any further mention of the strike through September and October.

105. Yonkers *Herald*, Jan 10, 1918, 1.

106. Yonkers *Herald*, Jan. 31, 1918, 1.

107. On the Red Scare, see John F. McClymer, "The Price of Failure: the Red Scare in New York State," in *War and Welfare: Social Engineering in America, 1890–1925* (Westport: Greenwood Press, 1980, 192–215; Robert K. Murray, *Red Scare: A Study in National Hysteria, 1919–1920* (Minneapolis: University of Minnesota Press, 1955); Burl Noggle, *Into the Twenties: the United States from Armistice to Normalcy* (Urbana: University of Illinois Press, 1974), 84–121.

108. There was some controversy over the meaning of "F.I.F." The speakers denied that it stood for "First Irish Families," and rather that it meant "Fratres in Fidelis." Yonkers *Herald*, March 14, 1919, 4.

109. Yonkers *Herald*, Mar. 19, 1919, 1.

110. Yonkers *Herald*, March 19, 1919, 1.

111. Yonkers *Herald*, May 1, 1919, 4.

112. Yonkers *Herald*, May 2, 1919, 6; June 27, 1919, 2.

113. Yonkers *Herald*, June 6, 1919, 1.

114. Yonkers *Herald*, July 28, 1919, 1.

115. Yonkers *Statesman*, Jan. 3, 1920, 1; Jan. 6, 1920, 1.

116. Yonkers *Statesman*, Jan 6, 1920, 1. Another pre-war unemployment reformer, Frances Kellor, joined the ranks of those aiming to "save America from Bolshevism," with a new organization, the Inter-Racial Council, whose aim was to strengthen the loyalties of immigrant workers. Korman, 165–166.

117. Yonkers *Statesman*, Jan. 7, 1920, 1; Jan. 8, 1920, 1.

118. *Survey* 41, 16 (Jan. 18, 1919), 535.

119. Yonkers *Statesman*, Jan. 8, 1920, 2.

120. Yonkers *Statesman*, Jan 12, 1920, 1.

121. In New York, the Associated Industries used the Red Scare atmosphere to its advantage in attacks on reform measures. Chambers, *Seedtime of Reform*, 25. See also McClymer, *War and Welfare*, 192–215.

8

Yonkers and the President's Conference on Unemployment: The Federal Government Embraces "the Community"

The rapid dismantling of the state apparatus to manage employment and labor markets in the immediate post-war years disappointed Progressive social workers and employment reformers. But they took part in the creation of a new approach to managing unemployment in the economic slump of 1921–1922. In this crisis, with more than five million unemployed workers, the concern with the "distribution of labor" and the notion of "reserve labor cities" which had been so prominent from 1914 through the end of the war, virtually disappeared. Labor exchanges still occupied a central role in reform thinking, but almost exclusively as local aids, not regional or national distribution clearinghouses. Prominent writers and speakers treated unemployment less as national problem than as "community" problem. Ironically, the agency most actively promoting this view was a conference marking the first active involvement of the federal government in the problem of unemployment: the President's Unemployment Conference of 1921, conceived and organized by Secretary of Commerce Herbert Hoover.[1]

Conference participants like Edward Devine, Mary Van Kleeck, and Henry Seager had responded earlier to the new, twentieth century social and economic arrangements which reduced locally-based elites' power to manage social crises arising from employment instability. Between the time of Leiserson's report and the various publications of the New York City Mayor's Unemployment Committee, they developed a two-tiered program, separating "problems of industry" from "problems of relief." The former, as we have seen, were to be addressed at the national level by broad stabilization efforts by the "the dominant forces in our American industrial life" (in Henry Bruere's words)—national financial and corporate managers. The state would supplement these efforts by generating and disseminating labor market information and by helping to transfer labor to where it was needed. With unnecessary unemployment eliminated, the local experts—social workers with their family caseloads—would be able to deal with the various problems in the community.[2]

The post-war program of the Unemployment Conference lent several new twists to this formulation. The new program was profoundly influenced by organized labor's wartime advances, which business organizations were now committed to rolling back, and by Herbert Hoover's commitment to an ideology of "American individualism." Like the earlier programs, the Conference addressed the problem of unemployment on two levels: one a broad, national, long-term campaign; the other an immediate, locally-based effort to deal with the casualties of the system.

Beveridge, the Webbs, and Leiserson had felt cyclical unemployment to be largely beyond the grasp of employment reform. Their long-term program focused rather on well-administered labor distribution and the elimination of seasonal and casual labor to reduce unemployment. The new long-term program targeted business cycles rather than labor distribution. Its innovations stemmed from recent advances in economic theory. By 1921–1922, Wesley Clair Mitchell's 1913 work on business cycles, and the Baldwin Committee's *How to Meet Hard Times* proposals began to receive enough circulation that reformers, backed by the research capabilities of new organizations like the National Bureau of Economic Research, felt ready to start tackling cyclical unemployment.[3]

The emergency program, on the other hand, sought to make the "community" the primary arena for immediate social and political stabilization efforts. In the name of "communication" among cities and towns, the Conference set up mechanisms to coordinate national surveillance. But more importantly, the "community" emphasis served an ideological purpose in bolstering the idea of individual initiative and community self-reliance, even in an economic system which apparently needed centralized, expert management of its debilitating business cycles. The Conference thus sought in the "community" means to suppress radicalism, to mitigate the deterioration of workers' discipline, and to stem challenges to the ideology of the self-reliant American individual, all of which loomed in a period of widespread unemployment. This ideological effort made the Conference literature read differently from the pre-War reform program.

While there was broad consensus on the importance of the "community" in dealing with the depression, there was disagreement about who would direct the community program. Herbert Hoover, who backed a role for experts as advisors at the national level, was unenthusiastic about relying on local social workers for leadership in the emergency. The opinions of metropolitan social workers notwithstanding, the ideological purposes of the emergency program were better served by local businessmen.

The peak of post-war employment came in the United States in the late spring of 1920, slightly earlier in New York State.[4] Employment declined precipitously shortly thereafter. The February 5, 1921 issue of *The Survey* contained an abridged version of the Baldwin Committee's *How to Meet Hard Times*. By August, the U.S. Department of Labor estimated that, compared to the 1920 peak, there were 5,735,000 fewer jobs.[5] In the Department of Commerce, Hoover tracked the steep drop in economic activity through data on production, inventory and sales gathered by his newly organized Survey of Current Business.[6] On August 20, 1921 he suggested to President Harding that he convene a presidential conference on unemployment, consisting predominantly of individuals "who can influence the action of employing forces [a strategy recalling Bruere's pre-war orientation] and who can influence public opinion [recalling the wartime campaigns]."[7] Harding approved and Hoover announced plans for the conference on August 29.

An Economic Advisory Committee met during the first weeks of September to prepare an agenda and materials for the full Conference. Most of its nineteen members—which included John Andrews, Bailey Burritt, and Henry Seager—were associated with university economics departments and almost one third were members of the executive committee of the American Association for Labor Legislation.[8] The Advisory Committee submitted its report to the full Conference when it convened on September 26.[9] As Carolyn Grin has observed, the Conference deliberations "were designed not to expand the work of the [Economic Advisory] committee, but rather to mobilize public opinion along the lines indicated."[10]

After one day of general sessions, the Conference broke into committees and hearings for three days. As planned in the pre-Conference sessions, the committees included Unemployment Statistics, "Municipal Organization and Employment Agencies and Registration," Public Works, various sectors of private industry, and the long-range "Unemployment and Business Cycles" committee. When they reconvened in general session September 30, the Conference adopted its first public statement, twelve points comprising "General Recommendations of the Conference for the Emergency Program." Unemployment, the statement affirmed, "is primarily a community problem. The responsibility for leadership is with the Mayor and should be immediately assumed by him." The Recommendations included a structure for community action, including a local Emergency Committee to develop a community plan for meeting the emergency, and a local public employment agency to register all those desiring work. The employment agency, it recommended, should "give priority in employment to residents." At the State level, the Emergency Program urged the governor to "unite all State agencies for support of the Mayors and, as the superior officer, [to] insist upon the responsibility of city officials." Remaining points involved recommendations for all levels of government to stimulate employment by freeing up money for public works, and for private industry to spread the available work by reducing hours, providing part-time jobs and undertaking plant construction, cleaning, and repairs during the winter months.[11] The "General Recommendations . . . for Measures for Permanent Recovery of Employment" followed towards the end of the Conference.[12]

While there was a flurry of public statements and press releases about the Conference, Hoover scrupulously avoided any appearance of expanded government activity at the federal level. As Carolyn Grin has observed, Hoover used the highly publicized conference itself as a means to achieve a managed economy without enlarging state institutions.[13] Hoover wanted it clearly understood that he did not intend to "to establish any extensive national organization." When the Conference adjourned on October 13 it left only a small "quasi voluntary" standing committee to oversee ongoing projects."[14]

Two major projects emerged directly from the Conference: the long-range study of business cycles and the local emergency campaign.[15] The Committee responsible for the former was chaired by Owen Young of General Electric.[16] The project developed into a collaboration between the Young Committee and the National Bureau of Economic Research, whose Director of Research, Wesley Mitchell, had sought funding for a new study of business cycles prior to the

Committee's formation. Mitchell became the Director of Research for the Young Committee.[17] The Committee would "sponsor" research undertaken by the NBER, with funding from the Carnegie Foundation.[18] The process of developing the report thus bore the stamp of Hoover's concern about any expansion of the state (he insisted on private funding for the "quasi voluntary" project) coupled with his desire to promote and disseminate neutral, scientific expert opinion on economic subjects.

Similarly, the Committee's conclusions concurred with Hoover's goal of developing mechanisms for promoting macroeconomic stability without directly expanding state institutions. The pre-eminent role in planning the national economy was reserved for private business, whose "enlarge[d] judgment . . . [would] greatly contribute to stability."[19] The state would simply recruit and distribute the necessary information upon which such judgments could be based.[20]

But while Hoover aimed to "eliminate waste in industry" largely by relying on the initiative of "individual businessmen," he understood that periods of economic distress undermined broad ideological commitment to this goal. The work of the Committee on Civic and Emergency Measures, which sought to demonstrate more immediately the efficacy of traditional voluntarism, was an antidote to this threat.[21]

President Harding announced the community program to the public on October 4:

> It is of national importance that every community should at once undertake organization [to provide work and assistance] in order that the Nation may be protected as a whole. . . . In order that there may be unity of action by all the forces which may be brought to bear . . . the Unemployment Conference is establishing an agency in Washington through which appropriate coordination can be promoted, and through which reports on progress and suggestions may be given general circulation and cooperation.[22]

After the Conference adjourned, Arthur Woods, Chairman of the Committee on Civic and Emergency Measures, remained in Washington to coordinate what Ellis Hawley has called "the most ambitious program of organized voluntarism since the war period."[23] A firm believer in the importance of building and maintaining "character" as the solution to social problems, Woods had dealt with unemployment as New York City Police Commissioner in the Mitchel administration, as Assistant Secretary of War in charge of maintaining an orderly demobilization in 1919, and most recently with related problems as chairman of the

American Legion's Americanization Committee.[24] From an office in the Department of Commerce, he "immediately began the work of furnishing the various municipal and State authorities with the necessary information to enable them to put into effect the emergency recommendations. . . ."[25] The information campaign began with distribution of three hundred reprints of *The Survey*'s summary of *How to Meet Hard Times*.[26] By October 21 Woods and his staff had written to 293 cities with populations over 25,000, inquiring about conditions and plans, and had received replies from 115.[27] This was the beginning of a stream of correspondence, much of it giving accounts of local activities and programs allegedly meeting with success in selected localities around the country.[28]

Mary Van Kleeck, a member of Woods' Committee at the Conference, and a member of the Standing Committee to oversee ongoing activity, soon began to express concern at the directions taken by Woods. While she did not object to the community focus itself, she felt that social workers were not sufficiently represented in the Conference follow-up. To make "local responsibility more workable," Van Kleeck suggested a committee composed "of those who will be recognized as having had long and effective experience in the problems of relief in local communities."[29] Woods responded:

> My own idea about the kind of people we should try to get on this Committee was rather that it would include people, who, from their personalities and their positions, might increase employment—like Presidents of Chambers of Commerce, National Manufacturers Associations, and etc.[30]

In a program concentrating on stimulating employment rather than relief, he argued, it made more sense to have the leadership of those who controlled jobs.

Undaunted, Van Kleeck explained that social workers "have done the most thinking and the most effective work in organizing their communities for just such preventive work as you desire to see emphasized," but that they "have so far not been drawn in in such a way as to enable them to contribute their part to the work of the conference."[31] Woods remained respectful but reluctant, and Van Kleeck eventually understood that he was not going to act on her criticism. Nevertheless, she thought the direction of his leadership was at least partially responsible for the shape of the local response. ". . . [T]hey are not following the injunction of the Conference to make the Mayor's Committee truly representative," she wrote. "They are appointing business men and leaving out both labor and the social workers."[32]

Like Van Kleeck, Samuel Gompers had no objection to community organization for emergency relief. He endorsed the recommendations of the Conference, while attacking the "representatives of organized greed and reaction" who "made almost superhuman effort to turn the tide of the conference in favor of measures that would have further enriched the beneficiaries of special privilege and that would have further intensified the suffering of the working people." He credited the Conference's success to Hoover's procedural organization: only unanimously supported committee reports came to general sessions of the Conference.[33] President Joseph Defrees of the United States Chamber of Commerce likewise supported the "community" orientation of the Conference, circulating the Emergency Program to his membership on October 1, before the Conference adjourned.[34] The New York Associated Industries, whose virulent campaign against unemployment insurance proposals attacked "the professors of economics and their allies (those who have made social welfare work a profession)," spared the Conference any criticism.[35]

Outright opposition to the Conference was initially mild, muted, or confined to relatively small radical organizations. One exception was Mayor William Thompson of Chicago, who responded to the recommendations as "a capitalistic move with the following objects: a blacklist, a refusal of charity to American union laboring men, a drive against union labor, a conspiracy to lower wages." Hoover responded noting the endorsements of the AFL, the Railway Brotherhoods, and the UMW.[36] In New York City, the *Volkszeitung* reported that two thirds of the conference

> are absolutely of one mind with President Harding, that the present foundation of the social system must not in any form be disturbed, and that the private employers cannot be held responsible for the hunger and misery. . . . [T]hese men know precisely what they want to prove—that the workmen demand too much and that the wages must be reduced.[37]

Also in New York City, a radical New York Unemployment Council operated through the winter, closely followed by the F.B.I. Secretary I. Amter wrote "respectfully" to President Harding, enclosing the Council's program, but making no specific reference to Hoover's

Conference.[38] At meetings on the Lower East Side, Amter urged the unemployed—as members of the working class which had produced all—simply to take what they deserved. Hoover received detailed reports on these activities through the F.B.I.[39]

While radical activity was by no means widespread in the aftermath of the Red Scare, the reports from towns and cities served to increase the urgency of Hoover's program for community action. As soon as the Conference approved of the Emergency Program, Hoover wrote to New York State's Governor Nathan Miller, "I am wondering if you would not take the leadership of all the governors in the country in calling upon the mayors of your towns to put this plan in action." It was of great importance to the administration, Hoover explained, "that we should get through this forthcoming winter with as little trouble as we possibly can . . . [and] most of the towns in the country are simply fooling with the explosives that lie under this situation."[40]

Ironically, Miller had entered office in January with a dramatic economy-in-government campaign, promising to cut the State budget from $201 million to $140 million by, among other things, closing branches of the State Employment Service and streamlining the Industrial Commission.[41] In June, the State's economy measures had added directly to the unemployment problem. As the Yonkers *Herald* reported, "A weary, disgruntled army of officially decapitated State employes wended their way out of the Capitol and branch State departments today to join the great army of unemployed."[42]

His own earlier measures notwithstanding, Governor Miller began to take some action at the time of the Conference. Just before it convened, he sent telegrams to New York mayors asking "what plans do you have in prospect or under way for meeting the present problem of unemployment in your city." Many reported expanded public works programs, hoping these would ease the burden.[43] In October, he supported the Conference by sending letters to all cities of the State asking mayors to appoint emergency committees. He emphasized the public works recommendations of the President's Conference, noting that funds had been made available for the repairs to public buildings of the State. "Every citizen who has work to do will render a patriotic service by having it done now," he intoned.[44] On October 19, Miller presided at a New York State Unemployment Conference, hosted by the Albany Chamber of Commerce.[45] Arthur Woods came from Washington for the occasion to deliver Hoover's message.

In his address Woods explained the President's Conference and its approach to unemployment in terms of the self-reliant American character (implicitly male), which faced a dual threat of unemployment and expanded government activity. The President's Unemployment Conference, said Woods, "was made up of just plain Americans . . . not representative of any particular groups, of any particular interests." At this classless, pragmatic Conference, "theory was cast aside . . ." because the participants would not "spend any time hunting for any particular big pill" that could cure unemployment. Nor did the Conference even have any "thought that it would be successful in developing anything particularly new about this question of unemployment."[46]

"I suppose," Woods ruminated, "that self-reliance is one of the dominant American traits." He sketched the picture of the self-reliant American out of work. "He does all he can for himself, and that is a sturdy American trait that needs no encouragement from people outside, because it is so deeply rooted in the American character." Personal resources exhausted, the American turned to relatives, neighbors, friends, church and fraternal organizations. (Woods did not mention unions.) Only after these avenues were tried, in Woods' picture, did the American lose his self-respect by having "to turn to the public."

If government assistance meant loss of character, government assistance must be minimized. To foster the unemployed "man's sturdy American self-reliance," Woods reported that "it seemed clear to the President's Conference that the question was primarily one for neighbors, and neighborhoods to handle." More government resources equaled less American self-reliance. City governments, close to the people, could devise innovative strategies for dealing with the emergency; Woods' function was merely to "transmit the experience of one city to another." And he cautioned, "not for the purposes of being in any way alarming," that "preachers of revolution" were taking advantage of the widespread unemployment.

Woods rounded out his American response to unemployment through a series lessons from the war. This was a "captain's battle," in which the mayors were the captains. Unemployment, like the wartime food crisis successfully met by Hoover's wartime Food Administration, demanded voluntary personal action and sacrifice, not more laws from Congress. And his own post-war "Spruce-Up" campaign to employ returning veterans might further serve as a model for the current crisis.

Woods closed with a rousing message "that Americans are called upon now to help fellow Americans in the American way, preserving the American virtues and hitting the problem with the old American aggressiveness and vigor." The mayors and Chamber of Commerce presidents responded with prolonged applause. An approach to unemployment based on localism, voluntarism, and "American character" found a favorable audience here.

Once again, Mary Van Kleeck had a rather different agenda: she urged Woods to use his visit to Albany to deliver "an urgent word" to State officials about employment statistics. While Governor Miller threatened to curtail the collection of employment statistics, Van Kleeck pointed to New York's leadership role, particularly since 1915, and asked Woods to press for expansion of statistical collection. Van Kleeck's concerns were, however, not those of Woods.[47]

Van Kleeck's aims were those of the technical expert, and she failed to appreciate Hoover and Woods' anti-statist ideological aims, around which the "community" project was organized. When Woods circulated an attack on British governmental involvement in unemployment relief, she called it a "'scare-head' about the . . . disadvantage of governmental responsibility." As always, Van Kleeck claimed authority on the basis of superior knowledge of the facts. She wrote Woods:

> I have recently had talks with representatives both of employers and of the labor movement who have come from England within the past few weeks and I am convinced that the situation there is far more complicated and the conclusions to be drawn from it more fundamental than is indicated in your letter. . . . I am quite frank to say that I think that many members of the President's Conference are not informed about conditions in England and, therefore, I would wish that if any information is sent to them it should be more inclusive and more fundamental. . . ."[48]

Woods, however, concerned mainly with the ideological impact of these messages, was as unmoved by this criticism as by earlier ones. Woods' view, and not Van Kleeck's, was reflected in the publication of the Associated Industries of New York, which claimed of the British situation: "Unemployment Benefits Make Chronic Idlers."[49]

After the Albany Conference, Governor Miller considered plans for a more extensive State organization to stimulate and coordinate local and state activities. At the same time, Woods appointed eighteen regional directors throughout the country, one for New York State in the person of Judge Randall LeBoeuf (on Miller's recommendation.) Miller subsequently decided that LeBoeuf's office was sufficient for state coordination.[50] LeBoeuf reported to Woods, at the end of January, that heads of Departments had done everything which a Special Committee could have done at the state level.[51]

For local activities in New York State, Woods relied not only on LeBoeuf, but on direct reports from the F.B.I. and from Lieutenant Fred W. Caswell. Having worked with Woods in the immediate post-war employment campaign, Caswell, now stationed at Plattsburg Barracks, New York, offered his assistance on the basis his "knowledge of conditions and past contact with the people you want to reach in the community."[52] Early in January, Woods appointed Caswell as one of several traveling trouble-shooters. He would use their reports not only to keep track of local conditions, but also for his circular bulletins on Mayors' Committees' activities in which he reported successful local projects to local correspondents. On January 23, Caswell met with LeBoeuf, Governor Miller, and other officials to plan his New York itinerary.[53] For the next two months, Caswell toured New York State, sending almost daily reports to Woods in Washington.

Monitoring radicals was one purpose of Caswell's tour. He supplemented F.B.I. reports on radical activity in Buffalo where, according to LeBoeuf, there was "very considerable unrest among the foreign element."[54] In Rome Caswell reported, "the foreign element gets nasty at times" and "radicalism has a couple of representatives," but "the S.S. men have a line on their post office boxes, etc."[55] In each case, however, Caswell reported what Woods already knew: he did not make a significant contribution to the surveillance mechanisms previously in place.

Caswell also reported the numbers of people unemployed as estimated by the various officials he met. In addition, he tried to establish the degree to which there was a problem with "floaters." For example, despite the effective cooperation of the Endicott-Johnson shoe company in providing jobs for residents, Binghamton reported trouble with transients.[56] "Floaters" on their way to New York or the West seemed to be a problem at Little Falls, but its size aided localism and surveillance, and Caswell wrote, "this city is so small that they have a very good line on their unemployed" and refused work or relief to the transients.[57] Transients concerned Caswell because they could undermine the community efforts already in place.[58] But there was a more troubling aspect to the problem.

Fear that provisions for the unemployed would attract transients either made some businessmen reluctant to take any action at all, or provided them an excuse for inaction. In Albany, both LeBoeuf himself and the Chamber of Commerce President were "against all publicity that might bring floaters into the town."[59] In Rochester "the Chamber of Commerce had the usual line . . . things were pretty good and they did not want to start a big useless movement to create jobs because all the floaters in America would flock here."[60] Some of Caswell's most critical judgments were reserved for these Chambers of Commerce.

Caswell also attacked the business attitude which, without particular reference to transients, claimed that there was no unemployment problem. In Syracuse, the Chamber of Commerce knew "nothing about the situation." "Everything is always lovely with these people," Caswell wrote, ". . . I am beginning to wonder just what these people are doing."[61] In Utica, Caswell found "the same old story of some of the biggest men trying to cover things up while the charity organizations are working overtime."[62]

Local businessmen taking this approach were failing to provide the supportive activity for the ideological campaign Hoover, Woods, and Caswell were waging. They needed above all to be able to point to local initiative to deal with unemployment. Caswell's most important task was to collect information on this activity to show its potential. Where there was no local activity, he was to stimulate it. The "spirit" with which businesses and local officials entered into the campaign were as important as concrete results.

That spirit was most evident in Schenectady where Mayor Lunn, described by Caswell as a "live wire," had "all kinds of schemes in mind."

> Everything possible is being done. . . . Everyone is awake to the situation. The wage scale, politics, religion and union labor figure in attacks on the mayor's efforts but he is doing *something*.

General Electric, the city's major employer (whose Owen Young was chairman of the Business Cycle Committee) established a relief plan for its laid off employees.[63]

The support of business was crucial in creating the appearance of local activity: where it did not cooperate, it threatened Hoover's ideological agenda. In Niagara Falls the President of the Trades Assembly, not the Chamber president, headed the local Unemployment

Committee. He reported that "his committee wasent worth a dam" [Caswell's spelling]. "The big employer now has his inning," he thought, "and is holding everything up in order to make labor come to terms."[64] The involvement of local social workers, assumed as a given, was less crucial than that of employers. In Buffalo, Caswell reported critically, the Unemployment Relief Committee was "a charity affair" and "no employment men or employers" were on it.[65]

Assuming the goal of Hoover's Unemployment Conference to be the reduction of unemployment, historians have been sceptical about its accomplishments. Hoover's own positive assessment of the results is more plausible, however, when we consider the goal—particularly of the "community" efforts—to have been ideological. Hoover did not really expect the local Chambers to have a major economic impact. He knew the depression was generated by forces beyond the locals' control and he supported the Business Cycle Committee's economic experts' work on the problem.[66] But he needed the cooperation of locals to maintain belief in the sturdy, self-reliant American character of which Woods spoke in Albany. Local Chambers had to acknowledge unemployment so that they could take the initiative in the crisis.[67] Accordingly, "spirit" and levels of activity, not rates of unemployment, were Caswell's ultimate measures of the Conference's local impact.

While the impact varied from community to community, it is suggestive to look more closely at one. In Yonkers, acknowledgement of the problem was slow in coming. The work of the Conference was crucial in changing local assessments of the situation and in stimulating local activities: its major impact was in the realm of perception and belief.

The first group to express concern about growing unemployment was, not surprisingly, the Yonkers Charity Organization Society. After the war, it faced the perennial problem of attracting contributions to meet its monthly disbursals, but now its budget was mushrooming. In 1913 the annual budget was $3,760, in 1918, $13,879, and by 1920 $25,997.[68] Bailey Burritt at first ascribed the growth in expenditures to the increased cost per family.[69] New leaders faced the problem: Julia Grandin had replaced the controversial Mary Jolly Van Hook as General Secretary in 1919. And in 1920, Walter M. Taussig succeeded Warren Kipp, president for the previous ten years. They clashed with Republican Mayor Wallin who felt that small relief payments were "a safeguard against too ready application for public relief."[70]

While problems of raising and distributing money were always central for the organization, Taussig and Grandin were largely occupied in the fall of 1920, with the organization of a central council of social agencies in Yonkers. Eager for the coordination within Yonkers which Van Hook had never achieved, Taussig noted that Van Hook's Social Service Exchange was used by only "five of the agencies and a mere handful of private individuals" and that therefore "the value of the Exchange was limited and its efficacy almost nullified."[71] On October 28, 1920, in his own home, Taussig chaired an organizing conference of representatives of about thirty of the seventy-eight organizations he had identified as being "engaged in some type of social endeavor." On Bailey Burritt's suggestion, the meeting unanimously chose Taussig chairman of a committee to draw up a constitution and continue the efforts. (Burritt stated that it was "hardly conceivable" that any one else should fill this position.)[72]

In November, Grandin noted an increase in appeals for relief from families of workers laid off by local factories. In the following months, emergency applications increased steadily, while efforts to find temporary work for the unemployed were fruitless. The Executive Committee of the Board of Directors considered instituting a system whereby they would obtain "refunds" from families whose wage-earners were temporarily out of work, but ultimately rejected it. The Department of Public Charities put additional pressure on the C.O.S. to support non-residents' applications which the Commissioner would not. With mounting emergency relief costs, Taussig appealed in January to Mayor Wallin to appoint a Committee on Unemployment.[73] But beyond the C.O.S., there was still little public expression of concern and thus little pressure on Wallin. The Yonkers *Herald* ran its own denial daily at the top of the front page: "There is little unemployment in Yonkers today. The merchant has business at hand who advertises for it."[74]

In January, the newspaper expressed approval of Governor Miller's economy-in-government message (it "has got the right ring to it: economy by cutting to the bone . . .") and recommended that the Yonkers Common Council do the same for the city.[75] Spring, which usually brought a decline in C.O.S. applications, brought further increases at the same time that Miller's economy measures closed the local office of the State Employment Service.[76]

In June, at the dedication of a new Salvation Army building, Mayor Wallin first acknowledged the problem in Yonkers, pointing out the "need of just such a building" in that there were 9,000 "men" out of work in the city and 3,000 working on part-time. "What the future holds for us we do not know," he declared, "the signs are none too hopeful."[77]

Indeed, Yonkers' industries were in poor shape. In May, with only 1,500 of the "normal force" of 2,500 at work at Otis, the company announced a ten to fifteen percent wage cut. Many of those working were already on part-time, working five or six hours a day, five days a week.[78] Things only got worse during summer: by the end of June, the plant was on a three-day week with a workforce of about 1,000. Seeing "no improvement for the rest of the year," Fitch closed Otis' employment office.[79] The carpet shops in Yonkers were less severely effected than the other local industries. But shortly after the summer bonus distribution, Alexander Smith announced wage cuts of an indeterminate percentage. The papers reported, "Work at the local plant is far from normal, yet it is far above the standard of other branches of industry in the city."[80] The Department of Labor published figures for September showing 8,350 out of work in Yonkers, a rate more than twice that of the New York State average, and greater than either New York City or Chicago.[81]

For the first time, the Otis and Waring managements expressed concern with the effects of the business depression upon their own workforces. Wishing to retain men in the city, Fitch promised that "should the occasion arise for employing any extra help, they will be recruited from those recently laid off" and he instituted a policy of transferring "the most valuable men now on the company roster" to different departments, in order to retain them in employment.[82] When the hat industry had a temporary resurgence of orders in mid-August, Waring found that "many of the employes who had been previously laid off, could not be located as they had gone to other parts in search of employment," and the firm claimed "difficulty in obtaining efficient help."[83]

After Wallin's Salvation Army speech, blaming workers for unemployment replaced outright denial of the problem. If there was some unemployment, the published analyses concurred, it was the workers' own fault. The *Statesman* (of which Wallin was Vice-President) ran editorials in September scoffing at "expressions of pity" for those "apparently out of work" in New York City. "If you want to know something about the actual number of men who really want work, "the editor challenged, "go out and try to hire somebody to do an odd job around your premises." It explained that the men sleeping in parks in Manhattan were "'tourists' . . . attracted by the white lights of Broadway" and that they could readily find work on farms if they wanted it. It called estimates of six million unemployed nationwide "perfectly ridiculous."[84]

An increase in workers' accounts with the Government Savings Associations was used as evidence that industrious workers—those who saved—still had jobs.[85] If workers themselves had saved more of their 1920 wages, another argument ran, "the country would not be facing a period of unemployment and industrial depression today."[86] And the most widespread analysis held that the high wages of workers caused unemployment. This argument, endorsed by the *Statesman*, promoted the "liquidation" of surplus labor by reducing its price—the wage.[87]

As national attention focused on the emergency in late September, the *Statesman* claimed that Yonkers was "not so bad off."[88] The paper greeted news of Hoover's Conference with skepticism, running an editorial entitled "Wasted Investigations" which discussed the tendency to spend resources on conferences "such as the current President's Conference on Unemployment" whose deliberations would not get translated into new policies.[89] But Woods' outreach to the cities had hardly been set into motion. Soon enough, the Republican city administration, the local Chamber of Commerce and even the *Statesman* began to see the problem in new ways.

At the end of September, on the day that the President's Conference held its first session, Mayor Wallin announced that he intended to form a local unemployment committee.[90] Rather than convening a wide range of civic leaders, Wallin called on Walter Taussig, as Chairman of the new Council of Social Agencies, his associate Rev. H.G. Richardson of the First Unitarian Congregational Church, and Robert Boettger, President of the Chamber of Commerce to constitute the committee.[91] Wallin himself did not take an active part, nor is there evidence of a larger committee meeting before the end of Wallin's term.

This was the first such committee since the Mayor's Relief Committee of 1893–1894, and the differences were significant. While the committee of the 1890s resulted from wealthy residents approaching the mayor, the 1921 committee was a creation of the Mayor, responding to the expression of concern at the State and federal government levels. The small size of the new committee was an indication of a new social service infrastructure within the city. Rather than a large *ad hoc* convocation of the philanthropically inclined business elites and church representatives, the new committee depended largely on the already established contacts of the organizations in Taussig's Social Service Council. Wallin needed only to appoint Taussig to mobilize its resources.[92]

In the first week of October, Mayor Wallin began to receive a stream of communications from the Conference. The first came from Edward Eyre Hunt, its secretary, who forwarded the recommendations for municipal action.[93] These underscored the mayoral responsibility for coping with the crisis.

> Whatever is done must take place in local communities, and the citizens of such communities are the ones responsible and capable of seeing that the necessary measures are carried out. This but repeats the first principle of American public life, reliance upon local initiative and obligation.[94]

Wallin responded that he had already formed a Committee and laid plans for a local Public Employment Agency.[95] On October 7, Herbert Hoover wrote to Wallin, as he did to mayors of all cities with populations greater than 25,000, asking him to report local activities and conditions to Woods.[96] Once again, Wallin confirmed that the City of Yonkers was "following out the plan outlined by the President's Conference in respect of the unemployment situation."[97]

In Yonkers, Hoover was widely associated with the humanitarian efforts he had spearheaded in Europe during and after the war. In recent months, Yonkers residents had held "Hoover Card Parties" and "Hoover Dinners" to raise funds for Eastern European relief. His name, according to the *Herald*, was "synonymous with humanitarian effort throughout the world."[98] His leadership of the publicity drive to stimulate local activity contributed significantly to its impact.

In a complete reversal of its stand over the previous months, the *Statesman* now called attention to the gravity of the crisis, not only in the country and in New York State, but also in Yonkers specifically. "It is apparent . . . that the situation is bad here," ran a new editorial. "A glance at the groups of idlers in the streets is all that is necessary to assure us of this." Not only did the paper reverse its assessment of the significance of the unemployed on the streets, but it also scrapped its skepticism about government investigation of the emergency:

> **Steps have been taken to open an employment bureau. . . . That may alleviate the situation but it cannot do more than scratch the surface. There is need for bigger measures. The situation demands a lot of study by the city administration.[99]**

Shortly thereafter, the *Statesman* called for Congressional passage of a $75,000,000 highways appropriation bill as "a small step in the relief of industrial idleness." "There is no more sensible thing that can be done by the Government or by any State," ran the editorial, "to help improve the situation than to engage in the construction of useful public works. . . ."[100]

Locally, Wallin announced plans to put unemployed men to work digging trenches for water mains and grading the grounds of a new fire hall. Wallin called a meeting of "local factory heads," attracting representatives from Otis, National (Warren Kipp), and Habirshaw Cable; these promised to give preference "to unemployed men who had previously worked for them," and said they "hoped gradually to take on others and thus relieve the situation. . . ."[101] But the employment bureau remained the major piece of evidence to show that local officials were confronting the emergency. It actually did little to ameliorate the situation.

The office opened on October 10 in a room donated by the Chamber of Commerce in its Getty Square office. A special "Community Fund" under the Mayor's control was used for supporting the agency.[102] On the first day fifty men applied, but the secretary, Anna Vanston, "refused to explain whether she had any actual jobs to offer."[103] Despite its office donation, some members of the Chamber of Commerce used the relatively small number of applicants to support their contention that the unemployment crisis had been exaggerated. "The unemployment situation in Yonkers is not as grave as has generally been thought," reported Secretary Hugh H. Thompson. "The government report of 8,000 in Yonkers is altogether too high." At the end of October, there had been 276 applicants at the agency, with only 67 given work. Thompson concluded, ". . . the men still seem to have in their veins the poison of war-time wages . . . many of those who applied could have received work if they had not been so exorbitant in the wage demands."[104] By January, there had been one thousand applicants, but only about 250 men [sic] placed.[105] Placements dropped off during the next month, with only fifty additional placements by the beginning of February.[106]

The Yonkers mayoral election coincided with the developing local acknowledgement of the unemployment crisis, but the latter was not a major campaign issue. The Democrats nominated the C.O.S.' Walter Taussig as their candidate, while Ulrich Wiesendanger replaced Wallin (who was finishing his second two-year term) as the Republican. The Democrats attacked Wiesendanger for luke-warm support for extending the New York City subway into Yonkers, and for his past performance as Westchester County Sheriff. He had been responsible for calling the National Guard in Hastings' National Conduit Strike of 1916, and the Democrats accused him both of incompetence in handling the situation and of collusion with the National Conduit owners.[107] They further accused him of profligate spending in the office. Walter Taussig won the election in November.[108]

Assuming office in January, he resigned as President of the Charity Organization Society but maintained his involvement, now as mayor, in the unemployment problem.[109] Where Wallin had delegated the task to his appointees, Taussig took personal responsibility for corresponding with officials of the President's Committee on Unemployment, and set out to enlarge the committee on unemployment with the help of Rev. Richardson.[110] But even with the increased interest, there is no evidence of a substantially different program for alleviating the problem. Taussig broke with his fellow Democrats on the city council in submitting a restraint budget approved by the Republicans and refused to commit the City to maintaining the Employment Agency on a permanent basis, despite Richardson's urging.[111] For the next several months, the local program largely took the form of helping the unemployed find temporary positions through the Employment Agency at the Chamber of Commerce, while emergency relief strained the C.O.S. to the limit of its resources.[112]

On February 9, Lieutenant Caswell arrived on the scene.[113] He brought a list of the accomplishments of the Conference's "community" program. At the top was the fact that 225 cities of more than 25,000 population had set up committees like that in Yonkers, and that many had set up employment bureaus. He also related news of "municipalities, schools, churches, and manufacturers (on a no-profit basis) putting people to work."[114]

Caswell reported to Woods that Yonkers looked "pretty fair," with the "carpet and sugar refining industries . . . going full force." He was impressed with Taussig, Richardson, and Vanston. His critical observations all related to the lack of "community" spirit. It was "some job," Richardson told him, to get the community working on the problems, because "half of the people here want to be classed as New Yorkers" and "do not give a darn about Yonkers." Secondly, local construction unions restricted the hiring of local unskilled labor, giving preference to "experienced out of town people." The third threat to a Yonkers "community" program to deal with unemployment came from floaters—"the riff raff from the big town and from upstate." But Mayor Taussig, his Police Chief, and the Charities Commissioner were all, Caswell reported approvingly, "eager to drive them out."[115]

Yonkers' recovery, of course, had nothing to do with community spirit. In the beginning of March Taussig reported to Woods, "our situation has improved to a certain extent."[116] A month later, the Chamber of Commerce asked that the Employment Agency be removed from its offices.[117] At the new location, the agency work blended into that of the Salvation Army.[118] New applications for work fell off, and the agency found it easier to place even the old applicants, some temporarily, but others permanently. By mid-April, 1350 applicants had registered, and 600 had been placed. On April 21, the secretary of the Bureau wrote to Woods to say that the unemployment situation in Yonkers had been "considerably reduced," and that there was "no longer an urgent need for the continuation of the City Employment Bureau."[119] By May, Taussig wrote to Hoover, the tide had turned and conditions improved to the point that "instead of the un-employed having difficulty in securing work the local industries as well as private individuals are experiencing trouble in securing needed help in practically all branches."[120] The *Statesman* declared the depression over when its editors received reports from the U.S. Department of Labor showing improvement in industry and increase in employment in every state.[121]

By October, 1922, with the promise of a huge new contract and a major expansion in the carpet shops, the mood in Yonkers was ebulient. The *Statesman* editorialized, "A period of great prosperity for Yonkers seems at hand, according to all indications. The outlook for extensive building operations next Spring is exceedingly bright."[122]

Hoover's "community" approach to maintaining faith in self-reliance and individual initiative at the same moment that he laid the groundwork for centralized economic planning placed a heavy ideological burden on the smaller local businesses which dominated the Chambers of Commerce. They had fewer resources than the large corporations like General Electric, Endicott-Johnson, and Otis. Nevertheless, their small contributions were important to Hoover's program. The Yonkers Chamber of Commerce with its close ties to Republican Mayor Wallin and the *Statesman* was not atypical in its response. The Chamber participated in the Mayor's committee and volunteered office space for an employment bureau while Hoover's local outreach campaign was operating in full force—but only during that time. Its members never fully subscribed to the idea that unemployment was an aspect of managerial inefficiency. Under pressure from higher levels of government the Chamber was reluctantly drawn into activities which reinforced the ideas both that local initiative counted and that local business could be counted on.[123]

The Conference's reliance on local businessmen in the "community" efforts puzzled social workers. Having been invited to play a central role in the Conference itself, social work activists encouraged the emphasis on the "community," because they had staked it out as the special domain of their own expert activity. At the Conference, they imagined that the community focus would provide them with a leading role in dealing with social problems. But Mary Van Kleeck's early concerns were echoed later in a Russell Sage Foundation study, *The Burden of Unemployment*, in which Philip Klein reported on efforts to deal with unemployment in fifteen cities between December, 1921 and May, 1922.

Like the Conference, Klein claimed that the community had to be the basis of emergency unemployment efforts.[124] But he rejected the mayor's emergency committees as the "basis of organization" of the community and concluded that the mayor was not at all "the natural leader in an unemployment situation. . . ."[125] Particularly troubling to Klein was the fact that the mayors' appointees represented particular "group interests in the population, which may or may not have had experience in dealing with unemployment."[126] He preferred the "neutral" expertise of the professional social workers. Klein considered the ongoing social welfare organizations of the city, and particularly welfare federations or social service councils as the most effective agents in an emergency.[127]

Edward Eyre Hunt, reading *The Burden of Unemployment*, noted its support for community organization. "The point that stands out very clearly is that . . . unemployment relief is a local problem and can only be handled locally." But he also noted Klein's criticism of the bypassing of social workers:

> I wish I felt sure that the social workers would have handled the problem better than the "business men" of the Conference, but Mr. Klein's book does not show that they did or could have done so. Naturally they are the source of most of his information, and may well have felt piqued at the formation of mayor's committees of amateurs and the resulting subordinate position of the professionals.[128]

Hoover wanted—and got—professional experts for the business cycle study. But in the local efforts, "amateur" businessmen were more important because only their participation could convey the ideological message which Hoover's "community" program sought to promote.

Mobilization for World War I raised the threat of a permanently enlarged federal government. Business leaders—even those who saw the need for national coordination of the economy—wanted to keep national planning in their own hands. Herbert Hoover's approach in sponsoring the Business Cycle study promised macroeconomic stabilization without expanding federal government controls or bureaucracies.

But the acknowledgment that the welfare not only of workers, but of smaller, locally based businesses was largely in the hands of managers of national corporations, financial institutions, and professional economists demanded a counterbalance from those—like Hoover—who were committed to an "American" ideology of individual initiative and opportunity. In Woods' hands, the "community" program became an ideological antidote to Hoover's centralized economic planning initiatives, conveying the message that individuals in the communities still had control over their own lives, still had the resources to maintain self-reliance.

The messages of the Unemployment Conference were thus curiously schizophrenic. They said that business cycle research in the hands of experts would help to stabilize chaotic economic conditions; but on the other hand, that ordinary citizens in the local communities would make all the difference in an emergency. Such inconsistencies were overlooked by the people who went back to work in 1922.

Notes

1. Historians' recent interest in the Unemployment Conference stems largely from Ellis Hawley's work on Hoover and the nineteen-twenties, and follows Hawley's work in its effort to revise the traditional picture of Hoover as a proponent of *laissez-faire*. With this orientation two recent studies—both by students of Hawley—call the Conference respectively "an experiment in national cooperative planning" and an attempt at "technocorporatist stabilization. "Carolyn Grin, "The Unemployment Conference of 1921: An Experiment in National Cooperative Planning," *Mid-America* 55, 2 (April, 1973), 83–107; Guy Alchon, *The Invisible Hand of Planning: Capitalism, Social Science and the State in the 1920s* (Princeton: Princeton University Press, 1985); Ellis Hawley, "Herbert Hoover and Economic Stabilization, 1921–1922," in Ellis Hawley, ed., *Herbert Hoover as Secretary of Commerce: Studies in New Era Thought and Practice* (Iowa City: University of Iowa Press, 1981), 43–79. Neither Carolyn Grin's overview of the Conference nor Guy Alchon's account of the construction of an apparatus for countercyclical economic planning outside of formal state institutions illuminates the strong interest in "community" which was at the center of the Conference's emergency unemployment program.

2. See chapters 3 and 4.

3. See Alchon, 52–63.

4. "Employment in Industrial Establishments in New York State and in the United States," Statistics Department, Federal Reserve Bank of New York, Nov.4, 1921, in Unemployment-Cities-New York-Misc., Box 629, CP-HHP. New York State Industrial Commission statistics indicate a beginning of the decline in employment in the State as early as April, 1920, becoming increasingly steep later in the year. See "Index of Employment in Factories in New York State, 1914–1923," New York State *Industrial Bulletin* 3,5 (Feb., 1924), 121. The Russell Sage study of the depression, completed in 1923, put the beginning at "late in the summer of 1920. Philip Klein, *The Burden of Unemployment* (New York: Russell Sage Foundation, 1923), 13.

5. "Report on Unemployment," August 12, 1921, Folder 20/145, Box 67, Chief Clerk's Files, General Records of the Department of Labor, R.G. 174, National Archives.

6. Alchon, 77.

7. President's Conference on Unemployment, *Report* (Washington: Government Printing Office, 1921), 15. Grin sets the date at August 12, but cites the Aug. 20 correspondence in the footnote, p. 86.

8. William Leiserson joined the full conference, but not the Economic Advisory Committee. President's Conference on Unemployment, *Report*, 7–14; Grin, 86. Alchon also notes the prominent representation from the Taylor Society and the National Bureau of Economic Research, 77.

9. President's Conference on Unemployment, *Report*, 16.

10. Grin, 89. Also see Alchon, 77; Hawley, "Herbert Hoover and Economic Stabilization, 1921–1922," in Hawley, ed., *Herbert Hoover as Secretary of Commerce: Studies in New Era Thought and Practice* (Iowa City: University of Iowa Press, 1981), 58.

11. President's Conference on Unemployment, *Report*, 19–22.

12. President's Conference on Unemployment, *Report*, 22–25.

13. Grin, 90.

14. H. Hoover to Governors, Oct. 11, 1921, printed in President's Conference on Unemployment, *Report*, 64–65.

15. In addition, Hoover and Edward Eyre Hunt continued to push recommendations to Congress for increased funding for the U.S.E.S., highways appropriations, and legislation permitting advanced planning of public works. Grin, 97–104.

16. Other members were Joseph Defrees, president of the U.S. Chamber of Commerce; Clarence Mott Woolley, American Radiator Co.; Mattew Woll, American Federation of Labor; Mary Van Kleeck, Russell Sage Foundation, with Hunt as Secretary. *Business Cycles and Unemployment*: Report and Recommendations of a Committee of the President's Conference on Unemployment Including An Investigation Made Under the Auspices of the National Bureau of Economic Research (New York: McGraw-Hill, 1923), v.

17. Alchon, 79–83; Hunt to Mitchell, Oct. 18, 1921; and Mitchell to Hunt, Feb. 28, 1922, Unemployment-Wesley C. Mitchell, Box 654, CP-HHP.

18. Hunt to Pritchett, Dec. 21, 1921, Unemployment-Unemployment Facts, Box 672, CP-HHP.

19. Herbert Hoover, Foreword to *Business Cycles and Unemployment*, vi.

20. Alchon, 72.

21. When the committee expressed confusion about its task, Hoover came to "indicate what he though was the function of this Committee, indicating also some measures which it seemed to him might be properly considered." "Progress Report of Committees," Sept. 28, 1921, Unemployment-Committee on Community, Civic and Emergency Measures, Box 637, CP-HHP. This committee was formed by a joining of two committees—Municipal Organization and Employment Agencies—established during the preliminary planning. "Suggestions for Committee on Community, Civic and Emergency Relief Measures," n.d., Unemployment-Committee on Community, Civic and Emergency Measures, Box 637, CP-HHP.

22. President's Conference on Unemployment, *Report*, 17.

23. Hawley, "Herbert Hoover and Economic Stabilization," 58. Bailey Burritt, incidentally, was Secretary of Woods' committee.

24. On Woods' background and activities, see Michael Pearlman, *To Make Democracy Safe For America: Patricians and Preparedness in the Progressive Era* (Urbana: University of Illinois Press, 1984), 106–107, 228–230.

25. President's Conference on Unemployment, *Report*, 18, 19.

26. Arthur Kellogg to Woods, Oct. 7, 1921, Unemployment-Mayors-Communications to, Box 654, CP-HHP.

27. Clark to Woods, Oct. 21, 1921, Unemployment-Committee on Community, Civic and Emergency Measures, Box 637, CP-HHP.

28. E.g., Woods to Mayors, Nov. 4, 1921, Unemployment-Committee on Community, Civic and Emergency Measures, CP-HHP; Grin, 92–93.

29. Van Kleeck to Woods, Oct. 8, 1921, Nov. 7, 1921, Unemployment-Van Kleeck, Mary, Box 672, CP-HHP.

30. Woods to Van Kleeck, Nov. 9, 1921, Unemployment-Van Kleeck, Mary, Box 672, CP-HHP.

31. Van Kleeck to Woods, Nov. 12, 1921, Unemployment-Van Kleeck, Mary, Box 672, CP-HHP.

32. Woods to Van Kleeck, Nov. 17, 1921; Van Kleeck to Woods, Dec. 6, 1921, Unemployment-Van Kleeck, Mary, Box 672, CP-HHP. Van Kleeck's criticisms did not stop at Woods. Secretary of the Conference, Edward Eyre Hunt recalled discussing them with Hoover, Hunt to Hoover, May 22, 1923, Unemployment-Committee on Community, Civic and Emergency Measures, Box 637, CP-HHP.

33. Samuel Gompers, "The Unemployment Conference—A Picture," Unemployment-AFL, Box 616, CP-HHP

34. Chamber of Commerce of the United States, "Emergency Program," Unemployment- 1921-Sept.Oct., Box 615, CP-HHP.

35. *The Monitor*, 8, 5 (Oct., 1921), 7–8.

36. Hoover to Thompson, Nov. 5, 1921, Unemployment–1921-Nov.Dec., Box 615, CP-HHP.

37. Translation from the Office of Radical Publications, *New Yorker Volkszeitung*, Sept. 28, 1921, Unemployment-Misc. Bolshevik Activities, Box 617, CP-HHP.

38. I. Amter to Harding, Dec. 1, 1921, Unemployment–1921-Nov.Dec., Box 615, CP-HHP.

39. F.B.I. reports from Jan. 16, 1922 to Feb. 6, 1922 in Unemployment-Misc. Bolshevik Activities, Box 617, CP-HHP.

40. Hoover to Miller, Oct. 1, 1921, Unemployment-Cities-New York-Misc., Box 629, CP-HHP.

41. Yonkers *Herald*, Mar. 4, 1921, 3; April 8, 1921, 6. On Miller's program, see Yonkers *Herald*, Jan. 5, 1921, 1, 6; on the announced end to the Service, COS Board Minutes, May 5, 1921, Box 2, Yonkers FSS Papers.

42. "2,500 Leave State's Employment Today," Yonkers *Herald*, June 30, 1921, 1; see also The N.Y. Associated Industries' *The Monitor*, 8, 5 (Oct., 1921), 8–11. Harding, of course, promised a similar retrenchment in federal government personnel.

43. "Extracts from telegrams sent by mayors of New York cities to Governor Miller in Response to his telegram of September 20, 1921," Folder: Unemployment 1920–1922, Box 2, American Association for Labor Legislation Papers, NYSSILR.

44. Press Release, Oct. 11, 1921, Unemployment-Cities-New York-Misc., Box 629, CP-HHP.

45. The Chamber of Commerce had invited all mayors, corporation counsels, school superintendents and Chamber of Commerce presidents in the State.James Watt to Nathan Miller, Oct. 13, 1921, Unemployment-Cities-New York-Misc., Box 629, CP-HHP. These officials would be in Albany at the same time for meetings of the State Conference of Mayors, etc. See Roy Smith to Woods, Oct. 12, 1921, loc. cit.

46. This, and the following, is from the typescript, "Address of Colonel Arthur H. Woods," Oct. 19, 1921, Unemployment-Unemployment Facts, Box 672, CP-HHP.

47. Van Kleeck to Woods, Oct. 15, 1921 and Nov. 26, 1921, Unemployment-Van Kleeck, Mary, Box 672, CP-HHP. See also Whiting Williams' observations of the inadequacy of omitting non-manufacturing sectors from employment statistics,

"Unemployment—Some General Considerations," Unemployment-Williams, Whiting, Box 673, CP-HHP.

48. Van Kleeck to Woods, Dec. 9, 1921, Unemployment-Van Kleeck, Mary, Box 672, CP-HHP.

49. The article by Davis Edwards on protests in England was widely reproduced in newspapers throughout the United States, according to *The Monitor*, 8, 6 (Nov., 1921), 24–26.

50. Miller to Woods, Nov. 12, 1921, and LeBoeuf to Woods, Dec. 23, 1921, Unemployment-Cities, New York -Misc, Box 629, CP-HHP.

51. LeBoeuf to Woods, Jan 24, 1922, Unemployment-Cities-New York-Misc., Box 629, CP-HHP.

52. Caswell to Woods, Oct. 5, 1921, Unemployment-Caswell, Fred. W., Box 621, CP-HHP. On Woods' connection to Plattsburg Barracks, see Pearlman, *To Make Democracy Safe for America*, Chapter 3. On Caswell in the Service Men's Welfare Organization, see above, chapter 7.

53. LeBoeuf to Woods, Jan. 24, 1922, Unemployment-Cities-New York-Misc., Box 629, CP-HHP.

54. LeBoeuf to Woods, Jan.24, 1922, Unemployment-Cities-New York-Misc., Box 629, CP, HHL; Unemployment-Cities-Conditions Reports-Improving-New York-Buffalo, Box 635, CP, HHL.

55. Caswell to Woods, March 2, 1922, Unemployment-Caswell, Fred W., Box 621, CP-HHP.

56. Caswell to Woods, Feb. 21, 1922, Unemployment-Caswell, Fred W., Box 621, CP-HHP. See also Gerald Zahavi, "Negotiated Loyalty: Welfare Capitalism and the Shoeworkers of Endicott-Johnson, 1920–1940," *JAH* 70, 3 (Dec., 1983), 602–620.

57. Caswell to Woods, Feb. 27, 1922, Unemployment-Caswell, Fred W., Box 621, CP-HHP.

58. Philip Klein, in a study for Russell Sage, concurred with Caswell's outlook. "The reciprocal and constructive helpfulness that plays so important a role in emergencies cannot be bred among rolling stones." Furthermore, ". . . in so far as each community is to care for its own unemployed it must be able to gain an idea of the size of its task and to see it through. . . . Adequate relief cannot be given to constantly swelling numbers attracted by the very fact of such adequacy" Klein, 85, 92.

59. Caswell to Woods, Jan.23, Jan. 24, 1922, Unemployment-Caswell, Fred W., Box 621 CP-HHP.

60. Caswell to Woods, Feb. 1, 1922, Unemployment-Caswell, Fred W., Box 621 CP-HHP.

61. Caswell to Woods, Feb. 2, 1922, Unemployment-Caswell, Fred W., Box 621 CP-HHP.

62. Caswell to Woods, Feb. 24, 1922, Unemployment-Caswell, Fred W., Box 621, CP-HHP. Another of Woods' agents found the same tendency: Whiting Williams noted that Chambers and Commerce and the press would "snatch at the slightest favorable indication." A common credo, he reported, was to "keep a stiff upper lip and lie." Whiting Williams, "Unemployment—Some General Considerations," March 4, 1922 Unemployment-Williams, Whiting, Box 673, CP-HHP.

63. Caswell to Woods, Jan. 27, 1922, Unemployment-Caswell, Fred W., Box 621 CP-HHP.

64. Caswell to Woods, Jan. 31, 1922, Unemployment-Caswell, Fred W., Box 621 CP-HHP. See also his report on Gloversville, Feb. 7, 1922.

65. Caswell to Woods, Jan. 30, 1922, Unemployment-Caswell, Fred W., Box 621 CP-HHP.

66. As influential as Van Kleeck was on the Business Cycle Committee, she made no headway with Woods in the Community efforts: she did not understand the ideological task, and he did).

67. Hoover's vision would have been reactionary—i.e. looked back to the community of the late nineteenth century and the position of paternalistic companies in the local social order—if he had really expected local businesses to take effective economic action. But, as explained above, he did not.

68. Yonkers *Statesman*, Oct. 20, 1921, 3.

69. Yonkers C.O.S. Board Minutes, Oct. 18, 1919, Box 2, Yonkers FSS Papers.

70. COS Board Minutes, May 6, 1920, Oct. 14, 1920, Box 2, Yonkers FSS Papers. Wallin later objected to the County welfare expenditures. "Mayor Believes County Pays Too Much for Social Welfare." Yonkers *Herald*, May 12, 1921, 1.

71. Yonkers COS Board Minutes, Sept. 23, 1920, 3, Box 2, Yonkers FSS Papers; Yonkers *Herald*, Oct. 30, 1920.

72. Yonkers *Herald*, Oct. 30, 1920.

73. COS Board Minutes, Dec. 2, 1920, Jan. 6, 1921, Feb. 3, 1921; Yonkers *Herald*, Jan. 12, 1921, 3.

74. E.g. Yonkers *Herald*, Jan. 14, 1921, 1. Klein refers to press blindness to the problem of unemployment in other cities, particularly in Pittsburgh where "hardly a trace of recognition of the fact came from the press," despite surveys showing severe unemployment. Local business interests were particularly interested in fostering a sense of optimism through periods of depression. Philip Klein, *The Burden of Unemployment*, 141, 240.

75. Yonkers *Herald*, Jan 5, 1921, 1,6.

76. Yonkers *Herald* Mar 4, 1921, 3; April 8, 1921, 6. On Miller's program, see Yonkers *Herald*, Jan. 5, 1921; on the announced end to the Service, COS Board Minutes, May 5, 1921, Box 2, Yonkers FSS Papers.

77. Yonkers *Herald*, June 13, 1921, 7. The fund-raising campaigns for the new Salvation Army building confirm the pattern of decreasing interest in local philanthropy by wealthy residents. Aiming for $25,000, the Salvation Army succeeded in raising only $12,000, consisting of one $500, one $400, one $200, and the remainder smaller donations. Such a pattern would have been unthinkable in a philanthropic campaign during the 1890s. Yonkers *Herald*, March 29, 1921, 1.

78. Yonkers *Herald*, May 11, 1921, 1; May 12, 1921, 1.

79. Yonkers *Herald*, June 24, 1921, 1; Yonkers *Statesman*, June 25, 1921, 1.

80. Yonkers *Statesman*, Aug. 11, 1921, 1. In its year-end summary, the *Herald* too, noted the relative health of the carpet industry. Yonkers *Herald*, Dec. 31, 1921, 2. It is hard to read backwards to the local situation from the State Department of Labor Report on this topic. Generally, carpet mill employment dropped 40 percent between May, 1920 and January, 1921, but there was virtually complete recovery by October, 1921. Moreover, according to the report, "a number of the carpet mills showed remarkable stability through the depression." New York State Department of Labor, "Course of Factory Employment in New York State From 1921 to 1930," Special Bulletin No. 171, Division of Statistics and Information, 1931, 78.

81. Yonkers *Statesman*, Oct. 5, 1921, 1 Oct. 6, 1921, 4.

82. Yonkers *Statesman*, June 25, 1921, 1. See also Yonkers *Herald*, Aug. 5, 1921, 9.

83. Yonkers *Herald*, Aug. 12, 1921, 1.

84. Yonkers *Statesman*, Sept. 16, 1921, 2. Although statistics were far from accurate, six million remains the best estimate of total unemployment at the time. The figure was based on a report to the U.S. Senate by the Secretary of Labor, who obtained figures from the U.S. Employment Service comparing employment in July, 1921 to that in January, 1920, assuming full employment at the latter date. A copy of the report is in Box 67, 20/145 (1913–1933), R.G. 174, General Records of the Dept. of Labor, Chief Clerk's Files, 1907–1942, National Archives.

85. Yonkers *Herald*, May 3, 1921, 6.

86. Yonkers *Statesman*, Feb. 9, 1921, 2.

87. Yonkers *Statesman*, Oct. 19, 1921, 4. W.R. Nigalls, quoted in the Washington, D.C. *Herald* said the main issue was "deflation in wages among the classes of labor whose stubbornness and stupidity are producing the jam." "Few High Wages Cause Depression," Nov. 27, 1921 Clipping in HHP-CP Box 672, Unemployment, Unemployment Facts. Arthur Woods heard the National Industrial Conference Board offer similar analysis: see Magnus Alexander to Arthur Woods, Dec. 31, 1921, HHP-CP Box 672, Unemployment, Unemployment Facts. These arguments followed A.C. Pigou's *Unemployment*. See Garraty, *Unemployment in History*, 142.

88. Yonkers *Statesman*, Sept. 27, 1921, 4.

89. Yonkers *Statesman*, Sept. 27, 1921, 4; Oct. 4, 1921.

90. It is unclear why Wallin appointed a committee at this point. Though Hoover had spoken in terms of local action, he had not yet specifically and publicly pointed to mayoral responsibility. Nor did the Republican *Statesman* seem to take the crisis seriously yet. Yonkers *Statesman*, Sept. 27, 1921, 4; Oct. 4, 1921.

91. W.J. Wallin to H. Hoover, Oct. 11, 1921, CP, HHL.

92. After establishing an employment agency, the next recommendation to local Emergency Committees was to "coordinate the work of the various charitable institutions." The structure for this task thus already existed in Yonkers. Philip Klein, summarizing the responses of the mayors in the cities he investigated, states that, "for the most part, they permitted the spontaneous formation of unemployment committees from among groups whose natural interests the year round brought them in contact with the problem," (38) rather than forming, or interfering with, the committees themselves. Yonkers was thus typical.

93. It is not decisively clear whether these were the "Recommendations" adopted by the plenary session of September 29, or the "Report of the Committee on Municipal Organization for Unemployment" which included "suggestions" to communities. For the following discussion, I have inferred the latter: Wallin's response of October 6, one day after the Committee "Report" was made public, expresses thanks for "the *suggestions* [my emphasis] of the President's Conference on Unemployment relative to municipal plans for meeting the present emergency." Wallin to Hunt, Oct. 6, 1921, Unemployment-Cities-New York-Yonkers, Box 630 CP-HHP; President's Conference on Unemployment, *Report*, 60–63.

94. "Report of the Committee on Municipal Organization for Unemployment," Oct. 5, 1921, printed in President's Conference on Unemployment, *Report*, 61.

95. W.J. Wallin to E.E. Hunt, Oct. 6, 1921, CP-HHP.

96. H. Hoover to Mayors, Oct. 7, 1921, printed in President's Conference on Unemployment, *Report*, 64.

97. W. J. Wallin to H. Hoover, Oct. 11, 1921, Unemployment-Cities-New York-Yonkers, Box 630 CP-HHP.

98. Yonkers *Herald*, Jan. 3, 21, 29, Mar.29, 1921.

99. Yonkers *Statesman*, Oct. 6, 1921, 4.

100. Yonkers *Statesman*, Oct. 22, 1921, 4. The highway bill was a result of the Conference, and passed in November. Grin, 98–99.

101. Yonkers *Herald*, Oct. 20, 1921, 1.

102. M.E. Santamorina to A. Woods, April 14, 1922, Unemployment-Cities-New York-Yonkers, Box 630 CP-HHP.

103. Yonkers *Statesman*, Oct. 10, 1921, 2.

104. Yonkers *Herald*, Oct. 28, 1921, 1. This newspaper report contains the only surviving information on those who applied, and it covers only Oct. 10 to Oct. 28. Of the 276 applicants, 113 were unskilled laborers, 64 factory workers and machinists, 47 clerical workers and store clerks, and 52 engineers and auto mechanics. 111 were married. In age, 23% were 15–20; 47% were 21–30; 25% were 30–50; and 5% were over 50. The C.O.S. directors offered a different explanation of the difficulties of the agency: "the City Employment Bureau does not seem to have the backing of the citizens at large." C.O.S. Board Minutes, Nov. 3, 1921, Box 2, Yonkers FSS Papers.

105. C.O.S. Board Minutes, Jan. 5, 1922, Box 2, Yonkers FSS Papers.

106. Report of John Updegrove Re: Yonkers Unemployment Situation, Feb. 7, 1922, CP-HHP.

107. Yonkers *Herald*, Oct. 21, 1921, 1; Oct. 31, 1921, 1; Nov. 2, 1921, 1.

108. Yonkers *Statesman*, Nov. 9, 1921, 1.

109. Yonkers C.O.S. Board Minutes, Jan. 5, 1922, Box 2, Yonkers FSS Papers.

110. W.M. Taussig to A. Woods, Jan. 12, 1922; H. Richardson to A. Woods, Jan. 9, 1922, Unemployment-Cities-New York-Yonkers, Box 630, CP-HHP.

111. Yonkers *Statesman*, Jan.3, 1922; H. Richardson to A. Woods, Jan. 9, 1922, CP-HHP.

112. W.M. Taussig to A. Woods, March 6, 1922, Unemployment-Cities-New York-Yonkers, Box 630, CP-HHP; Yonkers *Statesman*, Feb. 25, 1922.

113. Caswell's visit was reported in the Yonkers *Statesman*, Feb. 13, 1922, 12. His visit followed that of F.B.I. agent John C. Updegrove who spent six days in Yonkers. Updegrove reports, Feb. 3, 1922, Feb. 7, 1922, Unemployment-Cities-New York-Yonkers, CP-HHP.

114. Yonkers *Statesman*, Feb. 13, 1922, 12.

115. Caswell to Woods, Feb. 9, 1922, Unemployment-Caswell, Fred.W, Box 621, CP-HHP.

116. W.M. Taussig to A. Woods, March 6, 1922, Unemployment-Cities-New York-Yonkers, Box 630, CP-HHP.

117. Yonkers *Statesman*, March 31, 1922, 1; April 3, 1922, 5.

118. The evidence leaves some ambiguity about the formal end of the Agency. Taussig wrote to Herbert Hoover, June 19, 1922 "Our local Unemployment Bureau was discontinued about a month ago, but the work was continued at my personal request by the local branch of the Salvation Army." W.M. Taussig to H. Hoover, June 19, 1922, Unemployment-Cities-New York-Yonkers, Box 630, CP-HHP. Anna Vanston was

replaced by a Miss Santamarino in the new location. Yonkers *Statesman*, March 31, 1922, 1.

119. M.E. Santamorina to A. Woods, April 21, 1922, Unemployment-Cities-New York-Yonkers, Box 630, CP-HHP.

120. W.M. Taussig to H. Hoover, June 19, 1922, Unemployment-Cities-New York-Yonkers, Box 630, CP-HHP.

121. Yonkers *Statesman*, June 10, 1922, 6.

122. Yonkers *Statesman*, Oct. 12, 1922, 8, Oct. 16, 1922, 1.

123. In some cases, Hoover's efforts moved local Chambers closer to positions espoused by the more progressive managers of the large, national corporations. The Industrial Management Council of the Rochester Chamber issued its own study of Unemployment Insurance in 1922, concluding, "unemployment insurance has a fair chance to demonstrate its excellence, if not in the form of compulsory State insurance, at least when applied in individual plants or industries." "Unemployment Insurance at a Glance," August, 1922, in Unemployment 1920–1922, Box 2, AALL Papers.

124. Klein, 5.

125. Klein, 60, 216.

126. Klein, 46, 56.

127. Klein repeatedly emphasized the uniqueness of each city's situation. The Yonkers experience, where Walter Taussig, the organizer of the Social Service Council, became mayor in the middle of the crisis, was not repeated in any other city he investigated.

128. Draft of a letter by Hunt for Hoover to John Glenn, May 22, 1923, Unemployment-Committee on Community, Civic and Emergency Measures, Box 637, CP-HHP. (Hoover refused to sign the letter but did not object to Hunt's signing it. Emmet to Hunt, May 28, 1923, Unemployment-Committee on Community, Civic and Emergency Measures, Box 637, CP-HHP.)

Conclusion

Yonkers of the nineteen-twenties reverberated with some of the themes of the eighteen-nineties. Concerns with "floaters" and casual laborers echoed back to the earlier tramps. Hoover's "community" efforts recalled an earlier time when local factory owners contributed substantially to paternalistic measures during and between employment crises. But nobody could miss the vast differences which separated the depression of 1893 from that of 1921.

First and most fundamental was the fact that the owners of the largest factories themselves no longer lived in the city. The paternalism which they had demonstrated in the 1890s had been replaced by a social service infrastructure. The *ad hoc* and informal arrangements of the local factory owners of the 1890s were replaced by middle class organizations with full-time, paid officials. While these groups were active in a variety of social improvement campaigns, they were still clearly incapable of dealing with the problem of unemployment, which resulted from far larger forces.

Though the social service workers might claim expertise and commitment, they did not claim nor command the same position as community leaders as had their forerunners, the local factory owners. Nor, perhaps more importantly, did they have access to the same kind of financial resources. For these reasons, they looked outward to organizations beyond Yonkers to strengthen their claims to legitimacy and occasionally to obtain funding as well.

The ideas of a labor market stabilized and managed on a broad scale came from metropolitan reformers—not from the local setting. These reformers saw the management of capital markets and the organizational innovations of the corporate era and asked why labor markets should remain so decentralized, so information-poor, and so chaotic, particularly when their disorganization had such grave consequences for workers. The central plank of their reform platform involved a relatively small extension of state capacity to collect and disseminate employment information in public employment exchanges.

Employers and state officials became most interested in the reformers' program during the chaos of wartime labor shortages. Both the federal government's U.S.E.S. and the post-war New York State Employment Bureau operated on a scale which made a significant contribution to labor market dynamics. The experience taught all concerned that real labor market management involved more than simply matching workers with jobs: that issues of union recognition, wage rates, and employment conditions would all receive scrutiny if labor market conditions were to be stabilized. This understanding made employers more insistent than ever that the employment relationship remain firmly in their control.

While some embraced a return to laissez-faire after the war, others, like General Electric's Owen Young felt sufficiently convinced of the scope of their power and of the need for economic stabilization that they joined with reformers in devising strategies for economic coordination which would not encroach upon large employers' powers.

All of these developments—the demise of the local factory owners, the outward-looking social service organizations, the experiments with state involvement in labor policies, and the conferences to coordinate financial and industrial policies—forced recognition that the welfare of local workers was dependent on forces beyond the local community. But Progressives of the twenties, like Young in General Electric and Herbert Hoover in the Department of Commerce, mobilized the resources of the centralized, national institutions in which they wielded power to broadcast an ideological message underlining the continuing importance of individual initiative and community spirit.

Only two years after the elation of the 1922 recovery in Yonkers, Waring Hat's receivership was announced. The Y.M.C.A. called its permanent closing in October "the greatest industrial and financial tragedy that has happened in Yonkers in fifty years."[1] Waring's demise and "abnormal conditions in some of the other factories" sent "literally hundreds of young men, and boys, unemployed and walking the streets of the city."[2]

But the Waring collapse was only the first of three twentieth century industrial calamities in Yonkers. In the midst of a 1954 United Textile Workers strike at Alexander Smith, management announced the termination of work at the Yonkers shops and relocation in Greenville, Mississippi to take advantage of non-union labor and local tax incentives.[3]

In response to similar threats from the Otis Elevator Corporation in the ensuing years, civic leaders argued that it was "best to give Otis whatever it wanted."[4] The price was steep, but the incentives provided by the city were not enough to keep the corporation in Yonkers.[5] In 1975, Otis was taken over by United Technologies, a defense-oriented corporation looking for diversification in the mid–1970s.[6] Seven years later, it shut down the Yonkers operation as it expanded elevator manufactures overseas.[7]

The impact upon the social fabric of Yonkers of the factory shutdowns and high levels of unemployment are manifest as one walks among the idle men and women on Getty Square today. In 1987, the city still appears to be crumbling visibly. The worst fears of the Yonkers-boosters of eighty years ago could hardly have taken a more disastrous form. Yonkers as a local community was unable to compete with other communities, in the United States and elsewhere, which offered greater incentives to capital.

The early twentieth century reformers concerned with the debilitating effects of chronic underemployment, the ongoing human cost of the business cycle's troughs, and employment practices which abandoned workers in the competitive search for profits, would be similarly appalled by a stroll through Getty Square today. They too would see the embodiment of many of the worst of their fears. But in the late twentieth century, reformers would not see the "shifting sands" of mobile workers posing a threat. In Yonkers, as in many other manufacturing cities, the "shifting sands" have become a stagnant swamp. Not the unregulated mobility of workers but the unregulated mobility of capital now saps the "very basis of our national efficiency." That it does not also "germinate the seeds of revolution," is a tribute, in part, to the ongoing success of the kind of ideological campaigns pioneered during and after the First World War.

Notes

1. Yonkers *Herald*, July 15, 1924, 1–2. Yonkers Y.M.C.A. *Annual Report*, March 1, 1925, 4. This annual report was found at the Yonkers Y.M.C.A. which has few other surviving records.

2. Y.M.C.A. *AR* 1925, 4. Either the women and girls laid off by Waring did not walk the streets in response to unemployment, or the Y.M.C.A. officials had gender-blinders, or both.

3. "When the Mill Pulled the Rug Out From Under Yonkers," N. Y. *Times*, July 29, 1979, 15; Peter Zopes and Rick Beard, "In the Mill" Hudson River Museum pam., 1983, 9–10.

4. Jeff Coplon, "Parting Company," New York *Sunday News Magazine*, March 6, 1986, 8.

5. In addition to concessions in bonus and incentive rates, the City of Yonkers put together a $14 million package (over $11 million of which were federal and state aid) to buy nine acres adjacent to the plant, then occupied by offices, business, and black and Hispanic residences. The city demolished the buildings, and sold the land to Otis in return for $539,000 and the construction of a retaining wall. Coplon, "Parting Company," 6–13.

6. *Time Magazine*, Nov. 24, 1975, 92.

7. Coplon, "Parting Company," 6–13.

Bibliography

Primary Sources

Manuscripts and Archives

Alexander Smith Company Papers. Hudson River Museum (HRM). Yonkers, New York.

American Association of Labor Legislation Papers (AALL). Labor Management Documentation Center (LMDC), New York State School of Industrial Labor Relations (NYSSILR). Ithaca, New York.

American Association of Labor Legislation Papers, 1905–1943. (Microfilm Edition) Mary S. Arluck, ed., Cornell University Labor Management Documentation Center, 1974.

Bruere, Henry. *Reminiscences*. Columbia University Oral History Project. Columbia University Library. New York, New York.

Community Service Society Papers (CSS). Columbia University Library. New York, New York.

Hoover, Herbert Papers: Commerce Papers. Hoover Presidential Library. (CP-HHP) West Branch, Iowa.

Mayoralty Papers. Municipal Archives. New York, New York.

Mills, Abraham Gilbert Papers. New York Public Library.

New York City Merchants Association Archives. Chamber of Commerce. New York, New York.

Otis Elevator Corporation Papers. United Technology Corporation Archives. East Hartford, Connecticut.

Perkins, Frances Papers. Columbia University. New York, New York.

Perkins, Frances. *Reminiscences*. Columbia University Oral History Project. Columbia University Library. New York, New York.

Rubinow, Isaac M. Papers. Labor Management Documentation Center, New York State School of Industrial Labor Relations. Ithaca, New York.

Russell Sage Foundation Papers (RSF). Rockefeller Archive Center. Pocantico Hills, New York.

Socialist Party Papers. Tamiment Library. New York, New York.

United States Commission on Industrial Relations (CIR). Records. National Archives. Washington, D.C.

United States Department of Labor. Record Group 174. National Archives. Washington, D.C.

United States War Labor Policies Board. Record Group 1. National Archives. Washington, D.C.

Van Kleeck, Mary Papers (MVK). Sophia Smith Collection, Smith College. Northampton, Massachusetts.

Yonkers Chamber of Commerce Papers. Yonkers Chamber of Commerce. Yonkers, New York.

Yonkers Family Service Society Papers (FSS). Yonkers Family Service Society. Yonkers, New York.

Yonkers Historical Society Collections. Hudson River Museum. Yonkers, New York.

Yonkers Planning Bureau Records. Yonkers Planning Bureau. Yonkers, New York.

Yonkers Woman's Institute Papers (YWI). Yonkers Woman's Institute and Yonkers Chamber of Commerce. Yonkers, New York.

Yonkers Y.M.C.A. Papers. Yonkers Y.M.C.A. Yonkers, New York

Government Documents

Baruch, Bernard M. *American Industry in the War: A Report of the War Industries Board*. Washington, D.C.: GPO, 1921.

Brissenden, Paul F. *Earnings of Factory Workers 1899 to 1927: An Analysis of Payroll Statistics*. Census Monographs 10. Washington, D.C.: GPO, 1929.

Kube, Harold D. and Ralph H. Danhof. *Changes in Distribution of Manufacturing Wage Earners 1899–1939*. Washington, D.C.: GPO, 1942.

New York State Commission on Employers' Liability and Unemployment. *Third Report*. Albany: J.B. Lyon, 1911.

New York State Department of Labor. *Industrial Directory*. Albany: J.B. Lyon, 1912, 1913.

———. *Annual Reports of the Commissioner of Labor*. Albany: J.B. Lyon, 1900–1920. (Becomes *Annual Reports of the Industrial Commission*, 1915.)

———. *Bulletins*. Albany: J.B. Lyon, 1910–1918.

———. *Special Bulletins*. 58, 69, 73, 85, 93, 189. Albany: J.B. Lyon, 1914–1936.

———. *The Labor Market*. Albany: monthly, from Oct. 1915.

New York State Factory Investigating Commission. *Reports*. Albany: J.B. Lyon, 1912–1915.

New York State Board of Charities. *Annual Reports*.

President's Conference on Unemployment. *Report*. Washington: GPO, 1921.

Sargent, F.B. *Statistics of Unemployment and Work of Employment Offices*. Labor Bureau Bulletin 109, 1913.

U.S. Bureau of the Census. Compendium of the 11th Census (1890).
———. Compendium of the 12th Census (1900).
———. Compendium of the 13th Census (1910).
———. Compendium of the 14th Census (1920).
U.S. Bureau of Labor Statistics. "Unemployment in New York City." Bulletin 172 (April, 1915).
———. "Proceedings of the American Association of Public Employment Offices." Annual Meetings, 1913, 1914, 1915. Bulletin 192 (1916).
———. "Unemployment in the United States." Bulletin 195 (July, 1916).
———. "Proceedings of the Employment Managers Conference, Minneapolis Minnesota." Bulletin 196 (May, 1916).
———. "Welfare Work for Employees in Industrial Establishments in the United States." Bulletin 250 (1919).
U.S. Commission on Industrial Relations. *Final Report and Testimony*. Washington: GPO, 1916.
U.S. Department of Commerce. *Survey of Current Business*. Washington: GPO, monthly from July 1, 1921.
U.S. Department of Labor. "The Attitude of Women's Clubs and Associations Towards Social Economics." Bulletin 23 (July, 1899)
Waring, George E. *Report on the Social Statistics of Cities*. Washington: GPO, 1886. Rpr. New York: Arno Press and New York Times, 1970.

Periodicals

American Labor Legislation Review
New York Associated Industries *Monitor*
Yonkers *Herald*
Yonkers *Statesman*
The Survey

Primary Published Works

Abbott, Edith. *Women in Industry: A Study in American Economic History*. New York and London: Appleton, 1909.
Alexander, Magnus W. "Waste in the Hiring and Firing of Men," *Annals of the American Academy* 65 (May, 1916).
Allen, William H. *Efficient Democracy*. New York: Dodd, Mead, 1907.
Allison, Charles E. *The History of Yonkers*. New York: Wilbur B. Ketcham, 1896.
Andrews, John B. "A National System of Labor Exchanges." *New Republic* 1, 8 (Dec. 26, 1914) Part 2, 1–8.
———. "American Cities and the Prevention of Unemployment." pam. New York: The Civic Press (American City Pamphlets), 1916.

———. "A Practical Program for the Prevention of Unemployment." *American Labor Legislation Review* 5 (June, 1915).

Beveridge, William H. *Unemployment: A Problem of Industry*. London: Longman's, Green and Co., 1909.

Bliss, W.D.P., ed. *Encyclopedia of Social Reform*. New York: Funk and Wagnalls, 1908.

Bloomfield, Daniel, ed. *Selected Articles on Employment Management*. New York: Wilson, 1922.

Bloomfield, Meyer and Joseph H. Willets, eds. *Personnel and Employment Problems in Industrial Management*. Entire issue of *The Annals of the American Academy* 65 (May 1916).

Bogart, Ernest L. "The Housing of the Working People of Yonkers." *Economic Studies* 3, 5 (Oct. 1898): 273–348.

Brandeis, Elizabeth. "Labor Legislation." In John R. Commons and Associates. *History of Labor in the United States* 3. New York: Macmillan, 1935.

Brandt, Lillian. "The Causes of Poverty." *Political Science Quarterly* 23, 4

Brissenden, Paul and Emil Frankel. *Labor Turnover in Industry*. New York: Macmillan, 1922.

Brooks, John Graham. "The Future Problem of Charity and the Unemployed." *Annals of the American Academy of Political and Social Science* 5 (July, 1894), 14–15.

Bruere, Henry. "America's Unemployment Problem." *Annals of the American Academy* (Sept. 1915).

Bullock, Edna D., ed. *Selected Articles on Compulsory Insurance*. Minneapolis: H.W. Wilson, 1912.

Campbell, M. Edith. "Employment Bureaus for Women." *The Economic Position of Women: Proceedings of the Academy of Political Science* 1, 1 (Oct. 1910): 151–161.

Robert C. Chapin, The Standard of Living Among Workingmen's Families in New York City (New York: Russell Sage, 1909).

Closson, Carlos C., Jr. "The Unemployed in American Cities," *Quarterly Journal of Economics* 8 (Jan. 1894): 168–217, 257–258; (July 1894): 453–477, 499–502.

———. "Notes on the History of 'Unemployment' and Relief Measures in the United States." *Journal of Political Economy* 3 (Sept. 1895): 461–469.

Colvin, Fred H. *Labor Turnover, Loyalty and Output*. New York: McGraw Hill, 1919.

Commons, John R. *Unemployment Insurance: The Road to Prevention*. Madison, Wisconsin: Wisconsin Association for the Prevention of Unemployment, 1923.

Cooke, Morris Llewellyn. "Casual and Chronic Unemployment." *Annals of the American Academy* 59 (1915), 194–199.

———. "Scientific Management as a Solution of the Unemployment Problem." pam. Philadelphia, 1915.

Crowther, Samuel. *John H. Patterson: Pioneer in Industrial Welfare*. Garden City, N.Y.: Doubleday, Page, 1922.

Devine, Edward T. *Efficiency and Relief: A Programme of Social Work*. New York: Columbia University Press, 1906.

———. "Employment Bureau for the People of New York City." *Annals of the American Academy* 33 (March 1909): 225–238.

———. *The Family and Social Work*. New York: Survey Associates, 1912.

———. *Misery and Its Causes*. New York: Macmillan, 1909.

———. *Principles of Relief*. New York: Macmillan, 1904.

———. *Report on the Desirability of Establishing an Employment Bureau in the City of New York*. New York: Russell Sage Foundation, 1909.

———. *Social Forces*. New York: Charities Publication Committee, 1910.

Douglas, Paul H. "The Problem of Labor Turnover." *American Economic Review* 8 (June 1918), 308–316.

Elkus, Abram. "Value of Investigation as a Basis for Social Legislation." *Survey* 34 (April 24, 1915).

Feder, Leah Hannah. *Unemployment Relief in Periods of Depression: A Study of Relief Measures Adopted in Certain American Cities 1857–1922*. New York: Russell Sage Foundation, 1936.

Fitch, John A. "Labor Reconstruction: The Conference of the Academy of Political Science." *Survey* 41, 11 (Dec. 14, 1918): 335–342.

Forbes, James. "The Work of the Mendicancy Police in New York." *Charities* 11 (1903): 576–578.

French, Alvah P. *History of Westchester County, New York*. New York and Chicago: Lewis Historical Publishing Co., 1925.

Gurteen, S. Humphreys *A Handbook of Charity Organization*. Buffalo, New York: 1882.

Harrison, Shelby M., et al. *Public Employment Offices: Their Purpose, Structure and Methods*. New York: Russell Sage Foundation, 1924.

Hodges, Henry G. "Progress of the Public Employment Bureaus." *Annals of the American Academy*. 69 (Jan. 1917): 91–102.

Howe, Frederick C. "Unemployment: A Problem and a Program." *Century Magazine* 89 (1915): 843–848.

Howe, Frederick C. *Confessions of a Reformer*. New York: Scribner's, 1925.

Hunter, Robert. *Poverty*. New York: Macmillan, 1904.

Johnsen, Julia E., ed. *Selected Articles on Unemployment*. White Plains, N.Y. and New York: H.W. Wilson, 1915)

Kellogg, Charles D. "The Situation in New York City During the Winter of 1893–1894." *Proceedings of the National Conference of Charities and Correction* 1894.

Kellogg, Paul, ed. *The Pittsburgh Survey*. New York: Russell Sage Foundation, 1909–1914.

Kellor, Frances A. *Out of Work*. New York: Putnam, 1904. Revised, 1915. Rpr. New York: Arno, 1971.

———. "Is Unemployment a Municipal Problem?" *National Municipal Review* 3 (April 1914): 366–370.

———. *Unemployment: A Program for Relief* pam. repr. of *The Survey*: Feb. 1914.

Kelly, Edmond. *The Elimination of the Tramp*. New York: Putnam's Sons, 1908.

Kingsbury, John A. "Our Army of the Unemployed." *Review of Reviews* 49 (April 1914): 433–439. Rpr. Johnsen, Julia E., ed. *Selected Articles on Unemployment*. White Plains, N.Y. and New York: H.W. Wilson, 1915): 5–15.

Klein, Philip. *The Burden of Unemployment: A Study of Unemployment Relief Measures in Fifteen American Cities, 1921–1922*. New York: Russell Sage Foundation, 1923.

Laubach, Frank C. *Why There Are Vagrants: A Study Based Upon Examination of One Hundred Men*. New York: Columbia University Press, 1916.

Leiserson, William. *Unemployment in the State of New York*. New York: Columbia University Press, 1911.

———. "Theory of Public Employment Offices and the Principles of Their Practical Application." *Political Science Quarterly* 29 (March 1914): 28–46.

———. "A Federal Labor Reserve Board for the Unemployed." *Annals of the American Academy*. 69 (Jan. 1917): 103–117.

Lescohier, Don D. *The Labor Market*. New York, Macmillan, 1919.

Lewis, Orlando F. "Vagrancy in the United States." *Proceedings of the National Conference of Charities and Correction* 1907: 64-.

Lowell, Josephine Shaw. "The Unemployed in New York City, 1893–1894." *Journal of Social Science* 32 (Nov. 1894).

MacLean, Annie Marion. *Wage Earning Women*. New York: Macmillan, 1910.

McCook, J.J. "A Tramp Census and Its Revelations." *The Forum* (Aug. 1893): 753–766.

Merchants' Association of New York. "Report on Industrial Relations." pam. New York: 1919.

Mitchell, Wesley Clair. *Business Cycles*. Berkeley: University of California Press, 1913.

———. *Business Cycles: The Problem and Its Setting*. New York: National Bureau of Economic Research, 1927.

New York City Mayor's Committee on Unemployment. *Report*. New York: 1916.

———. "A Proposal in Reference to Unemployment in the Winter of 1914," pam. Prepared by Henry Bruere. New York: 1914.

———. "Report of the Bundle Day Committee." pam. New York, 1915.

———. *Report on Dock Employment in New York CIty and Recommendations for its Regularization*. New York: 1916.

———. *How to Meet Hard Times: A Program for the Prevention and Relief of Abnormal Unemployment*. New York: 1917.

Odencrantz, Louise. *Italian Women in Industry*. New York: Russell Sage Foundation, 1919.

Parker, Carleton H. *The Casual Laborer and Other Essays*. New York: Harcourt, Brace and Howe, 1920.

Person, Harlow. "Scientific Management and the Reduction of Unemployment." *Bulletin of the Taylor Society* 6 (Feb. 1921).

Presient's Conference on Unemployment. *Business Cycles and Unemployment: Report and Recommendations*. New York: McGraw Hill, 1923.

Richardson, Anne B. "Women in Philanthropy." *Proceedings of the National Conference of Charities and Correction* 1892: 216–223.

Ripley, Charles M. *Life in a Large Manufacturing Plant*. Schenectady, New York: General Electric Company Publication Bureau, 1919.

Rubinow, Isaac Max. *Social Insurance, with Special Reference to American Conditions*. New York: Henry Holt, 1913.

———. "Dependency Index of New York City, 1914–1917." *American Economic Review* 8, 4 (Dec. 1918): 713–740.

Seager, Henry R. *Social Insurance: A Program for Social Reform*. New York: Macmillan, 1910.

Sekely, Bela. *Minimizing Unemployment: A Plan for the Organization of the Labor Market*. New York: National Liberal Immigration League, 1916.

Smelser, David P. *Unemployment and American Trade Unions*. Baltimore: Johns Hopkins University Press (Studies in Historical and Political Science), 1919.

Slichter, Sumner. *The Turnover of Factory Labor*. New York: Appleton, 1919.

Solenberger, Alice Willard. *One Thousand Homeless Men: A Study of Original Records*. New York: Russell Sage Foundation, 1911.

Spargo, John. "Socialism as a Cure for Unemployment." *Annals of the American Academy* 59 (May 1915): 194–199.

Speek, Peter A. "The Psychology of Floating Workers." *Annals of the American Academy* 69 (Jan. 1917): 72–78.

Tead, Ordway. *Instincts in Industry: A Study of Working Class Psychology*. Boston: Houghton, Mifflin, 1918.

Van Kleeck, Mary. "The Effect of Unemployment on the Wage Scale." *Annals of the American Academy*. (Sept. 1915).

———. "Women Workers During Reconstruction." *American Labor Legislation Review* (March, 1919): 62–68.

Warner, Amos G. *American Charities: A Study in Philanthropy and Economics*. New York: Thomas Crowell, 1894.

Watson, Frank D. *The Charity Organization Movement in the United States: A Study in American Philanthropy*. New York: Macmillan, 1922.

Webb, Sidney and Beatrice, eds. *The Public Organization of the Labour Market: Being Part II of the Minority Report of the Poor Law Commission*. London: Longman's Green and Co., 1909.

Weitz, Louis. *Out of a Job?*. New York: Peoples' Educational Society, 1915.

Willits, Joseph H., ed. *Stabilizing Industrial Employment: Reducing the Labor Turnover*. Entire issue of *The Annals of the American Academy* 71 (May, 1917).

Yonkers Board of Trade. *Yonkers Illustrated*. Yonkers, 1902.

Yonkers Chamber of Commerce. *Yonkers: Next to the Largest City in the United States*. New York: Robert L. Stillson, 1912.

Yonkers Mayor's Honor Roll Committee. *Yonkers in the World War*. Norwood, MA: Plimpton Press, 1922.

Yonkers Fiftieth Anniversery Celebration Committee. *"Souvenir Issue" History of Yonkers, 1872–1922*. Yonkers: Fernhead and Bleakley, 1922.

Secondary Works

Adams, Graham. *The Age of Industrial Violence, 1910–1915*. New York: Columbia University, 1966.

Adams, Thomas, Harold M. Lewis, and Theodore T. McCrosky, eds. *Regional Survey of New York and Its Environs, Volume II: Population, Land Values and Government*. New York: Committee on Regional Plan of New York and Its Environs, 1929.

Alchon, Guy. *The Invisible Hand of Planning: Capitalism, Social Science and the State in the 1920s*. Princeton, NJ: Princeton University, 1985.

Alexander, John K. *Render Them Submissive: Responses to Poverty in Philadelphia, 1760–1800*. Amherst: University of Massachusetts, 1980.

Asher, Robert. "Failure and Fulfillment: Agitation for Employers' Liability Legislation and the Origins of Workmen's Compensation in New york State, 1876–1910." *Labor History* 24, 2 (Spring, 1983): 198–222.

Bender, Thomas. *Community and Social Change in America*. Baltimore: Johns Hopkins, 1978.

Berkowitz, Edward and Kim McQuaid. *Creating the Welfare State: The Political Economy of Twentieth-Century Reform*. New York: Praeger, 1980.

Bernstein, Irving. *The Lean Years: A History of the American Worker, 1920–1933*. Baltimore, MD: Penguin, 1966.

———. *Turbulent Years: A History of the American Worker, 1933–1941*. Boston: Houghton, Mifflin, 1969.

———. *A Caring Society: The New Deal, the Worker, and the Great Depression*. Boston, Houghton, Mifflin, 1985.

Boyer, Paul. *Urban Masses and Moral Order in America, 1820–1920*. Cambridge: Harvard University, 1978.

Brandes, Stuart. *American Welfare Capitalism, 1880–1940*. Chicago: University of Chicago, 1976.

Braverman, Harry. *Labor and Monopoly Capital: The Degradation of Work in the Twentieth Century*. New York: Monthly Review, 1974.

Bremer, William W. *Depression Winters: New York Social Workers and the New Deal*. Philadelphia: Temple University, 1984.

Bremner, Robert. *From the Depths: The Discovery of Poverty in the United States*. New York: New York University, 1956.

Brody, David. *Steelworkers in America: the Non-Union Era*. Cambridge: Harvard University, 1960.

———. *Workers in Industrial America: Essays on the Twentieth Century Struggle*. Oxford: Oxford University, 1980.

Buenker, John D. *Urban Liberalism and Progressive Reform*. New York: Scribner's, 1973.

Bukowczyk, John. "The Transformation of Working Class Ethnicity: Corporate Control, Americanization and the Polish Immigrant Middle Class in Bayonne, N.J., 1915–25." *Labor History* 25 (Winter, 1984).

Buhle, Mari Jo. *Women and American Socialism, 1970–1920*. Urbana: University of Illinois Press, 1981.

Burawoy, Michael. *Manufacturing Consent: Changes in the Labor Process Under Monopoly Capitalism*. Chicago: University of Chicago, 1979.

Burnham, Walter Dean. *The Current Crisis in American Politics*. New York: Oxford University, 1982.

Bustard, Bruce. "The Human Factor: Labor Administration and Industrial Manpower Mobilization During the First World War." PhD. Diss. University of Iowa, 1984.

Calhoun, Craig. *The Question of Class Struggle*. Chicago: University of Chicago, 1982.

Case, Josephine Young and Everett Needham Case. *Owen D. Young and American Enterprise*. Boston: David R. Godine, 1982.

Chambers, Clarke A. *Seedtime of Reform: American Social Service and Social Action, 1918–1933*. Minneapolis: University of Minnesota, 1963.

———. "Toward a Redefinition of Welfare History." *Journal of American History* 73, 2 (Sept. 1986): 407–433.

——— and Andrea Hinding. "Charity Workers, the Settlements and the Poor." in *Who Spoke for the Poor? 1880–1914*. New York: Family Service Association, 1968. (A reprint of Feb. 1968 *Social Casework*.)

Chandler, Alfred D. *The Visible Hand: The Managerial Revolution in American Business*. Cambridge: Harvard University, 1977.

Chern, Kenneth S. "The Politics of Patriotism: War, Ethnicity, and the New York Mayoral Campaign, 1917." *New York Historical Society Quarterly* 63, 4 (Oct. 1979).

Clement, Priscilla Ferguson. *Welfare and the Poor in Nineteenth Century City: Philadelphia, 1800–1854*. Rutherford, NJ: Fairleigh-Dickinson University, 1985.

Cole, Arthur H. and Harold F. Williamson. *The American Carpet Manufacture: A History and An Analysis*. Cambridge: Harvard University, 1941.

Conner, Valerie Jean. *The National War Labor Board: Stability, Social Justice and the Voluntary State*. Chapel Hill: University of North Carolina, 1983.

Cooper, John Milton, Jr. *The Warrior and the Priest: Woodrow Wilson and Theodore Roosevelt*. Cambridge: Belknap, 1983.

Cronin, James E. and Carmen Sirianni, eds. *Work, Community and Power: The Experience of Labor in Europe and America, 1900–1925*. Philadelphia: Temple University, 1983.

Crunden, Robert M. *Ministers of Reform: The Progressives' Achievement in American Civilization, 1889–1920*. New York: Basic Books, 1982.

Cuff, Robert D. "Business, The State and World War I: The American Experience." in J.L. Granatstein and R.D. Cuff, eds., *War and Society in North America*. Toronto: Thomas Nelson and Sons, 1971.

———. *The War Industries Board: Business-Government Relations During World War I*. Baltimore: Johns Hopkins University, 1973.

———. "Herbert Hoover, The Ideology of Voluntarism and War Organization During the Great War." *Journal of American History* 64 (1977): 358–372.

———. "Harry Garfield, the Fuel Administration, and the Search for a Cooperative Order During World War I." *American Quarterly* 30, 1 (Spring, 1978): 39–53.

———. "The Politics of Labor Administration During World War I." *Labor History* 21, 4 (Fall, 1980): 546–569.

Cumbler, Jonathon T. *Working-Class Community in Industrial America: Work, Leisure and Struggle in Two Industrial Cities, 1880–1930*. Westport, CT: Greenwood, 1979.

———. "The Politics of Charity: Gender and Class in Late 19th Century Charity Policy." *Journal of Social History* 14, 1 (Fall 1980): 99–112.

Davis, Allen F. *Spearheads for Reform: The Social Settlements and the Progressive Movement, 1890–1914*. New York: Oxford, 1967.

Dublin, Thomas. *Women at Work: The Transformation of Work and Community in Lowell, Massachusetts, 1826–1860*. New York: Columbia University, 1979.

Dubofsky, Melvyn. *When Workers Organize: New York City in the Progressive Era*. Amherst, MA: University of Massachusetts, 1968.

———. *We Shall Be All: A History of the Industrial Workers of the World.* Chicago: Quadrangle Books, 1969.

Dye, Nancy Schrom. *As Equals and As Sisters: Feminism, Unionism, and the Women's Trade Union League of New York.* Columbia: University of Missouri, 1980.

Edwards, Richard. *Contested Terrain: The Transformation of the Workplace in the Twentieth Century*. New York: Basic Books, 1979.

Ehrenberg, Ronald G. and Robert S. Smith. *Modern Labor Economics: Theory and Public Policy*. Glenview, IL: Scott, Foresman, 1982.

Eisner, J. Michael. *William Morris Leiserson: A Biography*. Madison, WI: University of Wisconsin, 1967.

Evans, Peter B., Dietrich Rueschemeyer and Theda Skocpol, eds. *Bringing the State Back In*. Cambridge: Cambridge University, 1985.

Fine, Sidney. *Laissez Faire and the General-Welfare State: A Study of Conflict in American Thought*. Ann Arbor: University of Michigan, 1956.

Finegold, Kenneth. "From Agrarianism to Adjustment: The Political Origins of New Deal Agricultural Policy." *Politics and Society* 11, 1 (1981): 1–27.

Fink, Leon. *Workingmen's Democracy: The Knights of Labor and American Politics*. Urbana: University of Illinois, 1983.

Fones-Wolf, Kenneth. "Revivalism and Craft Unionism in the Progressive Era: The Syracuse and Auburn Labor Forward Movements of 1913." *New York History* 63, 4 (Oct., 1982): 389–416.

Fraser, Derek. *The Evolution of the British Welfare State: A History of Social Policy Since the Industrial Revolution*. London: Macmillan, 1973.

Fraser, Steve. "From the 'New Unionism' to the New Deal." *Labor History* 25, 3 (Summer, 1984): 405–430.

Freeden, Michael. *The New Liberalism: An Ideology of Social Reform*. Oxford: Clarendon, 1978.

Gaffield, Chad. "Big Business, the Working-Class, and Socialism in Schenectady, 1911–1916." *Labor History* 19, 3 (Summer, 1978): 350–372.

Galambos, Louis. "The Emerging Organizational Synthesis in Modern American History." *Business History Review* 44 (1970): 279–290.

———. *The Public Image of Big Business in America, 1880–1940*. Baltimore: Johns Hopkins University, 1975.

Garraty, John A. *Unemployment in History: Economic Thought and Public Policy*. New York: Harper, 1978.

Gilbert, Bentley B. *The Evolution of National Insurance in Great Britain: The Origins of the Welfare State*. London: Michael Joseph, 1966.

Gilbert, James. *Designing the Industrial State: The Intellectual Pursuit of Collectivism in America, 1880–1940*. Chicago: Quadrangle, 1972.

Gilbert, Neil. *Capitalism and the Welfare State: Dilemmas of Social Benevolence*. New Haven: Yale University, 1983.

Gitelman, Howard M. *Workingmen of Waltham: Mobility in American Urban Industrial Development*. Baltimore: Johns Hopkins University, 1974.

———. "Being of Two Minds: American Employers Confront the Labor Problem, 1915–1919." *Labor History* 25, 2 (Spring, 1984): 189–215.

Glenn, John, Lillian Brandt and F. Emerson Andrews. *Russell Sage Foundation, 1907–1946*. New York: Russell Sage, 1947.

Gordon, David M. *Theories of Poverty and Underemployment: Orthodox, Radical and Dual Labor Market Perspectives*. Lexington, MA: D.C. Heath, 1972.

———, Richard Edwards, and Michael Reich. *Segmented Work, Divided Workers: The Historical Transformation of Labor in the United States*. New York: Cambridge, 1982.

Goodwyn, Lawrence. *Democratic Promise: The Populist Moment in American History*. Oxford: Oxford University, 1976.

Graebner, William. "Federalism in the Progressiv Era: A Structural Interpretation of Reform." *Journal of American History* 64 (1977): 331–357.

Greenwald, Maurine Weiner. *Women, War and Work: The Impact of World War I on Women Workers in the United States*. Westport, CT: Greenwood, 1980.

Grin, Carolyn, "The Unemployment Conference of 1921." *Mid-America* 55 (1973): 83–107.

Green, Bryan S. *Knowing the Poor: A Case-study in Textual Reality Construction*. London: Routledge and Kegan Paul, 1983.

Grubb, W. Norton and Marvin Lazerson. *Broken Promises: How Americans Fail Their Children*. New York: Basic Books, 1982.

Gutman, Herbert G. *Work, Culture and Society in Industrializing America: Esays in American Working-Class and Social History*. New York: Random House, 1966.

Hammack, David C. *Power and Society: Greater New York at the Turn of the Century*. New York: Russell Sage, 1982.

Hareven, Tamara and Randolph Langenbach. *Amoskeag: Life and Work in an American Factory-City*. New York: Pantheon, 1978.

———. *Family Time and Industrial Time: The Relationship Between Family and Work in a New England Industrial Community*. Cambridge: Cambridge University, 1982.

Harris, Jose. *Unemployment and Politics: A Study in English Social Policy, 1886–1914*. Oxford: Clarendon, 1972.

———. *William Beveridge: A Biography*. Oxford: Clarendon Press, 1977.

Hay, J.R. *The Origins of the Liberal Welfare Reforms, 1906–1914*. London: Macmillan, 1975.

———. "The British Business Community, Social Insurance and the German Example." in W.J. Mommsen, ed. *The Emergence of the Welfare State in Britain and Germany 1850–1950*. London: Croom Helm, 1981: 107–132.

Hayes, Samuel P. *The Response to Industrialism, 1885–1914*. Chicago: University of Chicago, 1957.

———. *Conservation and the Gospel of Efficiency: The Progressive Conservation Movement, 1890–1920*. Cambridge: Harvard University, 1959. [rpr. New York: Atheneum, 1975].

Hawley, Ellis. *The Great War and the Search for a Modern Order*. New York: St. Martin's, 1979.

———, ed. *Herbert Hoover as Secretary of Commerce: Studies in New Era Thought and Practice*. Iowa City: University of Iowa, 1981.

Hofstadter, Richard. *The Age of Reform*. New York: Vintage, 1955.

Horwitz, Morton. *The Transformation of American Law, 1780–1860*. Cambridge: Harvard University Press, 1977.

Huggins, Nathan Irvin. *Protestants Against Poverty: Boston's Charities, 1870–1900*. Westport, CT: Greenwood, 1971.

Israel, Jerry, ed. *Building the Organizational Society: Essays on Associational Activities in Modern America*. New York: Free Press, 1972.

Jacoby, Sanford M. "The Origins of Internal Labor Markets in American Manufacturing Firms, 1910–1940." PhD. Diss., University of California, Berkeley, 1981.

———. "Industrial Labor Mobility in Historical Perspective." *Industrial Relations* 22, 2 (Spring, 1983): 261–282.

———. *Employing Bureaucracy: Managers, Unions and the Transformation of Work in American Industry, 1900–1945*. New York: Columbia University, 1985.

Jaenicke, Douglas Walter. "Herbert Croly, Progressive Ideology, and the FTC Act." *Political Science Quarterly*. 93, 3 (Fall 1978): 471–493.

Johnson, Paul E. *A Shopkeepers' Millennium: Society and Revivals in Rochester, New York, 1815–1837*. New York: Hill and Wang, 1978.

Katz, Michael. *The People of Hamilton, Canada West: Family and Class in a Mid-Nineteenth Century City*. Cambridge: Harvard University Press, 1975.

———. *Poverty and Policy in American History*. New York: Academic Press, 1983.

———. *In the Shadow of the Poorhouse: A Social History of Welfare in America*. New York: Basic Books, 1986.

Katznelson, Ira. *City Trenches: Urban Politics and the Patterning of Class in the United States*. Chicago: University of Chicago, 1981.

Keller, Morton. *Affairs of State: Public Life in Late Nineteenth Century America*. Cambridge: Harvard University, 1977.

Kennedy, David M. *Over Here: The First World War and American Society.* Oxford: Oxford University, 1980.

Kessler-Harris, Alice. *Out to Work: A History of Wage-Earning Women in the United States.* New York: Oxford University, 1982.

Kerr, Thomas. "The New York Factory Investigating Commission and the Progressives." D.S.Sc. Thesis, Syracuse University, 1965.

Keyssar, Alexander. *Out of Work: The First Century of Unemployment in Massachusetts.* New York: Cambridge University, 1986.

Kolko, Gabriel. *The Triumph of Conservatism: A Reinterpretation of American History, 1900–1916.* New York: Free Press, 1963.

Korman, Gerd. *Industrialization, Immigrants and Americanizers: The View From Milwaukee, 1866–1921.* Madison, WI: State historical Society, 1967.

Kreader, J. Lee. "Isaac Max Rubinow: Pioneering Specialist in Social Insurance." *Social Service Review* 50, 3 (Sept. 1976):403–425.

Lasch, Christopher. "The Origins of the Therapeutic State." *New York Review of Books.* (June 12, 1980): 24ff.

Lears, T. Jackson. *No Place of Grace: Antimodernism and the Transformation of American Culture, 1880–1920.* New York: Pantheon, 1981.

Levine, Susan. "'Honor Each Noble Maid': Women Workers and the Yonkers Carpet Weavers' Strike of 1885." *New York History* (April, 1981): 153–176.

———. *Labor's True Woman: Carpet Weavers, Industrialization and Labor Reform in the Gilded Age.* Philadelphia: Temple University, 1984.

Lewinson, Edwin R. *John Purroy Mitchel, Boy Mayor of New York.* New York: Astra Books, 1965.

Leiby, James. *A History of Social Welfare in the United States.* New York: Columbia University, 1978.

Lubove, Roy. *The Progressives and the Slums: Tenement House Reform in New York City, 1890–1917.* Pittsburgh: University of Pittsburgh, 1963.

———. *The Professional Altruist: The Emergence of Social Work as a Career, 1880–1930.* Cambridge: Harvard University, 1965.

———. *The Struggle for Social Security, 1900–1935.* Cambridge: Harvard University, 1968.

Lustig, R. Jeffrey. *Corporate Liberalism: the Origins of Modern American Political Theory, 1890–1920.* Berkeley: University of California, 1982.

McClymer, John F. *War and Welfare: Social Engineering in America, 1890–1925.* Westport, CT: Greenwood, 1980.

McConnell, *Private Power and American Democracy.* New York: Random House, 1966.

McCormick, Richard L. *From Realignment to Reform: Political Change in New York State, 1893–1910.* Ithaca: Cornell University, 1981.

McDonald, Robert A.J. "The Business Elite and Municipal Politics in Vancouver, 1886–1914." *Urban History Review/Revue d'histoire urbaine* 21, 3 (Feb. 1983).

Miller, Harold L. "The American Bureau of Industrial Research and the Origins of the 'Wisconsin School' of Labor History." *Labor History* 25, 2 (Spring 1984): 165–188.

Monkkonen, Eric H. *The Dangerous Class: Crime and Poverty in Columbus, Ohio, 1860–1885*. Cambridge: Harvard University, 1975.

———. "A Disorderly People? Urban Order in the Nineteenth and Twentieth Centuries." *Journal of American History* 68,3 (Dec. 1981), 539–559.

———. *Police in Urban America, 1880–1916*. Cambridge: Cambridge University, 1981.

———, ed. *Walking to Work: Tramps in America, 1790–1935*. Lincoln, NE: University of Nebraska, 1984.

Montgomery, David. *Workers' Control in America: Studies in the History of Work, Technology, and Labor Struggles*. Cambridge: Cambridge University Press, 1979.

Nelson, Daniel. *Unemployment Insurance: The American Experience*. Madison: University of Wisconsin, 1969.

———. and Stuart Campbell. "Taylorism versus Welfare Work in American Industry: H.L. Gantt and the Bancrofts." *Business History Review* 46 (Spring 1972): 1–16.

———. *Managers and Workers: Origins of the New Factory System in the United States, 1880–1920*. Madison: University of Wisconsin Press, 1975.

Nielsen, Waldemar. *The Big Foundations: A Twentieth Century Fund Study*. New York Columbia University Press, 1972.

Noble, David F. *America by Design: Science, Technology and the Rise of Corporate Capitalism*. New York: Knopf, 1977.

Noggle, Burl. *Into the Twenties: The United States From Armistice to Normalcy*. Urbana: University of Illinois Press, 1974.

Ozanne, Robert. *A Century of Labor-Management Relations at McCormick and International Harvester*. Madison: University of Wisconsin Press, 1967.

Palmer, Bryan. *A Culture in Conflict: Skilled Workers and Industrial Capitalism in Hamilton, Ontario, 1860–1914*. Montreal: McGill-Queen's University, 1979.

Parrini, Carl P. and Martin Sklar. "New Thinking About the Market," *Journal of Economic History* 43, 3 (Sept. 1983): 559–578.

Patterson, James T. *America's Struggle Against Poverty, 1900–1985*. Cambridge: Harvard University, 1986.

Pearlman, Michael. *To Make Democracy Safe for America: Patricians and Preparedness in the Progressive Era*. Urbana: University of Illinois, 1984.

Peel, Mark. "On the Margins: Lodgers and Boarders in Boston, 1860–1900." *Journal of American History* 72, 4 (March, 1986): 813–834.

Piven, Frances Fox and Richard Cloward. *Regulating the Poor: The Functions of Public Welfare*. New York: Random House, 1971.

Preston, William, Jr. *Aliens and Dissenter: Federal Suppression of Radicals, 1903–1933*. Cambridge: Harvard University, 1963. [Rpr. New York: Harper and Row, 1966].

Ramirez, Bruno. *When Workers Fight: The Politics of Industrial Relations in the Progressive Era*. Westport, CT: Greenwood, 1978.

Reese, William J. *Power and the Promise of School Reform: Grassroots Movements During the Progressive Era*. Boston, London: Routledge, Kegan and Paul, 1986.

Ringenbach, Paul T. *Tramps and Reformers 1873–1916: the Discovery of Unemployment in New York*. Westport, CT: Greenwood, 1973.

Rebic, Michael P. *Landmarks Lost and Found: An Introduction to the Architecture and History of Yonkers*. Yonkers: Yonkers Planning Bureau, 1986.

Rodgers, Daniel T. *The Work Ethic in Industrial America, 1850–1920*. Chicago: University of Chicago, 1978.

———. "In Search of Progressivism," *Reviews in American History* 10,4 (Dec. 1982): 113–132.

Romanofsky, Peter. *Social Service Organizations*. Westport: Greenwood, 1978.

Rothman, David J. *Conscience and Convenience: The Asylum and Its Alternatives in Progressive America*. Boston: Little Brown, 1980.

Salvatore, Nick. *Eugene V. Debs: Citizen and Socialist*. Urbana: University of Illinois, 1982.

Sautter, Udo. "North American Government Labor Agencies Before World War One: A Cure For Unemployment?" *Labor History* 24, 3 (Summer 1983): 366–393.

———. Government and Unemployment: The Use of Public Works before the New Deal." *Journal of American History* 73, 1 (June 1986): 59–86.

Schatz, Ronald W. *The Electrical Workers: A History of Labor at General Electric and Westinghouse, 1923–1960*. Urbana: University of Illinois, 1983.

Schneider, David M. and Albert Deutsch. *The History of Public Welfare in New York State, 1867–1940*. Chicago: University of Chicago, 1941.

Shergold, Peter R. *Working-Class Life: The 'American Standard' in Comparative Perspective*. Pittsburgh: University of Pittsburgh, 1982.

Sicherman, Barbara. *Alice Hamilton, A Life in Letters*. Cambridge: Harvard, 1984.

Sicilia, David B. "Technological Risk in Manufacturing, 1850–1880, Yonkers, New York: A Case Study." Unpublished paper, Brandeis University, n.d.

Skocpol, Theda. "Political Reponse to Capitalist Crisis: Neo-Marxist Theories of the State and the Case of the New Deal." *Politics and Society* 10, 2 (1980): 155–201.

Skowronek, Stephen. *Building a New American State: The Expansion of National Administrative Capacities, 1877–1920*. Cambridge: Cambridge University, 1982.

Smith, Darrell Hevenor. *The United States Employment Service: Its History Activites and Organization*. Baltimore, MD: Johns Hopkins University, 1923.

Solow, Robert. "On Theories of Unemployment." *American Economic Review* 70 (March 1980): 1–11.

Stone, Katherine. "The Origins of Job Structures in the Steel Industry." in Michael Reich, David Gordon and Richard Edwards, *Labor Market Segmentation*. Lexington, MA: Heath, 1975.

Struthers, James. *No Fault of Their Own: Unemployment and the Canadian Welfare State, 1914–1941*. Toronto: University of Toronto, 1983.

Tentler, Leslie Woodcock. *Wage-Earning Women: Industrial Work and Family Life in the United States, 1900–1930*. Oxford: Oxford University, 1979.

Thernstrom, Stephan. *Poverty and Progress: Social Mobility in a Nineteenth Century City*. Cambridge: Harvard University, 1964.

———. *The Other Bostonians: Poverty and Progress in the American Metropolis, 1880–1970*. Cambridge: Harvard University, 1973.

Thompson, Edward P. *The Making of the English Working Class*. New York: Vintage, 1966 [1963].

Trachtenberg, Alan. *The Incorporation of America: Culture and Society in the Gilded Age*. New York: Hill and Wang, 1982.

Trattner, Walter I. *Homer Folks: Pioneer in Social Welfare*. New York: Columbia University, 1968.

———. *From Poor Law to Welfare State: A History of Social Welfare in America*. New York: Free Press, 1974.

Wallace, A.F.C. *Rockdale: The Growth of an American Village in the Early Industrial Revolution*. New York: Knopf, 1978.

Walkowitz, Daniel J. *Worker City, Company Town: Iron and Cotton-Worker Protest in Troy and Cohoes, New York, 1855–1984*. Urbana: University of Illinois, 1978.

Weinstein, James. *The Corporate Ideal in the Liberal State 1900–1918*. Boston: Beacon, 1968.

Wiebe, Robert H. *The Search for Order, 1877–1920*. New York: Hill and Wang, 1967.

Wilentz, Sean. *Chants Democratic: New York City and the Rise of the American Working Class, 1788–1850*. New York: Oxford University Press, 1984.

Wilson, James Q. "The Rise of the Bureaucratic State." *The Public Interest* 41 (Fall 1975): 77–103.

Wilson, Joan Hoff. *Herbert Hoover, Forgotten Progressive.* Boston: Little, Brown, 1975.

Woytinsky, W.S. *Three Aspects of Labor Dynamics.* Washington: Social Science Research Council, 1942.

Yans-McLaughlin, Virginia. *Family and Community: Italian Immigrants in Buffalo, 1880–1930.* Ithaca: Cornell University, 1971. [rpr. Urbana: University of Illinois, 1982.]

Yellowitz, Irwin. *Labor and the Progressive Movement in New York State, 1897–1916.* Ithaca: Cornell University, 1965.

Zahavi, Gerald. "Negotiated Loyalty: Welfare Capitalism and the Shoeworkers of Endicott-Johnson, 1920–1940." *Journal of American History* 70, 3 (Dec. 1983): 602–620.

Index